D0915388

QUANTITATIVE ANALYSES
OF BEHAVIOR

0) David W. Stephens
1) Sara Shettleworth
2) William Baum
3) John A. Nevin
4) Steven Lima
5) David Sherry (seated)
6) Allan Wagner
7) Lee Gass (seated)
8) Richard Herrnstein
9) Ronald Gendron
10) Nureya Abarca
11) Michael L. Commons
12) Alasdair Houston
13) Roger Mellgren

14) Thomas Caraco (seated)
15) Michael Rashotte
16) Edmund Fantino
17) Peter Cahoon
18) Donald Kilroy
19) Alejandro Kacelnik
20) Susan Dow
21) Timothy Moermond (seated)
22) Alan Kamil
23) John Krebs
24) John McNamara
25) H. Ronald Pulliam
26) Thomas Getty

QUANTITATIVE ANALYSES OF BEHAVIOR

Foraging

Volume VI

Edited by

MICHAEL L. COMMONS
Harvard University

ALEJANDRO KACELNIK
Oxford University

SARA J. SHETTLEWORTH
University of Toronto

LEA

LAWRENCE ERLBAUM ASSOCIATES, PUBLISHERS

1987   Hillsdale, New Jersey   London

Lawrence Erlbaum Associates, Inc., Publishers
365 Broadway
Hillsdale, New Jersey 07642

Library of Congress Cataloging in Publication Data
LC card number: 86-640678
ISBN: 0-89859-550-9

Printed in the United States of America
10 9 8 7 6 5 4 3 2 1

Volumes in the **QUANTITATIVE ANALYSES OF BEHAVIOR** series:

All volumes available from LAWRENCE ERLBAUM ASSOCIATES, PUBLISHERS

CONTENTS

ABOUT THE EDITORS

Michael Lamport Commons is a research associate in the Department of Psychology and Social Relations at Harvard University. He did his undergraduate work at the University of California at Berkeley, and then at Los Angeles, where in 1965 he obtained a B.A. in mathematics and psychology. In 1967 he received his M.A. and in 1973 his Ph.D. in psychology from Columbia University. Before coming to Harvard University in 1977, he was an assistant professor at Northern Michigan University. He has co-edited *Quantitative Analyses of Behavior: Volume I, Discriminative Properties of Reinforcement Schedules, Volume II, Matching and Maximizing Accounts, Volume III, Acquisition, Volume IV, Discriminative Processes, Volume V, The Effect of Delay and of Intervening Events on Reinforcement Value,* and *Beyond Formal Operations: Vol. 1. Late-Adolescent and Adult Cognitive Development.* His area of research interest is the quantative analysis of the construction and the understanding of reality, especially as they affect decision processes. This includes the subarea of utility, along with such topics as perception and knowledge of causal relations and of value, and how it develops in infrahumans and humans across the lifespan.

Alejandro Kacelnik studied zoology in Buenos Aires and obtained his Ph.D. from Oxford University in 1979, with research on foraging behavior and time budgeting in birds. He has worked in laboratories in Buenos Aires, Groningen (Netherlands), and in Oxford, where he is now a member of the Department of Zoology at the Edward Grey Institute of Field Ornithology. He is interested in several aspects of behavioral ecology, especially optimal foraging, parental effort, and learning among free-living wild birds.

Sara J. Shettleworth is a professor of psychology at the University of Toronto, where she has taught since 1972. She obtained her B.A. from Swarthmore College in 1965, her M.A. from the University of Pennsylvania, and, in 1970, her Ph.D. from the University of Toronto. In 1980-81 she was a Guggenheim Fellow in the Department of Zoology, Oxford University. Her long-standing interest has been the integration of the study of natural behavior in animals with the analysis of learning and memory processes.

LIST OF CONTRIBUTORS

Nureya Abarca
Escuela de Psicologia
Pontificia Universidad Católica de
  Chile

Steven W. Brown
Department of Psychology
University of Oklahoma

Peter Cahoon
Department of Zoology
University of British Columbia
  Now at:
Institute of Animal Resource Ecology
University of British Columbia

Thomas Caraco
Department of Biology
University of Rochester
  Now at:
Department of Biological Sciences
State University of New York,
  Albany

Julie S. Denslow
Departments of Zoology and Botany
University of Wisconsin
  Now at:
New York Botanical Garden

Veljko J. Djuric
Department of Psychology
The Florida State University
  Now at:
University of Belgrade

Susan M. Dow
Department of Zoology
University of Bristol
  Now at:
The Zoological Society of London
Regent's Park

Bruno Ens
Department of Zoology
University of Groningen, Netherlands

Edmund J. Fantino
Department of Psychology
University of California at San Diego

Alasdair I. Houston
Department of Zoology
Cambridge University
  Now at:
Edward Grey Institute of Field
  Ornithology
Department of Zoology
Oxford University

Masato Ito
Department of Psychology
City University of Osaka

Alejandro Kacelnik
Edward Grey Institute of Field
  Ornithology
Oxford University

John R. Krebs
Edward Grey Institute of Field
  Ornithology
Oxford University

Stephen E. G. Lea
Department of Psychology
Washington Singer Laboratories
University of Exeter

Douglas J. Levey
Department of Zoology
University of Wisconsin

Steven L. Lima
Department of Biology
University of Rochester

John M. McNamara
School of Mathematics
University of Bristol

Roger L. Mellgren
Department of Psychology
University of Oklahoma

Timothy C. Moermond
Department of Zoology
University of Wisconsin

Jeffrey M. O'Connell
Department of Psychology
The Florida State University

Michael E. Rashotte
Department of Psychology
The Florida State University

Eduardo Santana-Castellon
Department of Wildlife Ecology
Unversity of Wisconsin

David F. Sherry
Department of Psychology
University of Toronto

Sara J. Shettleworth
Department of Psychology
University of Toronto

PREFACE

The study of behavior has consisted of a number of somewhat separate traditions. One set of traditions arose in psychology, another set in biology. The first psychological tradition, starting with Thorndike and then continuing with Skinner, has experimentally analyzed the control of behavior by events that occur subsequent to it. The second psychological tradition, starting with Bechterev and Pavlov and coming down to the present through Watson, Hull, Spence, and others, has analyzed the control and transfer of control by events that precede behavior.

The biological traditions have a longer history, and include work by Darwin, Tinbergen, Lorenz on ethology; and the work on quantitative behavioral ecology by MacArthur and Pianka, and more recently by Maynard Smith and Krebs.

After the 1920s both psychological approaches became more quantitative. In the experimental analysis of behavior, quantifiable variables, such as the rate of responding, were used to represent the behavioral outcomes. At the same time, more elaborate quantitative studies were carried out in the Hullian approach. Quantifiable measures, such as response probability and latency, were introduced. In that period, and extending through the 1950s, mathematical models were developed by Hull, Spence, Estes, Bush and Mosteller, and Logan, among others. Both groups carried out some parametric studies in the tradition of psychophysics. By the early 1960s mathematical psychology had developed to the point where it could deal with problems from a number of domains. In each domain, explicit mathematical models were proposed for the processes by which performances were acquired and maintained within that domain. Although the models generated a number of experiments, they were of limited generality.

Quantitative analysis now generally refers to the fact that theoretical issues are represented by quantitative models. An analysis is not a matter of fitting arbitrary functions to data points. Rather, each parameter and variable in a set of equations represents part of a process that has both a theoretical and an empirical interpretation. Quantitative analysis has forced researchers to represent explicitly their notions and to be economical in the number of parameters that must be estimated. The matching law, a model of maintained performance is one example from the analysis-of-behavior tradition. The Rescorla-Wagner model of acquisition processes is a second example. These models represent effects of interactions of environmental and behavioral events. Because neither model requires otherwise, the possibility exists that both the organism and the environment modify each other. The rules of such interaction may be represented by an arithmetic that accounts for the results from a large class of studies.

The models are designed to account for the maximal amount of variance found in a number of experimental situations to which the processes described by a given one of those models apply. Some parameter estimates should be the same regardless of the situation. The adequacy of a model can be tested by examining how well that model fits the data or by comparing obtained data to the theoretically simulated values. These methods are to be contrasted with the testing of relatively simple hypotheses. Because the models can be quite complex, however, only portions of them are tested by single sets of studies. As in other areas of science, looking for the generality of a formulation has made these models more testable. Independent routes of verification are possible because of the increased scope of the models.

The volumes in the present series have been written for behavioral scientists. Those concerned with issues in the study of how behavior is acquired and then allocated in various environments—biologists, psychologists, economists, anthropologists, and other researchers, as well as graduate students and advanced undergraduates in those areas—should find volumes in this series to be state-of-the-art readers and reference works. They are also intended for use in seminars.

Each volume of the series examines a particular topic that has been discussed at the annual Symposium on Quantitative Analyses of Behavior held at Harvard University. The topic of Volume I was the discrimination of schedules of reinforcement. It was chosen because it represents an area that has been highly quantified through the application of psychophysical methods and analyses of maintained performances.

Volume II explored matching and maximizing accounts of the allocation of behavior, another area that has been highly quantified. It explored the generality of such formulations and how they apply to animal behavior in both the field and the laboratory and to human behavior in choice situations in economics.

Acquisition models and data were considered in Volume III. These models dealt with the roles that various events play in different conditioning situations and how those events interact to produce conditioning or to retard it. Also considered were aspects of the conditioning situation that go beyond the simple notions of temporal contiguity between the stimulus to be conditioned and the unconditioned stimulus.

Volume IV presented studies of discrimination processes. How discriminations are acquired and the role of various events within the discrimination situation were considered.

Volume V addressed the topic of how reinforcement value is affected by delay and intervening events. Self-control studies were also presented and discussed.

The present volume addresses issues in foraging. Included is an examination of optimal-foraging theory and its alternatives, as well as an examination of how the detectibility of prey controls the choice to pursue those prey.

Volume VII will address the biological determinants of reinforcement and memory.

Tentative future volumes will include pattern recognition and concepts in animals, people, and machines, economic approaches to human and animal choice, and stimulus control.

The contents of the present volume were first prepared for and presented at the Sixth Symposium on Quantitative Analyses of Behavior, held at Harvard University. Subsequently, a portion of the chapters has been revised, updated, and rearranged into the five topical parts found herein.

The symposium out of which this volume has arisen was organized by Michael L. Commons and John A. Nevin with assistance from Alan Kamil and Mark S. Snyderman. The symposium was supported in part by the Society for the Quantitative Analyses of Behavior, The Department of Psychology and Social Relations at Harvard University, and by the Dare Association, Inc.

Local arrangements were made by Patrice M. Miller and Dean Gallant, with assistance from Queen Booker, Robert A. Buhlman, Rosemarie DeBiase, Robert Hoyt, Joseph Patrick McNamara, Susan Warning, and Marion Wentworth.

For help in reviewing the chapters for stylistic and organizational improvements we thank the staff of the Dare Institute. The index was prepared by Katherine G. McCarthy.

Michael L. Commons
Harvard University

INTRODUCTION

Alejandro Kacelnik

The contributors to this volume work in equal number in association with departments of psychology and zoology. Nevertheless, many of them would find it difficult to define themselves as belonging exclusively to one or the other field of research, primarily because the study of foraging behavior, as it has developed in recent years and, hopefully, as it is presented in this volume, is a fruitful, but uneasy *menage à trois* of ecology, ethology, and experimental psychology. Each of these fields contributes its own tradition, know-how, and aims. From ecology, the study of foraging behavior has inherited a view of organisms and environments as unitary systems, and a concern for the consequences of individual behavior for population and community dynamics. From ethology, comes the legacy of simultaneous concern for the traditional aims of the discipline: the study of causes (mechanisms), development, survival value, and the phylogenetic history of behavior (Tinbergen, 1960). Experimental psychology is the most recent associate in this synthesized field. It contributes its emphasis on thorough analyses of behavior in simplified—hence, rigorously controlled—environments. The assumption that underlies psychological studies of foraging is that properties of behavioral mechanisms present in simple laboratory situations must also be present, albeit potentially masked, in complex natural environments.

The term *optimality* refers to different notions. In psychology it refers to a mechanism for making choice that maximizes the amount of prey obtained. In biology, two notions exist side by side. The first is that of maximizing energy obtained from prey selection under both internal and external contraints. The other notion does not specify a particular meaning for optimality but leaves it an undefined concept in the program of applying evolutionary theory.

Optimality techniques are another characteristic feature of foraging research, but their status is qualitatively different, because optimality is a subordinate methodology within the three founding fields, rather than a more or less independent discipline with its own subject matter. Curiously, in view of its subordinate role, it has been optimality techniques that have produced the greatest controversy. In spite of many polemic pages having been written about the scientific respectability of optimality views in biology and psychology (see, e.g., Cheverton, Kacelnik, & Krebs, 1984; Gould & Lewontin, 1979; Gray, in press; Janetos & Cole, 1981; Kacelnik & Cuthill, in press; Maynard Smith, 1978; Mazur, 1981; Ollason, 1980; Rachlin, 1982; Rachlin, Green, Kogel, Battalio, 1976; Synderman, in press; Staddon & Hinson, 1983), the issue remains unsettled. The main source of the differences expressed in the debate is the lack of agreement on whether optimality hypotheses can be tested.

Opponents of optimality usually fall into two categories: those who implicitly assume that optimality is subject to empirical testing and that it is refuted by available data (e.g., Herrnstein, 1982; Mazur, 1981; Vaughan, 1982), and those who maintain that it is untestable and hence inappropriate as a scientific source of hypotheses (e.g., Gray, in press; Ollason, 1980). Symmetrically, users and defenders of optimality either believe that empirical observations can—and do—provide evidence about the optimality of organisms (Rachlin, 1978) or that, even though optimality itself is untestable, it nevertheless remains useful (e.g., Cheverton et al., 1984; Kacelnik & Cuthill, in press; Maynard Smith, 1978). The alert reader finds these views permeating the various chapters in this collection, and even on occasions coexisting uneasily within a single chapter. This coexistence does deserve attention, but it need not lead to apologies. Scientists, like most other people with the probable exception of philosophers, are better at doing things than at reflecting on and understanding what they are doing. Just as successful tightrope walkers may be unable to explain how they maintain their balance, valid contributions to science often come from people not entirely aware of all the underlying assumptions involved in their research program (their scientific ideology).

The topics mentioned in this introduction are illustrated, rather than explicitly discussed, by the different chapters of this collection. Part I discusses alternative currencies in foraging theory, the limitation of some early models of maximization of energy gain in patchy environments, and the difference between causal and functional levels of explanation of foraging behavior.

Part II groups a number of laboratory studies of foraging behavior under changing conditions of food availability. This type of study reflects a recent revival of interest in the study of acquisition, after a period during which psychological attention was almost monopolized by the analysis of steady-state behavior. It is ironic that in this context there has been some degree of role reversal. Although Roger Mellgren, a former contributor to the purely psychological study of the partial reinforcement-extinction effect, co-authors a laboratory simulation of foraging in patches, researchers with experience in ecological research on foraging in patches, such as John Krebs and myself, find themselves intruding timidly into the experimentation and interpretation of the partial reinforcement-extinction effect, albeit from a patch-exploitation point of view.

Part III shows how a number of aspects of foraging behavior can be discussed and understood in the framework of classical and operant conditioning. This kind of research may fill an important gap in current modelling of optimal behavior. The emphasis on functional analysis of the consequences of behavior has led behavioral ecologists away from the study of causation, and, consequently, uninformed guesses about what animals can do are often included among the assumptions of many optimality models.

Part IV illustrates that there can be more to foraging than obtaining artifical rewards for immediate consumption. Although it contains laboratory rather than field studies, this work points to aspects of foraging that, in spite of their relevance to psychological topics such as memory or choice, have been largely overlooked by the bulk of psychological research. Finally, Part V concludes the book with a methodological contribution toward greater objectivity in the accumulation of behavioral data where complex patterns of movement are involved.

The paths of different disciplines concerned with the study of behavior are starting to converge, and the study of foraging behavior can be an appropriate arena for this meeting. The research reported in the chapters included here should be but the tip of the iceberg.

REFERENCES

Cheverton, J., Kacelnik, A., & Krebs, J. R. (1985). Optimal foraging: Constraints and currencies. In B. Holldobler & M. Lindauer (Eds.), *Experimental behavioral ecology and sociobiology. Fortschritte der Zoologie* (Vol. 31, pp. 109–126). Stuttgart: Fischer Verlag.

Gould, S. J., & Lewontin, R. C. (1979). The spandrels of San Marco and the panglossian paradigm: A critique of the adaptionist programme. *Proceedings of the Royal Society, B 205,* 581–598

Gray, R. (in press). Faith and foraging: A critique of the "paradigm argument from design." In A. Kamil, J. R. Krebs, & R. Pulliam, *Foraging behavior.*

Herrnstein, R. J. (1982). Melioration as behavioral dynamism. In M. L. Commons, R. J. Herrnstein, & H. Rachlin (Eds.), *Quantitative analyses of behavior: Vol. II, Matching and maximizing accounts* (pp. 433–458). Cambridge, MA: Ballinger.

Janetos, A. C., & Cole, B. S. (1981). Imperfectly optimal animals. *Behavioral Ecology and Sociobiology, 9,* 203–209.

Kacelnik, A., & Cuthill, I. C. (in press). Optimal foraging: Just a matter of technique. In A. Kamil, J. R. Krebs, & R. Pulliam, *Foraging behavior.*

Maynard Smith, J. (1978). Optimization theory in evolution. *Annual Review of Ecological Systems, 9,* 31–56.

Mazur, J. (1981). Optimization theory fails to predict performance of pigeons in a two-response situation. *Science, 214,* 823–825.

Ollason, J. G. (1980). Learning to forage—optimally? *Theoretical Population Biology, 18,* 44–56.

Rachlin, H. (1978). A molar theory of reinforcement schedules. *Journal of the Experimental Analysis of Behavior, 30,* 345–360.

Rachlin, H. (1982). Economics of the matching law. In M. L. Commons, R. J. Herrnstein, & H. Rachlin (Eds.), *Quantitative analyses of behavior: Vol. II, Matching and maximizing accounts* (pp. 347–374). Cambridge, MA: Ballinger.

Rachlin, H., Green, L., Kagel, J. H., Battalio, R. C. (1976). Economic demand theory and psychological studies of choice. In G. Bower (Ed.), *The psychology of learning and motivation* (Vol. 10). New York: Academic Press.

Snyderman, M. (1986). Prey selection and self-control. In M. L. Commons, J. E. Mazur, J. A. Nevin, & H. Rachlin (Eds.), *Quantitative analyses of behavior: Vol. V, Reinforcement value: The effect of delay and of intervening events on reinforcement value.* Hillsdale, NJ: Lawrence Erlbaum Associates.

Staddon, J. E. R., & Hinson, J. M. (1983). Optimization: A result or a mechanism? *Science, 221,* 976–977.

Tinbergen, L. (1960). The natural control of insects in pinewood. *Archives Néerlandaises de Zoologie, 13,* 265–343.

Vaughan, W., Jr. (1982). Choice and the Rescorla-Wagner moedel. In M. L. Commons, R. J. Herrnstein, & H. Rachlin (Eds.), *Quantitative analyses of behavior: Vol. II, Matching and maximizing accounts* (pp. 263–279). Cambridge, MA: Ballinger.

ASPECTS OF OPTIMAL-FORAGING THEORY

1 Survival, Energy Budgets, and Foraging Risk

Thomas Caraco
Steven L. Lima
Department of Biology
University of Rochester

The foraging economy of most animals includes elements of stochastic variation. Learning may reduce the uncertainty associated with problems of information, but the uncertainty induced by risk may be independent of the forager's experience. In the first case the forager may be uncertain about resource quality, so that the acquisition of information becomes important. By sampling available alternatives, the forager can update its probabilistic assessments of profitability (Green, 1980; Kacelnik, 1979; McNamara, 1982; Oaten, 1977). For this reason, an animal's foraging efficiency may depend on its sampling efficiency (Houston, Kacelnik, & McNamara, 1982; Krebs, Kacelnik, & Taylor, 1978; Lima, 1984). Several contributions to this volume indicate the scope and intensity of current interest in ecological questions concerning information in foraging processes.

In stationary environments, (i.e., when resource quality is not a function of time), or when a forager can recognize distinct resource types (e.g., different prey species) prior to exploitation, sampling is less important. In effect, the organism may acquire "total information." However, the problem of risk remains when the outcome of a foraging decision is a random variable; that is, the forager may possess full information concerning the probability distributions of benefits and costs associated with available options, but the variation in those benefits and costs may still impose survival (and sometimes fecundity) risk (Caraco, 1980; McNamara & Houston, 1982; Pulliam & Millikan, 1982; Real, 1981; Stephens & Charnov, 1982). This chapter deals solely with this second aspect of foraging in stochastic environments.

To study preference over levels of risk, we initially characterize a probability distribution of a foraging currency by its statistical moments: mean, variance (or standard deviation), and skew. We usually take reward size as the random

1

variable in experiments. But the logic we develop applies to problems where either the cost of obtaining a required amount of food (Caraco, 1981a) or the rate of energy intake (Stephens & Charnov, 1982) is the random variable of interest.

For each member of a set of benefit or cost distributions, we relate the statistical moments to the probability that the forager will obtain less than its physiologically required intake in the time available for feeding. We take the probability of an energetic deficit as the proxy attribute for fitness in our models. For nonbreeding animals this probability is functionally related to the probability of starvation (Caraco, Martindale, & Whittam, 1980; Pulliam & Millikan, 1982). We assume that natural selection favors discrimination abilities (e.g., Commons, 1981; Commons, Woodford, & Ducheny, 1982) and decision rules that promote survival in nonbreeders. Therefore, a forager should always prefer the benefit distribution associated with the smallest attainable probability of an energetic deficit (Caraco et al., 1980; Houston & McNamara, 1982; Pulliam & Millikan, 1982; Stephens & Charnov, 1982). Furthermore, these probabilities should allow one to predict a preference ranking over available foraging options (Caraco, 1983). Perhaps the most interesting departure of the theory of risk-sensitive foraging from deterministic foraging theory is the relationship predicted between choice and energy budgets. The risk-sensitive forager's preference for one reward versus another need not be fixed but can depend (in the manner described in the following) on a comparison of required and expected food intake (Caraco et al., 1980; Houston & McNamara, 1982; Stephens, 1981; for a related phenomenon see de Villiers & Herrnstein, 1976).

A MINIMIZATION PREMISE

The models presented here employ optimization, though it is in no way anticipated that optimal behavior will be commonly realized. Optimization provides a logical, quantitative means to generate testable hypotheses based on assumptions about natural selection. Properly interpreted, optimization models make no unreasonable expectations of nature. The purpose of such models is to elucidate the consequences of possible selective forces governing Darwinian evolution (Hinson & Staddon, 1983; Maynard Smith, 1978; Pyke, Pulliam, & Charnov, 1977).

Suppose an animal exploiting a stochastic environment has n foraging opportunities during a finite time interval (a day for convenience). Denote the reward at trial i ($i = 1, 2, \ldots, n$) with the independent random variable x_i. The mean and variance of each x_i are finite: $E[x_i], V[x_i] < \infty$. $Y = \sum_{i=1}^{n} x_i$ is the total reward acquired during the day. Then $E[Y] = \sum_{i=1}^{n} E[x_i] = \mu_Y$, and $V[Y] = \sum_{i=1}^{n} V[x_i] = \sigma^2_Y$. $F(Y)$ is the distribution function; $F(y) = Pr[Y \leq y]$. As long as one x_i does not dominate the sum, and the x_i's are not uniformly skewed (see following), Y should approach normality for sufficiently large n by the central-limit theorem.

Assume that the forager must accumulate a total reward exceeding R to satisfy daily physiological requirements. Let $F(R) = Pr[Y \leq R]$ be the probability of an energetic deficit. For simplicity we assume that selection on survival might favor minimizing this probability. More complex relationships between energy intake and fitness (Caraco, 1980; McNamara & Houston, 1982) are discussed later.

Following Stephens and Charnov (1982), we use a simple transformation as a useful characterization of the forager's problem. Because Y approaches normality, the random variable z, where $z = (Y - \mu_Y)/\sigma_Y$, is approximated by the standard normal distribution. Minimizing $F(R)$ is then equivalent to minimizing

$$Pr[z \leqslant (R - \mu_Y)/\sigma_Y] = \phi(z_R). \qquad (1)$$

Suppose the forager (fully informed by assumption) must choose to allocate its time to one of k elements (that is, reward probability distributions) of a set S_1. S_1 might consist of k foraging habitats situated so that the cost of switching habitats during the day would be prohibitive. In making the choice, larger means are always attractive, because $\partial\phi(z_R)/\partial\mu_Y < 0$. The influence of the standard deviation depends on the sign of $(R - \mu_Y)$; that is,

$$\partial\phi(z_R)/\partial\sigma_Y > 0, \text{ if } \mu_Y > R \qquad (2)$$

$$\partial\phi(z_R)/\partial\sigma_Y < 0, \text{ if } \mu_Y < R. \qquad (3)$$

When a forager can expect its intake to exceed its requirement ($\mu_Y > R$, a positive energy budget), increasing variance decreases an option's value. But when the forager can expect an energetic deficit ($\mu_Y < R$, a negative energy budget), increasing reward variance enhances the value of an option (Caraco et al., 1980; Houston & McNamara, 1982; Pulliam & Millikan, 1982; Stephens & Charnov, 1982).

We can immediately form some hypotheses from (2) and (3). Consider an animal presented with experimental choices between a constant reward ($\sigma_Y = 0$) and a variable option ($\sigma_Y > 0$) with an expected value equal to the constant reward. According to (2), the animal should prefer the constant reward if its expected energy budget is positive. However, according to (3), the animal should prefer the variable option if its expected energy budget is negative. These predicted behaviors usually are termed, respectively, risk-aversion and risk-proneness (Keeney & Raiffa, 1976), because risk ordinarily is assumed to depend on a measure of variability (e.g., Pollatsek & Tversky, 1970).

Next, presume an animal is presented with a series of choices constructed from all combinations of the elements taken two at a time from a set S_2; that is, if S_2 contains k elements, one considers the $k!/2[k - 2)!]$ different choice situations. Each reward probability distribution $f_i \in S_2$ has the same expected value (and no skew) and a unique standard deviation. Because the assumed overall objective is the minimization of $\phi(z_R)$, i.e.,

$$\min_{f_i \in S_2} \phi(z_R|\mu, \sigma_i), \qquad (4)$$

expressions (2) and (3) predict that the animal's preference ranking over the elements of S_2 should exhibit a strictly monotone ordering (Caraco, 1983). For positive energy budgets ($\mu_Y > R$), preference rank should decrease strictly as σ_Y increases about the common mean. If the forager can expect a negative energy budget ($\mu_Y < R$), preference rank should increase strictly as the standard deviation increases. In either case, the minimal $\phi(z_R)$ should be preferred over all other outcomes, but the preference ordering reverses if the sign of the quantity ($R - \mu_Y$) is changed.

The analysis of the preceding paragraph yields the same predictions if risk is characterized in terms of reward variance. However, the minimization of $\phi(z_R)$ and variance-discounting models (see following) make different predictions in terms of the interaction of mean reward with variability. Suppose the forager can choose across a large number of options that differ in both mean reward and standard deviation (under the assumption of no skew). The distribution(s) preferred over all others should be the (μ_Y, σ_Y) combination(s) minimizing the probability of an energetic deficit; that is, the distributions should be ranked from minimal to maximal $\phi(z_R)$ for a particular energy budget. For fixed R, consider a set of reward distributions yielding the same $Pr[Y \leq R]$. The forager should be indifferent between (i.e., prefer equally) any two of these distributions, because they enhance survival equally (which assumes that indifferences will be transitive). Because the $F(R)$ are equal, each such distribution must have the same z value (say z^*) according to (1). Then the various (μ_Y, σ_Y) elements of this indifference set determine the indifference curve (Stephens & Charnov, 1982):

$$\mu_Y = R - \sigma_Y z^*. \tag{5}$$

Given a preference ordering in terms of $\phi(z_R)$, an indifference set defines a straight line in the μ–σ plane. The marginal rate of substitution of σ_Y for μ_Y along this indifference curve is

$$-(\partial z^*/\partial \mu_Y)/(\partial z^*/\partial \sigma_Y) =$$
$$(1/\sigma_Y)\,(\sigma_Y^2/[\mu_Y - R]) = -(z^*)^{-1}, \tag{6}$$

a constant. Linearity of indifference curves holds whether the forager avoids or prefers reward variability. The sign of the slope of (5) is negative in the first case and positive in the second, and z^* has the sign opposite to the sign of the slope of the indifference curve.

If indifference curves are linear in the μ–σ plane, mean and variance (σ_Y^2) must trade off nonlinearly. Equation (5) implies that the forager that ranks options in terms of $\phi(z_R)$ should exhibit decreasing risk-sensitivity (Keeney & Raiffa, 1976). Analyzing the marginal rate of substitution of variance for mean along an indifference curve (constant z^*) shows that

$$-(\partial z^*/\partial \mu_Y)/(\partial z^*/\partial \sigma^2_Y) = -2\sigma_Y/z^*. \tag{7}$$

Therefore, the trade-off between μ_Y and σ^2_Y depends on the value of the mean, because σ_Y fixes μ_Y for a given R and z^*. The consequences of (7) are the following:

For a positive energy budget ($\mu_Y > R$), a forager should accept a larger increase in variance for a given increase in mean as the mean itself increases along an indifference curve (constant z^*);

For a negative energy budget ($\mu_Y < R$), a forager should accept a smaller increase in variance for a given increase in mean as the mean itself increases along an indifference curve.

General points concerning variable (i.e., decreasing and increasing) risk-sensitivity are found in Pratt (1964) and in Keeney and Raiffa (1976). For applications to foraging theory, see Caraco et al. (1980) or Caraco (1981b, 1982).

Variance-discounting models of foraging preference (Oster & Wilson, 1978; Real, 1980, 1981) portray risk-sensitivity a bit differently. The basic assumption of these models is that the value (U) of a reward probability distribution is a linear combination of mean and variance. They take

$$U = \mu_Y - \alpha\sigma^2_Y, \tag{8}$$

where α is a constant. $\alpha > 0$ if the forager should avoid reward variability (Real, 1980), and $\alpha < 0$ if the forager should prefer variability. The criterion of optimality is the maximization of U over available reward distributions. Variance discounting predicts indifference curves (constant U) that are linear in the $\mu-\sigma^2$ plane (Real, Ott, & Silverfine, 1982) and, consequently, nonlinear in the $\mu-\sigma$ plane. Under variance discounting, the mean-variance trade-off is independent of the value of the mean; that is,

$$-(\partial U/\partial\mu_Y)/(\partial U/\partial\sigma^2_Y) = 1/\alpha, \tag{9}$$

a condition that necessarily implies constant risk-sensitivity (Keeney & Raiffa, 1976). Therefore, minimizing $\phi(z_R)$ and variance discounting (maximizing $\mu_Y - \alpha\sigma^2_Y$) predict different isopreference sets over (μ_Y, σ_Y) combinations, but the two theories can predict exactly the same response to variation about a fixed mean reward. Note that one cannot directly compare the efficiency of minimizing $\phi(z_R)$ with variance discounting, because the two models assume a different currency of fitness.

Caraco and Chasin (1984) extend the analysis of risk-sensitivity to reward skew (the third moment about the mean, $E[(Y - \mu_Y)^3]$). When each x_i is uniformly skewed, or when the forager experiences a rare event of very large absolute value (an extremely large or extremely small x_i), the probability distribution of total daily intake can be skewed (Drake, 1967). The analysis was suggested by the observation that foragers in nature often encounter skewed reward distributions (e.g., Feinsinger, 1978; Gill & Wolf, 1975). If reward skew can influence survival, skew may also influence foraging preference (Oster & Wilson, 1978; also see Pollatsek & Tversky, 1970).

Caraco and Chasin (1984) develop two simple models for preference over levels of reward skew. One model employs an expected utility argument (as a normative surrogate for expected fitness) and indicates some general conditions that could induce preference for positive or negative skew. When the forager seeks to avoid reward variability, either decreasing or constant risk-sensitivity is a sufficient condition for positive skew (i.e., $E[Y - \mu_Y{}^3] > 0$) to increase expected utility. Increasing risk-sensitivity is a necessary, but not sufficient, condition for negative skew to increase expected utility when the forager avoids variance. Analogous conditions are given for foragers preferring reward variability.

The logic of the second model is similar to that used previously; that is, the forager is assumed to select a strategy that minimizes the probability of an energetic deficit. Caraco and Chasin (1984) examine the special case in which the forager has two options. Each reward distribution has the same mean and standard deviation (to control for responses to these parameters). The absolute values of the third moments are equal, but one distribution is skewed positively and the other is skewed negatively. Analysis of this model predicts that for sufficiently positive or sufficiently negative energy budgets, positive skew provides a lower probability of an energetic deficit. However, when the value of R is close to the common mean, negative skew should be preferred. The two models are reconciled by observing that, when R increases through an interval centered on the common mean of the distributions, the forager should switch from avoiding to preferring reward variability, as predicted by expressions (2) and (3). This shift in preference amounts to increasing risk-sensitivity near the mean, which is just the necessary condition for preferring negative skew under the expected utility model.

This section of the chapter has advanced some ideas relating reward stochasticity and energy budgets to foraging preference. Before critiquing the model and discussing some extensions of the major premise (that selection might favor behaviors minimizing the probability that total energy intake is less than the daily requirement) of this section, we summarize some predictions deduced from the premise:

1. A forager should avoid (prefer) variability about a given mean reward when its expected daily energy budget is positive (negative).

2. When skewless reward distributions differ in standard deviation, but not in mean reward, a forager should rank the distributions by preference in a strictly monotone order. The distribution associated with the smallest probability of an energetic deficit should be preferred over all others. If the forager's expected energy budget is positive, the distributions should be ordered preferentially from smallest to largest standard deviation. If the forager's expected energy budget is negative, the ranking should proceed from largest to smallest standard deviation.

3. For skewless distributions, a set of equally valued foraging options should define a linear indifference curve in the μ–σ plane.

4. A forager that can expect to meet its physiological requirement easily should prefer a positively skewed distribution over a negatively skewed distribution when the two reward distributions have equal means and equal standard deviations.

PROBLEMS WITH THE MINIMIZATION PREMISE

Evolutionary ecologists like to believe that an empirically estimable index of foraging performance (e.g., daily food intake) maps at least monotonically into fitness (see Oster & Wilson, 1978). Fitness, as well as its close relative inclusive fitness, can be an elusive quantity (see Stearns, 1976). In terms of life history theory, the best foraging strategy is that associated with the maximization of reproductive value at every age (see Schaffer, 1983), where reproductive value is related to the objective functional of dynamic programming (Bellman, 1957). For a forager outside of its breeding season, reproductive value becomes a combination of current survival plus expected future reproductive success (over the organism's lifetime) weighted appropriately by the inverse of the population's growth rate (Schaffer, 1983). Basically, ecologists hope that a foraging currency indicates something reasonable about an animal's immediate survival and its chance of later reproduction.

Deterministic foraging models characterize available options by expected values only. This necessarily implies that expected fitness is a linear function of the foraging currency. Various theoretical objections to determinism (e.g., Caraco, 1980; McNamara & Houston, 1982; Oster & Wilson, 1978; Real, 1980; Stephens & Charnov, 1982) argue that expected fitness depends on the probability distribution of the foraging currency. Each of these studies concludes that the fitness function will not be linear. Furthermore, empirical measures of utility or effective value indicate that foragers do not scale levels of random rewards linearly (e.g., Caraco et al., 1980; Commons, Woodford, & Ducheny, 1982).

The minimization premise developed previously for a nonbreeding forager considers only immediate (i.e., daily) survival and takes fitness (W) as a step function of total daily food intake; that is,

$$W = 0, \text{ if } Y \leqslant R$$
$$W = 1, \text{ if } Y > R. \tag{10}$$

$E[W]$ then becomes $Pr[Y > R]$.

McNamara and Houston (1982) point out that the step function (10) neglects the effect of one day's food intake on future survival (and reproduction); that is, all foragers with a daily food intake exceeding the physiological requirement need not be equally "fit." When energy can be stored on one day and used the next, it is very possible that $dW/dY > 0$ for at least some $Y > R$. Caraco (1980) and McNamara and Houston (1982) adopt a convex–concave fitness function, where $dW/dY > 0$, and

$$d^2W/dY^2 > 0 \text{ for } Y < R \tag{11}$$

$$d^2W/dY^2 < 0 \text{ for } Y > R. \tag{12}$$

Expressions (11) and (12) are analogous, respectively, to (3) and (2) in that convexity implies that expected fitness increases with reward variability and concavity implies that expected fitness decreases with reward variability (via Jensen's inequality; see Caraco et al., 1980). Caraco (1980) assumed that W has the convex–concave form of (11) and (12). McNamara and Houston (1982) provide a rigorous justification of this type of fitness function.

A second problem with the minimization premise of the preceding section is that the optimization procedure is static rather than dynamic. Minimizing $\phi(z_R)$ supposes that the forager makes one decision and receives the outcome of that decision at the end of the foraging day. Therefore, there is no feedback from the forager's progress through the day on the animal's strategy. If a forager can switch from one available option to another during the day without incurring prohibitive costs, feedback may decrease the $Pr[Y \leq R]$. Houston and McNamara (1982) discuss the optimal dynamic policy when there is no cost to switching between options that have the same mean, but different levels of reward variability. Their analysis yields a surprisingly simple result. As long as the forager can expect to meet requirements, it should favor the option with lower variability. However, whenever the forager can expect an energetic deficit, it should choose the more variable option. Consequently, the optimally controlling forager may switch back and forth between levels of variability as its local success rate changes due to random reward variation. A similar policy, but with delayed switching, should emerge if the forager incurs a nonprohibitive cost for switching between resources (McNamara, personal communication, 1983).

The solutions to these two problems of the minimization premise (i.e., its oversimplification of the fitness function and its static optimization criterion) do not substantially alter the predictions suggested by the minimization of the probability of an energetic deficit. For simplicity, we retain the $Pr[Y \leq R]$ as our predictive criterion in discussing some tests of risk-sensitive foraging.

TESTING THE PREDICTIONS
OF THE MINIMIZATION PREMISE

We begin this section by outlining methods used in our experimental analyses of foraging under risk. Subjects have included yellow-eyed juncos (*Junco phaeonotus*), dark-eyed juncos (*J. hyemalis*) and white-crowned sparrows (*Zonotrichia leucophrys*). All birds are caught in the wild and can easily be maintained in the laboratory.

A bird is kept in a large aviary equipped with two feeding stations (1 meter apart). A partition separates the stations so that a bird's choice of one station versus the other is unequivocal. An experimenter, positioned behind a two-way mirror, presents small dishes containing predetermined numbers of millet seeds (*Panicum miliaceum*) at the stations.

Birds quickly learn to perch on the midline between the feeding stations. The perch is located 2.2 meters from each station. We regularly test for position preference (see Caraco et al., 1980) and test for foraging preference only with subjects that have demonstrated indifference in a choice between left and right sides of their aviary.

Several factors govern a bird's daily energy budget (see Caraco, 1981b). A simple estimation procedure for dark-eyed juncos is outlined. For a more sophisticated physiological analysis of energy intake and metabolism, see Caraco et al. (1980).

A 19 gram junco experiences a constant ambient temperature of 10°C and a photoperiod of 10 hours (0730–1730 hours). The exact number of seeds consumed during each half hour over the course of the 10-hour foraging day is counted. Pre-experimental deprivation always begins at 0900. During the first 1.5 h of the day (0730–0900), the average number of seeds consumed is 171.2 ± 7.72 (*SE*, $N = 24$). Over the 10 h day the average consumption is 771.6 ± 34.2 (*SE*, $N = 18$). Most of the variability in seed consumption results from within-individual variation across repeated samples, rather than from differences among subjects. Consequently, we assume that each junco requires 600.4 (i.e., 771.6 − 171.2) seeds after deprivation to meet its daily requirement. However, if the birds learn to anticipate the deprivation, 600.4 seeds may be an overestimate (see Kacelnik, 1979).

The bird's expected energy budget can be manipulated by adjusting the length of pre-experimental deprivation (D, in hours) and the average feeding rate (f, in seeds/hour) during an experiment. If $(8.5 - D)f > 600.4$, the junco can expect a positive energy budget. $D = 1.5$ and $f = 120$ are taken to assure an expectation of a positive energy budget. If $(8.5 - D)f < 600.4$, the junco can expect a negative energy budget. $D = 4$ and $f = 60$ are taken to achieve this condition. If $D = 2$ and $f = 90$, then $(8.5 - D)f = 600$. This treatment has been referred to elsewhere (Caraco, 1981b) as a balanced energy budget, which implies that the bird barely attains its requirement if it spends all available time foraging.

The simplest way to describe current experimental procedures is to give an example. A coin toss assigns a certain reward of 3 seeds to one feeding station. At the other station the bird obtains either 1 or 5 seeds with equal probability. Mean rewards are identical, but the levels of variability differ. The experiment consists of 24 forced-choice learning trials followed immediately by 30 preference trials.

Food is presented at only one station on each learning trial. Subjects reliably respond to the appearance of the food dish in the sense that they visit the "correct" station when food is available at only one station. The bird visits each station 12 times during the learning trials. The subject receives the same total number of seeds at each station during these trials (unless an experiment examines the trade-off between mean and variability). Twenty-four learning trials presumably allow the junco sufficient experience to discriminate between the two reward distributions (e.g., Commons, 1981) and should reduce sampling in the subsequent preference test (Krebs et al., 1978; Lea, 1979; Shettleworth, 1978).

Consider a positive energy budget as an example. The delay between each trial (learning and preference) is 1.5 minutes, so that $f = 120$ seeds/hour. Caraco et al. (1980) and Caraco (1981b) used a variable delay between trials, but this difference does not appear to influence the results. During each preference trial the two food dishes are presented simultaneously. The bird selects one feeding station and the other dish is removed.

The null hypothesis assumes indifference (equal preference), which implies that choice probabilities over the 30 preference trials will not differ significantly from 0.5. Heterogeneity tests consistently fail to reject the hypothesis that choices made during sequential trials are statistically independent (Caraco, 1981b, 1982, 1983; Caraco & Chasin, 1984; Caraco et al., 1980). From the binomial distribution with parameters 30 and 0.5, a significant preference (i.e., $p < 0.05$) occurs when a bird chooses one station during 21 or more of the preference trials.

We divide the discussion of our laboratory work with foraging birds into five subsections.

1. Response to Variation about a Given Mean.   Caraco et al. (1980) examined foraging preferences of yellow-eyed juncos at both positive and negative energy budgets. Metabolic rate was estimated from measures of oxygen consumption, and the energetic value of seeds was estimated by bomb calorimetry. In some of the experiments birds were presented with choices of a constant reward or a variable option with a mean equal to the constant reward. The juncos most often preferred the constant reward at positive energy budgets but most often preferred the variable reward at negative energy budgets. Figure 1.1 summarizes the average choice probabilities observed in these experiments.

In further experiments utility functions (DeGroot, 1970; Keeney & Raiffa, 1976) were estimated in order to describe preference over levels of the random variable (reward size). Utility functions were obtained for several birds at each energy budget. The constant reward was titrated above or below the mean of a given variable reward until indifference was noted. Then the utility of the constant reward was taken as equal to the expected utility of the variable reward. The estimated functions were concave when the birds avoided variability and convex when the birds preferred variability about a given mean (as predicted by expressions 11 and 12). The utility functions and associated risk premiums (dif-

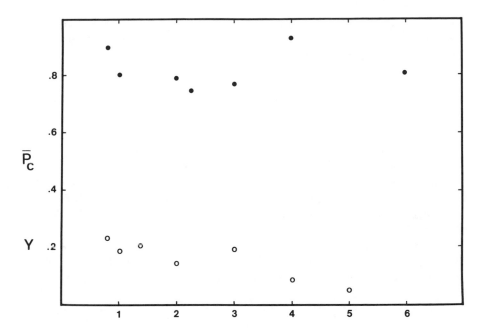

FIG. 1.1.   Average choice probabilities for yellow-eyed juncos at positive- and negative-energy budgets. Each experiment involved a series of choices between a constant reward and a variable reward with a mean equal to the constant reward. The abscissa is the variance to mean ratio of the variable reward. $\bar{p}_c$ represents the average proportion of trials where the constant reward was selected. Closed circles (means of five subjects) represent choices made at positive-energy budgets; the constant reward is preferred. Open circles (means of four subjects) represent choices made at negative-energy budgets; the variable reward is preferred.

ference between the associated indifference point and the mean of a given probability distribution; see Keeney & Raiffa, 1976) indicated decreasing risk-sensitivity, whether the juncos avoided or preferred reward variability. Each result is fully consistent with the minimization premise (expressions 2, 3, and equation 5).

Caraco (1981b) studied dark-eyed juncos. In all experiments mean rewards were equal. One reward was a constant number of seeds, whereas the other was variable. Given estimates of seed consumption through the day, pre-experimental deprivation and feeding-rate combinations were chosen to achieve positive, balanced (where, in theory, $\mu_Y = R$), and negative expected energy budgets. Most experiments at positive energy budgets resulted in significant preference for the constant reward (see Fig. 1.2). Indifference was the most common result at balanced energy budgets, but preference for the constant reward remained more common than preference for the variable reward. Most experiments at negative energy budgets resulted in significant preference for the variable reward (see Fig. 1.2). Essentially, the juncos' aversion to reward variation decreased as their expected daily energy intake decreased, until they came to prefer variability whenever they expected an energetic deficit.

2. Between-Patch and Within-Patch Choice. White-crowned sparrows were the subjects in Caraco (1982). These birds weigh approximately 50% more than a junco. The white-crowned sparrows were subjected to the same experiments that had resulted in aversion to variable rewards in dark-eyed juncos. Seed-consumption estimates assured positive energy budgets. No significant difference was detected in comparing choice probabilities of the two species, a result consistent with the minimization premise; that is, response to reward variability was just as strong in the larger subjects, even though expected time until starvation increases with body size in wintering birds (Calder, 1974; Downhower, 1976).

All experiments discussed to this point involved choices between the two feeding stations with rewards available on a discrete-trial basis. It was presumed that the procedures just described mimic patch or microhabitat choice by a bird

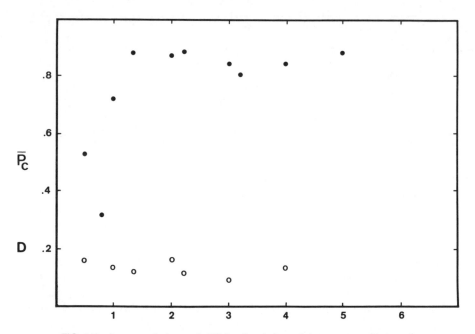

FIG. 1.2. Average choice probabilities for dark-eyed juncos at positive, and negative-energy budgets. Axes and symbols are the same as in Fig. 1.1. Each entry is the mean choice probability for three individuals. For positive-energy budgets (closed circles), the certain reward is preferred whenever the variance of the variable reward is at least as great as its mean. For negative-energy budgets (open circles), the variable reward is preferred.

perched midway between food sources. Risk-sensitivity may also influence diet selection, the choice of food types within a patch (Real, 1981; Waddington, Allen, & Heinrich, 1981). We attempted to simulate this problem by placing a large number of petri dishes on the floor of an aviary. Constant and variable rewards were covered by differently colored pieces of paper. The two reward types were equally abundant, and the mean of the variable reward equalled the constant reward. Feeding rates assured positive energy budgets, and 21 of 27 experiments resulted in significant preference for the constant reward. The sparrows often learned to discriminate between the two reward types after sampling only 10 to 15 total dishes. We conclude that risk-sensitivity may influence foraging choice at both between-patch and within-patch (diet) levels.

3. Preference Ordering over Reward Variability. All the experiments we have discussed so far in this section involved choices between a constant and a variable reward. But discrimination among, and preferential choice over, elements of a set of variable rewards is necessary, if risk-sensitive foraging is to have significance in nature. In Caraco (1983) white-crowned sparrows were presented with five series of two-choice experiments. In half of the preference tests both rewards were variable; mean rewards were always equal. Preference for the lower standard deviation was the most common response at positive energy budgets. Preference for the greater standard deviation predominated at negative energy budgets.

Over the course of these experiments, subjects faced choices over all possible pairs of elements of a set of probability distributions differing in standard deviation (but not in mean reward). Two-thirds of the preference rankings over reward standard deviation indicated a monotone ordering, as predicted by the minimization premise. These results generally support the survival model, particularly with respect to predicted aversion to or preference for reward variability. The weaker result for preference orderings suggests that more complex models may be required to account for individual variation and temporal change in preference (Coombs & Huang, 1976; Luce & Suppes, 1965; van Santen, 1978).

4. Reward Skew. Caraco and Chasin (1984) presented white-crowned sparrows with choices where minimization of the $Pr [Y \leq R]$ predicts preference for positive skew. The two rewards in any particular experiment did not differ in either mean or standard deviation. Absolute values of the third moment were equal but differed in sign. Figure 1.3 summarizes average choice probabilities. The birds preferred positive skew in 42 of 72 experiments. Indifference occurred in 22 experiments, but the negatively skewed reward was preferred significantly in only 8 experiments. The response to skew was weaker than response to standard deviation noted in some of the same subjects. However, analysis of the results does suggest that reward skew can influence preference when skew influences the probability of an energetic deficit.

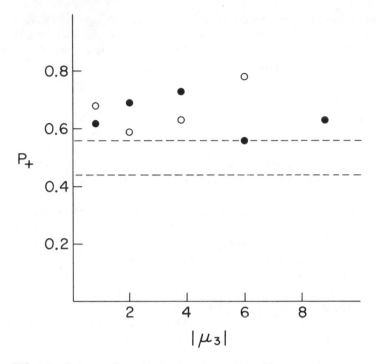

FIG. 1.3.   Preference for positively skewed rewards in white-crowned sparrows. Each experiment involved a series of choices between two variable rewards. Means and standard deviations were equal. The absolute values of the third moments (the abscissa in the figure) were equal, but one reward was skewed positively while the other was skewed negatively. The ordinate is the mean proportional choice of the positively skewed reward. Each entry is the mean choice probability for eight experiments. The dashed lines indicate the indifference band (p_+ not significantly different from 0.5). The open circles represent experiments involving higher mean rewards. Eight of nine mean choice probabilities show preference for the positively skewed reward. Increasing the mean reward (open cirlces) had no significant influence on choice probabilities.

5. *Mean-Variance Trade-off.*   Caraco and Lima (1985) studied the interaction of mean reward size and reward-size variability in dark-eyed juncos' foraging preferences. The procedure resembled that used by Real et al. (1982). Each experiment involved discrete-trial choices between a constant and a variable reward. In a particular series of experiments, the constant reward always had the same value (2 seeds in the first series; 3 seeds in the second series). By systematically exploring different (μ, σ) combinations, one locates three sets of reward distributions: (a) a set where the constant reward is preferred over each element, (b) a set where each element is preferred over the constant reward, and (c) an indifference set. Ideally, the experiments would distinguish between the predic-

tions of constant risk-sensitivity (equations 7 and 8) and the form of decreasing risk-sensitivity assumed in the minimization of $\phi(z_R)$ (equations 5 and 6).

All experiments involved dark-eyed juncos experiencing positive energy budgets. Results in both series of experiments support the qualitative predictions of risk-aversion. At a given value of μ, preference for the certain reward increases as σ increases. At a given value of σ, preference for the certain reward decreases as μ increases. These patterns support both the minimization premise and variance discounting (i.e., both decreasing and constant risk-aversion predict these behaviors). By considering only the two separate indifference sets, we cannot distinguish a better statistical correlation between μ and σ than between μ and σ^2. However, after the constant reward was increased from 2 seeds to 3 seeds, the juncos' aversion to a given level of reward variability decreased (Caraco & Lima, 1985). This result suggests decreasing risk-aversion (see Caraco et al., 1980), though not necessarily the specific form predicted by minimizing $\phi(z_R)$.

DISCUSSION

We believe that our experiments present reasonable evidence that foragers in nature respond not just to mean rewards, but also to variability within available rewards. Furthermore, a forager's preferences may vary as its energetic condition varies, and the scaling of expected rewards in relation to physiological requirements may predict that variation in preference (Barnard & Brown, 1985; Caraco, 1983). The potential for labile risk-sensitive foraging preferences may be common in small homeotherms that must regulate their food intake over relatively short periods of time. In larger animals, where variation in survival probabilities should be less dependent on variation in daily food intake, response to risk may be less dependent on a forager's expected 24-hour energy budget (J. H. Kagel, personal communication, 1984).

The experiments presented here involve an open economy (Hursh, 1980), in that the birds had ad lib access to food both before and 1 hour after an experimental session. In a closed economy (Collier, Hirsh, & Hamlin, 1972; Hursh, 1980), an animal's total daily ration is acquired during an experiment (e.g., within an operant chamber). The contrasting procedures may, in some cases, result in different responses to foraging risk (Fantino & Abarca, 1985). However, the open- versus closed-economy issue probably does not bear directly on our work with small birds, because the subjects' response to risk changed as their expected energy budget changed.

When we observe a significant preference in our experiments, we seldom observe exclusive choice of the preferred alternative (see Figs. 1.1–1.3). Depending on subject and experiment, the average choice probability for the preferred reward lies between 0.8 and 0.93 (given a significant preference). If the minimization premise is taken as the criterion of performance, nonexclusive choice represents a departure from optimality. Again, we do not test to see whether animals perform optimally. They do not. Instead, we test predictions of models employing optimization techniques to gain some insight into the economics of behavior. In this sense our preference/indifference results offer strong qualitative support for the assumptions embedded in an optimality model. Still, the near ubiquity of nonexclusive choice in our experiments may deserve some comment.

Caraco (1983) lists several possible explanations for the lack of exclusive choice. The more plausible of these suggestions are reviewed as follows:

1. Animals ordinarily exposed to temporally varying rewards should sample currently less preferred, but potentially profitable, resources (e.g., Caraco, 1980; Gill & Wolf, 1977; Krebs et al., 1978; Real, 1981). Consequently, sampling behavior may constrain choice probabilities adaptively. However, this possibility would invoke a constraint not included in the model in order to "explain away" deviations from a quantitative prediction. Therefore, we cannot propose its acceptance until the model has been appropriately modified and tested accordingly.

2. Preference requires discrimination between possible outcomes. The length of training and preference tests in our experiments is rather short in comparison to lengths used in most operant studies. Nonexclusive choice might somehow be related to incomplete discrimination of rewards or spatial locations of rewards. Perhaps lengthier sessions would have resulted in exclusive choice over the last n preference trials, although we seldom observe trends within a session. This possibility is simpler than the explanation offered previously. However, it involves relaxing the model's assumption of complete information in order to explain away nonexclusive choice. Lack of discrimination may influence our results, but no reason for accepting this possibility has yet been demonstrated.

3. Nonexclusive choice may result simply from stochasticity in behavior over the course of 30 preference trials, so that neither an adaptive explanation nor a claim of lack of information per se need be invoked (Caraco, 1982). We can perhaps view the subject as a black box with an environmental input and a random output (behavior). In terms used by Luce and Suppes (1965), we may need to replace an algebraic theory of choice with a probabilistic theory.

Consider two distributions of total reward f_1 and f_2. Let $a \, p \, b$ designate a relationship "a is preferred to b"; let i in place of p (i.e., $a \, i \, b$) represent indifference. The development described previously has been an algebraic theory, essentially a strong-utility model. The minimization premise predicts binary relationships of the form

$$Pr[Y \leqslant R|f_1] > Pr[Y \leqslant R|f_2]$$
$$\Rightarrow Pr[f_1 \, p \, f_2] = 0 \tag{13}$$

$$Pr[Y \leq R|f_1] = Pr[Y \leq R|f_2]$$
$$\Rightarrow f_1 \ i \ f_2 \Rightarrow Pr[f_1 \ p \ f_2] = 1/2 \tag{14}$$

$$Pr[Y \leq R|f_1] < Pr[Y \leq R|f_2]$$
$$\Rightarrow Pr \ [f_1 \ p \ f_2] = 1. \tag{15}$$

Under the algebraic theory, if the forager must choose between two options, only exclusive choice of one option (13 and 15) or equiprobable utilization (indifference, 14) is predicted. This sort of choice behavior is predicted by unconstrained natural selection on preference behavior. But suppose that preference is constrained by the animal's biology so that choice is stochastic. Then the animal's behavior is portrayed more realistically with a probabilistic, or weak-utility, model. (15) could be replaced with

$$Pr[Y \leq R|f_1] \leq Pr[Y \leq R|f_2]$$
$$\Rightarrow Pr[f_1 \ p \ f_2] \geqslant 1/2. \tag{16}$$

If f_1 advances survival more than f_2, there is a tendency to prefer f_1. As the difference, in terms of $Pr[Y \leq R]$, between f_1 and f_2 increases, the tendency to choose f_1 presumably increases. As the strength of selection acting on choice behavior increases, choice probabilities should more closely approach the strong-utility model's predictions.

It is suspected that each of these three possibilities, and perhaps weak position bias as well, influences these results. However, no basis has been established for estimating their relative importance.

Our observation that foraging birds may prefer the more variable reward when arithmetic means are equal should not surprise operant psychologists dealing with foraging rewards (e.g., Commons et al., 1982; Leventhal, Morrell, Morgan, & Perkins, 1959; Young, 1981). However, our subjects sometimes prefer the less variable reward. Furthermore, ecological studies of risk-sensitive foraging in nectar-feeding insects also have indicated preference for constant over variable rewards (Real, 1981; Real et al., 1982; Waddington et al., 1981). Subjects in operant studies are sometimes deprived to the level of as little as 80% of their normal body weight. But, like Krebs, Stephens, and Sutherland (1983), we feel it is too simplistic to attribute the contrasting results to differences in energy budgets alone. Subject species, apparatus, and procedures differ a great deal across these operant and ecological studies. One can only conclude that the results are not comparable in any rigorous and clear manner. Operant studies scaled to physiological requirements may provide useful bases of comparison.

Both psychologists (e.g., Commons et al., 1982; Herrnstein & Vaughan, 1980; Hinson & Staddon, 1983; Staddon, 1980) and ecologists (e.g., Gilliam, Green, & Pearson, 1982; Stephens & Charnov, 1982; Templeton & Lawlor, 1981; Turelli, Gillespie, & Schoener, 1982) are sometimes concerned about whether short-term or long-term (that is, molecular or molar) reward rate better predicts choice behavior. Most of our results have no relationship to this question. The option with the lesser (greater) variability on any one trial produces the lesser (greater) variability in total rewards across all preference trials. In the future we hope to test risk-sensitivity to foraging costs in a manner that can distinguish molecular from molar responses.

We have attempted to be quite conservative in interpreting the significance of our results and in comparing our results to those of other studies. However, we conclude with a highly speculative comment. Our results indicate that foraging birds prefer reward variability when they expect a net energetic loss but avoid the same variability when they expect an energetic profit. Friedman and Savage (1962) developed an aggregate utility function for human economic preferences over the random variable consumption stream (essentially, the amount of money the individual can spend on goods and services per unit of time). The economic analysis finds that humans tend to avoid or prefer variable options (e.g., gambling), depending on what Friedman and Savage (1962) call socioeconomic level. Below a certain level, variability is preferred, whereas above that level variability is avoided (cf. Tversky, 1967). If a particular level of consumption were perceived within a culture as being "required" or "just adequate," a parallel with the birds' foraging behavior might follow (loosely).

Tversky and Kahneman (1981) posed hypothetical questions concerning "gains and losses" contingent upon strategies intended to combat disease. They offered two variable options. Each would save the same average number of lives (and consequently lead to the same average number of deaths), but the variances differed. When the options were described in terms of lives to be saved (gains), the less variable option was preferred. When the options were described in terms of lives to be lost, the more variable option was preferred (Tversky & Kahneman, 1981). Shifting the context from expected gains to expected losses shifted preference from avoiding to preferring variability. Of course, no claim is made here that there is any functional relationship among these observations. But we do suggest that theories concerned with preference over stochastic benefits and/or costs may often be enhanced by scaling the random variable(s) in relation to some ecologically significant criterion of performance.

ACKNOWLEDGMENTS

This research was supported by National Science Foundation grants BNS–8020717 and BNS–8312154. We thank the Sixth Harvard Symposium on Quantitative Analyses of Behavior coordinators, A. I. Houston, J. H. Kagel, and L. L. Wolf for useful comments.

REFERENCES

Barnard, C. J., & Brown, C. A. J. (1985). Risk-sensitive foraging in common shrews (*Sorex araneus* L.). *Behavioral Ecology and Sociobiology, 16,* 161–164.
Bellman, R. (1957). *Dynamic programming.* Princeton: Princeton University Press.

Calder, W. A. (1974). Consequences of body size for avian energetics. In R. A. Paynter (Ed.), *Avian energetics* (pp. 86–144). Cambridge: Nuttal Ornithological Club.

Caraco, T. (1980). On foraging time allocation in a stochasic environment. *Ecology, 61,* 119–128.

Caraco, T. (1981a). Risk-sensitivity and foraging groups. *Ecology, 62,* 527–531.

Caraco, T. (1981b). Energy budgets, risk and foraging preferences in dark-eyed juncos (*Junco hyemalis*). *Behavioral Ecology and Sociobiology, 8,* 213–217.

Caraco, T. (1982). Aspects of risk-aversion in foraging white-crowned sparrows. *Animal Behaviour, 30,* 719–727.

Caraco, T. (1983). White-crowned sparrows (*Zonotrichia leucophrys*): Foraging preferences in a risky environment. *Behavioral Ecology and Sociobiology, 12,* 63–69.

Caraco, T., & Chasin, M. (1984). Foraging preferences: Response to reward skew. *Animal Behaviour, 32,* 76–85.

Caraco, T., & Lima, S. L. (1985). Foraging juncos: Interaction of reward mean and variability. *Animal Behaviour, 33,* 216–224.

Caraco, T., Martindale, S., & Whittam, T. S. (1980). An empirical demonstration of risk-sensitive foraging preferences. *Animal Behaviour, 28,* 820–830.

Collier, G. H., Hirsch, E., & Hamlin, P. H. (1972). The ecological determinants of reinforcement in the rat. *Physiology and Behavior, 9,* 705–716.

Commons, M. L. (1981). How reinforcement density is discriminated and scaled. In M. L. Commons & J. A. Nevin (Eds.), *Quantitative analyses of behavior, Vol. I: Discriminative properties of reinforcement schedules* (pp. 51–85). Cambridge, MA: Ballinger.

Commons, M. L., Woodford, M., & Ducheny, J. R. (1982). How reinforcers are aggregated in reinforcement-density discrimination and preference experiments. In M. L. Commons, R. J. Herrnstein, & H. Rachlin (Eds.), *Quantitative analyses of behavior, Vol. II: Matching and maximizing* (pp. 25–78). Cambridge, MA: Ballinger.

Coombs, C. H., & Huang, L. C. (1976). Test of the betweenness property of expected utility. *Journal of Mathematical Psychology, 13,* 323–337.

DeGroot, M. H. (1970). *Optimal statistical decisions.* New York: McGraw–Hill.

de Villiers, P. A., & Herrnstein, R. J. (1976). Toward a law of response strength. *Psychological Bulletin, 83,* 1131–1153.

Downhower, J. F. (1976). Darwin's finches and the evolution of sexual dimorphism in body size. *Nature, 263,* 558–563.

Drake, A. (1967). *Fundamentals of applied probability theory.* New York: McGraw-Hill.

Fantino, E., & Abarca, N. (1985). Choice, optimal foraging, and the delay-reduction hypothesis. *Behavioral and Brain Sciences, 8,* 315–330.

Feinsinger, P. (1978). Ecological interactions between plants and hummingbirds in a successional tropical community. *Ecological Monographs, 48,* 269–287.

Friedman, M., & Savage, L. J. (1962). The utility analysis of choices involving risk. In E. J. Hamilton, A. Rees, & H. G. Johnson (Eds.), *Landmarks in political economy* (pp. 297–336). Chicago: University of Chicago Press.

Gill, F. B., & Wolf, L. L. (1975). Foraging strategies and energetics of East African sunbirds at mistletoe flowers. *American Naturalist, 109,* 491–510.

Gill, F. B., & Wolf, L. L. (1977). Nonrandom foraging by sunbirds in a patchy environment. *Ecology, 58,* 1284–1296.

Gilliam, J. F., Green, R. F., & Pearson, N. E. (1982). The fallacy of the traffic policeman: A response to Templeton and Lawlor. *American Naturalist, 199,* 875–878.

Green, R. F. (1980). Bayesian birds: A simple example of Oaten's stochastic model of optimal foraging. *Theoretical Population Biology, 18,* 244–256.

Herrnstein, R. J., & Vaughan, W. (1980). Melioration and behavioral allocation. In J. E. R. Staddon (Ed.), *Limits to action: The allocation of individual behavior* (pp. 143–176). New York: Academic Press.

Hinson, J. M., & Staddon, J. E. R. (1983). Hill-climbing by pigeons. *Journal of the Experimental Analysis of Behavior, 39,* 25–47.

Houston, A., Kacelnik, A., & McNamara, J. (1982). Some learning rules for acquiring information. In D. McFarland (Ed.), *Functional ontogeny* (pp. 140–191). London: Pitman.

Houston, A., & McNamara, J. (1982). A sequential approach to risk-taking. *Animal Behaviour, 30,* 1260–1261.

Hursh, J. R. (1980). Economic concepts for the analysis of behavior. *Journal of the Experimental Analysis of Behavior, 34,* 219–238.

Kacelnik, A. (1979). *Studies of foraging behaviour in great tits (Parus major).* Doctoral dissertation, University of Oxford.

Keeney, R. L., & Raiffa, H. (1976). *Decisions with multiple objectives: Preferences and value tradeoffs.* New York: Wiley.

Krebs, J. R., Kacelnik, A., & Taylor, P. (1978). Test of optimal sampling by foraging great tits. *Nature, 275,* 27–31.

Krebs, J. R., Stephens, D. W., & Sutherland, W. J. (1983). Perspectives in optimal foraging. In A. H. Brush & G. A. Clark, Jr. (Eds.), *Perspectives in ornithology* (pp. 165–221). Cambridge, England: Cambridge University Press.

Lea, S. E. G. (1979). Foraging and reinforcement schedules in the pigeon: Optimal and non-optimal aspects of choice. *Animal Behaviour, 27,* 875–886.

Leventhal, A. M., Morrell, R. F., Morgan, E. F., Jr., & Perkins, C. C., Jr. (1959). The relation between mean reward and mean reinforcement. *Journal of Experimental Psychology, 57,* 284–257.

Lima, S. L. (1984). Downy woodpecker foraging behavior: Efficient sampling in simple stochastic environments. *Ecology, 65,* 166–174.

Luce, R. D., & Suppes, P. (1965). Preference, utility and subjective probability. In R. D. Luce, R. R. Bush, & E. Galanter (Eds.), *Handbook of mathematical psychology* (Vol. 3, pp. 249–410). New York: Wiley.

Maynard Smith, J. (1978). Optimization theory in evolution. *Annual Review of Ecology and Systematics, 9,* 31–56.

McNamara, J. (1982). Optimal patch use in a stochastic environment. *Theoretical Population Biology, 21,* 269–288.

McNamara, J., & Houston, A. (1982). Short-term behaviour and lifetime fitness. In D. McFarland (Ed.), *Functional ontogeny* (pp. 60–87). London: Pitman.

Oaten, A. (1977). Optimal foraging in patches: A case for stochasticity. *Theoretical Population Biology, 12,* 263–285.

Oster, G. F., & Wilson, E. O. (1978). Caste and ecology in the social insects. *Monographs in Population Biology, 12,* 1–352.

Pollatsek, A., & Tversky, A. (1970). A theory of risk. *Journal of Mathematical Psychology, 7,* 540–553.

Pratt, J. W. (1964). Risk aversion in the small and in the large. *Econometrica, 32,* 122–136.

Pulliam, H. R., & Millikan, G. C. (1982). Social organization in the non-reproductive season. In D. S. Farner & J. R. King (Eds.), *Avian biology* (Vol. 6, pp. 169–197). New York: Academic Press.

Pyke, G. H., Pulliam, H. R., & Charnov, E. L. (1977). Optimal foraging: A selective review of theory and tests. *Quarterly Review of Biology, 52,* 137–154.

Real, L. A. (1980). Fitness, uncertainty, and the role of diversification in evolution and behavior. *American Naturalist, 115,* 623–638.

Real, L. A. (1981). Uncertainty and pollinator-plant interactions: The foraging behavior of bees and wasps on artificial flowers. *Ecology, 62,* 20–26.

Real, L. A., Ott, J., & Silverfine, E. (1982). On the trade-off between the mean and the variance in foraging: An experimental analysis with bumblebees. *Ecology, 63,* 1617–1623.

Schaffer, W. M. (1983). The application of optimal control theory to the general life history problem. *American Naturalist, 121,* 418–431.

Shettleworth, S. J. (1978). Reinforcement and the organization of behavior in golden hamsters: Punishment of three action patterns. *Learning and Motivation, 9,* 99–123.

Staddon, J. E. R. (1980). Optimality analyses of operant behavior and their relation to optimal foraging. In J. E. R. Staddon (Ed.), *Limits to action, the allocation of individual behavior* (pp. 101–141). New York: Academic Press.

Stearns, S. C. (1976). Life-history tactics: A review of the ideas. *Quarterly Review of Biology, 51,* 3–47.

Stephens, D. W. (1981). The logic of risk-sensitive foraging preferences. *Animal Behaviour, 29,* 628–629.

Stephens, D. W., & Charnov, E. L. (1982). Optimal foraging: Some simple stochastic models. *Behavioral Ecology and Sociobiology, 10,* 251–263.

Templeton, A. R., & Lawlor, L. R. (1981). The fallacy of the averages in ecological optimization theory. *American Naturalist, 117,* 390–393.

Turelli, M., Gillespie, J. H., & Schoener, T. W. (1982). The fallacy of the fallacy of the averages in ecological optimization theory. *American Naturalist, 119,* 879–884.

Tversky, A. (1967). Utility theory and additivity analysis of risky choices. *Journal of Experimental Psychology, 75,* 27–36.

Tversky, A., & Kahneman, D. (1981). The framing of decisions and the psychology of choice. *Science, 211,* 453–458.

van Santen, J. P. H. (1978). A new axiomization of portfolio theory. *Journal of Mathematical Psychology, 17,* 14–20.

Waddington, K. D., Allen, T., & Heinrich, B. (1981). Floral preferences of bumblebees (*Bombus edwardsii*) in relation to intermittent versus continuous rewards. *Animal Behaviour, 29,* 779–784.

Young, J. S. (1981). Discrete-trial choice in pigeons: Effects of reinforcer magnitude. *Journal of the Experimental Analysis of Behavior, 35,* 23–29.

2

Foraging in Patches: There's More to Life than the Marginal Value Theorem

John M. McNamara
School of Mathematics
University of Bristol

Alasdair I. Houston
Department of Zoology
University of Cambridge
Current address: Dept. of Zoology, University of Oxford

INTRODUCTION

Optimal-foraging theory (OFT) has been dominated by two paradigms—prey choice and patch use (see, for example, Krebs, 1978; Krebs, Stephens, & Sutherland, 1983; Pyke, Pulliam, & Charnov, 1977). In the patch-use paradigm, the forager is faced with a series of well-defined patches that contain food (although the same ideas can be applied to other resources; see Parker & Stuart, 1976). The forager has to decide when to leave a patch and spend time travelling to a new (and possibly better) patch.

Charnov (1976) modeled this decision problem by assuming that the forager obtains a smooth flow of rewards from a patch. Let γ^* denote the maximum possible long-term average reward rate. Charnov considered a procedure (called by Oaten, 1977, the *equal-rates procedure*) in which the forager leaves a patch as soon as its reward rate on the patch falls to γ^*. Charnov showed that when the reward rate on a patch decreases with time, this equal-rates procedure achieves the maximum possible rate γ^*. This result is known as the marginal value theorem (MVT).

Although it is sometimes realistic to model food as constituting a smooth flow (e.g., nectar), many attempts at a quantitative use of the MVT have been based on patches that contain discrete reward items. In some cases it is possible to use a

23

discrete version of the MVT—we illustrate this with an example later in the chapter (see also Houston, this volume). But usually another approach has been adopted. Some form of smoothing of the rewards over time is carried out, for example by finding the average cumulative reward obtained after a given time in the patch. Using such a rate as part of an equal rates procedure does not necessarily maximize the long-term rate (McNamara & Houston, 1985; Oaten, 1977). Some other difficulties that arise from averaging are discussed by McNamara (1982).

Krebs, Ryan, and Charnov (1974) tried to apply the MVT by measuring the giving-up times (GUTs) of black-capped chickadees. The GUT is defined as the time between the forager finding the last prey item that is taken from a patch and the forager leaving the patch. Krebs et al. argued that, if all prey items have the same value, then the reciprocal of the GUT approximates the reward rate in the patch and hence concluded that the long-term rate was maximized by having the same GUT in all patches. As McNair (1982) shows, this conclusion is false.

The MVT, by its association with the equal-rates procedure, has diverted attention from other phenomena that may be important when an animal exploits patches of food. In particular, excessive preoccupation with it has encouraged the view that the effect of rewards can be understood just by calculating the reward rate. Such a view ignores the fact that rewards may also provide information about the type of patch that is being exploited. Oaten (1977) stressed the importance of such information and showed that when use could be made of it the equal rates procedure did not maximize reward rate. Unfortunately, the mathematical complexity of Oaten's paper prevented its message from being taken to heart; most empirical papers that emerged after it paid lip-service to it without attempting to address the issues that it raised.

Our aim in this chapter is to demonstrate that there is more to patch use than the MVT. Attention is drawn to various aspects of patch use that have been neglected but may be important. Optimality theory is used to motivate an analysis of foraging and learning. This use of optimality theory as a framework is not to be taken as implying that animals are always optimal.

An Idealized Model

Consider a rather idealized environment in which (a) food is found only in well-defined patches or clumps; (b) food occurs in the form of discrete items rather than as a continuous flow. For the sake of simplicity it is assumed that all items are identical; and (c) the items that an animal finds are its only indication of the value of the current patch. Assumption (c) implies that an animal can potentially gain information on how much more food it is likely to find on the current patch from the items that it has already found and their time of discovery, but not from quantitites such as the size of the patch or its smell.

It is assumed that patches in the environment can be classified into distinct patch types E_0, E_1, E_2, . . . which occur with frequency α_0, α_1, α_2, . . .

respectively. On leaving one patch an animal chooses the next patch at random from the collection of patches, so that the (a priori) probability that the patch chosen is type E_i is α_i. It is assumed that patches are not revisited.

The mean travel time between patches is denoted by τ, and the maximum long-term average reward rate that can be achieved in a particular environment will be denoted by γ^*.

The environment that has just been outlined is the one considered by Oaten (1977). In special cases of this environment, the optimal policy has been found by Green (1980, 1984), McNamara (1982), and McNamara and Houston (1985). The environment provides a reasonable model of some of the laboratory and field investigations of patch use (e.g., Cowie, 1977; Krebs et al., 1974; Lima, 1983, 1984).

What Can an Animal Learn About the Environment?

The model that has been presented here describes the environment as being composed of a number of distinct patch types. There is, however, no reason to suppose that the forager "knows" this before it starts foraging or can learn it while foraging. The analysis therefore starts by considering what an animal could possibly learn about its foraging environment. It must be realized that an animal can effectively learn about something without acquiring the same sort of knowledge that a mathematician would use to represent the problem (see also Houston, this volume). This point is illustrated with the following example.

Environment A

This environment has two patch types, E_0 and E_1, present in equal proportions. Type E_0 does not contain any food items. Type E_1 has one item. A searching animal finds this item after an exponentially distributed time with a mean of one time unit.

In a randomly selected patch in this environment, the probability that an animal searching a patch finds an item by time t is given by $F(t) = .5 \, [1-\exp(-t)]$. An animal that searches a patch in this environment will either give up and move to another patch without having found an item, or, having found an item, will eventually stop searching for a second item. It seems reasonable to argue that after spending some time in the environment the animal could estimate the distribution of time to wait for the first item, that is it could estimate F, and learn that, once an item has been found in a patch, another is never found. In contrast to these properties of reward probabilities, the animal has no direct experience of the fact that there are two distinct patch types and may not be able to learn this. In a more complex environment with many different patch types this conclusion must hold all the more strongly. An animal in such an environment could potentially learn such things as, for example, the expected number of rewards found in the first unit of time and the dependence of the expected number found after time $t = 1$ on the number found before $t = 1$. For example, the animal might be able to learn whether the expected number found after $t = 1$ is an increasing or decreasing function of the number found before this time. The probability distribution of the number of rewards found, the time of their capture, and the dependence of the capture times on one another are referred to here as the *joint distribution of capture times*. It is reasonable to assume that the animal can learn about aspects of this joint distribution.

Optimal Decisions

To be optimal in all the environments that it encounters, an animal must respond to: (1) its experience on the current patch, (2) either (a) the mean interpatch travel time τ, or equivalently (b) the maximum rate γ^*, and (3) either (a) the patch types E_i and their frequency of occurrence α_i, or equivalently (b) the joint distribution of capture times on a randomly chosen patch.

An animal that ignored its experience in a patch would always leave after spending some fixed time in the patch. Rules based on fixed-patch residence times are only optimal in certain environments (Breck, 1978; McNair, 1982; Stewart-Oaten, 1982).

From a knowledge of 3(a) it is possible to calculate 3(b), and vice versa. In this sense, 3(a) and 3(b) are equivalent. Given either 3(a) or 3(b), τ can be found from γ^*, and vice versa. In this sense τ and γ^* are equivalent.

An animal has to respond to (1), (2), and (3) if it is to be optimal in all possible environments. An animal that failed to respond to one or more of these might be optimal in some environments but not in others. For example, an animal using the giving-up time rule can respond to experience on the patch and to τ or γ^* but cannot respond to the joint distribution of capture times. This rule is therefore not optimal in general, although it may be optimal in certain special cases (Breck, 1978; McNair, 1982).

What Do Animals Respond To?

Despite the popularity of the patch-use paradigm, there is little detailed evidence on how animals make decisions about when to leave a patch. This section reviews some of the data.

Response to Experience on the Current Patch

As has been stated, a bird that ignores its experience on a patch will on each occasion leave the patch after spending the same mean time there. There is some direct evidence that this does not always occur. The results of Krebs et al. (1974), working with black-capped chickadees, and Cowie (1979), working with great tits, suggest that birds in a given environment spend more time in the better patches. For example, Cowie (1979) investigated two artificial environments, each containing three patch types. In both of the environments the amount of time spent in the patch increased with patch quality, but the trend was not significant. Clearer evidence for differences in the response to patch type emerged from the GUTs. Cowie found a significant effect of patch quality, with shorter GUTs in the better patches. Subsequent work on great tits by Ydenberg (1984) indicates that the decision to leave a patch may depend on runs of bad luck. Lima (1984) reports that when downy woodpeckers found no rewards in a patch they stayed for a relatively short time, but that once a reward was found the birds were more persistent even if no further rewards were found. From all this it can be concluded that animals do respond to experience on a patch, and that they do not necessarily use a giving-up time rule that requires a constant GUT in all the patches of the environment.

Response to τ and γ^*

If an environment is altered by increasing the mean travel time between patches while keeping the patches the same, then it becomes optimal to spend more time in each patch visited. This result is well known when patches yield a smooth decreasing flow of rewards (Krebs, 1978), but the result holds quite generally (McNamara, 1982).

In an aviary study of the foraging behavior of great tits, Cowie (1977) varied travel time by making it harder for the birds to open the pots ("patches") that contained mealworms. He found that the mean patch residence time increased with travel time.

A much more extensive investigation of the influence of travel time is possible in field studies. Kacelnik (1984) presented the same progressive interval schedule to starlings at various distances from their nests. (In this case parents are bringing back food to their young rather than feeding themselves, but the logic of the problem is the same as that of the standard patch-use problem.) Kacelnik found that the number of prey items brought back per trip increased as round-trip travel time increased (see also Houston, this volume, Fig. 3.1).

From these examples it may be concluded that animals can respond to aspects of the environment as a whole, and in a way that appears to be adaptive. It cannot be concluded, however, that they are responding directly to the average inter-patch travel time that they have experienced. They may be responding to some other function of the travel times that they have experienced, or to quantities related to the reward rate that they have experienced. Because mean reward rate decreases with increasing mean travel time, it is logically possible that the birds are responding directly to a decrease in the number of obtained rewards per unit time. There are circumstances in which it seems that animals either cannot form an estimate of the overall reward rate or at least cannot act so as to maximize this rate (Mazur, 1981; see also Houston, this volume). Conversely, the results of

Krebs et al. (1974) suggest that the birds in their experiment did respond to something like the overall rate. Krebs et al. varied patch quality while keeping the travel time fixed. They found that mean GUTs were significantly longer in poor environments, and that there was a tendency for patch residence time to be longer as well. Of course, this is not unequivocal evidence of a response to reward rate, because the birds could have responded to the variation in patch quality.

The Importance of the Joint Distribution of Capture Times

To illustrate the importance of using information about the distribution of capture times, the optimal behavior is compared in two hypothetical environments, A and B, which have the same mean interpatch travel time τ and maximum reward rate γ^*. Patches are of three types, E_0, E_1, and E_2, defined as follows:

Type E_0 - No item present.
Type E_1 - One item present. The search time for this item has an exponential distribution with mean one time unit.
Type E_2 - Two items present. The search time for each item has an exponential distribution with mean one time unit. Thus, the time required in order to find the first item is exponentially distributed with mean one half a time unit, and the time required in order to find the second item is exponentially distributed with mean one time unit.

Environment A has been described earlier in the chapter. It contains patches of type E_0 and type E_1 in equal proportions and has a mean interpatch travel time of one time unit. Environment B has all three patch types, with the proportion of types E_0, E_1, and E_2 being 0.6450, 0.1775, and 0.1775, respectively. The mean interpatch travel time is again one time unit.

Both environments have a maximum reward rate of $\gamma^* = 0.1816$. The optimal policy for each environment is illustrated in Fig. 2.1. In Environment A it is optimal to leave immediately after a reward is found, and to leave after a time $t_0^* = 1.505$ if no reward has been found by that time. The decision to leave without a reward can be understood in terms of the change in the probability that the patch contains a prey item (McNamara & Houston, 1980, 1985). When the animal starts searching a patch, the (a priori) probability that the patch contains an item (i.e., is type E_1) is 0.5. As unsuccessful search time increases, this probability falls and eventually becomes so small that it is worth travelling to a new patch, whose probability of containing an item is once again 0.5.

In Environment B it is optimal to leave after time $t_0^* = 0.951$ if no item has been found by that time. If an item is found before this time, then it is worth searching for a second item until time $t_1^* = 2.199$. In this environment, if no

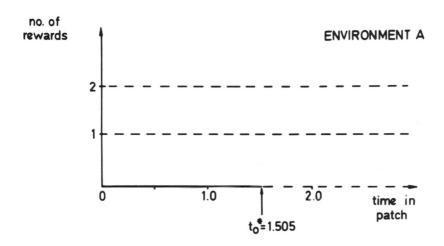

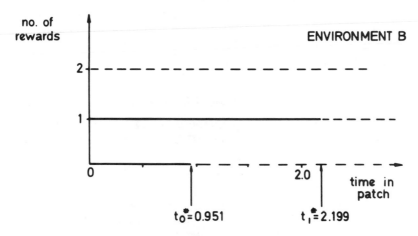

FIG. 2.1. The optimal policy in Environments A and B, illustrated by a plot of items found against time spent searching. It is optimal to leave a patch as soon as a broken line is reached. In Environment A this occurs when the first item is found, or when a time $t_0^* = 1.505$ has been spent in unsuccessful search. In Environment B it is optimal to leave after a time $t_0^* = 0.951$ if no item has been found. If an item is found before this time, then it is optimal to leave after a total time $t_0^* = 2.199$ if no second item has been found. If a second item is found, it is optimal to leave immediately.

29

reward is found then the probability that the patch is type E_2 drops rapidly with increasing search time and the probability that the patch is type E_0 rises. Because the initial probabilities of the patch being type E_1 or E_2 are low, it is optimal to leave after a shorter time than in Environment A. If a reward is found before t_0^*, then it becomes likely that the patch is of type E_2 and that a second item is present. It is therefore worth spending time searching for this item. (These intuitive explanations are given partly in terms of patch type. In the next section an explanation is given directly in terms of information about the distribution of joint capture times.)

Environments A and B differ radically in their associated joint distribution of capture times, and this is reflected in the fact that, although both environments have the same τ and γ^*, the optimal response to a given experience is very different in Environment A as compared to Environment B. For example, it is optimal to leave a patch after the first reward in Environment A, whereas it is optimal to carry on searching in Environment B.

The optimal policy for Environment A would perform poorly in Environment B and vice versa. This illustrates an important general point. An animal that cannot gain information on the joint distribution of capture times in an environment may do well in a narrow range of environments but will do badly in very different environments. In contrast, an animal that can learn about the joint distribution of capture times may be able to perform well in a wide range of environments. Thus there is a selective advantage in using information about the joint distribution of capture times, and this advantage increases with the range of environments that the animal encounters.

Response to Joint Distribution of Capture Times

There is some evidence that animals can respond to aspects of the joint distribution of capture times. For example, Cowie (1979) found that when it is optimal to leave a patch after finding a reward, great tits are able to learn the optimal behavior. The results of Catania and Reynolds (1968) indicate that pigeons are sensitive to the way in which the probability of reinforcement depends on the time since the last reinforcement. When this probability is constant, so is the bird's response rate, but when the probability increases with time since the last reinforcement, then so does the response rate.

The results reported by Lima (1984) suggest that animals can acquire information about patch types. The woodpeckers' behavior on an empty patch depended on the other patch types available in the environment. Although this supports the view that the animals were able to learn about the range of patch types, it is possible that the animals were responding to γ.

This chapter does not offer a review of all the data on patch use. The examples are chosen to show that animals can respond to all the necessary environmental parameters. There has, however, been no systematic investigation of the limits of abilities.

Sampling a Patch

It would be very useful for an animal searching a patch to know exactly what rewards it would receive in the immediate future. Clearly such knowledge is impossible. But knowledge of the probability of a reward or the expected reward in the immediate future could potentially be estimated from an animal's experience on previous patches. In particular, an animal could potentially estimate the stochastic reward rate r defined by

$$r = \text{limit as } \delta \text{ tends to zero} \left(\frac{\text{Expected reward in the next } \delta \text{ time units}}{\delta} \right).$$

This rate is the natural stochastic analogue of the deterministic reward rate used by Charnov (1976) in the MVT. It is the rate used by Oaten (1977) and is not based on a smoothing out of previously obtained rewards but is defined in terms of future expectations. In general the stochastic reward rate depends on the time spent in the patch so far, the number of rewards found, and their time of capture as well as environmental parameters. The two environments A and B can be used to illustrate this point.

In Environment A the longer an animal has searched a patch unsuccessfully, the less likely it is that a reward will be found in the immediate future, so that the reward rate decreases with time. It can be shown (McNamara & Houston, 1985) that after time t of unsuccessful search the rate is

$$r_0(t) = \frac{1}{e^t + 1}.$$

This rate is illustrated in Fig. 2.2(a). Of course the rate is zero once a reward has been found.

In Environment B the rate drops much more rapidly with unrewarded search but jumps upwards when a reward is found. This is illustrated in Fig. 2.2(b).

Environments A and B are examples of the general type of environment considered by Iwasa, Higashi, and Yamamura (1981). They consider an environment in which patches may vary in the number of prey items they contain, but where the time to find each item has an exponential distribution. These times are all independent with the same mean. Let $e(n,t)$ denote the expected number of items left in a patch given that n items have been found by search time t (Iwasa et al. denote this by $r(n,t)$.) Because the rate at which items are found is proportional to the number left, we see that r is proportional to e in such an environment, and the two measures are equivalent as assessors of current patch quality.

Iwasa et al. (1981) show that e drifts downwards in the time between the finding of items and jumps when items are found. If the patches are highly variable in the number of items they contain (a contagious distribution of prey number), e jumps upwards when an item is found, whereas if patches do not vary a lot (a regular distribution), e jumps downwards. Thus r exhibits the same behavior as e. Environment A is of regular type whereas Environment B is of

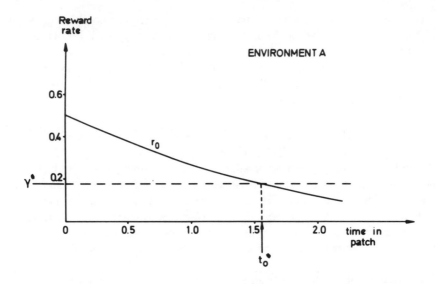

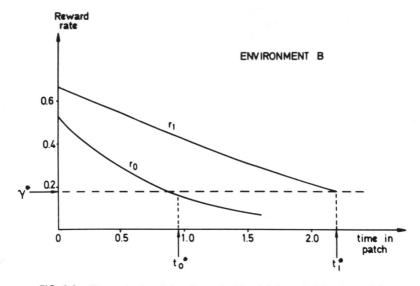

FIG. 2.2. The optimal policies shown in Fig. 2.1 expressed in terms of the stochastic reward rate. r_0 is the reward rate before an item is found. In Environment A, the reward rate jump to zero once an item has been found, and it is optimal to leave immediately. If no item is found, it is optimal to search until time t_0^*, at which r_0 is below γ^*. Thus the equal-rates procedure is not optimal in this case.

mixed type: r jumps upwards on finding the first item and downwards on finding the second.

In view of the Marginal Value Theorem it is natural to consider the policy given by: continue foraging while $r > \gamma^*$, leave when r falls to γ^* or below. The stochastic equal rates procedure is not optimal in general as Oaten (1977) showed. In Environment A r decreases monotonically with time in the patch and the procedure is optimal: An optimal forager leaves at time t_0^* at which the reward rate is γ^* [see Fig. 2.2(a)]. In contrast r is not monotone decreasing in Environment B but can jump upwards. As Fig. 2.2(b) shows, it is optimal to continue searching for the first item even when r falls below γ^* in this environment. One can think of r as providing an assessment of current patch quality. In Environment B finding the first item not only gives a reward but also improves the assessment of patch quality. It is optimal to continue foraging when r falls to γ^* because the number of items present is uncertain and it is worth continuing awhile to see whether the patch is better than the current estimate, r, suggests.

This argument applies to all environments in which the finding of a prey item increases the probability of a subsequent capture. It is optimal to incur an immediate expected loss in order to sample the patch and find out whether it is better than current estimates suggest.

The model presented by Green (1980) illustrates the failure of the equal rates procedure. In Green's model a patch consists of n bits, i.e., locations that may contain a prey item. Each bit has a probability p of containing an item, but p varies from patch to patch. The predator searches the patch systematically and has to decide on the basis of the bits that it has searched whether or not to move to a new patch. Green found the best strategy and also considered instantaneous rate (IR) strategies, which involve leaving a patch when the IR falls to some critical rate. The IR is defined as the probability of finding an item in the next bit and hence is a discrete version of the stochastic reward rate. Green showed that the best IR startegy is to use a rate below γ^*, and that this strategy fails to achieve γ^*. This result implies that the equal rates procedure is not optimal, and that it can be improved upon by remaining on the patch even when the rate falls below γ^*.

The failure of the equal rates procedure explains the difficulty experienced by Pyke (1981) in analyzing the foraging behavior of honeyeaters. Pyke (1978) proposed a discrete version of the equal rates procedure when rewards occur at discrete locations in a patch (e.g., flowers on an inflorescence). The rule (called *Pyke's rule*) is to continue if and only if the expected rate for the next item is greater than the overall rate. This argument seemed successful when applied to hummingbirds (Pyke, 1978), but not when applied to honeyeaters (Pyke, 1981). In the latter case, the optimal policy was found by a numerical calculation of various rules. The best rule found did not follow the discrete version of the equal rates procedure. The reason for this failure is easily found. There is a correlation between the nectar volume of the flowers on an inflorescence, so that as the bird probes flowers it can gain information about the quality of the inflorescence. The optimal policy may well require the forager to tolerate quite low amounts of nectar from the first few flowers because of the chance that the inflorescence might be good. This can be seen in the policy found by Pyke in which decisions about when to leave a patch are based on the mean volume of all the flowers on the inflorescence that the bird has probed. In can be seen that the critical mean threshold below which it is optimal to leave increases with the number of flowers probed (Pyke, 1981, Table 1). To illustrate this effect in more detail, a simple model of the sort of problem that bees or nectar-eating birds may encounter is presented.

When to Leave an Inflorescence—the Effect of the Number of Flowers

Consider the following special case of the foraging environment defined previously:

1. The environment consists of patches (inflorescences), each patch containing n flowers (where n is deterministic).
2. Although each inflorescence in a given environment has the same number of flowers, the inflorescences vary in quality. To be specific, each inflorescence has an associated parameter θ that determines its quality. The n flowers of an inflorescence yield rewards of magnitude $X_1, \ldots, X_n$ where the X_i are independent and normally distributed with mean θ and variance σ^2.
3. θ varies from inflorescence to inflorescence with a normal distribution with mean μ and variance σ^2. (The same variance for X_i and θ simplifies the mathematics.)
4. The animal takes one time unit to consume the nectar from a flower, and no time to move between flowers. (It is easy to modify this to include the time needed to move between flowers.) In reality, the time required to consume nectar may well depend on nectar amount (especially for bees see, for example, Hodges & Wolf, 1981), but such complications are ignored. It would be relatively easy to include such effects.
5. The animal takes a time τ to travel between inflorescences and the maximum achievable rate is γ^*.

The optimal policy is found by means of dynamic programming (Bellman, 1957). The problem is simplified by assuming a value for γ^* and eventually finding the value of τ (cf. our preceding remarks on the equivalence of γ^* and τ and Green, 1980, Houston & McNamara, 1985). The optimal policy can be expressed in two ways; either in terms of the expected reward on the next flower or in terms of the average reward obtained so far on the inflorescence. The first characterization involves a sequence $b(1)$, $b(2)$, . . ., $b(n - 1)$ of critical values. After the nectar on the jth flower has been consumed, it is optimal to continue to the next flower on the inflorescence if the expected reward from it is greater than $b(j)$. In the second characterization it is optimal to continue to the next flower if the sample mean $(X_1 + . . . + X_j)/j$ is greater than the critical value mean (j). Table 2.1 shows the value of $b(j)$ for a series of environments that differ in the number of flowers on an inflorescence. It can be seen that when there is just one flower left unvisited on an inflorescence, then the critical expected reward rate is γ^*. (Recall that one unit of time is taken to consume the nectar in a flower, so an expected nectar volume of 2.00 units is equivalent to an expected rate of 2.00.) In other words, Pyke's rule is optimal for the last possible decision on an inflorescence. But the table shows that it is not optimal for any of the other decisions. Two effects can be seen in the table. As long as there are more than two flowers per inflorescence, the successive critical expected rewards that must be obtained from a flower increase (effect of j for a given n). Secondly, the critical expected reward after a given number of flowers has been visited decreases with increasing number of flowers unvisited (effect of n for a given j).

TABLE 2.1
The Optimal Policy for Leaving Inflorescences

j	$n = 2$ $\tau = 1.004$	$n = 3$ $\tau = 1.512$	$n = 4$ $\tau = 2.022$	$n = 5$ $\tau = 2.534$	$n = 6$ $\tau = 3.047$	$n = 10$ $\tau = 5.104$	$n = 25$ $\tau = 12.854$
1	2.00	1.90	1.84	1.80	1.76	1.65	1.46
2		2.00	1.93	1.89	1.85	1.76	1.60
3			2.00	1.95	1.91	1.82	1.68
4				2.00	1.95	1.87	1.73
5					2.00	1.90	1.77
6						1.93	1.80
7						1.95	1.83
8						1.97	1.85
9						2.00	1.87
10							1.88
12							1.90
14							1.92
16							1.94
18							1.95
20							1.97
22							1.98
24							2.00

Note: The critical expected reward $b(j)$ as a function of number of flowers visited, j, for various values of the number of flowers per inflorescence, n. It is optimal to continue to the next flower if the expected reward is greater than $b(j)$. Prior mean reward $\mu = 3.00$ with standard deviation $\sigma = 0.8$. The travel time τ is adjusted so as to keep $\gamma^* = 2.00$

TABLE 2.2
Effect of Variability on the Optimal Policy

j	$\sigma = .2$ $\tau = 5.000$	$\sigma = .5$ $\tau = 5.008$	$\sigma = .8$ $\tau = 5.104$	$\sigma = 1.1$ $\tau = 5.292$
1	1.91(.82)	1.78(.56)	1.65(.30)	1.52(.04)
2	1.94(1.41)	1.85(1.27)	1.76(1.14)	1.67(1.00)
3	1.95(1.60)	1.89(1.52)	1.82(1.42)	1.76(1.34)
4	1.96(1.70)	1.92(1.65)	1.87(1.58)	1.82(1.52)
5	1.97(1.76)	1.94(1.72)	1.90(1.68)	1.86(1.63)
6	1.98(1.81)	1.95(1.77)	1.93(1.75)	1.90(1.71)
7	1.98(1.83)	1.97(1.82)	1.95(1.80)	1.93(1.77)
8	1.99(1.86)	1.98(1.85)	1.97(1.84)	1.96(1.83)
9	2.00(1.88)	2.00(1.88)	2.00(1.88)	2.00(1.88)

Note: Critical values $b(j)$ of the expected reward on the next flower, together with the corresponding critical means in brackets. It can be seen that as variability increases the critical values decrease ($\gamma^* = 2.00$, $n = 10$, prior mean = 3.00)

The general principle is that the greater the possibilities of improvement, the lower the threshold for leaving. At the last decision on the inflorescence there is no room for improvement and so Pyke's rule is optimal.

Whereas Table 2.1 illustrates the idea of possible improvement with differences in the number of flowers still to be visited, Table 2.2 illustrates it with differences in the variability of inflorescences. As variability increases, the critical expected rewards decrease.

Discussion

All that has been said so far has been based on the idea that foraging behavior should maximize the long-term rate of energetic gain. Some other factors that may be important are now considered. At the most fundamental level, it is not necessarily the case that fitness is maximized by maximizing the net rate of energetic gain (Caraco & Lima, this volume). The minimization of the probability of starvation requires a consideration of both the mean and the variance of a foraging strategy. Stephens and Charnov (1982) apply this idea to the problem of patch use.

Even if fitness is maximized by the maximization of the long-term rate of energetic gain, realistic models should take account of the fact that the forager might be interrupted while foraging. The resulting effects depend crucially on the nature of the interruptions. If the animal is not able to resume foraging after an interruption, then future rewards must be discounted (Houston, Kacelnik, & McNamara, 1982). This leads to the animal putting more weight on immediate gain, and, hence, tends to result in longer patch residence times than a model with no interruptions. Even though most laboratory experiments do not involve interruptions, the animal may use a rule that incorporates the possibility of interruptions and hence behave as if there were interruptions.

It also is important to remember that animals have other preoccupations in addition to food. The early optimal-foraging models assumed that the animal under consideration was not engaged in any activities other than looking for food and eating it, but subsequent work often has considered the problem of reaching a compromise between the demands of several activities. For example, as well as looking for food, an animal may be under pressure to spend time looking out for animals that might eat it (see Milinski & Heller, 1978; Pulliam, Pyke, & Caraco, 1982), or evicting conspecifics from its territory (see e.g., Davies & Houston, 1981). The balance between feeding and responding to conspecific intruders was investigated by Kacelnik, Houston, and Krebs (1981). Male great tits in an aviary had access to two progressive ratio schedules (see Houston, this volume) that represented depleting patches. At the start of some trials the experimental bird was presented with a rival male at a location that could not be viewed from either patch but could be seen when the experimental bird travelled between the patches. On such trials the birds tended to spend less than the optimal number of trials in the patch. This change can be seen in terms of the bird sacrificing energetic gain in order to increase the opportunities to check for the presence of an intruder. Ydenberg (1982) replicated the basic result and also considered the effect of satiation. Just as in the case of interruptions, animals may behave as if predators and intruders are present even under laboratory conditions.

Intruders, predators, and the need to perform other activities may often influence the amount of time that an animal spends in a patch. The reason for this is that around the optimum the reward rate does not in general vary much with changes in behavior, so that deviations from the optimum are cheap. As a result, if behavior is approximately optimal, effects other than rate of gain are likely to predominate.

Although patch use is one of the two basic paradigms of optimal-foraging theory, our knowledge of the rules that animals use while foraging on patches is depressingly meagre. Although the MVT is useful in providing a feel for how optimal behavior depends on, say, travel time, its popularity has led to many aspects of patch use being ignored. This chapter considers an animal's rules in terms of an optimality criterion. Such an analysis provides a functional account for results that are already known and suggests many issues that ought to be investigated. Using optimality theory in this way can be fruitful, but we do not wish to claim that it provides a complete account of what animals do. Some aspects of behavior may not be explainable in terms of the maximization of fitness, and a narrow-minded obsession with optimality theory may lead to these aspects being ignored. Nevertheless, some sort of framework for thinking about behavior is necessary, and we believe that optimality theory provides a powerful initial framework for organizing ideas about patch use.

ACKNOWLEDGMENTS

We thank the editors and Dr. Richard Green for their comments and advice.

REFERENCES

Bellman, R. (1957). *Dynamic programming.* Princeton, NJ: Princeton University Press.

Breck, J. E. (1978). *Suboptimal foraging strategies for a patchy environment.* Unpublished doctoral dissertation, Michigan State University.

Catania, A. C., & Reynolds, G. S. (1968). A quantitative analysis of the responding maintained by interval schedules of reinforcement. *Journal of the Experimental Analysis of Behavior, 11,* 327–383.

Charnov, E. L. (1976). Optimal foraging: The marginal value theorem. *Theoretical Population Biology, 9,* 129–136.

Cowie, R. J. (1977). Optimal foraging in great tits (*Parus major*). *Nature, 268,* 137–139.

Cowie, R. J. (1979). Foraging behaviour of the great tit (*Parus major* L) in a patchy environment. Unpublished doctoral dissertation, University of Oxford.

Davies, N. B., & Houston, A. I. (1981). Owners and satellites: The economics of territory defence in the pied wagtail (*Motacilla alba*). *Journal of Animal Ecology, 50,* 157–180.

Green, R. F. (1980). Bayesian birds: A simple example of Oaten's stochastic model of optimal foraging. *Theoretical Population Biology, 18,* 244–256.

Green, R. F. (1984). Stopping rules for optimal foragers. *American Naturalist, 123,* 30–40.

Hodges, C. M., & Wolf, L. L. (1981). Optimal foraging in bumblebees: Why is nectar left behind in flowers? *Behavioural Ecology and Sociobiology, 9,* 41–44.

Houston, A. I., Kacelnik, A., & McNamara, J. M. (1982). Some learning rules for acquiring information. In D. J. McFarland (Ed.), *Functional ontogeny* (pp. 148–191). London: Pitman.

Houston, A. I., & McNamara, J. M. (1985). A general theory of central-place foraging for single prey loaders. *Theoretical Population Biology, 28,* 233–262.

Iwasa, Y., Higashi, M., & Yamamura, N. (1981). Prey distribution as a factor determining the choice of optimal foraging strategy. *American Naturalist, 117,* 710–723.

Kacelnik, A. (1984). Central place foraging in starlings (*Sturnus vulgaris*) I: Patch residence time. *Journal of Animal Ecology, 53,* 283–300.

Kacelnik, A., Houston, A. I., & Krebs, J. R. (1981). Optimal foraging and territorial defence in the great tit (*Parus major*). *Behavioural Ecology and Sociobiology, 8,* 35–40.

Krebs, J. R. (1978). Optimal foraging: Decision rules for predators. In J. R. Krebs & N. B. Davies (Eds.), *Behavioural ecology* (pp. 23–63). Oxford, England: Blackwell Scientific Publications.

Krebs, J. R., Ryan, J., & Charnov, E. L. (1974). Hunting by expectation or optimal foraging? A study of patch use by chickadees. *Animal Behaviour, 22,* 953–964.

Krebs, J. R., Stephens, D. W., & Sutherland, W. J. (1983). Perspectives in optimal foraging theory. In A. H. Brush & G. Clark, *Perspectives in ornithology* (pp. 165–216). Cambridge, England: Cambridge University Press.

Lima, S. L. (1983). Downy woodpecker foraging behavior: Foraging by expectation and energy intake rate. *Oecologia, 58,* 232–237.

Lima, S. L. (1984). Downy woodpecker foraging behavior: Efficient sampling in simple stochastic environments. *Ecology, 65,* 166–174.

Mazur, J. E. (1981). Optimization theory fails to predict performance of pigeons in a two-response situation. *Science, 214,* 823–825.

McNair, J. N. (1982). Optimal giving-up times and the marginal value theorem. *American Naturalist, 119,* 511–529.

McNamara, J. M. (1982). Optimal patch use in a stochastic environment. *Theoretical Population Biology, 21,* 269–288.

McNamara, J. M., & Houston, A. I. (1980). The application of statistical decision theory to animal behaviour. *Journal of Theoretical Biology, 85,* 673–690.

McNamara, J. M., & Houston, A. I. (1985). A simple model of information use in the exploitation of patchily distributed food. *Animal Behaviour, 33,* 553–560.

Milinski, M., & Heller, R. (1978). Influence of a predator on the optimal foraging behaviour of sticklebacks (*Gasterosteus aculeatus*). *Nature, 275,* 642–644.

Oaten, A. (1977). Optimal foraging in patches: A case for stochasticity. *Theoretical Population Biology, 12,* 263–285.

Parker, G. A., & Stuart, R. A. (1976). Animal behaviour as a strategy optimizer: Evolution of resource assessment strategies and optimal emigration thresholds. *American Naturalist, 110,* 1055—1076.

Pulliam, H. R., Pyke, G. H., & Caraco, T. (1982). The scanning behavior of juncos: A game-theoretical approach. *Journal of Theoretical Biology, 95,* 89–103.

Pyke, G. H. (1978). Optimal foraging in hummingbirds: Testing the marginal value theorem. *American Zoologist, 18,* 739–752.

Pyke, G. H. (1981). Honeycater foraging: A test of optimal foraging theory. *Animal Behaviour, 29,* 878–888.

Pyke, G. H., Pulliam, H. R., & Charnov, E. L. (1977). Optimal foraging: A selective review of theory and tests. *Quarterly Review of Biology, 52,* 137–104.

Stephens, D. W., & Charnov, E. L. (1982). Optimal foraging: Some simple stochastic models. *Behavioural Ecology and Sociobiology, 10,* 251–263.

Stewart-Oaten, A. (1982). Minimax strategies for a predator-prey game. *Theoretical Population Biology, 22,* 410–424.

Ydenberg, R. C. (1982). *Territorial vigilance and foraging behaviour: A study of trade-offs.* Unpublished doctoral dissertation, University of Oxford.

Ydenberg, R. C. (1984). Great tits and giving-up times: Decision rules for leaving patches. *Behaviour, 90,* 1–24.

3

The Control of Foraging Decisions

Alasdair I. Houston
Department of Zoology
University of Cambridge
Current address: Department of Zoology, Oxford, U.K.

The behavior of an animal can be explained on many levels. Tinbergen (1951) distinguished four sorts of explanation, based on development, phylogeny, causal factors, and evolutionary advantage. The last two are of fundamental importance to this chapter. An explanation based on causal (proximate) factors relates behavior to immediate stimuli, whereas an explanation based on evolutionary advantage (known as a functional or ultimate explanation) attempts to explain why evolution by natural selection might have resulted in the observed behavior. Failure to observe this distinction has done much to hinder attempts to unify the psychological and ecological approaches to foraging behavior. This chapter starts by arguing that the control of foraging decisions can be understood in terms of simple rules that perform well in some evolutionary sense. There follows an attempt to review what is known about these decisions and to use the results to discuss various rules that have been proposed.

OPTIMALITY AND OPTIMAL-FORAGING THEORY

The application of optimality to behavior is reviewed by Krebs and McCleery (1984). The application of optimality to foraging behavior is known as optimal-foraging theory (OFT). OFT is reviewed by Krebs (1978), Krebs, Stephens, and Sutherland (1983) and Pyke, Pulliam, and Charnov (1977). It often involves the assumption that the fitness of a forager is maximized by the maximization of its net rate of energetic gain, E/T. (One alternative currency is the probability of avoiding starvation; see Caraco & Lima, this volume; McNamara & Houston, 1982; Stephens & Charnov, 1982.) When energetic costs can be ignored and all food items (or rewards) are of equal value, the maximization of E/T is equivalent to the maximization of overall reward rate or, in "operant" language, reinforcement rate, R/T.

Some OFT models suggest that E/T (or R/T) is the currency for foraging decisions, but it does not follow that E/T (or R/T) is the variable that actually controls these decisions. Herrnstein and Vaughan (1980) call such a view *literal optimization*. A literal optimizer would compare various options in terms of the optimality criterion, say R/T, and choose the option with the highest overall rate.

It has been pointed out often that the use of optimality principles in the study of behavior does not require that animals are literal optimizers. Even if the analysis requires an explicit and perhaps complicated maximization, animals may actually be using simple rules ("rules of thumb") that approximate the optimal solution (e.g., Cowie & Krebs, 1979; Green, 1980; Houston, 1980; Krebs & McCleery, 1984; Lea, 1981; McNamara, 1982; McNamara & Houston, 1980; Maynard Smith, 1982; Staddon & Motheral, 1978). A consequence of this view is that the animals may perform badly in conditions that are very different from those that have been responsible for selecting the animal's rule over evolutionary time. This distinction between the optimality analysis and the rule that the animal uses is no more than the traditional distinction between functional (ultimate) and causal (proximate) explanations. In other words, optimality theory is not a theory about the immediate control of behavior, but a theory about the factors that influence its evolution. Behavioral ecologists use the statement "animals maximize reward rate" as an abbreviation for the statement "natural selection has evaluated foraging behavior in terms of resulting reward rate."

Rachlin, Battalio, Kagel, and Green (1981) argue that animals are literal optimizers. It is clear that animals do not always maximize R/T (Herrnstein & Heyman, 1979; Mazur, 1981; Vaughan, Kardish, & Wilson, 1982). Rachlin et al. (1981) therefore claim that animals allocate their time in such a way that their utility is maximized, where utility includes the value of leisure. This position also has been put under pressure (Boelens, 1984; Houston, 1983a; Vaughan & Miller, 1984). If animals are not literal optimizers, then these failures of maximization theory are not unexpected. An animal using a simple behavioral rule cannot maximize its gains in all experimental procedures. This is what Herrnstein and Vaughan (1980) and Vaughan and Herrnstein (in press) conclude, but they tend to see the discrepancy between the predictions of optimality and the data as a failing on the part of optimality theory. Many people working in behavioral ecology would prefer to blame the discrepancy on "unnatural" experimental procedures. There is some truth in both views. If an account of behavior that will work under all conditions is desired, then a causal rather than a functional (optimization) account is needed (unless animals are literal optimizers). Animals cannot be expected to behave optimally under conditions that are very different from those that have shaped their decision rules over evolutionary time.

It should not be imagined that the optimality analysis is an attempt to remove the need to look at what animals actually do. Indeed if the investigator's only interest is what the animal does in a particular situation, he does not need to perform an optimality analysis or to consider various rules of thumb. He should start with the actual behavior. The first law of model-making is that for any set of data there is at least one model (Kalman, 1968). The relevant question is therefore not "can a model be found?" but "what does one want from a model?" For an introduction to this area see Metz (1974, 1977).

Matching

Herrnstein (1961) proposed the matching law as a description of the behavior of pigeons working on concurrent variable-interval schedules. In its generalized form it can be written as:

$$B_i/B_j = b(R_i/R_j)^s,$$

where B_i and B_j are the total number of responses delivered to schedule i and schedule j, respectively, R_i and R_j are the total number of reinforcements obtained from schedule i and schedule j, respectively, and b and s are parameters that indicate bias and sensitivity (Baum, 1974, 1979). The sensitivity parameter has been linked to the sort of VI schedule used (Taylor & Davison, 1983) and to the sort of reinforcer (Rachlin, Kagel, & Battalio, 1980). The matching law can also be based on measures of time allocation (e.g., Baum & Rachlin, 1969), in which case its generalized form is:

$$T_i/T_j = b(R_i/R_j)^s$$

where T_i and T_j are the total times spent on schedule i and schedule j, respectively. When animals are presented with two different variable-ratio schedules, they tend toward an exclusive choice of the schedule with the smaller ratio (e.g., Herrnstein & Loveland, 1975; Krebs, Kacelnik, & Taylor, 1978). Such exclusive preference is still matching, because the proportion of responses (or time) allocated to each schedule equals the proportion of reinforcements obtained from it.

Melioration

Matching is consistent with the exclusive choice of either variable ratio in the experiment described by Herrnstein and Loveland (1975), yet the birds invariably preferred the schedule with the smaller ratio. To explain this, Herrnstein and Vaughan (1980) suggest a principle that they call melioration, and which is defined as a moment-to-moment tendency to increase the time allocated to the alternative with the higher local rate of reinforcement. As such the principle is not specific enough to be a decision rule, but the model analysed by Myerson and

Miezin (1980) can be thought of as a particular example. Unfortuantely this model simplifies the nature of the schedule and treats a stochastic process in terms of a deterministic equation based on averages—an approach that is widespread in discussions of melioration.

Immediate Maximization

Immediate maximization involves making the best choice at each decision, rather than making the series of choices that is best in overall terms. When all reinforcements are of equal value, such a principle might take the form of choosing the alternative with the highest probability of yielding a reinforcement or the alternative that leads to a reinforcement in the shortest possible time. Shimp (1969) gave a general statement: Each choice maximizes the momentary value, where value is the momentary probability of reinforcement, weighted by reinforcement value.

The Relationship Between Long-Term and Immediate Maximization

In discrete-trial concurrent procedures (e.g., Nevin, 1969), the maximization of reinforcement probability on each trial does not necessarily maximize the long-term R/T (Houston & McNamara, 1981; Staddon, Hinson, & Kram, 1981). McNamara and Houston (1983) reformulate the problem of choosing the inter-response time on a single variable-interval schedule that maximizes net rate (E/T) in terms of patch use and the marginal value theorem (Charnov, 1976). The analysis shows that making a response as soon as it will yield a net gain does not maximize the long-term rate. In the example of patch use discussed by Janetos and Cole (1981), immediate rather than long-term maximization is used, but the underlying equations are incorrect. Houston and McNamara (1984) correct the equations and show that immediate maximization does not maximize the long-term rate.

Experimental work on patch use does not always enable a distinction between immediate and long-term optimization to be made. To clarify the two forms of maximization, consider an environment consisting of deterministic patches in which rewards are found at times t_1, t_2, . . ., t_i with $t_{i+1} > t_i$ for all i. All rewards are of equal value, and the travel time between patches is τ. (A discrete-trial version of this problem is illustrated in Fig. 3.2.) If an animal leaves all patches after n rewards, then its long-term rate $R(n)/T(n)$ is given by the equation:

$$R(n)/T(n) = \frac{n}{\tau + \sum_{i=1}^{n} t_i}.$$

The choice of n that maximizes $R(n)/T(n)$ can be found by the rule of leaving the patch as soon as:

$$\frac{n}{\tau + \sum\limits_{i=1}^{n} t_i} > \frac{n+1}{\tau + \sum\limits_{i=1}^{n+1} t_i},$$

i.e., as soon as staying for a further reward lowers the long-term rate. This condition can be simplified to the rule:

$$\frac{n}{\tau + \sum\limits_{i=1}^{n} t_i} > \frac{1}{t_{n+1}}.$$

The left-hand side is $R(n)/T(n)$; the right-hand side can be thought of as a "local" rate—it is the reward rate over the next reward item, in units of rewards/time. (It is easy to extend this argument to include differences in reward value to obtain the rule proposed by Pyke, 1978. See also McNamara & Houston, this volume.)

A "short-term" animal might only be concerned with local rates and always choose the option with the higher rate. In other words, it would leave the patch as soon as:

$$\frac{1}{\tau + t_1} > \frac{1}{t_{n+1}}.$$

(The left-hand side here is the local reward rate for moving to a new patch.)

Although these two conditions are logically distinct, they often will predict the same value of n. (In the Appendix it is shown that immediate maximization requires the animal to stay for at least as long as long-term maximization.) Some

TABLE 3.1
Immediate Maximization (IM) versus Long-term Maximization (LTM)
on Progressive Schedules

| Paper | IM and LTM Make Same Predictions | | |
	Procedure	Subjects	Agree with IM & LTM
Findley (1958)	Ratios, Skinner Box	Pigeons	No-stay too long
Kacelnik et al. (1981)	Ratios, aviary	Great Tits	Mode as predicted
Ydenberg (1982)	Ratios, aviary	Great Tits	Sometimes stay too long

| Paper | IM and LTM Make Different Predictions | | |
	Procedure	Subjects	Better Currency
Hodos & Trumbule (1967)	Ratios, response panel	Chimps	LTM
Cowie (1979)	Ratios, aviary	Great Tits	LTM
Kacelnik (1984)	Intervals, field	Starlings	LTM

examples are given in Table 3.1. The best evidence for long-term, rather than immediate, maximization is in Hodos and Trumbule (1967, Fig. 3) and Kacelnik (1984) as analyzed in Fig. 3.1.

Matching and Maximizing

A review of this topic would require a chapter to itself, and a long chapter at that. The following statements are an attempt to summarize the facts:

1. Immediate maximization tends to result in matching in various concurrent procedures (Hinson & Staddon, 1983; Houston & McNamara, 1981; Shimp, 1969; Staddon et al., 1981).
2. Maximizing R/T does not necessarily result in matching (Houston & McNamara, 1981), but it comes close to it (Houston, 1983a). Under some models of responding, maximization does lead to matching (Staddon & Motheral, 1978).
3. Matching can come close to maximizing R/T provided that the switching rate is high (Houston, 1983a; Houston & McNamara, 1981).

The comparison between matching and maximizing on concurrent variable interval schedules is really not very informative, in that deviations from the optimum result in very small drops in reward rate (Heyman, 1982; Houston, 1983a; Houston & McNamara, 1981; Prelec, 1982). But even in cases with a "sharp" optimum, it can be argued that explicit comparisons of matching and maximizing as accounts of behavior (e.g., Baum, 1981; Prelec, 1982) can be misleading because they compare completely different sorts of explanation. The maximization of R/T is a functional account that exactly specifies the behavior for given parameter values. In contrast, matching is an empirical generalization that relates variables that are under the animal's control. Even in its original form, with bias and sensitivity equal to one, it does not uniquely specify the behavior that will be observed under given conditions. For example in the equation proposed by Heyman and Luce (1979), there is an infinite set of stay times compatible with matching. The only way to obtain a definite prediction about behavior on the basis of matching is to add an extra feature. In the Heyman–Luce formulation this is a constraint on an index I of interswitch time.

Expensive Deviations are Rare

In those circumstances in which animals appear to come close to maximizing R/T, there is usually considerable spread of behavior about the optimum. It often is found that the frequency of a given deviation from the optimum is proportional

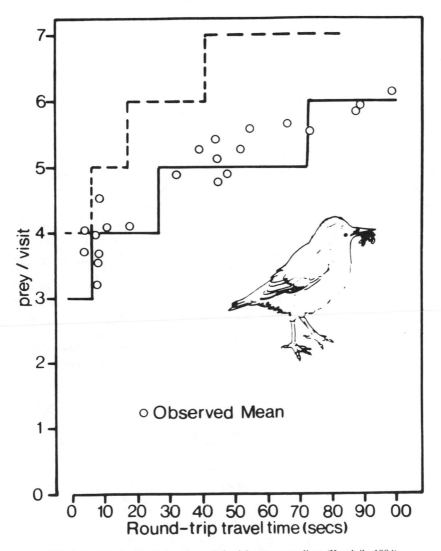

FIG. 3.1. The data on the load brought back by parent starlings (Kacelnik, 1984) reanalysed to compare the predictions of immediate maximization (broken line) and long-term maximization (solid line). The circles are the means of the observed loads.

to how costly the deviation is in terms of a loss in R/T. For example, Kacelnik (1984) presented mealworms to starlings on a progressive interval schedule. The load that a starling brings back to its nest should increase with its travel time to the nest if the rate at which energy is delivered to the young is to be maximized. Kacelnik found that the prey taken back to the nest per visit was approximately given by what he called "profitability matching," that is to say the relative frequency of a load size is equal to its relative profitability.

In a similar vein, Rechten, Krebs, and Houston (1981) found that the extent to which great tits reject inferior prey types is proportional to the increase in R/T that would result from not taking such items. These and other cases are summarized in Table 3.2.

There are various possible reasons for this finding (Kacelnik, 1984; Kacelnik, Houston, & Krebs, 1981). One tempting idea is that the deviations result because a learning process has not had time to converge on the optimum. It might be expected that learning would be rapid when the differences in payoff between options is large, and so costly deviations would be eliminated before less costly ones. Snyderman (1983) pointed out that many studies of prey choice have involved relatively few sessions, so that transients in choice might not have been eliminated. By running pigeons on an operant simulation of prey choice until various stability criteria were met, he obtained almost total rejection of small items when this was required for the maximization of R/T. Synderman showed that the proportion of small items taken may decrease rather slowly as a function of number of sessions.

On the other hand, Kacelnik (1984) found no trend towards the optimum load size becoming more frequent either within or across sessions. It is possible that a

TABLE 3.2
Rarity of Costly Deviations from Optimality

Paper	Procedure		Subject
Fantino (1966)	Skinner Box	Self-control	Pigeons
Lea (1979)	" "	"Prey choice"	" "
Abarca & Fantino (1982)	" "	" "	" "
Kaufman (1979) [in Collier (1981)]	" "	" "	Rats
Herrnstein & Loveland (1975)	" "	VR–VR	Pigeons
Rider (1979)	" "	VR–FR	Rats
Krebs et al. (1977) Houston et al. (1980) Erichsen et al. (1980) Analysed in Rechten et al. (1981)	Conveyor Belt	Prey choice	Great Tits
Kacelnik et al. (1981)	Aviary	Patch use	Great Tits
Kacelnik (1984)	Field	Patch use	Starlings
Davies (1977)	Field	Foraging Strategy	Flycatchers

certain amount of variability is unavoidable, and that it should be incorporated as a constraint (Houston & McNamara, 1985).

Rules of Thumb

It has been argued that even if animals are optimal in the sense understood in behavioral ecology, they are not expected to calculate optimal behavior in the way that a mathematician would. It is much more reasonable to expect them to follow simple rules. To find out what these rules are, it is necessary to describe what animals actually do. Why then is so much effort being devoted to the investigation of rules of thumb? Three justifications can be offered. The first is that it may be worth demonstrating that a simple rule can perform quite well on a complex problem. The phrase ''perform quite well'' means that the results achieved by the rule are close to the optimum. In terms of foraging, ''results'' may mean rate of energetic gain or probability of survival. It is results that must be compared, not behavior, for even if the behavior of a rule is very different from the optimal behavior, it may achieve close-to-optimum results.

The second justification is that some problems may be too complex for us to solve analytically or computationally. In such cases it might still be possible to get a feel for the best sort of behavior by analyzing a range of simple rules. The problem of maximizing the number of rewards obtained from a given number of trials on two unknown variable-ratio schedules (the ''two-armed bandit problem'') provides a suitable example. It is simple to state but difficult to solve, and yet many simple rules perform well (Houston, Kacelnik, & McNamara, 1982). The optimal behavior is actually a deterministic function of the outcomes of the previous trials, but most of the successful rules have a stochastic element in their decision making (Houston et al., 1982).

The third justification is that investigating different rules may indicate which evidence is necessary to distinguish between possible rules that an animal might be using.

After presenting the view that rules of thumb are proximate (causal) explanations, Krebs, Stephens, and Sutherland (1983) go on to suggest an alternative view that they call the *Continuum of Strategy sets*. According to this view, a rule of thumb is not ''imperfectly optimal'' (Janetos & Cole, 1981) but is optimal under constraints that limit the options that are available to the animal. Such a view can be dangerous, in that it encourages a blurring of the distinction between causal and functional accounts. Furthermore, it seems to be worth preserving a distinction between a rule that approximates the optimal solution, and the best behavior under constraints. Note that the best behavior under constraints can be found without actually specifying a mechanism. For example, the marginal value theorem can be viewed as the best behavior for certain patch problems when no use of information is allowed. The solution to a constrained optimization problem is therefore not necessarily on the same explanatory level as a rule of thumb.

Learning

The early optimal-foraging models assumed that the forager "knew" the parameters of the foraging problem. Subsequent work has tried to consider learning within the framework of optimality. There have been two lines of approach: (a) the formulation of learning in terms of the optimal use of information (see McNamara & Houston, this volume) and (b) the use of decision rules to explore the way that a forager's gain depends on the way in which it learns. This section reviews some aspects of the second approach.

Many of the rules of thumb that have been used to investigate learning are based on the idea of a linear operator, as expounded in the classic book by Bush and Mosteller (1955). They consider choices that are made at discrete times ("trials") and represent learning as an operator that acts on the probability p of choosing an alternative on trial n to yield the probability of choosing the same alternative on trial $n + 1$. An operator L is linear if this new probability, denoted by Lp, is given by an equation of the form:

$$Lp = a + mp,$$

where a and m are constants that depend on the outcome of the choice on trial n (e.g., whether a reward was obtained).

Bush and Mosteller (1955) discuss various alternative formulations of a linear operator Q_i when a choice is to be made between two alternatives. What they call the *fixed-point form* is:

$$Q_i p = \alpha_i p + (1 - \alpha_i) \lambda_i,$$

where α_i and λ_i depend on the outcome of trial n.

The requirement that p and $Q_i p$ must always lie between 0 and 1 inclusive imposes restrictions on the possible values of α_i and λ_i (Bush & Mosteller, 1955). This, together with the intuitive condition that α_i is non negative, gives:

$$0 \leq \lambda_i \leq 1$$

and

$$0 \leq \alpha_i \leq 1.$$

The term *fixed-point form* arises because λ_i is a fixed point in the map from p to $Q_i p$, i.e., when $p = \lambda_i$, $Q_i p = p = \lambda_i$. If the operator Q_i is repeated n times, then the resulting probability, $Q_i^n p$, is given by the equation:

$$Q_i^n p = \alpha_i^n p + (1 - \alpha_i^n) \lambda_i.$$

As long as α_i is less than 1, α_i^n will tend to zero as n tends to infinity, and so the limiting value of $Q_i^n p$ is λ_i.

In the linear operator appraoch of Bush and Mosteller (1955), the probability of choosing an alternative on trial $n + 1$ is completely determined by the probability of choosing the alternative on trial n and the outcome of trial n. This property is known as "independence-of-path," because the path to a given probability has no effect on subsequent behavior. Houston, Kacelnik, and McNamara (1982) point out that effects that result from partial reinforcement violate the principle of independence-of-path (see also Kacelnik, Krebs, & Ens, this volume). Bush and Mosteller (1955) dealt with this problem by abandoning what they call *event invariance*, i.e., the parameters for a given event, such as nonreward, can depend on context.

Linear operators, or their continuous time equivalents, are the basis for many models of learning and motivation (see Kacelnik et al., this volume; Lea & Dow, this volume; Shettleworth, this volume). In the rule proposed by Harley (1981) and called by him the relative payoff sum (RPS) rule, there is a decision variable $S_i(n)$ associated with alternative i on trial n. The following linear operator determines changes in the variables:

$$S_i(n + 1) = xS_i(n) + (1 \text{ I-}x)r_i + P_i(n),$$

where $O < x < 1$ is a constant (the memory factor) and r is a constant (the residual). $P_i(n)$ is the payoff received from option i on trial n. $P_i(n)$ is zero if alternative i is not chosen on trial n, or if it is chosen but no reward is obtained. For the sort of problems that are considered here, $P_i(n) = 1$ if alternative i is chosen and a reward is obtained. The probability $Pr_i (n + 1)$ of choosing alternative i on trial $n + 1$ is given by $S_i(n)$ over the sum of the $S(n)$'s for all the alternatives, including i. Thus when there are just two alternatives,

$$Pr_1(n + 1) = \frac{S_1(n)}{S_1(n) + S_2(n)}.$$

Because the probability of a choice depends on both S_1 and S_2, the independence-of-path property does not hold. Despite this, the model still has difficulty accounting for the effects of partial reinforcement (see Kacelnik, Krebs, & Ens, this volume).

An example is now given of a foraging problem on which the RPS rule performs badly. The problem is that of choosing between two deterministic depleting patches. In operant terms, each patch is a progressive ratio schedule (Findley, 1958). Working on one patch resets the other to its minimum ratio. The optimal behavior in such circumstances has been given previously. Figure 3.2 gives the graphical solution to a particular schedule that was used in some simulations of the RPS rule that were carried out by Brian Sumida. The results are summarized in Fig. 3.3. For two travel times (of 6 time units and 10 time units, respectively) the upper part of the figure shows the reward rate of the RPS rule for $x = .99$ and $x = .7$, together with the optimal reward rate, and the lower part of the figure shows the corresponding switching rates. Two points can be made: the performance of the RPS rule is considerably worse than the optimal performance, and the memory factor of 0.7 results in a rather better rate than that

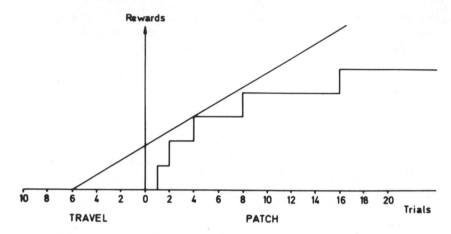

FIG. 3.2.   An illustration of the discrete-trial progressive ratio used to investigate the relative-payoff sum rule. A reward is obtained on the first, second, fourth, and eighth trials. The figure also shows that when the travel time is six trials, it is optimal to leave the patch after four trials—the slope of the line from a travel time of six trials to the cumulative reward curve is the maximum possible long-term reward rate. If immediate maximization is taken in this context to be making the choice that obtains a reward in the shortest number of trials, then immediate maximization is achieved by staying until the fourth reward is obtained.

of .99. The reason for the second point is that when $x = .99$ too much weight is given to previous experience, and the rule results in too few trials being spent in a patch. Decreasing x means that more weight is given to current experience, and so more time is spent in a patch, as is shown by the switching rates. Thus in this particular example, a poor memory performs better than a good one, even though the environment is constant. Why does the RPS rule perform badly in this case? It is not enough to say that the optimal behavior is deterministic whereas the rule is stochastic. The optimal behavior on the two-armed bandit problem is deterministic, and yet the RPS rule, and other stochastic rules, perform well (Harley, 1981; Houston et al., 1982). A better answer is to say that the RPS model should not be formulated in terms of which patch to visit, but in terms of possible values of the number of trials spent on a patch. In the terms used by Herrnstein and Vaughan (1980), the rule has been given the wrong set of response classes. There are, however, an infinite number of response classes, so it is not clear how to proceed. What is interesting is that for some problems it does not seem to be important to define the right response classes. For example, on the discrete-trial concurrent VI–VI on which Harley (1981) tested the RPS rule, the form of the optimal policy is "make one trial on the worse VI, followed by n trials on the better side," where n depends on the schedule parameters (Houston & McNamara, 1981). Harley formulated the RPS rule so that it enabled a choice to be made between the schedules on each trial. For typical schedule parameters,

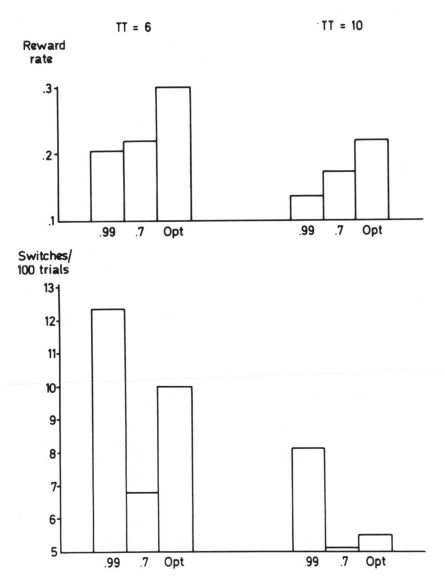

FIG. 3.3. The performance of the relative-payoff sum (RPS) rule on the schedule shown in Fig. 3.2. The upper part of the figure shows the reward rate of the optimal policy together with that of the RPS rule for two values of the memory factor, x, ($x = .7$ and $x = .99$) at two travel times ($TT = 6$ trials and $TT = 10$ trials). It can be seen that the RPS rule achieves a rate well below the optimal rate, and that the better memory ($x = .99$) has a worse performance.

The lower part of the figure shows the switching rate under the same conditions as were used in the upper part of the figure. When $x = .99$ the rule switches more frequently than is optimal, and when $x = .7$ it switches less frequently than is optimal.

however, it turns out that the performance of the rule is virtually identical to the optimal reward rate (Houston & Sumida, in preparation). This is no longer true if a changeover delay (COD) is incorporated. The longer the COD, the greater n should be, and when n is large the stochasticity inherent in the RPS rule can no longer produce a pattern of choice that performs well. Even when the COD is 3 seconds, the reward rate of the RPS rule is significantly less than the optimal rate (Houston & Sumida, in preparation).

Matching and Optimality Yet Again

Harley's treatment of the general properties of an evolutionarily stable (ES) learning rule is now considered. An ES learning rule is an extension of the idea of an evolutionarily stable strategy (ESS) (Maynard Smith, 1982). In ESS theory, animals are considered to play various "games" against other members of their species and against nature. The concept of the ESS was introduced to analyze frequency-dependent games, i.e., games in which the payoff to a strategy depends on the frequency of the various strategies in the population. In such cases an attempt to analyze the action of natural selection by asking which strategy is the best is not possible, beacuse the best strategy depends on the mixture of strategies that is present. Instead of looking for the best strategy, it is necessary to look for stable strategies. An ESS is defined as a strategy that, if adopted by all the members of a population, prevents any other strategy from increasing in the population by the action of natural selection (Maynard Smith, 1982). An ES learning rule is defined in just the same way.

Harley (1981) has made the claim that the equilibrium behavior of an ES learning rule is characterized by the matching law. In frequency-independent games the ESS can be found by the usual optimization techniques (Maynard Smith, 1978), so Harley's claim amounts to saying that matching is always optimal in such circumstances.

The "proof" (Harley, 1981) rests only on the law of large numbers and a standard result in ESS theory, which requires the payoff of all co-existing strategies to be equal. As matching is not in general optimal (aforementioned), Houston (1983b) concluded that Harley's use of the equal payoff condition was incorrect. In reply Harley (1983) starts by saying that the ESS might not involve the maximization of reward rate because of certain constraints. This is true, but totally irrelevant to the argument, in that his "proof" makes no mention of how constraints might limit its applicability. In fact, his argument is completely general. He then goes on to elaborate on why he thinks that his application of the equal payoff condition is correct. His argument (Harley, 1983) is that at equilibrium the payoff to all behaviors must be equal; otherwise the behavior with the highest payoff would increase in frequency. But it is not behaviors (in the sense of choices) that invade, but strategies. The distinction can be illustrated with the aid of the concurrent variable-interval variable-ratio procedure. Following Harley

(1981), it is assumed that an animal has a repertoire of simple behaviors B_i that it may display. In this case the ratio schedule is assumed to be on the right key of a skinner box and the interval schedule is assumed to be on the left key. The two simple behaviors are making a response on the left key, denoted by B_L, and making a response on the right key, denoted by B_R. A strategy is a sequence made up of B_L's and B_R's. A sequence may be given by a deterministic rule (e.g., "three B_R's followed by one B_L") or by a stochastic rule (e.g., "if the last response was B_L, then choose B_R with probability μ_L, if the last response was B_R then choose B_L with probability μ_R." This sort of rule is analysed by Heyman and Luce, 1979). When the payoff to a strategy does not depend on the frequency of strategies in the population, then the ESS can be found by optimization, i.e., the ESS is the strategy that maximizes payoff (Maynard Smith, 1978). Operant procedures involving interval schedules can be called frequency dependent, in that the expected payoff (reinforcement probability) for one schedule depends on the frequency with which the schedule is chosen. This frequency dependence at the level of behavioral options must not be confused with frequency dependence at the level of strategies. In the former case the frequency dependence arises from the fact that reinforcement probability depends on the time since the last response on the schedule, so *temporal contingency* may be a better term than frequency dependence. In standard operant procedures, there is no frequency dependence in the ESS sense, the payoff to a strategy does not depend on the frequency of the strategy in a population of foragers. To illustrate that there is a real danger of confusion here, note that Harley (1981) refers to the concurrent variable-interval procedure as a frequency-independent individual game, whereas Maynard Smith (1982), in his description of Harley's work, refers to the procedure as a frequency-dependent individual game. In the terminology advocated here, it is a frequency-independent individual game in which the behavioral options have temporal contingencies. The concurrent variable-interval variable-ratio procedure is also in this category, and so the ESS is the strategy that maximizes payoff (assumed to be R/T in this case). In a population adopting the ESS strategy S^*, no mutant strategy can invade because S^* results in the maximum possible payoff. When S^* is adopted, the rate on the interval schedule is higher than the rate on the ratio schedule (Herrnstein & Heyman, 1979; Houston, 1983a), and so the expected payoff for B_L is greater than the expected payoff for B_R. There is, however, no contradiction with ESS theory. A strategy in which the frequency of B_L was greater than the frequency of B_L in S^* would result in a decrease in reinforcement rate and hence would not increase in frequency. B_L and B_R coexist in the behavioral repertoire of each animal of a population adopting the ESS.

Although behavioral alternatives do not replicate in the sense that phenotypic stretegies replicate from generation to generation in ESS theory, it is possible that behavioral alternatives "replicate" during a behavioral sequence. Vaughan and Herrnstein (in press) make just such a claim, suggesting that the frequency of behavioral alternatives in an animal's repertoire will change until an equilibrium is reached at which all the alternatives are being reinforced at equal rates. As they point out, such a process will not necessarily maximize the long-term (overall) rate R/T. Vaughan and Herrnstein use the analogy between their view of behavior and ESS theory to suggest that stability analysis rather than optimality analysis should be used in the study of behavior. Their argument is misleading. What they do not draw attention to is that a stability analysis of the foraging schedules that they consider would result in the ESS being the strategy that maximizes reward rate (provided reward rate is the appropriate currency).

The distinction between the behavioral choices and a strategy as a series of choices is illustrated by the example of the performance of the RPS rule on the patch problem based on progressive ratios (Fig. 3.2 and 3.3). The payoffs for individual decisions to stay on a patch are not equal at the optimal strategy. Now consider the level of the strategy. Because the same strategy is used on all patches it always has the same payoff. Taking this idea a stage further, the simple "proof" that optimization always results in matching is obtained. The optimal solution is some strategy S^*, and when this is always adopted all rewards (reinforcements) are obtained from S^*, so the frequency of occurrence matches the frequency of rewards obtained (cf. the discussion of matching on ratio schedules). Of course, what this argument really shows is that the optimal stretegy is the optimal strategy, and if response classes are not defined in advance they can always be redefined in such a way that matching holds. It is hard to see how matching can be successfully applied to patch use without some special definition of response class or reinforcement rate.

It has been argued that matching in terms of the basic behavioral options is not a property of an ES learning rule. The properties of such rules may depend very much on the particular problem, and in general it will be necessary to analyze various competing rules. This approach has already been adopted by Axelrod (1980a, 1980b, 1981) in an elegant investigation of the repeated Prisoner's Dilemma game.

Some Tentative Conclusions

It is easy to say that animals always maximize utility or equalize reinforcement rate across response classes. It is rather harder to specify the relationship between observed measures of rewards and "utility" or "reinforcement" or to know what the response classes will be for a given organism in a given procedure. Either a literal optimality account or a matching account can be produced after the outcome of any given experiment. For example, the effects of hunger on foraging decisions (reviewed by Caraco & Lima, this volume) can be handled by making reinforcement value depend on the animal's state. But behavioral ecology tries to go beyond such a redescription by attempting to understand why evolution has favored these state-dependent choices. The analysis in terms of the danger of starvation provides an answer to this question, but it does not answer the question of how animals actually make such decisions. Operant psychology provides techniques for understanding how decisions are made. Behavioral ecology can tell us why they are made. The approaches can complement each other to the mutual benefit of all concerned.

APPENDIX

Minimizing the time to the next reward results in staying in a patch for at least as many rewards as is required to maximize the overall rate.

There is a travel time τ between patches. Once in a patch, it takes time t_i to obtain the ith reward, with $t_{i+1} > t_i$ for all i.

Let n^* be the number of rewards taken from each patch that results in the maximum possible rate γ^*, i.e.,

$$\gamma^* = \frac{n^*}{\tau + \sum_{i=1}^{n^*} t_i}.$$

Let m be the number of rewards taken from a patch if the animal minimizes the time to the next reward. It follows that

$$\tau + t_1 > t_m$$

and

$$\tau + t_1 < t_n \text{ for all } n > m.$$

Now assume that $m < n^*$. It follows that

$$\tau + t_1 < t_n^*.$$

Consider the overall rate for a cycle of staying for $n^* - 1$ rewards on a patch, travelling to a new patch and staying for just one reward. This behavior has a rate $\hat{\gamma}$ that is given by the equation

$$\hat{\gamma} = \frac{n^*}{\tau + \sum_{i=1}^{n^*-1} t_i + \tau + t_1}$$

If γ^* is written as

$$\gamma^* = \frac{n^*}{\tau + \sum_{i=1}^{n^*-1} t_i + t_n^*}.$$

then because $t_n^* > \tau + t_1$, it follows that $\hat{\gamma} > \gamma^*$. This contradicts the assumption that γ^* is the maximum possible rate, and so it can be concluded that m cannot be less than n^*.

ACKNOWLEDGMENTS

My thanks to the editors and Richard J. Herrnstein for their helpful comments and to Madeline Mitchell for typing several drafts of the chapter. I was supported by the Science and Engineering Research Council.

REFERENCES

Abarca, N., & Fantino, E. (1982). Choice and foraging. *Journal of the Experimental Analysis of Behavior, 38,* 117–123.

Axelrod, R. (1980a). Effective choice in the prisoner's dilemma. *Journal of Conflict Resolution, 24,* 3–25.

Axelrod, R. (1980b). More effective choice in the prisoner's dilemma. *Journal of Conflict Resolution, 24,* 379–403.

Axelrod, R. (1981). The emergence of cooperation among egoists. *The American Political Science Review, 75,* 306–318.

Baum, W. M. (1974). On two types of deviation from the matching laws: Bias and under-matching. *Journal of the Experimental Analysis of Behavior, 22,* 231–242.

Baum, W. M. (1979). Matching, undermatching and overmatching in studies of choice. *Journal of the Experimental Analysis of Behavior, 32,* 269–281.

Baum, W. M. (1981). Optimization and the matching law as accounts of instrumental behavior. *Journal of the Experimental Analysis of Behavior, 36,* 387–403.

Baum, W. H., & Rachlin, H. E. (1969). Choice as time allocation. *Journal of the Experimental Analysis of Behavior, 12,* 861–874.

Boelens, H. (1984). Melioration and maximization of reinforcement minus costs of behavior. *Journal of the Experimental Analysis of Behavior, 42,* 113–126.

Bush, R. R., & Mosteller, F. (1955). *Stochastic models for learning.* New York: Wiley.

Charnov, E. L. (1976). Optimal foraging: The marginal value theorem. *Theoretical Population Biology, 9,* 129–136.

Collier, G. H. (1982). Determinants of choice. In D. Bernstein (Ed.), *Nebraska symposium on motivation* (pp. 69–127). Lincoln: University of Nebraska Press.

Cowie, R. J. (1979). *Foraging behavior of the great tit (Parus major) in a patchy environment.* Unpublished doctoral dissertation, University of Oxford.

Cowie, R. J., & Krebs, J. R. (1979). Optimal foraging in patchy environments. In R. M. Anderson, B. D. Turner, & R. L. Taylor (Eds.), *Population dynamics* (pp. 183–205). Oxford, England: Blackwell Scientific Publications.

Davies, N. B. (1977). Prey selection and the search strategy of the spotted flycatcher (*Musciapa striata*), a field study on optimal foraging. *Animal Behaviour, 25,* 233–234.

Erichsen, J. T., Krebs, J. R., & Houston, A. I. (1980). Optimal foraging and cryptic prey. *Journal of Animal Ecology, 49,* 271–276.

Fantino, E. (1966). Immediate reward followed by extinction vs. later reward without extinction. *Psychonomic Science, 6,* 233–234.

Findley, J. D. (1958). Preference and switching under concurrent scheduling. *Journal of the Experimental Analysis of Behaviour, 1,* 123–144.

Green, R. F. (1980). Bayesian birds: A simple example of Oaten's stochastic model of optimal foraging. *Theoretical Population Biology, 18,* 244–256.

Harley, C. B. (1981). Learning the evolutionarily stable strategy. *Journal of Theoretical Biology, 89,* 611–633.

Harley, C. B. (1983). When do animals learn the evolutionarily stable strategy? *Journal of Theoretical Biology, 101,* 179–181.

Herrnstein, R. J. (1961). Relative and absolute strength of response as a function of reinforcement. *Journal of the Experimental Analysis of Behavior, 4,* 267–272.

Herrnstein, R. J., & Heyman, G. N. (1979). Is matching compatible with reinforcement maximization on concurrent variable interval variable rate? *Journal of the Experimental Analysis of Behavior, 31,* 209–224.

Herrnstein, R. J., & Loveland, D. H. (1975). Maximizing and matching on concurrent ratio schedules. *Journal of the Experimental Analysis of Behavior, 24,* 107–116.

Herrnstein, R. J., & Vaughan, W., Jr. (1980). Melioration and behavioral allocation. In J. E. R. Staddon (Ed.), *Limits to action* (pp. 143–176). New York: Academic Press.

Heyman, G. M. (1982). Is time allocation elicited behavior. In M. Commons (Ed.), *Quantitative analyses of behavior,* Vol. II. *Matching and maximizing accounts* (pp. 459–490). Cambridge, MA: Ballinger.

Heyman, G. M., & Luce, R. D. (1979). Operant matching is not a logical consequence of maximizing reinforcement rate. *Animal Learning and Behavior, 7,* 133–140.

Hinson, J. M., & Staddon, J. E. R. (1983). Hill-climbing by pigeons. *Journal of the Experimental Analysis of Behavior, 39,* 25–47.

Hodos, W., & Trumbule, G. H. (1967). Strategies of schedule preference in chimpanzees. *Journal of the Experimental Analysis of Behavior, 10,* 503–514.

Houston, A. I. (1980). Godzilla vs. the creature from the black lagoon. In F. M. Toates & T. R. Halliday (Eds.), *The analysis of motivational processes* (pp. 297–318). London: Academic Press.

Houston, A. I. (1983a). Optimality theory and matching. *Behaviour Analysis Letters, 3,* 1–15.

Houston, A. I. (1983b). Comments on "Learning the evolutionarily stable strategy." *Journal of Theoretical Biology, 105,* 175–178.

Houston, A. I., Kacelnik, A., & McNamara, J. M. (1982). Some learning rules for acquiring information. In D. J. McFarland (Ed.), *Functional ontogeny* (pp. 140–191). London: Pitman.

Houston, A. I., Krebs, J. K., & Erichsen, J. T, (1980). Optimal prey choice and discrimination time in the great tit (*Parus major* L.). *Behavioural Ecology and Sociobiology, 8,* 35–40.

Houston, A. I., & McNamara, J. (1981). How to maximize reward rate on two variable-interval paradigms. *Journal of the Experimental Analysis of Behavior, 35,* 367–396.

Houston, A. I., & McNamara, J. M. (1984). Imperfectly optimal animals: A correction. *Behavioral Ecology and Sociobiology, 15,* 61–64.

Houston, A. I., & McNamara, J. M. (1985). The variability of behaviour and constrained optimization. *Journal of Theoretical Biology, 112,* 265–273.

Houston, A. I., & Sumida, B. H. (in prep). *An evaluation of some simple learning rules.*

Janetos, A. C., & Cole, B. J. (1981). Imperfectly optimal animals. *Behavioural Ecology and Sociobiology, 9,* 203–209.

Kacelnik, A. (1984). Central place foraging in starlings (*Sturnus vulgaris*) I: Patch residence time. *Journal of Animal Ecology, 53,* 283–300.

Kacelnik, A., Houston, A. I., & Krebs, J. R. (1981). Optimal foraging and territorial defence in the great tit (*Parus major*). *Behavioral Ecology and Sociobiology, 8,* 35–40.

Kalman, R. E. (1968). New developments in systems theory relevant to biology. In M. D. Mesarovic (Ed.), *Systems theory and biology* (pp. 222–232). Berlin: Springer–Verlag.

Kaufman, L. W. (1979). *Foraging strategies: Laboratory simulations.* Unpublished doctoral dissertation, Rutgers University.

Krebs, J. R. (1978). Optimal foraging: Decision rules for predators. In J. R. Krebs & N. B. Davies (Eds.), *Behavioural ecology* (pp. 23–63). Oxford, England: Blackwell Scientific Publications.

Krebs, J. R., Erichsen, J. T., Webber, M. I., & Charnov, E. L. (1977). Optimal prey selection in the great tit (*Parus major*). *Animal Behaviour, 25,* 30–38.

Krebs, J. R., Kacelnik, A., & Taylor, P. (1978). Test of optimal sampling by foraging great tits. *Nature, 275,* 27–31.

Krebs, J. R., & McCleery, R. H. (1984). Optimization in behavioural ecology. In J. R. Krebs & N. B. Davies (Eds.), *Behavioural ecology* (2nd ed., pp. 91–121). Oxford, England: Blackwell Scientific Publications.

Krebs, J. R., Stephens, D. W., & Sutherland, W. J. (1983). Perspectives in optimal foraging theory. In A. M. Brush & G. A. Clark, Jr. (Eds.), *Perspectives in ornithology* (pp. 165–216). Cambridge, England: Cambridge University Press.

Lea, S. E. G. (1979). Foraging and reinforcement schedules in the pigeon: Optimal and nonoptimal aspects of choice. *Animal Behaviour, 27,* 875–886.

Lea, S. E. G. (1981). Correlation and contiguity in foraging behaviour. In P. Harzem & M. H. Zeiler (Eds.), *Advances in the analysis of behaviour* (Vol. 2, pp. 355–406). Chichester: Wiley.

Maynard Smith, J. (1978). Optimization theory in evolution. *Annual review of Ecology and Systematics, 9,* 31–56.

Maynard Smith, J. (1982). *Evolution and the theory of games.* Cambridge: Cambridge University Press.

Mazur, J. E. (1981). Optimization theory fails to predict performance of pigeons in a two-response situation. *Science, 214,* 823–825.

McNamara, J. M. (1982). Optimal patch use in a stochastic environment. *Theoretical Population Biology, 21,* 269–288.

McNamara, J. M., & Houston, A. I. (1980). The application of statistical decision theory to animal behaviour. *Journal of Theoretical Biology, 85,* 673–690.

McNamara, J. M., & Houston, A. I. (1982). Short-term behaviour and life-time fitness. In D. J. McFarland (Ed.), *Functional ontogeny* (pp. 60–87). London: Pitman.

McNamara, J. M., & Houston, A. I. (1983). Optimal responding on variable interval schedules. *Behaviour Analysis Letters, 3,* 157–170.

Metz, H. A. J. (1974). Stochastic models for the temporal fine structure of behaviour sequences. In D. J. McFarland (Ed.), *Motivational control systems analysis* (pp. 5–86). London: Academic Press.

Merz, H. A.J. (1977). State space models for animal behaviour. *Annals of Systems Research, 6,* 65–109.

Myerson, J., & Miezin, F. M. (1980). The kinetics of choice: An operant systems analysis. *Psychological Review, 87,* 160–174.

Nevin, J. A. (1969). Interval reinforcement of choice behavior in discrete trials. *Journal of the Experimental Analysis of Behavior, 12,* 875–885.

Prelec, D. (1982). Matching, maximizing, and the hyperbolic reinforcement feedback function. *Psychological Review, 89,* 189–230.

Pyke, G. H. (1978). Optimal foraging in hummingbirds: Testing the marginal value theorem. *American Zoologist, 18,* 739–752.

Pyke, G. H., Pulliam, H. R., & Charnov, E. L. (1977). Optimal foraging: A selective review of theory and tests. *Quarterly Review of Biology, 52,* 137–154.

Rachlin, H., Battalio, R., Kagel, J., & Green, L. (1981). Maximization theory and behavior. *The Behavioral and Brain Sciences, 4,* 371–388.

Rachlin, H., Kagel, J. H., & Battalio, R. C. (1980). Substitutability in time allocation. *Psychological Review, 87,* 355–374.

Rechten, C., Krebs, J. R., & Houston, A. I. (1981). Great tits and conveyor belts: A correction for non-random prey distribution. *Animal Behaviour, 29,* 1276–1277.

Rider, D. P. (1979). Concurrent ratio schedules: Fixed vs. variable response requirements. *Journal of the Experimental Analysis of Behaviour, 31,* 225–237.

Shimp, C. P. (1969). Optimal behaviour in free-operant experiments. *Psychological Review, 76,* 97–112.

Snyderman, M. (1983). Optimal prey selection: The effects of food deprivation. *Behaviour Analysis Letters, 3,* 359–369.

Staddon, J. E. R., Hinson, J. M., & Kram, R. (1981). Optimal choice. *Journal of Experimental Analysis of Behavior, 35,* 397–412.

Staddon, J. E. R., & Motheral, S. (1978). On matching and maximizing in operant choice experiments. *Psychological Review, 85,* 436–444.

Stephens, D. W., & Charnov, E. L. (1982). Optimal foraging: Some simple stochastic models. *Behavioural Ecology and Sociobiology, 10,* 251–263.

Taylor, R., & Davison, M. (1983). Sensitivity to reinforcement in concurrent arithmetic and exponential schedules. *Journal of the Experimental Analysis of Behavior, 39,* 191–198.

Tinbergen, N. (1951). *The study of instinct.* Oxford, England: Clarendon Press.

Vaughan, W., Jr., & Herrnstein, R. J. (in press). Stability, melioration and natural selection. In L. Green & J. Kagel (Eds.), *Advances in behavioral economics* (Vol. 1).

Vaughan, W. Jr., Kardish, T. A., & Wilson, M. (1982). Correlation versus contiguity in choice. *Behaviour Analysis Letters, 2,* 153–160.

Vaughan, W., Jr., & Miller, H. L., Jr. (1984). Optimization versus response-strength accounts of behavior. *Journal of the Experimental Analysis of Behavior, 42,* 337–348.

Ydenberg, R. C. (1982). *Territorial vigilance and foraging behaviour: A study of trade offs.* Unpublished doctoral dissertation, University of Oxford.

II FORAGING IN A CHANGING ENVIRONMENT

4

Foraging in a Changing Environment: An Experiment with Starlings (*Sturnus vulgaris*)

Alejandro Kacelnik*
Department of Zoology
University of Groningen, Netherlands

John R. Krebs
Department of Zoology
Edward Grey Institute of Field Ornithology

Bruno Ens
Department of Zoology
University of Groningen, Netherlands

INTRODUCTION

Many models of foraging behavior assume that animals have complete knowledge of their environment (see review in Krebs, Stephens, & Sutherland, 1983; Pyke, 1984). Animals could behave as if they have complete knowledge either by using a fixed rule that does perfectly in a wide variety of situations (e.g., Cheverton, Kacelnik, & Krebs, 1985), or by always learning the appropriate features of the environment. In the latter case the process of learning about the environment can be revealed by exposing the animal to new conditions or to a change in the environment. By studying the process of acquisition following a change one can evaluate possible models of learning. In the experiment described here, captive starlings were given a choice between two operant feeding devices (patches) in an aviary. The patches differed in reinforcement probability, but the difference was not signaled to the birds. The birds soon learned to discriminate between the two and responded almost exclusively in the patch offering the higher probability. At a time unpredictable to the birds an unsignaled step change in the environment was introduced by reducing the reward proba-

---

*Present address: Dept. of Zoology, University of Oxford

bility at the better site to zero. Both the data on initial learning at the start of the experiment and that on the response of the birds to the change were used in order to evaluate descriptive models of learning.

Learning Models

The "learning" discussed in this chapter consists of adjusting behavioral allocation to changes in rates of reinforcement in simultaneously available food sources. The models described in this section have in some cases been proposed in slightly different contexts, but the only concern here is how they apply to this issue.

We examine how well various models derived from the linear-operator model of Bush and Mosteller (1951) account for our results. Although models of this kind can be criticized for their inability to account for the quantitative details of acquisition (e.g., Mazur & Hastie, 1978) and to distinguish different temporal patterns of reinforcement with the same overall average, they remain a useful framework to analyze the integration of previous and current present experience during learning. In the past few years several variants of the linear-operator model have been proposed in connection with foraging behavior of individuals (Commons et al., 1982; Dow & Lea, this volume; Harley, 1981; Killeen, 1982, 1984; Lea & Dow, 1984; Myerson & Miezin, 1980; Pulliam & Dunford, 1980) and of social units (Lester, 1984; Milinski, 1984; Regelmann, 1984; see Kacelnik & Krebs, 1985, for discussion), with the common property that behavioral allocation between options is a function of an exponentially weighted moving average (EWMA) (Killeen, 1982) of past and recent experience. The general equation on which these models are based is:

$$P_i(t + 1) = \alpha \, Q_i(t) + (1 - \alpha) \, P_i(t) \qquad (1)$$
$$0 < \alpha < 1.$$

In this expression P_i represents a variable that determines the probability of responding on behavioral option i in the interval or response (t). Q_i represents a measure of the amount of reinforcement obtained during interval or response t. α represents a parameter that determines the relative weight of recent and past experience. A large value of α (i.e., α close to 1) implies that behavior is controlled mostly by the very recent experience, with little weight given to the memory of past experience.

In Bush and Mosteller's original model P_i represented the probability of responding (or the rate of responding) in variable i, but later versions have incorporated an intervening process by which the probability of choice of option i is determined by some "decision rule" (Houston, Kacelnik, & McNamara, 1982) that operates on the P value of all available options. P_i is now seen as a "state variable" associated with option i and can be intuitively seen as the subject's current estimate of the value of the given option.

Two commonly considered decision rules are *maximizing* (the subject responds at time (or response number) t on the option with the highest value of P at the time) and *matching* (responses are allocated to behavioral option i with probability $P_i(t)$ / $\Sigma P_j(t)$). This use of the term matching is different from its use in the matching law (Herrnstein, 1970). Matching is used here as an allocation mechanism rather than as a molar description of allocation throughout a whole session.

Table 4.1 summarizes various versions of the linear-operator model and reveals that there are various points of difference.

Firstly, the models differ in how they update the estimates (P). The value of P corresponding to each option may be updated after arbitrary time intervals, as in the work of Lester (1984) and Regelmann (1984), who used 10 minutes and 2 seconds, respectively, or every time a response (e.g., Pulliam & Dunford, 1980) or a reward occurs. In Killeen's (1982, 1984) model the estimate of P is updated at every response, but the value of the memory parameter α is dynamically varied with readjustments every time a reward is obtained. The main difficulty of updating P after arbitrary intervals is that, unless the length of the interval for updating is chosen to be much shorter than the shortest interval between two observed choices (responses), the length of the updating interval is effectively an extra free parameter that may be important in generating patterns of choice. This objection is specially relevant to Lester's study because he used an updating interval during which the experimental animals (goldfish in a tank with a feeding site in each half) could change feeding patch several times, and thus the (model) subject's experience of food availability at each place is a function of the length of the interval. However, the use of time is hard to avoid for allocation problems where individual responses cannot be identified. An alternative approach for this kind of problem is that developed by Ollason (1980), who proposes a continuous time model instead of the discrete time updating common to all versions of the linear operator. On the other hand, updating P only after responses have occurred ignores the fact that response rate does change, and it assumes that the subjects will consider the world to be "frozen" between responses even when response rate is low and responses are spaced out. Killeen's (1984) approach is more realistic and derived from the finding that his rule is more efficient than various other alternatives in accounting for behavior observed by Gibbon, Farrell, Locurto, Duncan, and Terrace (1980). The cost of realism is an increase in complexity that entails some loss of heuristic value for the model.

Secondly, there are differences regarding the "prior" expectation. In order to compare the predictions of the linear-operator model to any particular set of experimental results, it is necessary to introduce an assumption about the value of each behavioral option before any response is made, i.e., a value has to be assigned to $P_i(O)$. This value is named the *prior expectation,* and it is supposed to be related to the previous experience of the subject in the environment as a whole. In the case of the Relative Pay-off Sum model (Harley, 1981; Re-

TABLE 4.1
Summary of Linear-Operator Learning Models

Source	Model	Decision Rule	Step*	Updating P When Unattended	Comments
Harley, 1981	$P' = \alpha P + (1 - \alpha)R + Q$	Matching	resp	yes	R = Residual value of P
Lester, 1984	$P' = \alpha Q + (1 - \alpha)P$	Matching	time	yes	Q can differ from 0,1
Pulliam & Dunford, 1980	$P' = \alpha Q + (1 - \alpha)P$	Maximizing	resp	—	
Killeen, 1984	$P' = \alpha' Q + (1 - \alpha')P$ $1/\alpha' = \gamma \, cT + (1 - \gamma) \, 1/\alpha$	Matching $\sqrt{P}$	P:resp α:rews	—	T = inter-reward interval C = empirical constant
This paper	$A = P' \, C'^{k}$ $P' = \alpha Q + (1 - \alpha)P$ $C' = 1$ if $Q = 1$, else $C (1 - P)$	Maximizing	resp	no	

P: subjective reward probability; Q: reward obtained in previous response; α: memory factor; γ: memory factor for dynamic memory; A: Attractiveness; C: Confidence; k: free parameter. Variables with an apostrophe (') refer to response to be made $(t + 1)$, without it to response just made (t)*; *step* refers to the updating of the value of P; in this column *resp* stands for updating P every response and *rews* for updating α (in Kileen's model) every reward. —: information not available. The two models using Maximizing are deterministic, in that choice is univocally determined by history and state, whereas the remaining models are probabilistic: They specify the probability of choices.

66

gelmann, 1984), the prior expectation (residual) is retained in the learning equation as a separate entity, so that when one of the alternatives does not provide rewards for a relatively long time the P value of this option decays to the residual rather than to zero as in the other models. This retention of the prior makes the RPS model somewhat more sensitive to the (arbitrary) initial values than the other models and implies that no option reaches zero probability of response.

Thirdly, different things may happen to the value of options that are not used. The value of $P_i(t + 1)$ when the response at time t has taken place in an option other than i can be assumed to remain unchanged $(P_i(t + 1) = P_i(t)$. Alternatively, some authors generate a new value of $P_i(t + 1)$ according to equation 1 even when the option is not tried, assuming that the situation is equivalent to having made an unrewarded response in this option $(Q_i(t) = 0$ if response t has occurred in an option other than $i)$. This "pessimistic" assumption, incorporated by Harley, Regelmann, and Lester, implies that the animals ignore information potentially available: No distinction is made between an option not tried for n intervals or responses and one tried but with no rewards. In the standard form of equation 1 the pessimistic assumption leads to:

$$P_i(t + 1) = \alpha P_i(t),$$

whereas in the RPS model used by Harley and by Regelmann it leads to:

$$P_i(t + 1) = \alpha P_i(t) + (1 - \alpha) R,$$

where R is the value of the residual. In other words, the value of unvisited options drops exponentially to zero in the standard version of the linear operator and drops to the residual in the RPS model.

Fourthly, there is the possibility of changing the weight of memory. Killeen (1982, 1984) includes the idea that the memory factor itself (α in eq. 1) could be variable and dependent on capture rate. His model assumes that the subjects give relatively more weight to immediate experience when reward rate is high. This change implies the addition of one extra parameter, responsible for the rate of adjustment of the memory factor. The memory factor itself, (α_i), is postulated to change as an exponentially weighted moving average (see Table 4.1), and because of this the predictions of this model for the context of the present experiments are fundamentally different from the other versions of the linear operator.

Finally, there are differences with respect to the decision rule. Whereas Harley, Lester, and Killeen use forms of matching as the decision rule, Pulliam and Dunford use maximizing.

In order to compare the predictions of the models to the present results, Harley's, Lester's, and Killeen's models, as well as an additional two-parameter model described later, were simulated. The values of the parameters were taken from these experiments. We are grateful to Peter Killeen and Nigel Lester for having run the simulations of their respective models themselves. Among the other available versions of linear-operator based models simulations of Harley's model were included because, in contrast with the other models, which have been formulated as potentially accurate descriptions of choice, the RPS rule was presented as a nearly optimal decision rule (Harley, 1981, 1983; Maynard Smith, 1982, 1984) albeit not without objections (Houston, 1982; Krebs & Kacelnik, 1984).

EXPERIMENT I. RANDOM RATIOS

Materials and Methods

Subjects.   Three adult starlings (*Sturnus vulgaris*) with previous experience in similar experiments were used. They lived individually in the experimental aviaries, feeding exclusively from the operant dispensers described in the following section, except for a 4-hour gap between experiments every second day. During this period they received fish-food pellets ad libitum, plus 20 mealworms per bird. Water was always freely available.

Apparatus.   Each aviary contained two feeding discs (Krebs, Kacelnik, & Taylor, 1978) each with an associated perch, separated by 1.5 meters. The birds could obtain food from the discs by perch-hopping. The disc-plus-perch unit is referred to here as a foraging "patch." In addition, there was a third perch placed midway between the two patches and oriented along the main axis of the aviary, so that when the bird sat on this central perch its body was at right angles to the direction of either patch. The bird was required to return to the central perch between each response to either of the feeding patches, which ensured that each response was effectively an independent trial. Food rewards consisted of 0.08 grams of fish food pellets, and water was available continuously in a bottle by the central perch.

Schedules.   The foraging sequence began with the bird sitting on the central perch, which turned on cue lights in both patches. In the "lights on" state both patches were active and a hop in either patch could result in a reward being delivered according to the programmed probability for that patch. A hop in either patch deactivated both patches and turned both cue lights off, so that the bird had to return to the central place to start again, equidistant from the two patches. The reward schedules were random ratios, i.e., each hop had the same probability of delivering a reward. In one patch ("stable", randomly assigned for each session) the probability remained at 0.08 throughout, whereas the other patch ("unstable") started off with a high probability, 0.25 or 0.75 in either of two different treatments, and eventually changed in a single step to zero.

Protocol.   Each experimental session lasted approximately 44 hours and was run in a "closed economy" (Collier & Rovee-Collier, 1981). Sessions started at about 14:00 and ran through the following day until about 10:00 on the third day. The change in reward probability of the "unstable" patch from either 0.25 or 0.75 to 0.00 occurred at an uncued time between 10:00 and 15:00 of the second day (Fig. 4.1). The time of the change was chosen so that it occurred at random, with the constraint that more than 100 rewards (not necessarily successive rewards) had been obtained on the unstable side prior to the drop to zero. Due to this constraint the change to zero did not occur earlier than at about 133 responses in the 0.75 treatment and at about 400 responses in the 0.25 treatment. In three out of 56 sessions, the bird failed to reach the criterion by 15:00 hours on day 2, either by not making enough responses or by strongly preferring the 0.08 side. These sessions are not included in the analysis.

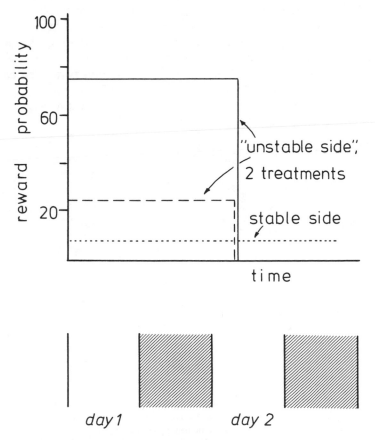

FIG. 4.1.   A diagram of the experimental design.

Each bird was tested 10 times with each treatment (20 sessions per bird). Four replicates were lost due to recording errors and three were discarded as explained before, which left 53 sessions for analysis.

Results

Acquisition.   Figure 4.2 shows that in both treatments of the random ratio experiment there is a gradual rise in preference for the better patch from the start of each session. The rise is steeper for the 0.75 treatment. The figure shows the averaged data for the three animals. All showed the same trend, although between sessions the results were highly variable. In both treatments the birds approached complete commitment to the better side before the change to zero. In the 0.25 treatment the asymptotic value (taken as the last 100 responses before the change) was 98.37% and in the 0.75 treatment it was 99.20%. This difference is not significant (analysis of variance, treatment effect: $F = 2.95$, $df = 1$, $p = 0.09$). Notice that this result may be biased towards complete commitment because of the requirement of obtaining at least 100 rewards on the unstable side before the change, whereas no constraint was imposed on the 0.08 side.

Table 4.2 shows the number of responses that the birds performed on each side before the drop to zero during the 0.25 and the 0.75 sessions. There were more responses before the drop to zero in the 0.25 treatment than in the 0.75 treatment, both on the stable and on the unstable sides.

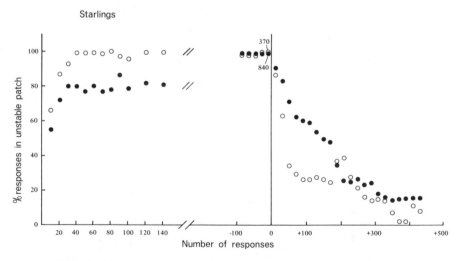

FIG. 4.2.   A summary of the results of the random-ratio experiment. Data for three birds and 53 sessions are averaged. The vertical line at zero on the abscissa indicates the point at which the unstable patch was changed to zero reward probability. All sessions have been aligned at this point, and data are shown for bins of 20 responses. The results are analysed statistically in Fig. 4.3. Open circles: 0.75 treatment; closed circles: 0.25 treatment.

TABLE 4.2
Responses in Each Patch Before Reward-Probability Change to Zero
in the Unstable Patch ($\bar{x} \pm SD$)

	Stable		Unstable	
TREATMENT	25	75	25	75
BIRD				
A	222.6 ± 24	16.6 ± 25	547.4 ± 24	298.7 ± 89
B	274.3 ± 31	103.0 ± 15	695.5 ± 21	382.9 ± 12
C	47.6 ± 61	16.5 ± 26	742.7 ± 30	320.7 ± 13
Mean	181.5 ± 11	45.5 ± 50	661.9 ± 10	334.1 ± 44

Effect of the Drop to Zero. The main aim of this experiment is to examine how the birds responded to the stepwise change to zero reward probability in the unstable patch. Figure 4.2 shows that in data averaged for all birds the switch in preference after the drop to zero is more rapid in the 0.75 treatment than in the 0.25 treatment. In both cases the birds shifted their commitment (defined as percentage of responses in successive blocks of 10 responses) from the unstable to the stable patch, but they did so more rapidly following a big change (0.75–0.00) than following a smaller one (0.25–0.00). All three birds performed in a similar way when analyzed for the molar level of commitment over 100 responses before and after the drop to zero (treatment effect: $F = 9.94$, $df = 1$, $p = 0.003$, Fig. 4.3a). In molecular terms, the number of responses after the drop to zero before the first switch to the stable side was larger in the 0.25–0.00 treatment than in the 0.75–0.00 treatment for all three birds, but the variance was large, and the result is not significant (treatment effect: $F = 1.88$, $df = 1$, $p = 0.17$, Fig. 4.3b).

Predictions of the Models. The predictions of three of the models in Table 4.1 were compared with two aspects of the results: (a) the difference in asymptotic commitment before the change in the two treatments and (b) the difference in adjustment to the change. Our analysis is concerned with the qualitative rather than with the quantitative aspects of the data, so the two effects the models have to account for are (a) nearly equal and almost exclusive commitment before the change (with the asymptote reached earlier for the 0.75 treatment), and (b) more rapid reversal of preference after the change in the 0.75 than in the 0.25 treatment. Figure 4.4 shows the simulations of Harley's, Lester's, and Killeen's models. The parameters used are explained in Table 4.1 and their values are given in the figure legend. In simulating Lester's model a single response was used as the time bin. This made it similar to Pulliam and Dunford's (1980) model, except with matching instead of maximizing as the decision rule and with the "pessimistic" assumption referred to earlier as a premise. Also, whereas

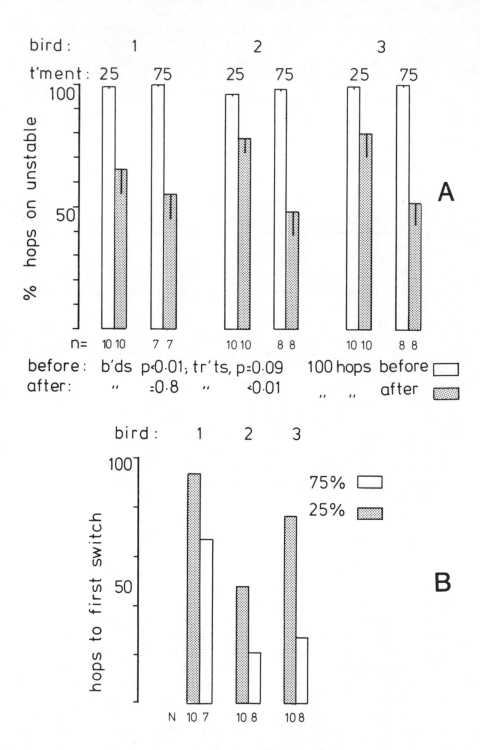

Lester's original model predicted fraction of time spent on each side during each time interval, this simulation predicted probability of responding on each side instead. None of the three models describes successfully the similarity of commitment in the two treatments at the end of the period *before* the change (i.e., during acquisition), when it is assumed that the amount of experience of the models is the same as the average number of responses that the birds performed before the drop in reward probability. Harley's and Lester's models also produce the opposite of the present results *after* the change, namely a more rapid reversal of preference in the 0.25 than in the 0.75 treatment. Killeen's model is more successful in accounting for the behavior of the birds after the change to zero. Because the model updates its memory more rapidly when reinforcement rate is high, it predicts more rapid shifting of preference in the 0.75–0.00 treatment than in the 0.25–0.00 treatment. For reasons of space, a sensitivity analysis of the models shall not be presented, but the qualitative trends are quite robust and not easily modified by changing the parameters of the models. Results from all models are shown with favorable parameter values. It is worth noting parenthetically that in order to make Killeen's model produce a reasonable description of our data it was necessary to use a somewhat ad hoc decision rule (see legend for Fig. 4.4).

An Alternative Model.   Given the failure of existing learning models to account for the observed pattern of both the acquisition and the reversal of preference, a new two-parameter model was developed. It should be emphasized that this is a descriptive model designed to account for obtained results, and thus its success in doing so is not surprising. Its interest, however, lies in the apparent need to use at least two parameters and the relevant implications for what animals might learn about experimental situations. It is also interesting to note that this new model bears a formal resemblance to a Bayesian statistical decision model (see appendix, and also McNamara & Houston, 1980).

The model was designed to take into account the nature of the experimental protocol, i.e., that there is a stepwise, unpredictable change to zero in one of the patches. The learning process was modeled with two components, one a linear operator that yields an estimate of reward probability and the other an estimate of

---

FIG. 4.3.   Experiment I: (a) Commitment (= % of responses) to the unstable patch averaged for 100 responses before (open histograms) and after (shaded histograms) the change to zero. All three birds show the same pattern and an analysis of variance reveals that there is no significant *treatment* effect before the change ($p = 0.69$), whereas there is one after the change ($p < 0.01$); (b) the number of responses before the first switch away from the unstable side (first response to stable side after last reward on the unstable side) following the change to zero. The latency is not significantly shorter in the 0.75 than in the 0.25 treatment ($p = 0.17$). Numbers under the bars are the number of sessions involved.

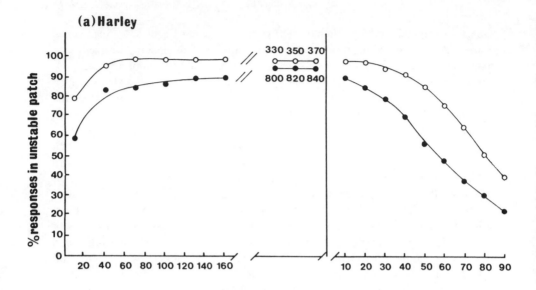

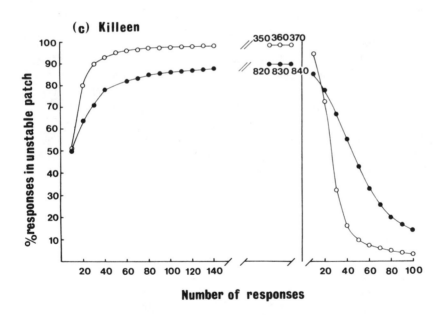

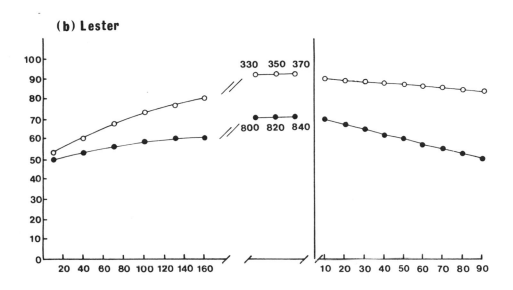

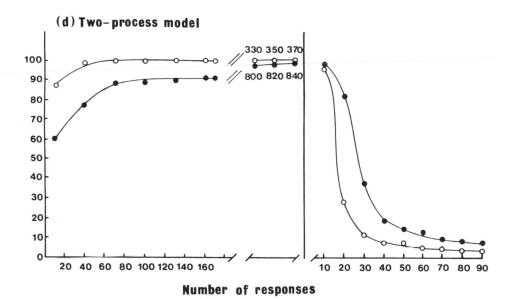

Number of responses

FIG. 4.4. Simulations of four learning models (Table 4.1). (a) Harley's relative-payoff sum model, $\alpha = 0.95$, $R = 0.20$; (b) Lester's dynamic-matching model, $\alpha = 0.99$, prior = 0.10; (c) Killeen's adaptive-clock model, $T = 340$ sec. for 0.75, 480 sec. for 0.25, $\gamma = 0.005$, $c = 5.364$, response rule = matching to square-root transformed estimates of payoff; (d) the two-process model, $\alpha = 0.99$, prior = 0.2, $k = 0.1$.

the probability that the sudden change in payoff has not yet occurred. Each success or failure gives information about both aspects.

The linear-operator estimate of reward probability is updated at a given site after each response according to equation 1. If a site is not visited, there is no change in the estimate, i.e., the "pessimistic" assumption used by Lester and Harley was not incorporated.

The second component of this model, the estimate of the probability that *no* drop to zero in the value of a site has occurred, is given by:

$$C_i(t + 1) = C_i(t)(1 - P_i(t)) \tag{2}$$

when no reward is obtained at trial t in patch i and:

$$C_i(t + 1) = 1 \tag{3}$$

when a reward is obtained at trial t in patch i.

These equations imply that when a run of nonrewards is obtained, the animal's "confidence" that no change has occurred will diminish in a way that is related to the estimated likelihood of getting such a run of bad luck, given the value of P_i. For example, if the value of P_i changes extremely slowly (α is close to 0.00 in equation 1), the probability of n unsuccessful consecutive responses after each reward is given by $(1 - P_i(t))^n$, which would be the same as the value of C after n unsuccessful responses calculated by equation (2). The value of C is updated only when a site is visited, so that "confidence" does not change when the animal is elsewhere.

Finally the model combines the two components given by equations (1) and either (2) or (3) to give an estimate of overall "attractiveness" of a site. This is done as follows:

$$A_i(t + 1) = P_i(t + 1) \, C_i \, (t + 1)^k \tag{4}$$

where A is "attractiveness" and k is a scaling constant to weight the relative emphasis put on confidence and assessed reward probability ($k > O$). Due to the multiplication, $O \leqslant A \leqslant 1$.

In contrast to the linear-operator model, this model allows the value of attractiveness to change more rapidly with nonrewards on a site with a high value of assessed reward probability than in one with a lower value. If P_i is high, the value of C_i will decline rapidly with a run of nonrewards [equation (2)] and if k is not too small this will produce a rapid change in $AH?\phi\mathring{a}*_i$. In the simulations of this two-process model A_i is translated into behavioral responses using a rule of maximizing ("at time $t + 1$ go to the site with the higher value of A"). A range of values of k and α were used in simulations, and the results shown are those that gave a good description of the results. It should be noted parenthetically that the component C of our model is applicable only to a decrease in reward probability. When there is an increase the model behaves as a linear operator.

Figure 4.4d shows that this model mimics the animal's behavior successfully in both aspects referred to earlier. The prechange asymptote in commitment to the unstable site is similar and near 100% in the two treatments after the appropriate number of responses. Also, the response to the step change is more rapid in the 0.75 than in the 0.25 treatment.

EXPERIMENT II. FIXED RATIOS

Methods

A second experiment was carried out with two of the subjects, using fixed instead of random ratios. The design was similar to that of the previous experiment with the exception that the starting reward ratios on the unstable patch were 1.0, 0.5, and 0.25 rewards per response in three different treatments. Two other procedural differences were as follows: (a) Between experimental sessions the birds were "neutralized" with respect to patch preference by forced alternation after each reward (only one of the patches was activated for each trial, switching between patches after each reward) until the subject had obtained 10 rewards per patch; and (b) the unstable side was changed to zero after at least 50 rewards (excluding those obtained during neutralisation) had been obtained instead of after 100 (with the fixed ratios the birds tended to absorb on the unstable side more rapidly than with random ratios). The aim of this experiment was to analyze the response to the change to zero when the schedule left no ambiguity, i.e., the subjects could (in theory) know exactly when a reward was due.

Each treatment (Fixed ratios 1, 2, and 4) was replicated 7 times (sessions) per bird, following a random order.

Results

The results are summarized in Table 4.3. As in the random-ratio experiment, there was no between-treatment difference in commitment to the unstable side before the change, although in this case the percentage of responses to this side was around 90% instead of nearly 100% as in the previous experiment. Two differences in the protocol can explain this difference: the birds were biased towards switching between patches during the "neutralization" at the beginning of the test (see methods) and the amount of experience required for the change to take place was shorter, so that the birds might not have reached their asymptotic commitment when the change occurred. These possibilities mean that it is not possible to attribute an intrinsic difference in equilibrium behavior to the different schedules. The aim of this experiment, however, was to characterize the behavior of potentially omniscient animals after the change to zero. If the birds were fully acquainted with the details of the experimental protocol, they could "know" that reward probabilities never changed during a test other than for the higher of them to drop to zero. Under the fixed-ratio schedule the change to zero could have been unambiguously detected after the first reward had failed to be

TABLE 4.3
Summary of Results of the Fixed-Ratio Experiment ($\bar{x} \pm$ S.D.).
($n = 7$ for All Experimental Treatments)

Treatment	Bird	Percentage Responses in Unstable Patch		Responses Before Drop in Reward Probability	
		100 BEFORE	100 AFTER	STABLE	UNSTABLE
FR1 (100%)	A	88.4 ± 18.1	41.7 ± 28.7	18.8 ± 40	87 ± 42
	C	93.4 ± 8.8	59.9 ± 22.9	5 ± 10	81
FR2 (50%)	A	84.0 ± 16.5	55.1 ± 29.0	54.5 ± 71	172 ± 47
	C	96.1 ± 3.2	59.7 ± 32.5	5 ± 18	120 ± 18
FR4 (25%)	A	94.9 ± 7.9	61.1 ± 30.3	51.5 ± 64	257 ± 49
	C	93.9 ± 9.1	71.3 ± 22.7	44.5 ± 56	250 ± 80

delivered on completion of the ratio. The reversal in preference after the change ought to have been dramatically shortened with respect to the random-ratio experiment. Actually the reversal in preference of omniscient animals (a strategy potentially realizable in the fixed-ratio experiment) ought to be total after the first, second, and fourth unrewarded responses in the fixed ratios 1, 2, and 4, respectively, with scores of commitment in the 100 responses after the change of 1, 2, and 4%, respectively. Table 4.3 shows that the results were far away from these values, with mean commitments after the change of 50.8, 57.4, and 66.2, respectively. Thus, even though statistical comparison between the two experimental situations is inappropriate because of the differences in procedure, it is apparent that the results not only show the same trend in both cases (slower reversal for lower prechange rate of reinforcement), but they are also of the same order of magnitude (means in the random-ratio experiment were 51.2 and 74.6% for commitments after drops from 0.75 and 0.25 reward probability, respectively, see Fig. 4.3).

DISCUSSION

The main conclusion of our experiment is as follows. When there is a stepwise, unpredictable, and unsignaled drop to zero reward probability at the better of two feeding sites, starlings switch to the alternative more rapidly when the drop to zero is from a higher initial probability. This holds for both random and fixed ratios. This result is qualitatively contrary to the predictions of single-parameter learning models based on smooth averaging of past and recent experience. Although Killeen's (1984) model with a varying memory factor can account for this aspect of our data, it does not mimic the allocation of responses before the change in reward probability. In this paper, a two-parameter model that accounts for the obtained results was proposed. This model hypothesizes that the animals estimate both the reward probability at each site and the probability that a sudden change has occurred. This implies that the subjects learn the general nature of the experimental protocol. In the ensuing discussion, some limitations in the experimental design are considered, and then the results are discussed in relation to (a) the partial reinforcement extinction effect (PREE) and (b) a Bayesian statistical decision model of response to changes in the environment. Finally, some changes in response rate in the course of the experiments are briefly considered.

Confounding Variables

Three independent variables are confounded in these experiments: initial reward probability, size of the drop in reward probability, and amount of experience on the better side before the drop. As the main aim of the experiments was to test if some learning models could account for the results obtained given the experimental protocol, the general conclusions are not affected by the fact that these variables are confounded.

The Partial Reinforcement Extinction Effect

The present results might appear to be as expected from the partial reinforcement extinction effect (PREE). The PREE consists of greater resistance to extinction (slower drop in response rate) following partial than following continuous reinforcement, or following low instead of high partial reinforcement (see Tarpy, 1982, for a review). Before attempting to assess the present results in relation to PREE, it is worth pointing out that there are many procedural differences between these experiments and conventional PREE studies, and that procedure has an important effect on the outcome, to judge from the existing literature. PREE studies usually measure rates of responding rather than choice (for an exception, see Elam & Tyler, 1958) and are usually done with maze running, with short sessions, and with comparisons between subjects. In contrast, a "free operant" procedure was used here, choice and not rate was measured, and the comparisons are within subjects. It is therefore more appropriate to compare these data with the operant literature on extinction than with the conventional maze-running literature.

Nevin (1979; see also Mellgren & Olson, 1983) points out that operant studies of PREE are ambiguous in their results. Some show conventional PREE whereas others show the reverse effect. For example, in some variable-interval schedule experiments there is more rapid extinction following low than high rates of reinforcement, whereas with variable ratios (as in our experiment) there is more rapid extinction following higher probabilities of reward (Jenkins, 1978). These data refer to rates of responding, and Nevin (1979) concludes that there are too few data for concurrent schedules to draw any firm conclusions about choice. In short, one could not predict with confidence the outcome of the present experiments from the existing data on PREE, but the relation between this effect and these experiments deserves further analysis.

Can existing theoretical accounts of PREE be applied to the data reported here? Nevin (1979) proposes that resistance to extinction depends on a combination of two things, response strength and discriminability. The higher the response strength (an increasing function of reward rate or reward probability), the greater the resistance to extinction. On the other hand, the higher the discriminability of the change in schedule, the less resistance to extinction there should be. Nevin applies this verbal model to the literature by suggesting that when the reward probabilities used in an experiment are high (e.g., 0.5 or 1.0, as in many maze studies) the main factor influencing the speed of extinction is the ability of the animal to detect the drop to zero reward probability. This ability increases with larger initial probability of reward. In contrast, when the initial probability is very low (as in a variable interval experiment when a very small proportion of responses is rewarded), detectability of the change to extinction is always low and the major factor influencing persistance is the response strength, which as mentioned is assumed to increase with reinforcement rate. It is apparent that Nevin's verbal model could be considered to be analogous to our mathematical two-process model: Response strength being equivalent to our estimated reward probability (P) and detectability being analogous to our value of "confidence" (C).

The most widely accepted theory of PREE for maze studies is Capaldi's sequential theory (1966), which hypothesizes that the animal on a partial reinforcement schedule learns that nonrewards are sometimes followed by rewards and therefore persists during extinction. Although this idea could be applied to the reversal of preference in the results reported here (not surprisingly, it would predict the PREE-compatible behavior observed, because it was designed to describe such effects), it is not comparable to the post hoc model of learning developed in this chapter, because it does not account for initial acquisition as well as for adjustments in choice after a drop in reward probability.

Detecting the Change: A Bayesian Approach

McNamara and Houston (1980) point out that the PREE could be explained in terms of information acquisition (equivalent to Nevin's idea of detectability). If the animal is viewed as sampling at each response to detect whether a drop to zero has occurred, a longer run of nonrewarded responses is required to detect the drop to zero if the initial probability is low than if it is high. Although it is intuitively obvious that this would lead to the qualitative effect observed, it is unlikely that the quantitative pattern could be accounted for by an optimality model of sampling. This can perhaps be seen most clearly in the case of the fixed-ratio experiments. When the fixed ratio is 2, the animals experience rewards and nonrewards in a determinstic alternating sequence, so that a run of two or more nonrewards signals with certainty that the drop to zero has occurred.

However, the animals persist in responding to the unstable patch for much longer than two hops after the drop to zero (Table 4.3), so the pattern of response cannot be explained solely in terms of estimating the probability of a drop to zero. (It could of course be argued that the birds never learn the deterministic nature of the fixed-ratio schedule, but even with random ratios they are far too persistent for the information hypothesis to account for their response to the drop to zero.)

A Bayesian model of optimal sampling for this experiment is presented in the appendix. The model does not specify an actual learning rule and therefore cannot be used to compare with the data, but its value lies in suggesting a functional analog to the descriptive post hoc model described previously. The Bayesian model analyzes how the animal ought to assess whether the reward probability at a feeding site has dropped to zero. As the appendix shows, this assessment should depend on both the estimated reward probability and an estimate of "confidence" that the probabilities have not changed. These are the same two factors that entered into the descriptive model, so it can be inferred that the descriptive model may make functional sense from the standpoint of information acquisition, even though the quantitative details of behavior cannot be explained purely in information terms.

Variations in Response Rate

Attention is now turned to the problem of rate of responding. How should response rate (responses/time) be affected by the changes in reward probability experienced during these experiments? There are two views in the literature, one represented by researchers who consider long-term consequences of behavior in closed economies (Collier, Hirsch, & Hamilin, 1972; Hirsch & Collier, 1974 (see review in Collier, Hill, & Kaufman, 1984); Mellgren, this volume; Rashotte et al., this volume), and the other by those (more numerous) who are concerned with short-term experiments and open economies. According to the first view, rate of responding should be negatively related to reward probability. According to the second, it should be positively related (for an attempt to reconcile these two views, see Staddon, 1983 and in press). Actually, neither view on its own is satisfactory to account for long-term control of behavior in free-living animals.

First consider the view that there is a positive relationship between reward probability (which, everything else being equal is positively related to reward rate) and response rate. This view implies a positive feedback that, in the long term, can lead to either of two states: maximum rate of responding or not responding at all. Only the second state is totally stable, because a slight decrease in response rate on a fast-responding animal would lead to a decline in reward rate, and the system would spiral down to total lack of responding. In short, there would be a positive feedback and animals would die of starvation.

The view that response rate must decline with increases in reward rate also has problems, especially in a changing environment. It does not allow for making use of temporary abundance of food. Short-term negative feedback (satiation) would cause animals to slow response rate as soon as food becomes readily available, instead of taking advantage of good conditions.

Thus, satisfactory accounts of the relationship between reward probability (directly related to reward rate) and response rate must include both positive and negative components, probably acting with different time constants.

The results of the random-ratio experiment show, on the whole, a negative relationship between reward probability and response rate (Fig. 4.5). During the two periods when differences in reinforcement availability can be compared (i.e., the comparison between treatments in the period before the drop to zero and the comparison between the periods after and before the drop to zero within each treatment), response rates were higher the lower the reward probability. Nevertheless, short-term variations in the other direction were also present. When the birds were responding almost exclusively on the side giving no re-

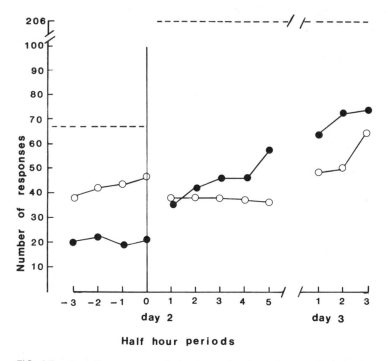

FIG. 4.5.   Overall response rate during the course of experiment I. Open circles represent the mean between the three animals in the 0.25 treatment and closed circles the same score for the 0.75 treatment. Responses were counted in half hour intervals and synchronized for the plotting with respect to the moment of the change to zero reward probability on the unstable side. The broken lines indicate response rate required under 0.25 (before the change to zero) or 0.08 (after the change to zero) reward probabilities to get a reward rate equal to that obtained under 0.75 reward probability.

wards at all (immediately after the change to zero probability in the formerly better side), they lowered their response rate as expected from all previous studies of extinction.

The models discussed in this chapter refer to choice among alternatives rather than to rate of responding, but one of them, Killeen's model, which is based on the incentive effect of reinforcement, predicts more rapid responding for greater reward availability. As previously said, this kind of model cannot account for long-term adjustments in rate, and it predicts the opposite of what the results show. The problems of both choice and rate of responding could be modeled so as to take into account short-term effects of arousal and long-term negative feedback, but such models would have to have extra free parameters specifying the relative weight of these effects. Their heuristic value would therefore be limited.

Models of Sampling

Finally, a brief comment on possible future developments. The descriptive models that have been discussed represent only one possible approach to the problem of how animals respond to fluctuations in reward rate or reward probability. The experimental results have revealed that a major class of descriptive models of choice, those derived from a linear-operator model, is unable to account for adjustments to a very simple kind of environmental change, and it has been shown how an ad hoc addition to these descriptive models can be made to allow the resulting model to account for the observed results. An alternative approach, which has not been developed here, would be to model the animal's behavior as a problem in information acquisition (Houston & McNamara, 1980; Krebs et al., 1978; Stephens, 1982; appendix). By asking how animals ought to sample their environment in order to acquire information about payoffs in a maximally efficient manner one may generate deeper insight into the way in which animals assess reinforcement rate than has been possible with a purely descriptive approach. This kind of modeling may also carry with it interesting implications about the cognitive capacities of animals.

APPENDIX (BY DR. CHARLES LEWIS, GRONINGEN UNIVERSITY)

What would a Bayesian statistican do if ordered to work on a multiarmed bandit machine, if he knew that each arm had a constant reward probability that could suddenly drop to zero at an unpredictable moment in time? For the present purposes only the updating of information is considered. Because updating of information on one arm is independent of what happens to other arms, it is possible to consider one arm only. Before each trial there will be two hypotheses on the state of the arm: (a) $H_0(t)$: the reward probability is zero at time t. (b) H_1 (t): the reward probability is greater than zero and equal to the value during the previous trials. For the experimental conditions,

$$P[H_1(t)] + P[H_0(t)] = 1, \tag{A1}$$

where $P[H_i(t)]$ denotes the prior probability that $H_i(t)$ is true. Let $Q(t)$ denote the value of the reward obtained at t. It takes the value 1 when a reward has been obtained and 0 when no reward has been obtained. When $H_0(t)$ is true, the probability that a reward will be obtained is zero:

$$P[Q(t) = 1 \mid H_0(t)] = 0. \tag{A2}$$

The main interest lies in $P[Q(t) = 1]$, the prior probability of getting a reward at t, because it will determine the subject's willingness to visit the site. Due to (A1),

$$P[Q(t) = 1] = P[Q(t) = 1 \mid (H_0(t)]. \, P[H_0(t)] +$$
$$P[Q(t) = 1 \mid H_1(t)].P[H_1(t)]. \tag{A3}$$

Writing $P[Q(t) = 1 \mid H_1(t)] = \theta(t)$ and taking (A_2) into account,

$$P[Q(t) = 1] = \theta(t).P[H_1(t)]. \tag{A4}$$

By definition, $P[H_1(t)]$ is the probability that the arm hasn't changed for the worse since the last trial. It is now shown that $\theta(t)$ can be interpreted as the estimate of the reward probability when nonzero, thereby demonstrating the significant resemblance between equations (4) and (A4).

Let $f(\theta \mid H_1(t))$ denote the prior probability density function (equal to the posterior distribution of the previous trial) that the reward rate is θ, given that it is not zero. One obtains:

$$\theta(t) = P[Q(t) = 1 \mid H_1(t)] = \int_0^1 \theta f(\theta \mid H_1(t)) \, d\theta, \tag{A5}$$

which we set out to prove. For the present purposes there is no need to actually specify $f(\theta \mid H_1(t))$, but a likely choice would be a beta distribution.

The next problem is to show what is needed in order to calculate $[H_1(t)]$. When a reward was obtained on trial $t - 1$ it is clear that $H_0(1), \ldots, H_0(t - 1)$ must have been false. Assume that the probability that the machine will be turned off at the next trial $(P[H_0(t) \mid Q(t - 1) = 1])$ is constant and denote it with P_0. When on h occasions no reward was obtained after the last rewarded visit occurred at time n, the prior probability $P[H_0 (n + h + 1) \mid Q(n) = 1, Q(n + 1) = 0, \ldots, Q(n + h) = 0]$, is denoted with P_h. The next aim is to calculate the posterior probability $P[H_0(n + h + 1) \mid Q(n) = 1, Q(n + 1) = 0, \ldots, Q(n + h) = 0, Q(n + h + 1) = 0]$. Due to the experimental protocol, this posterior probability can be taken as the prior probability for the next trial. Hence, it can be denoted as P_{h+1}.

Applying Bayes' theorem, it is found that:

$$P_{h+1} = P_h/[P_h + (1 - P_h)(1 - \theta(n + h + 1))].$$ (A6)

This can be written in terms of P_0:

$$P_h = P_0/(P_0 + (1 - P_0) \prod_{i=1}^{k} [1 - \theta(n + i)]).$$ (A7)

Thus, to calculate $P[H_1(t)]$ it is necessary to know how many nonrewards were obtained since the last reward, as well as to assign a value to P_0. Without specifying a decision rule it is impossible to know if the preceding equations lead to PREE in a multiarmed bandit problem. The following derivation shows that at least under certain circumstances the behavior of the updating process is such that PREE is likely to result. When $\theta(t)$ changes little with time and is close to the real reward probability (as it should be if it is a decent estimator), we may assume $\theta(t)$ to be constant: θ_c. Then,

$$P_k = P_0/(P_0 + (1 - P_0) (1 - \theta_c)^k).$$

Because $0 \leq 1 - \theta_c \leq 1$ it is clear that $(1 - P_0) (1 - \theta_c)^k$ will tend to zero more quickly when θ_c is large. P_k (which is to say $P[H_0(t)]$) will approach one more rapidly and $P[H_1(t)]$ will go to zero more quickly, as will $P[Q(t) = 1]$. There comes a point when $P[Q(t) = 1]$ is judged to be too low to justify another visit to the site. When this will happen depends on the costs and benefits of particular behaviors, which we have not specified. However, this derivation shows that when appropriate decision rules are used, PREE is likely to occur.

ACKNOWLEDGMENTS

We thank the Netherlands Research Council (BION) and the UK Natural Environment Research Council for financial support. The experiments were carried out in the Department of Zoology, University of Groningen, with the technical assistance of Gerda Bloem. We thank Dr. S. Daan, Dr. R. Drent, and Professor G. Baerends for their hospitality and support. Hans Reddingius helped B. E. with modeling and Charlie Lewis developed the Bayesian model described in the appendix. Peter Killeen ran the simulation of his model for us and Nigel Lester made helpful suggestions for his model. Alasdair Houston, John A. Nevin, Roger Mellgren, Michael L. Commons, Hans Reddingius, and Sara J. Shettleworth commented on the manuscript.

REFERENCES

Bush, R. R., & Mosteller, F. (1951). A mathematical model for simple learning. *Psychological Review, 68,* 313–323.

Capaldi, E. J. (1966). Partial reinforcement: A hypothesis of sequential effects. *Psychological Review, 73,* 459–477.

Cheverton, J., Kacelnik, A., & Krebs, J. R. (1985). Optimal foraging: Constraints and currencies. In B. Hölldobler & M. Lindauer (Eds.), *Experimental behavioral ecology and sociobiology* (pp. 109–126). New York: Fischer Verlag.

Collier, G. H., Hill, W., Kaufman, L. W., & Johnson, D. (in press). The economics of the law of effect. *Journal of the Experimental Analysis of Behavior.*

Collier, G. H., Hirsch, E., & Hamilin, P. (1972). The ecological determinants of reinforcements in the rat. *Physiology and Behavior, 9,* 705–716.

Collier, G. H., & Rovee-Collier, C. K. (1981). A comparative analysis of optimal foraging: Laboratory simulations. In A. C. Kamil & T. D. Sargent (Eds.), *Foraging behavior* (pp. 39–76). New York: Garland STPM Press.

Commons, M. L., Woodford, M., Boitano, B. A., Ducheny, J. R., & Peck, J. R. (1982). Acquisition of preference during shifts between terminal links in concurrent chain schedules. In M. L. Commons, R. J. Herrnstein, & A. R. Wagner, *Quantitative Analyses of Behavior: Vol. III, Acquisition* (pp. 391–426). Cambridge, MA: Ballinger.

Elam, C. B., & Tyler, D. W. (1958). Reversal learning following partial reinforcement. *American Journal of Psychology, 71,* 583–586.

Gibbon, J., Farrell, L., Locurto, C. M., Duncan, H. J., & Terrace, H. S. (1980). Partial reinforcement in autoshaping with pigeons. *Animal Learning & Behavior,* 845–59.

Harley, C. B. (1981). Learning the evolutionarily stable strategy. *Journal of Theoretical Biology, 89,* 611–633.

Harley, C. B. (1983). When do animals learn the evolutionarily stable strategy? *Journal of Theoretical Biology, 105,* 179–181.

Herrnstein, R. J. (1970). On the law of effect. *Journal of the Experimental Analysis of Behavior, 131,* 243–266.

Hirsch, E., & Collier, G. (1974). The ecological determinants of reinforcement in the guinea pig. *Physiology and Behavior, 12,* 239–249.

Houston, A. I. (1982). Comments on "learning the evolutionarily stable strategy." *Journal of Theoretical Biology, 105,* 175–178.

Houston, A. I., Kacelnik, A., & McNamara, J. (1982). Some learning rules for acquiring information. In D. J. McFarland (Ed.), *Functional ontogeny* (pp. 140–191). Boston: Pitman.

Houston, A. I., & McNamara, J. (1980). The application of statistical decision theory to animal behaviour. *Journal of Theoretical Biology, 85,* 673–690.

Jenkins, P. E. (1978). Resistance to extinction and satiation following training on random ratio schedules of reinforcement. *Psychological Record, 28,* 471–478.

Kacelnik, A., & Krebs, J. R. (1985). Learning to exploit patchily distributed food. In R. M. Sibly & R. H. Smith (Eds.), *Behavioural ecology: Ecological consequences of adaptive behaviour* (pp. 189–205) Oxford, England: Blackwell's Scientific Publications.

Killeen, P. R. (1982). Incentive theory. In D. Bernstein (Ed.), *Nebraska symposium on motivation* (pp. 169–216). Lincoln: University of Nebraska Press.

Killeen, P. R. (1984). Incentive theory III: Adaptive clocks. *Annals of the New York Academy of Sciences, 423,* 515–827.

Krebs, J. R., & Kacelnik, A. (1984). Optimal learning rules. *The Brain and Behavioral Sciences, 7,* 109–110.

Krebs, J. R., Stephens, D. W., & Sutherland, W. J. (1983). Perspectives in optimal foraging. In A. H. Brush & G. Clark (Eds.), *Perspectives in ornithology* (pp. 165–216). Cambridge, England: Cambridge University Press.

Krebs, J. R., Kacelnik, A., & Taylor, P. (1978). Test of optimal sampling by foraging great tits. *Nature, 275,* 27–31.

Lea, S. E. G., & Dow, S. M. (1984). The integration of reinforcements over time. *Annals of the New York Academy of Sciences, 423,* 269–277.

Lester, N. (1984). The feed: feed decision: How goldfish solve the patch depletion problem. *Behaviour, 89,* 175–199.

Maynard Smith, J. (1982). *Evolution and the theory of games.* Cambridge, England: Cambridge University Press.

Maynard Smith, J. (1984). Game theory and the evolution of behavior. *The Brain & Behavioral Sciences, 7,* 95–125.

McNamara, J., & Houston, A. I. (1980). The application of statistical decision theory to animal behaviour. *Journal of Theoretical Biology, 85,* 673–690.

Mazur, J. E., & Hastie, R. (1978). Learning as accumulation: A reexamination of the learning curve. *Psychological Bulletin, 85,* 1256–1274.

Mellgren, R. L., & Olson, W. M. (1983). Mazes, Skinner boxes, and feeding behavior. In R. L. Mellgren (Ed.), *Animal cognition and behavior* (pp. 223–252). Amsterdam: North Holland.

Milinski, M. (1984). Competitive Resource Sharing: An experimental test of a learning rule for ESSs. *Animal Behaviour, 32,* 233–242.

Myerson, J., & Miezin, F. M. (1980). The kinetics of choice: An operant systems analysis. *Psychological Review, 87,* 160–174.

Nevin, J. A. (1979). Reinforcement schedules and response strength. In M. D. Zeiler & P. Harzem, (Eds.), *Advances in the analysis of behaviour, Vol. 1: Reinforcement and the organization of behaviour* (pp. 117–158). Chichester and New York: Wiley.

Ollason, J. G. (1980). Learning to forage–optimally? *Theoretical Population Biology, 18,* 44–56.

Pulliam, H. R., & Dunford, C. (1980). *Programmed to learn: An essay on the evolution of culture.* New York: Columbia University Press.

Pyke, G. H. (1984). Optimal foraging theory: A critical review. *Annual Review of Ecology and Systematics, 15,* 523–575.

Regelmann, K. (1984). Competitive resource sharing: A simulation model. *Animal Behaviour, 32,* 226–232.

Staddon, J. E. R. (1983). *Adaptive behavior and learning.* Cambridge, England: Cambridge University Press.

Staddon, J. E. R. (in press). Adaptation to reward. In A. Kamil, J. R. Krebs, & R. Pulliam (Eds.), *Foraging behavior.* New York: Plenum Press.

Stephens, D. W. (1982). *Stochasticity in foraging theory: Risk and information.* Unpublished doctoral dissertation, Oxford University.

Tarpy, R. (1982). *Principles of animal learning and motivation.* London: Scott, Foresman.

5 Foraging in a Changing Environment: Simulations in the Operant Laboratory

Susan M. Dow
Department of Zoology, University of Bristol

Stephen E. G. Lea
Department of Psychology, University of Exeter

The study of foraging has been approached from two sides. One strategy, which can be termed the *ethological approach,* involves observing natural foraging behavior and trying to determine its controlling variables. The other strategy, the *laboratory approach,* takes the animal into the laboratory and tries to control the variables that are believed to determine foraging. The two approaches are thus mirror images of each other, and each derives validity from the other. The laboratory approach can be very profitable, provided that some aspects of the animal's foraging situation are either maintained or mimicked. To do this requires a knowledge of the animal's foraging ethology.

This chapter describes two series of experiments that were performed using the laboratory approach, with pigeons as subjects in conventional operant apparatus. They formed part of a more extended study (Dow, 1984), in which pigeons were also studied in more natural foraging situations. These experiments, together with published work (e.g., Baum, 1974; Morgan, Fitch, Holman, & Lea, 1976), make it clear that pigeons will incorporate operant responding into a natural sequence of feeding, selecting or abandoning an operant food station according to the abundance or exhaustion of the food supply it offers, and the other sources of food in the environment. We therefore felt justified in using this situation to study the effects of changes in prey density, and the ways in which pigeons learn about such changes.

THE PROBLEM OF THE UNSTEADY STATE

The study of learning is of course inextricably linked with the study of changing prey density within a patch (which, in the operant laboratory, is simulated by changing reinforcement frequency within a schedule component; in this chapter we use these two terminologies interchangeably). Until very recently, both learning and changing prey density have been oddly ignored, in operant psychology and in behavioral ecology. Many of the early optimal-foraging models considered the animal to have a wide knowledge of its environment but said nothing of how this knowledge is gained. In operant experiments, the effects of changes in schedules of reinforcement have rarely been studied; instead, each condition has usually been kept in force until "steady-state" behavior is achieved. This bypasses the problem of learning; it may also restrict the range of choice behaviors that the animal will show. In environments that they have experienced as totally stable, animals may show behavior that is quite different from what would be appropriate in a more rapidly changing (and, surely, more natural) environment.

The experiments reported here involved concurrent schedules, with reinforcement frequencies that changed in two different ways. First, the frequencies associated with each component of the schedule changed unpredictably from day to day. The situation thus mimicked that of a forager that must learn, each day, the density of prey in a well-known patch. This situation occurs commonly in natural environments. For example, earthworms are a common prey of foxes in southern England, and their density varies as a function of temperature and humidity (MacDonald, 1976); the density of mussels available to herring gulls varies with the state of the tide (Sibly & McCleery, 1983). A similar situation is typically faced by foragers that scavenge in human waste, and this is a common behavior of feral pigeons.

Secondly, in some conditions, the reinforcement frequency in a component fell as a function of the time for which the subject exposed itself to that component. This mimics the "depleting patch" situation, which has been extensively discussed by ecologists from Charnov (1976) on. Any nonsystematic forager will gradually reduce the density of prey in the patch it is currently exploiting; if it forages with companions, this depletion may be very rapid. Pigeons commonly feed in flocks, and in any relatively rich patch of food (for example, where grain is mixed with gravel or human waste) they give every appearance of feeding unsystematically.

THEORIES OF FORAGING IN A CHANGING ENVIRONMENT

A laboratory simulation of foraging behavior, however plausible in terms of the subjects' ethology and behavior, is not interesting in itself. It is only worth doing if the resulting behavior can be compared with that of theoretical models that specify the supposed controlling variables of natural foraging. This kind of comparison is the main purpose of the present chapter.

In an uncertain world, the forager has to pursue two goals, which may not be entirely compatible. In the short term, it must try to gain as many prey as possible from the environment, per unit time spent foraging. In the longer term, the estimates of prey density on which the short-term behavior is based must be acquired and kept up to date (cf. McNamara & Houston, 1980; Oaten, 1977). A theory of foraging in a changing environment must specify how the compromise between these two goals is reached.

In rough but not perfect correspondence to these two goals, most theoretical models so far proposed have two components. The first is an information acquisition rule, which specifies how significant events (reinforcement, or time or responses elapsing without reinforcement) are used to update estimates of reinforcement frequency. The second is a performance principle (cf. Tolman, 1955), the decision rule that determines what response, if any, will be emitted given the current set of reinforcement frequency estimates. Houston (this volume) and Kacelnik et al. (this volume) discuss in greater detail what is required if a model is to be able to describe the mechanisms of foraging in a changing environment. For our purposes, fairly simple and qualitative specifications are sufficient.

Models of Information Acquisition

Consider first the estimates of reinforcement frequency, and the way in which they are updated. The estimates must be a function of the forager's past history of prey captures. In a changing environment, these estimates must be liable to change, but they must not change too drastically in response to moment-to-moment experiences: Even in a rich environment there will be some intervals without prey capture, and even in a poor one there will be occasional captures. Any model will involve a compromise between these two necessities.

There are two simple ways of effecting this compromise. The first, proposed by Cowie (1977), is a "memory window": The animal "remembers" perfectly all events that occurred during the last w time units and forgets totally all events occurring longer than w ago. Killeen (1981) calls this the "moving average" principle. The second is the exponentially weighted moving average (EWMA; Killeen, 1981), in which the estimate of past prey density is averaged with a new value based on current events, with a weighting a being given to the past and a weighting $(1 - a)$ being given to the present. The EWMA solution, which is a variant of the linear operator model of Bush and Mosteller (1951), is much the more mathematically and computationally satisfying and has been almost universally adopted, so much so that Lea and Dow (1984) call it the "common model." Houston, Kacelnik et al., Pulliam, and Shettleworth all use variants of it in their chapters in this volume. It has also been used by Bobisud and Voxman (1979), Commons, Woodford, Ducheny, and Peck (1982), Harley (1981), Lester (1984), and Myerson and Miezin (1980)—and this is not an exhaustive list. It is easy to show, moreover, that under a EWMA model, there is a value of a that roughly corresponds to any given value of w under Cowie's model. A unit current reinforcement will tend to increase the EWMA density estimate by $1/(1$

− a) units, which is just what it would do under Cowie's model with a memory window $1/(1 - a)$ units long. Thus, while working with a EWMA model, we refer to the quantity $1/(1 - a)$ as the "memory window."

In addition to these two models of density estimate updating, we also need to consider one other possibility, which is implicit in much previous work in both ecology and psychology: The possibility that the subject does not update its estimates, because it always has perfect knowledge of them (presumably because the environment is perfectly stable).

Cutting across these different models of the updating process are further questions about the estimates of reinforcement frequency. Are these to be based on *time spent* or *responses made?* And are they to be *local* (i.e., estimates of reinforcements per time spent in a schedule component), or *global* (reinforcements per total time or responses in the foraging situation)? Further, what triggers updating? Does it occur after every response, or only after every reinforcement? These three factors create at least eight possibilities, all of which are compatible at least with the memory window and EWMA updating rules; thus there are at least 17 possible ways in which reinforcement frequency estimates could be updated.

It is fairly obvious that both the memory window and the EWMA model allow parametric variation. A judicious choice of parameters, moreover, may make possible a satisfactory compromise between obtaining prey and obtaining information. If the forager lives in a generally stable environment, it should presumably use a wide memory window (high w), or give a heavy weighting to the past (high a). It is even possible for w or a to be varied, either as a function of such foraging constraints as time of day, or within a session, as the animal becomes more certain about current prey densities (cf. Killeen, 1984).

Principles of Performance

At least five kinds of decision rule are of interest. The first is the "maximizing" rule, under which the animal always goes to the patch for which its current estimate of prey density is greatest. The second is the "matching" rule, under which the subject divides its time or responses between patches in the same proportions as its current estimates of their prey densities. The third is the "satisficing" rule (cf. Simon, 1957), according to which the subject stays in any patch for which the current estimate of prey density is suffficient to enable it to obtain its required food intake for the day, given the expected session length.

The fourth possibility is rather different. It is the "optimal sampling" rule (Krebs, Kacelnik, & Taylor, 1978), according to which the forager maximizes food intake over the day, by choosing the patch that gives the optimal combination of immediate prey and information about prey densities.

The final possibility is at the opposite extreme: The animal may ignore (or not have) prey density estimates and behave entirely at random, or according to some fixed rule such as regular alternation. Although this is not a plausible model, it does form a useful null hypothesis against which to compare the behavior of more plausible models and of real animals. Purely random behavior can be instructively effective under some conditions.

Models to be Investigated

Seventeen updating rules multiplied by five decision rules suggests that we should be considering at least 85 models. Fortunately, it is not necessary to consider all the combinations: Some of them are either not possible or not distinct (a random performance principle leads to random behavior, regardless of the updating rule), and not all the possible ones are interesting. Less fortunately, not all the interesting models lend themselves to analytical treatment, though some of course do. We are therefore forced to investigate the properties of some models by Monte Carlo techniques, using computer simulations. For comparability's sake, this technique is used consistently in this chapter.

We have selected five models for comparison with our data. They are chosen to represent a range of performance principles, combined with what seems to be the most interesting updating rule, the EWMA model, and to come close to models that have been widely used to analyze data from more static environments.

1. The Omniscient Forager. This is a first generation optimal-foraging model. The forager is assumed to "know" the details of the structure of the foraging situation, including the prey densities in force, but does not know exactly when the next prey item will be delivered. Although this strategy is not available to real foragers in the kind of environment we are studying, its behavior provides an estimate of, for example, the maximum number of prey that could be gained.

The next three models all involve the EWMA updating rule. They are all used in this chapter with the assumption that updating occurs after every response, though this assumption is not an inherent part of any of them.

2a. A Dynamic Meliorator. In this model, the EWMA updating principle is combined with the maximizing performance rule, so that the animal always switches towards the patch for which its current EWMA estimate of local prey density is higher. This model thus describes a dynamic version of the "melioration" principle of Herrnstein and Vaughan (1980), according to which animals switch to the schedule component with the highest local rate of reinforcement. In the original application of melioration, these local rates were, of course, taken as constant.

2b. A Dynamic Version of Herrnstein's Matcher. This model uses the EWMA principle to obtain estimates of *global* reinforcement rates, and the matching rule to determine its response rates. It is thus a dynamic version of the animal that obeys Herrnstein's (1961, 1970) matching law (normally only considered in static environments). It is closely similar to the models used by Harley (1981), Maynard Smith (1984), and Lester (1984).

2c. A EWMA Satisficer.   According to this model, the EWMA rule is used to obtain estimates of prey density, and the animal then remains in any patch whose current density estimate, extrapolated for the rest of the expected session time, would give the required daily intake of food.

The next two models have no updating principle, because they do not use estimates of prey density. The names used for them here imply an environment in which there are only two kinds of patch; that was true of our experiments, but the models could be generalized in obvious ways for more complex situations.

3a. The Alternator.   This model simply switches between patches after every response throughout a foraging session, regardless of the prey gained, and thus distributes its time (or responses) equally between patches.

3b. The Session Halver.   This model also divides its time or responses equally between patches, but in effectively the opposite way: It stays in one patch for half the session and then switches to the other for the remainder.

Note that the optimal sampler, in the sense of Krebs et al. (1978), is not included in our discussions. We believe that this model overestimates the problems faced by the subject (cf. Dow & Lea, in press). However, all the EWMA models allow at least some degree of optimization, in that the parameter a can be set at the value that maximizes overall reward.

EXPERIMENTAL METHOD

Optimal-foraging theory was originally formulated to describe behavior in the natural environment. Although our data come from fairly conventional operant conditioning apparatus (the subjects were pigeons, pecking keys for food grain reward in standard commercial Skinner boxes), the problems discussed are set in an ecological context, and the general structure of the situation the birds faced was designed to mimic natural foraging conditions. In the following descriptions of our experimental techniques, therefore, a mixture of ecological and psychological language is used.

Two experiments are described here, involving sequences of four and two subexperiments, respectively. Because the methods and analyses used were closely similar throughout, the two experiments are described together here. More detailed descriptions are given in Dow (1984, Experiments 2 and 3).

Subjects and Apparatus

The subjects were pigeons (domesticated *Columba livia*) of racing stock. They were kept in large single-sex groups in an indoor aviary, at around 90% of their caged free-feeding weights; on days when they were to be tested, they were caged in the morning. Fifteen pigeons were used for experiment 1, and these birds were experimentally naive. Thirteen birds were used for experiment 2. These birds had some previous experience of operant procedures, but not of the sorts of schedules of reinforcement used in these experiments. The apparatus consisted of six commercial three-key operant chambers, controlled by a minicomputer.

General Procedure

Following conventional pretraining, the pigeons were faced with the sort of concurrent schedules of reinforcement described by Findley (1958). The pigeons had two pecking keys available to them, the right key and the center key. The center key was always backlit with white light, whereas the right key was backlit with either red or green light. Pecks to the right key were occasionally rewarded with brief (3-second) access to a food hopper containing preferred grains, according to schedules of reinforcement described in more detail later. Pecks to the center key did not result in food access, but instead changed the color displayed on the right key, and hence the schedule of reinforcement in force there. A single center-key peck was sufficient to change the right-key color, and no changeover delay was used. Sessions were designed to terminate after 960 pecks but were terminated if 20 minutes elapsed without a peck (typically, sessions lasted 20–30 minutes). Each bird was given one session per day, so far as possible at the same time of day, 5 days per week.

Component Schedules (Patch Types)

The schedules were designed to simulate three kinds of changing patch density a forager might encounter in the natural environment. The first type actually involves no change at all: It is a nondepleting patch, whose density remains constant regardless of the forager's activities. This is presumably rare in nature, but it is of course common in operant experimentation, and in any case it forms a useful control procedure. The second type has a patch density that falls gradually in a way that is directly determined by the forager's success: As each prey item is "found" (i.e., as each reinforcement is delivered), the probability of finding the next item falls. The third type has a constant prey density until a certain number of prey items have been found, after which its density falls immediately to zero.

We call this the *sudden death* situation; in the natural environment, it is faced by a forager working systematically through patches of limited size.

These patch types were implemented as schedules of reinforcement in the following way, using the minicomputer. At the start of an experimental session, each patch consisted of a number of cells, typically 1,000. A few of these cells were designated as containing "prey." Each time the pigeon pecked the right key, one of the cells was chosen at random. If, and only if, the chosen cell contained a prey item, the pigeon was rewarded. This basic procedure allows several variations, which can be used to implement different patch types, as follows.

The first variation concerns what happens to a cell after it has been chosen. It could either become inaccessible or remain available for future sampling; statisticians would call these sampling without and with replacement, respectively. The first of these possibilities gives a nondepleting patch, since the ratio of empty to prey-containing cells remains roughly constant; the second requires further specification.

If cells once sampled remain available, the second variation becomes relevant. It concerns what happens when a prey-containing cell is found. The prey item could either be replaced or it could disappear, the cell now becoming empty. If prey are replaced, we have another way of implementing the nondepleting patch. If they are not, we have a patch that depletes gradually, in the same way as a naturally occurring patch in which a single forager works at random.

The third variation concerns what happens to a patch once the subject leaves it. It could either revert to the state it was in when last entered, or it could remain in the state it was in when left. We call these refreshing and nonrefreshing patches, respectively. With refreshing patches, the two schedule components correspond to two generic types of patch: Once the forager leaves one patch of a given type, it has the possibility of finding another that will have the same initial density of prey as the first one. With nonrefreshing patches, the two components correspond to two patches. If the forager leaves one and subsequently returns, it will find its density unchanged.

A fourth variation concerns the number of cells in a patch, relative to the number of pecks allowed in a session. If there are fewer cells than pecks allowed, sampling is without replacement, and patches do not refresh, then the patch is liable to be totally exhausted before the end of the session; that is to say, we have a sudden death patch. Similar conditions, but with sampling with replacement and prey not replaced once found, give a patch that depletes smoothly but relatively rapidly.

Finally, and obviously, the more prey are put in the patch, the higher the prey density (reinforcement frequency).

Clearly, patches implemented in this way are, in operant terms, random-ratio schedules, possibly with decreasing reinforcement probabilities.

Experimental Design

In each part of each experiment, there were two patches (corresponding to red and green key colors). One of these was arbitrarily designated as patch 1; for odd-numbered birds, patch 1 was associated with the green key, for even-numbered birds with the red key. Four initial densities were used with each patch, in all possible combinations, so there were 16 conditions. The initial prey densities used in each experiment were chosen so as to give overall reinforcement rates that would be high enough to maintain steady pecking throughout a session of 960 pecks, but not so high as to lead to premature satiation. In practice, these two constraints gave relatively little room for maneuver.

The patch types in use, and the right key color correlated with each patch, remained constant from day to day, so as to allow the birds to learn the overall structure of the problem they were given. The prey densities in the patches, on the other hand, changed from day to day, because the birds were only exposed to each condition for a single day. Each bird worked through the 16 conditions in a different order, so that the experiment followed a modified Latin-square design. Note that it would be impossible for a bird to predict from one session to the next which key color would be associated with the higher prey density. On the other hand, it was possible for the birds to form a general estimate of the kinds of prey density that were likely to be available, and on the basis of results reported by Dow and Lea (in press), it was to be expected that they would do so.

Experiment 1. The first experiment involved four parts, designated experiments 1a to 1d. Throughout, patches consisted of 1,000 cells, so that total exhaustion of a patch was impossible in a session of 960 pecks. The initial prey densities used were 20, 30, 45, and 70 prey/1,000 cells. In experiment 1a, patch 1 was nondepleting, while patch 2 involved sampling with replacement of cells and nonreplacement of prey, so that its density depleted; it was not refreshed. In experiment 1b, both patches depleted, but patch 2 refreshed while patch 1 did not. In experiment 1c, both patches depleted and refreshed, while in experiment 1d both patches depleted and neither of them refreshed. Figure 5.1 illustrates the kinds of changes in prey density these various arrangements of patches made possible.

Experiment 2. The second experiment involved two parts. In both of them, patch 1 consisted of 320 cells, and patch 2 of 200 cells, so both patches could be exhausted in a session of 960 pecks. The initial numbers of prey used in patch 1 were 10, 14, 22, and 34; in patch 2 they were 13, 20, 30, and 45. In experiment 2a, patch 1 involved sampling without replacement of cells, so that prey density remained constant until all the prey had been removed and then fell to zero; patch 2 involved sampling with replacement of cells but without replacement of prey, so that prey density fell continuously and rapidly but not necessarily to zero.

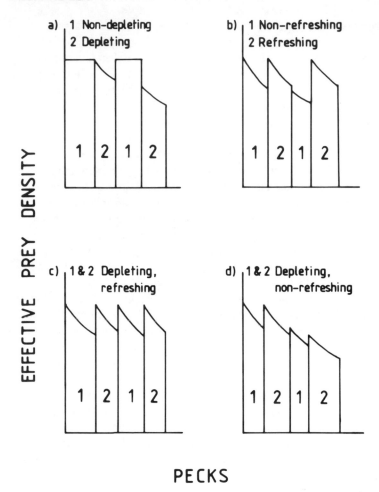

FIG. 5.1.   Idealized representation of the effects of behavior on effective prey density in the four combinations of patch types used in experiment 1. Vertical lines represent changes between patches.

Neither patch refreshed when re-entered. In experiment 2b, the patches were of the same types as in experiment 2a, but were refreshed when re-entered.

SELECTED EXPERIMENTAL RESULTS

It is impossible to describe all the results of all these experiments in full here; further details are to be found in Dow (1984). Here, we concentrate on two questions: How did the birds respond to different patch types, and what did they respond to? In the subsequent discussion, a third question is taken up: How did the birds' behavior compare with simulations using the six models introduced earlier in the chapter?

General Observations

Experiment 1 was started with 13 birds. Of these, two birds could not be pretrained and were dropped, and one could not be maintained at a stable weight except during part (b), and was excluded from the data for the other parts of the experiment. Two birds were added to parts (c) and (d) to replace these losses. Thus, the data reported for the four parts of the experiment are based on 10, 11, 12, and 12 birds, respectively. All these birds normally completed 960 pecks in a session. In experiment 2, one bird repeatedly failed to complete 960 pecks and was dropped. One or two other birds stopped responding following their first encounters with totally exhausted patches. This pattern of behavior disappeared after a few sessions, however, so the analyses for this experiment are based on 12 birds.

Throughout the experimental series, where the two patches were of different types (experiments 1a, 1b, 2a, and 2b), there were obvious differences in the birds' behavior to the two patches. When a new subexperiment was started, the change in patch types was followed, within at most a session or two, by obvious changes in the birds' pattern of behavior. For these reasons, data were aggregated over all 16 sessions in each part of each experiment.

In experiments 1a and 1b, some birds changed between patches very infrequently. The introduction of two refreshing patches in experiment 1c, however, led to a rapid increase in switching. Levels of changeover were, however, relatively low in all conditions, the means across birds and conditions for the four parts of experiment 1 being 5.0, 7.7, 12.1, and 7.2 changeovers per session. The corresponding figures for the two parts of experiment 2 were 10.6 and 10.6.

Peck and Time Distribution Between the Patches

The simplest measure of behavior is the distribution of responses and time between the patches. Throughout these experiments, the time distributions (measured by the time for which the two key colors were on) were very similar to the keypeck distributions, so only the latter are reported here. The time distributions are given by Dow (1984).

Figure 5.2 shows how the percentages of responses made in patch 1 varied with the initial densities of the patches in each part of experiment 1; Fig. 5.3 shows similar information for experiment 2. In these figures, data are averaged over all sessions in which a given initial density was used. Figure 5.4 shows the results of experiment 1a in more detail, giving results for each of the 16 combinations of initial patch densities. However, analysis of variance (using the initial

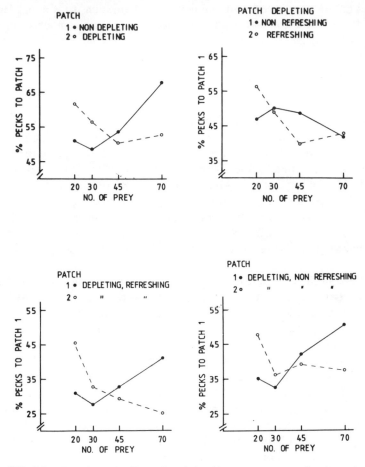

FIG. 5.2.   Experiment 1: effects of patch densities on percentages of pecks made in patch 1, averaged over all birds. Solid lines and closed symbols show the effect of the density of patch 1, averaged over all densities of patch 2, while broken lines and open symbols show the effect of the density patch 2, averaged over all densities of patch 1. The four panels give results from the four subexperiments.

densities of patch 1 and patch 2 as sources of variation) showed that the interaction of patch 1 density and patch 2 density was not significant for any part of either experiment, so the overall effects shown in Fig. 5.2 and 5.3 are representative of the more detailed data. The main effects of patch 1 and patch 2 density were significant in several cases, and the F values are given in Table 5.1.

The following general trends can be extracted from Fig. 5.2 and 5.3. In experiment 1a, the nondepleting patch (patch 1) was preferred to the depleting patch, and in experiment 1b the refreshing patch (patch 2) was preferred to the

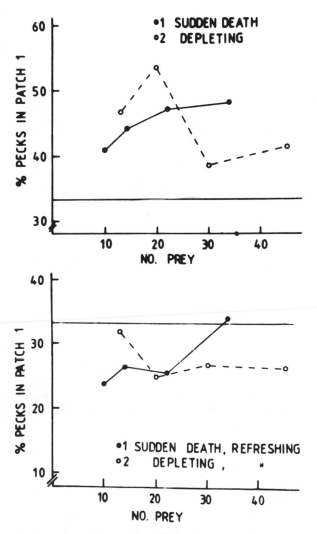

FIG. 5.3. Experiment 2: effects of patch densities on percentages of pecks made in patch 1, averaged over all birds. Solid lines and closed symbols show the effect of the density of patch 1, averaged over all densities of patch 2, while broken lines and open symbols show the effect of the density patch 2, averaged over all densities of patch 1. The two panels give results from the two subexperiments.

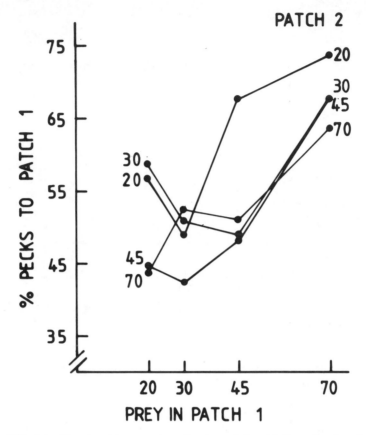

FIG. 5.4.   Experiment 1a: percentage of pecks made in patch 1, as a function of prey density in patch 1, with prey density in patch 2 as parameter. Results are averaged over all birds. Patch 1 prey densities were constant, while patch 2 prey densities depleted as prey were found.

nonrefreshing patch. In both parts of experiment 2, preference was for the gradually depleting patch over the sudden death patch, except at the highest initial prey densities of the latter.

In virtually all situations, the percentage of responses made in a patch tended to increase with its initial density. The most obvious exception was in experiment 1b, where the initial density of the nonrefreshing patch (patch 1) had little effect on the distribution of pecks.

One or two exceptions to these trends deserve comment. In experiment 1c, where both patches depleted and refreshed, the situation allowed idiosyncratic behavior (perhaps due to color preferences) to emerge: Two birds made most of their pecks to one color, with occasional brief spells in the other patch. Their behavior (and similar, but less extreme, tendencies in the other birds) caused the

TABLE 5.1
F-Values for Main Effects of Patch Densities on Percentage of Pecks
Made in Patch 1

| Experiment | Source of Variation | | Degrees of Freedom |
	Patch 1 Density	Patch 2 Density	
1a	3.82*	1.21	3,27
1b	.33	2.84	3,30
1c	2.85	6.27**	3,33
1d	6.91**	1.74	3,33
2a	1.22	5.71**	3,33
2b	2.27	1.22	3,33

$*p < .05.$ $**p < .01.$

mean distribution of pecks to show a preference for patch 2, which cannot be accounted for by the contingencies in force. A similar, but less extreme, tendency emerged in experiment 1d, where again the schedules in the two patches were identical, but a preference for one patch would result in a lowered reinforcement frequency.

Change in Preference Within a Session

The experiments were founded on the assumption that the birds would learn about prey densities within a session. The fact that they generally made more responses in the objectively better patch, as shown in the previous section, supports this assumption. It was tested further by calculating a correlation statistic, which reflected the change in preference within a session. This analysis gave results that supported those just described: The greater the initial density of a patch, and the more advantageous a type of patch, the greater the tendency for an increasing number of pecks to be made in it as a session advanced. Details of these results are given by Dow (1984).

Reinforcements Obtained

If the proof of a pudding is in the eating, the proof of a foraging strategy is in the prey consumed, or, in operant language, the reinforcements obtained. The first part of Table 5.2 shows the mean total reinforcements obtained under each condition of experiment 1, and the first part of Table 5.3 shows similar data for experiment 2. In experiment 1, the picture is fairly clear: With the lowest densities, the birds obtained a high proportion of the available reinforcements; as initial densities (in either patch) increased, so did the total reinforcements obtained, but the proportion of available reinforcements obtained fell off. When

TABLE 5.2
Mean Numbers of Reinforcements Obtained by the Experimental Birds and by 10 Simulations of Each of Six Models of Foraging Behavior, Under the Conditions of Experiment 1

	Subexperiment															
	1a				*1b*				*1c*				*1d*			
Patch 2 Density	*Patch 1 Density (Prey/1,000 Cells)*															
(Prey/1,000 Cells)	20	30	45	70	20	30	45	70	20	30	45	70	20	30	45	70
Experimental birds																
20	17	21	35	53	15	17	25	27	16	21	24	37	14	17	22	35
30	18	23	31	51	17	22	27	32	24	24	28	39	18	20	27	32
45	26	29	37	50	26	27	33	39	30	34	35	41	26	27	32	39
70	35	38	43	59	35	36	44	46	41	46	50	53	37	38	41	48
Omniscient forager																
20	21	28	43	64	18	21	28	42	16	29	41	64	14	20	26	43
30	21	27	44	62	27	28	32	41	28	32	45	63	20	20	29	44
45	27	30	45	65	39	41	44	48	46	38	39	59	26	30	34	46
70	45	44	47	68	63	64	66	68	58	65	66	67	44	42	42	52
Dynamic meliorator																
20	16	23	35	60	13	16	26	37	12	17	25	41	13	16	23	40
30	20	22	29	53	17	18	22	32	14	18	26	38	16	19	25	36
45	25	27	30	42	21	23	27	34	23	23	27	51	24	24	28	36
70	36	39	43	52	41	38	38	43	39	39	35	45	37	33	40	40
Dynamic matcher																
20	16	24	40	68	17	19	27	43	15	19	30	52	12	18	23	39
30	19	22	38	55	19	21	29	43	20	23	34	51	18	20	25	37
45	27	30	31	52	31	32	32	47	29	31	36	34	23	27	32	40
70	39	41	43	64	51	50	54	50	55	51	52	58	43	43	42	46
EWMA satisficer																
20	16	22	37	68	15	21	25	40	16	20	31	42	14	19	24	42
30	18	24	40	63	21	22	27	43	20	22	32	43	18	20	26	41
45	25	31	31	59	29	31	29	43	28	30	31	43	27	26	28	41
70	40	41	39	49	45	44	42	44	46	41	38	42	43	43	41	42
Alternator																
20	17	21	29	41	18	21	26	32	20	24	34	48	15	17	25	33
30	20	24	31	44	21	26	30	40	21	27	34	46	19	23	27	41
45	27	28	38	53	32	31	38	51	31	36	43	52	25	27	32	42
70	36	39	45	59	39	47	51	57	39	49	54	66	32	42	42	50
Session-halver																
20	19	21	30	42	15	19	24	34	13	18	26	32	14	18	22	29
30	20	23	33	44	18	21	30	36	19	23	27	38	16	23	28	36
45	26	32	39	40	23	26	33	41	25	28	34	43	23	27	33	43
70	36	40	46	57	35	35	42	54	32	37	44	50	33	26	42	53

Note: All values are rounded down to the nearest integer.

TABLE 5.3

Mean Numbers of Reinforcements Obtained by 10 Experimental Birds
and by 10 Simulations of Each of Six Models of Foraging Behavior,
Under the Conditions of Experiment 2

	Subexperiment							
	2a				2b			
Patch 2 Density	Patch 1 Density (Prey/320 Cells)							
(Prey/200 Cells)	10	14	22	34	10	14	22	34
Experimental birds								
13	19	24	30	42	34	37	44	60
20	26	28	35	45	47	50	54	62
30	38	38	43	53	63	73	69	77
45	49	49	56	65	95	88	92	99
Omniscient forager								
13	22	26	34	46	61	65	75	107
20	29	32	41	53	89	83	91	114
30	38	42	50	62	126	127	135	139
45	52	56	65	77	183	183	184	196
Dynamic meliorator								
13	20	24	32	43	22	24	39	51
20	25	29	37	50	30	29	38	47
30	35	37	45	58	42	41	45	53
45	48	50	56	67	58	62	52	68
Dynamic matcher								
13	17	19	29	39	30	39	47	73
20	23	26	34	43	47	50	65	92
30	32	34	38	55	70	71	68	96
45	45	48	52	62	101	93	107	126
EWMA satisficer								
13	20	23	27	35	25	25	26	37
20	25	25	26	37	26	27	27	32
30	29	29	27	31	30	30	27	33
45	44	45	42	43	45	45	45	43
Alternator								
13	22	26	33	46	45	50	65	84
20	27	32	40	52	63	64	81	101
30	37	41	48	61	81	91	107	118
45	50	54	63	74	123	127	136	157
Session halver								
13	21	26	34	45	21	26	34	46
20	27	32	40	52	28	31	40	52
30	35	41	50	61	37	40	49	61
45	50	54	62	75	21	26	34	46

Note: All values are rounded down to the nearest integer.

one patch density was at its highest value, the density of the poorer patch made little difference to the total reinforcements obtained.

In experiment 2a, total reinforcements obtained again varied with the densities of both patches. More detailed analysis (not reported here) showed that the birds obtained most of the rewards available from the sudden-death patch (in fact they obtained all of them in 60–70% of sessions), and the number taken did not vary with the initial density of the other (gradually depleting) patch. At its lower densities, the depleting patch also had most of its prey removed. In experiment 2b, the number of rewards taken from the sudden-death patch fell, but the number taken from the gradually depleting patch rose.

Giving-Up Times and Pecks

In the ecological literature, much importance has been attached to the giving-up time, the time from the capture of the last prey in a patch to the forager's abandoning that patch. Tables 5.4 and 5.5 show, for experiments 1 and 2, respectively, the mean giving-up pecks (pecks from last reinforcement until leaving patch) in each patch in each condition of each subexperiment; giving-up

TABLE 5.4
Experiment 1: Mean Giving-Up Pecks in Patch 1 and Patch 2
as a Function of Initial Prey Densities in Each Patch (Prey/1,000 Cells)

	Patch 2 Density	Patch 1 Density							
		20		30		45		70	
Experiment 1a									
	20	15	25	41	14	56	40	70	36
	30	33	14	42	3	32	13	51	44
	45	14	22	41	33	30	33	70	23
	70	36	32	42	41	42	12	52	26
Experiment 1b									
	20	32	30	23	13	30	35	45	23
	30	22	13	21	19	39	40	38	48
	45	39	30	38	38	20	21	27	16
	70	32	36	39	37	32	47	55	38
Experiment 1c									
	20	4	4	4	5	11	6	12	28
	30	4	5	2	5	11	4	19	14
	45	11	10	19	11	11	20	34	28
	70	12	26	18	18	19	27	26	26
Experiment 1d									
	20	4	6	11	21	5	12	18	22
	30	3	12	4	12	15	30	10	12
	45	5	28	19	20	2	19	11	20
	70	19	17	12	11	31	44	30	40

TABLE 5.5
Experiment 2: Mean Giving-Up Pecks in Patch 1 and Patch 2,
as a Function of Initial Prey Densities in Each Patch

Patch 2 Density (Prey/200 Cells)	Patch 1 Density (Prey/320 Cells)							
	10		14		22		34	
Experiment 2a								
13	14	15	10	11	11	19	25	12
20	4	10	9	8	11	20	24	9
30	8	0	11	10	18	2	42	30
45	4	26	6	10	2	5	26	4
Experiment 2b								
13	8	4	7	7	11	0	14	10
20	21	0	1	3	9	13	8	10
30	14	1	19	2	8	1	8	10
45	17	2	13	9	13	25	7	19

times were also analyzed but gave essentially similar results, so they are not presented here.

Tables 5.4 and 5.5 do not show any very clear trends, but the following generalizations seem to be justified. Where any consistent pattern was shown, it was for giving-up pecks in *each* patch to increase with the initial prey density in *both* patches; this was seen in experiments 1c and 1d, where both patches were of the same type. Secondly, giving-up pecks tended to be longer in nondepleting than in depleting patches, and shorter in refreshing patches than in nonrefreshing ones.

DISCUSSION

The experimental birds' behavior may be loosely summarized as showing adaptation to the varied experimental conditions to which they were exposed. With conditions changing both within and between daily sessions, the birds reliably made the majority of their pecks in the more productive patch, whether its productivity was due to a higher initial prey density or a more advantageous patch type. At least at the lower prey densities, they extracted a high proportion of the prey available. Thus, the birds clearly learned about the conditions in force each day, and they were clearly quite effective foragers. But did they learn in the ways suggested by the EWMA model? And were they optimal foragers?

These questions can be tackled in two ways. First, various kinds of learning model, and various kinds of optimal-foraging theory, make qualitative predictions that can be compared with our data. Secondly, the data can be compared with simulations of the various models described earlier in this chapter.

Qualitative Predictions of the EWMA Model

The EWMA model makes many predictions, and they cannot all be considered here. One crucial one, however, concerns refreshing patches. If a patch refreshes, the forager needs to abandon its previous estimate of that patch's density on every re-entry, and within the EWMA model this can only be achieved by a low value of a (the weighting given to the past). But once within the patch, a low a may be inappropriate, if depletion is fairly slow, or the variance of intercapture intervals is high. Under these circumstances, the EWMA model might well be outperformed by a more "cognitive" account, which would allow the forager to "understand" the structure of the situation, or by a model of the kind advanced by Silberberg, Hamilton, Ziriax, and Casey (1978), in which higher order response properties such as interchangeover times are treated as reinforcible entities.

In experiment 1, giving-up pecks were lower in refreshing than in nonrefreshing patches, with similar initial prey densities and depletion rates. Under the EWMA model, reduced giving-up pecks imply lower a values. The data thus have two implications. First, the value of a must be different for the two patches, and this is a considerable, and unwelcome, complication of the EWMA model (cf. Lea & Dow, 1984). Secondly, however, the EWMA model is supported in that its prediction of a low a to accommodate the refreshing patch situation is borne out. There is no obvious reason (and certainly no reason within optimal-foraging theory: Charnov, 1976) for the giving-up behavior to be different in the two kinds of patches.

Optimal-Foraging Theory

Optimal-foraging theory, too, exists in many versions and makes many predictions. But one of the simplest versions is Charnov's (1976) Marginal Value Theorem, with its simple prediction that all patches in an environment should be reduced to the same density, with the same giving-up time recorded in each, that time being a decreasing function of the densities of all patches exploited.

The results of experiment 1 contradict this prediction in at least two ways. First, as just noted, the giving-up pecks in experiment 1c were different in the two types of patch. However, the data reported here are mean giving-up pecks across a session, whereas it could be argued that Charnov's prediction refers only to conditions towards the end of a session. But the second contradiction cannot be resolved so easily. Increases in patch density were found to cause increases, not decreases, in giving-up pecks, both in the patch concerned and in the alternative patch. This is what one would expect from the EWMA or other learning models, in which a high estimate of prey density would take longer to decay under nonreinforcement. It is clearly contrary to the Marginal Value Theorem, and to any related form of optimal-foraging theory.

Comparisons with Models

To a certain extent, these qualitative comparisons are beside the point. As the introduction to this chapter made clear, any model that can cope with a changing environment has many properties that have to be specified more or less arbitrarily. It will be hard to get conclusive evidence against any one of them. This last section of the discussion, therefore, adopts the alternative strategy of taking the handful of completely specified models introduced earlier in this chapter and comparing their behavior with that of our experimental birds. Because the number of reinforcements obtained in a session is, from an adaptive point of view, the crucial output of any foraging strategy, it is adopted here as the criterion variable.

All the models were used in the same way. A computer program[1] was written to obey the rules of the model precisely (except that a constant pecking rate was assumed; no attempt was made to model the rates of pecking within a patch). In addition, the program simulated the patches used in the experiments, so that the behavior of the models in these patches could be studied. EWMA models require a value of a to be set, and suitable values were found by trial and error, exposing the models to patches of the types and densities used in the experiments and finding a values that reproduced the gross behavior of the experimental birds (proportion of pecks to patch 1, number of changes between patches) as closely as possible. The value chosen for a was 0.98; this corresponds to a memory window of 50 pecks, which seems reasonable for the patch densities in use in the experiment. The EWMA satisficer was set the target of obtaining 20 reinforcements within the session. All six models were then subjected to the 16 conditions of each part of each experiment, 10 times (corresponding to the 10–12 birds whose data were used in the preceding analyses).

Qualitative results from some of these simulations have been discussed by Lea and Dow (1984). It is the quantitative data that are of interest here. Tables 5.2 and 5.3 report the number of reinforcements obtained by the six models in these simulations, along with those obtained by the experimental birds. Among the conclusions that can be drawn from these tables are the following.

Under almost all conditions, the experimental birds and all the models do substantially worse than the omniscient forager. The only exception is found in experiment 2a, where with two rapidly depleting, nonrefreshing patches, the two nonlearning models (alternator and session-halver) both succeeded in finding most of the prey that were available. Under these conditions, the most successful strategy is to divide behavior reasonably equally between the two patches, and the learning models tended not to do this. The experimental birds were no more successful, and the satisficer was distinctly worse than them, and than the

---

[1]The program was written in Pascal and executed on an Apple II microcomputer. Listings may be obtained from S. E. G. Lea.

matcher or meliorator. In all other parts of the experiments, the birds were clearly disadvantaged by their lack of knowledge of the prey densities in the patches, and we have found no learning model that would have enabled them to overcome this disadvantage.

Secondly, there is no model that gives comparable results to the experimental birds under all conditions. The nearest is the dynamic matcher, which fits the data quite well except in experiment 2b, where it (and the alternator) find far more prey than the birds, whereas the meliorator, satisficer, and session-halver find far fewer. The matcher also finds consistently more prey than the birds did under those conditions in experiments 1a and 1b in which the initial density of patch 1 (the nondepleting patch) was highest.

Thirdly, there is no model that consistently finds most prey. With refreshing patches (as in experiments 1b, 1c, and 2b), the matcher tends to be the most successful of the three learning models, but with the rapidly depleting, non-refreshing patches of experiment 2a, it is outperformed by the meliorator on every combination of prey densities. A similar relation exists between the alternator and the session-halver, and this suggests that the key to the matcher's relative success with refreshing patches is its greater tendency to change patches.

Fourthly, the learning models (matcher, meliorator, and satisficer) do not consistently find more prey than the much simpler alternator and session-halver.

Finally, in every subexperiment, there is at least one model that tends to do worse than the experimental birds, and at least one that tends to do better. As would be expected from the last two points, these are not the same models in each case.

Obviously, the data reported in Tables 5.2 and 5.3 do not make possible a full comparison of the birds' performance with these simulations. To do that would require analysis of the models' distribution of behavior between the patches, numbers of changeovers, and giving-up behavior. Nor do the present simulations constitute a thorough test of the models: That would require, at least, repeated simulations with varying parameter values for the learning models. Furthermore, as has already been said, there are many other models that might be tested. We have carried out exploratory analyses in all these directions, and we believe that the results reported here, and the generalizations listed earlier, are representative of those models that behave at least approximately like the real birds.

One way in which all the models (and others we have tested) failed to approximate the birds' behavior was in the number of changeovers they made. As already reported, the birds tended to change between patches rather rarely. Except for the session-halver, which of course always changed exactly once, all the models changed very frequently. There are two possible explanations for this disparity. First, the models did not assign any cost to changing over, whereas in the experiments there was at least a cost of one keypeck, and the birds' general behavior suggested that the effective cost was considerably higher. Alternatively, the assumption (made in all the simulations) that updating (and a new decision about which patch to be in) occurs after every response may be inappropriate. The exploration of alternative assumptions would clearly be worthwhile, but we have not yet attempted it.

CONCLUSIONS

At a theoretical level, EWMA models still seem to be the most attractive way of modeling behavior in changing environments. There obviously are problems, however, in deciding which of the many possible versions to use, and in deciding on parameter values. The present results, moreover, are not very encouraging at the practical level. Qualitatively, it appears that the number of parameters to be specified must be increased: The crucial weighting factor a seems to be a function of the current patch or schedule component, rather than a fixed property of the organism or of the overall situation. Quantitatively, in some situations the EWMA models seemed to do worse than much cruder models (the alternator and the session-halver).

Of course, these simpler models fail to reproduce other aspects of the birds' behavior, such as their ability to make most of their pecks in the better patch. A detailed examination of models obviously should not concentrate only on the gross output statistics of number of prey gained. But it is these gross statistics that provide the raw material for natural selection. If the patches studied here are at all reasonable approximations of the conditions pigeons have faced in their natural environments during the evolutionary past, it will not be reasonable to argue for one learning mechanism over another on the grounds that it gives rise to foraging behavior that is precisely optimal. On the evidence presented here, there is scarcely enough selective pressure available to drive the evolution of a dynamic meliorator from a session-halver. The chances of producing a true optimal sampler, with its very much greater computational requirements, seem small indeed.

In one way, the birds seem to be more adaptable than the models tested in this chapter. Although they never performed as well as the best model, the birds never did as badly as the worst—and the best and the worst model varied between situations. This suggests that no one model will succeed in describing animals' behavior in changing environments. The birds may well have available a range of strategies, and the capacity to choose the best for each situation. This will inevitably impose costs; generalists never do as well as specialists in the environment to which the specialist is ideally adapted. But the generalist is much less likely to be trapped into disastrously maladaptive behavior in an unusual or unnatural situation.

ACKNOWLEDGMENT

The experimental work described here was carried out while S. M. Dow held a Research Studentship from the UK Science and Engineering Research Council.

REFERENCES

Baum, W. M. (1974). Choice in free-ranging wild pigeons. *Science, 185,* 78–79.

Bobisud, L. E., & Voxman, W. L. (1979). Predator response to variation of prey density in a patchy environment: A model. *American Naturalist, 144,* 63–75.

Bush, R. R., & Mosteller, F. (1951). A mathematical model of simple learning. *Psychological Review, 58,* 313–323.

Charnov, E. L. (1976). Optimal foraging: The marginal value theorem. *Theoretical Population Biology, 9,* 129–136.

Commons, M. L., Woodford, M., Ducheny, J. R., & Peck, J. R. (1982). The acquisition of performance during shifts between terminal links in concurrent chain schedules. In M. L. Commons, R. J. Herrnstein & A. R. Wagner (Eds.), *Quantititative analyses of behavior, Vol. III: Acquisition* (pp. 391–426). Cambridge, MA: Ballinger.

Cowie, R. J. (1977). Optimal foraging in great tits (*Parus major*). *Nature, 268,* 137–139.

Dow, S. M. (1984). *Foraging, reinforcement and learning in pigeons.* Unpublished doctoral dissertation, University of Exeter.

Dow, S. M., & Lea, S. E. G. (in press). Sampling of schedule parameters by pigeons; tests of optimising theory. *Animal Behaviour.*

Findley, J. D. (1958). Preference and switching under concurrent scheduling. *Journal of the Experimental Analysis of Behavior, 1,* 123–144.

Harley, C. B. (1981). Learning the evolutionarily stable strategy. *Journal of Theoretical Biology, 89,* 611–633.

Herrnstein, R. J. (1961). Relative and absolute strength of response as a function of reinforcement. *Journal of the Experimental Analysis of Behavior, 4,* 267–272.

Herrnstein, R. J. (1970). On the law of effect. *Journal of the Experimental Analysis of Behavior, 13,* 243–266.

Herrnstein, R. J., & Vaughan, W. (1980). Melioration and behavioral allocation. In J. E. R. Staddon (Ed.), *Limits to action* (pp. 143–176). New York: Academic Press.

Killeen, P. R. (1981). Averaging theory. In C. M. Bradshaw, E. Szabadi, & C. F. Lowe (Eds.), *Quantification of steady state operant behaviour* (pp. 21–34). Amsterdam: Elsevier.

Killeen, P. R. (1984). Incentive theory III: Adaptive clocks. *Annals of the New York Academy of Sciences, 423,* 515–527.

Krebs, J. R., Kacelnik, A., & Taylor, P. J. (1978). Test of optimal sampling by foraging great tits. *Nature, 275,* 27–31.

Lea, S. E. G., & Dow, S. M. (1984). The integration of reinforcements over time. *Annals of the New York Academy of Sciences, 423,* 269–277.

Lester, N. P. (1984). The feed–feed decision—how goldfish solve the patch-depletion problem. *Behaviour, 89,* 175–199.

MacDonald, D. W. (1976). Nocturnal observations of tawny owls *Strix aluco* preying upon earthworms. *Ibis, 118,* 579–580.

Maynard Smith, J. (1984). Game theory and the evolution of behavior. *The Behavioral and Brain Sciences, 7,* 95–125.

McNamara, J., & Houston, A. I. (1980). The application of statistical decision theory to animal behaviour. *Journal of Theoretical Biology, 85,* 673–690.

Morgan, M. J., Fitch, M. D., Holman, J. G., & Lea, S. E. G. (1976). Pigeons learn the concept of an "A." *Perception, 5,* 57–66.

Myerson, J., & Miezin, F. M. (1980). The kinetics of choice: An operant systems analysis. *Psychological Review, 87,* 160–174.

Oaten, A. (1977). Optimal foraging in patches: A case for stochasticity. *Theoretical Population Biology, 12,* 263–285.

Sibly, R. M., & McCleery, R. H. (1983). The distribution between feeding sites of herring gulls breeding at Walney Island, U.K. *Journal of Animal Ecology, 52,* 51–68.

Silberberg, A., Hamilton, B., Ziriax, J. M., & Casey, J. (1978). The structure of choice. *Journal of Experimental Psychology: Animal Behavior Processes, 4,* 368–398.

Simon, H. A. (1957). *Models of man.* New York: Wiley.

Tolman, E. C. (1955). Principles of performance. *Psychological Review, 62,* 315–326.

6

Learning and Foraging in Pigeons: Effects of Handling Time and Changing Food Availability on Patch Choice

Sara J. Shettleworth
University of Toronto

This chapter is divided into three parts. The first part consists of some remarks on the relationship between foraging theory and the experimental analysis of learning. The next two parts of the chapter present two examples from my laboratory of one way in which foraging theory and learning theory can interact.

FORAGING THEORY AND THE ANALYSIS OF LEARNING

Discussions of the relationship between studies of foraging behavior and psychologists' studies of learning and choice have become common in recent years (e.g., Baum, 1983; Kamil, 1983; Lea, 1981; Shettleworth, 1984; Staddon, 1980). Indeed, many of the chapters in this volume are based on the premise that foraging theorists and animal-learning psychologists have much in common. Both types of researchers are interested in the behavior of animals working for food. The laws and processes revealed by the behavior of animals working for food on schedules of reinforcement in the laboratory and of those foraging for food in the wild might be expected to be similar, if not identical. Thus, operant psychology might provide understanding of the mechanisms through which animals forage, whereas foraging theory might provide an ecological justification for studying schedules of reinforcement in the laboratory (Lea, 1981).

Many psychologists nowadays would probably agree that the ability to learn is an evolved adaptation. In the context of this assumption, optimal-foraging theory is important to the study of learning because it provides a rigorous derivation of immediate outcomes of behavior from explicit first principles of biology. From specific immediate outcomes one can work back one step more to infer the properties that learning or other behavioral mechanisms ought to have. The rigor and explicitness of this process contrasts with the loose and ad hoc attempts to relate the properties of learning to its function that, according to Domjan and Galef (1983), have characterized work on "biological constraints on learning."

The relationship between optimal-foraging theory and causal studies of behavior is depicted schematically in Fig. 6.1. The ultimate selective force on behavior is the impact of that behavior on inclusive fitness, but, for the sake of simplification, behavioral ecologists identify specific immediate outcomes of behavior that can reasonably be mapped into inclusive fitness fairly directly. For foraging theory this has often been net rate of energy intake per unit time spent foraging, or E/T. The type of behavior that leads to the maximization of this variable can be derived for specific situations like patch choice, item selection, and so on (Krebs, Stephens, & Sutherland, 1983; Pyke, Pulliam, & Charnov, 1977). Optimal-foraging theory usually stops with testing whether behavior actually has the predicted properties. However, those interested in the mechanisms underlying behavior can go one step further and ask what the properties of perception, memory, learning, and so on would have to be for the predicted outcomes to be attained. There are three possible sorts of answers to this question.

In some cases the expected psychological mechanisms are ones that are already well understood. Here, in effect, foraging theory says, "This is what

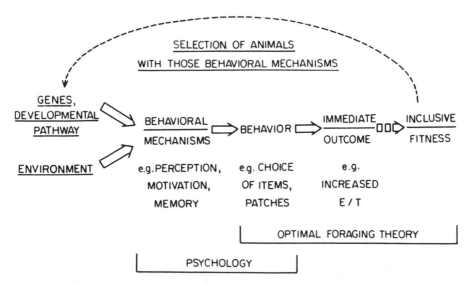

FIG. 6.1. Schematic representation of the relationship between natural selection and behavioral mechanisms, like learning and memory, and of the relationship between the psychology of learning and optimal-foraging theory.

ought to happen," and learning theory can say, "This is how it does happen." As a crude example, a high density of food should be preferred to a low density of food. Fantino, Abarca, and Ito (this volume) discuss how choice among items with different handling times may be accounted for by the same delay-reduction principle that accounts for choice among different delays to reinforcement in concurrent schedules.

In other cases, the known properties of perception, memory, or learning place constraints on what outcomes or mechanisms of achieving them are plausible. Here, when foraging theory says, "This is what ought to happen," psychological theory can say, "This is why it doesn't or shouldn't." One example of this kind of relationship comes from investigations of optimal-diet selection. According to a classical model of optimal-diet selection (Charnov, 1976), choices of foragers offered items of different profitabilities (energy yield per unit handling time or E/h) should be determined by the abundance of the most profitable items. Above a threshold abundance of the more profitable of two item types, foragers should specialize on it; below this, greater E/T is attained by generalizing, taking all items of both types that are offered. The predicted shift from generalizing to specializing is thus stepwise or all-or-none (Krebs, Erichsen, Webber, & Charnov, 1977; Lea, 1979).

When great tits are offered large (profitable) and small (unprofitable) pieces of mealworm moving past on a conveyor belt, they do not show the predicted abrupt shift in preference. Although they shift from generalizing to specializing as the rate of encounter with large pieces increases, they show partial preferences at intermediate encounter rates (Krebs et al., 1977). One functional explanation for this result is that the birds are "sampling," rejecting the current best choice to gain information about alternatives. However, analysis of the great tits' deviations from optimal choice shows that they can better be understood as mistakes, due to less than perfect discrimination of the two prey types. Signal-detection theory accounts very well for the pattern of errors (Rechten, Avery, & Stevens, 1983). Thus, in this case failure of an optimality model to account for observed behavior can be understood in terms of a familiar psychological theory about the mechanisms underlying discrimination and choice. New optimality models can then be formulated that take psychological constraints such as imperfect descriminability into account. It may be true in general that intrinsic variability in perception and memory will constrain how close animals can come to the predictions of classical, unconstrained, optimal-foraging models (Orians, 1981).

In these two sorts of cases, psychologists can provide explanations of how animals could achieve or fail to achieve outcomes predicted by optimal-foraging models. A third possibility, and in some ways the most interesting one, is that optimal-foraging theory can suggest what problems animals should be built to solve while the mechanisms for their solution remain to be discovered. Indeed, foraging theory can suggest ways of solving foraging problems that conflict with existing ideas about learning. One example is the idea mentioned earlier that animals should sample the environment even if they sacrifice immediate reward in doing so. Although "sampling" does not seem to account for the errors made by great tits in conveyor-belt experiments, this is not to say that it does not occur in other situations.

Another example is discussed by Caraco and Lima (this volume). Under some conditions, the optimal choice of patches depends on the time horizon, or time available for foraging. For instance, a small bird in winter needs to have enough energy reserves by the end of the day to keep it through the night. Near evening, if it has the choice between an option of constant value too small to make up its reserves and a variable option that has the same mean but that sometimes takes on a value high enough to keep it through the night, it should choose the variable option. When the time horizon is longer (say, in the morning), it should be less risk prone. In terms of foraging theory, it should be risk prone when time horizon is short and be risk averse otherwise (Stephens, 1981). This analysis throws new light on the problem of choice between fixed and variable reinforcement schedules with the same mean (Gibbon, 1977). It also suggests that session length, rather than being a matter only of convenience, might sometimes influence the outcomes of operant-choice experiments.

In pointing to the possible importance of such things as sampling or sensitivity to time horizon for rate of energy gain, optimal-foraging theory can enrich the study of learning by suggesting investigations of variables and processes that are not yet well understood. In the remainder of the chapter this kind of interaction between foraging theory and the study of learning is illustrated with two examples of research from my laboratory. The full details of each example can be found elsewhere (Lester, Beeby, & Shettleworth, 1985; Shettleworth, 1985).

Item Size and Profitability

In order to maximize rate of food intake, animals should choose among food items according to their profitabilities, where profitability is the ratio of energy yield to handling time, E/h. Items of relatively low profitability should be rejected when more profitable items are sufficiently abundant (Krebs et al., 1977). Some of the most extensive laboratory studies of item selection have been conducted with pigeons working on reinforcement schedules that simulate item-selection problems (Fantino et al., this volume; Lea, 1979). One of the concerns behind the research to be described here was to what extent these simulations tap into the same mechanisms pigeons use in selecting real food items like those they might normally eat.

In all the operant simulations of item selection that have been reported, "items" are discriminative stimuli on the pecking key, each correlated with a different delay and/or amount of food. When an "item" is presented, the bird can peck to obtain it. Failure to peck leads to continued "search" until another "item" of the same or a different kind is presented. Profitability of these simulated items (ratio of time available for feeding to total time out from searching) has been varied in three ways. In Lea's (1979) pioneering simulation, delay to a constant reward constituted the handling time. Snyderman (1983) equated handling times across items and varied hopper time and delays before and after the food within each "item presentation." Sigmundi and Shettleworth (in preparation) made handling times and amounts of food the same across items and varied the probability that food would be delivered when an item was chosen.

As can be seen, in each of these cases E/h is varied across "items." Although these variations have identical effects on item profitability, it need not be the case that animals respond to all these means of varying profitability in the same way. Moreover, none of these simulations captures the item-selection problem that confronts pigeons and other animals feeding on small items like seeds that can be snapped up instantaneously. In this case, whereas energy yields are greater for large items, handling times are equally short for large and small items. Thus, large items should be chosen over small ones that are available simultaneously, as indeed they are by many animals (see the review by Lea, 1981). In addition, a single large item should be chosen over a collection of small ones when the aggregate energy value of the small items is the same as that of the large one and all the items are available simultaneously. If there are n small items they will require approximately n times as much handling time as the single large item. The overall rate of feeding will be lowered if the animal chooses to feed on clumps of small items rather than single large items of equivalent energy value, but not because it experiences any differential delays between encounter and the initiation of consumption. In both cases, unlike the case in the operant simulations of item selection, consumption can begin as soon as food is encountered.

Conventional studies of the effects of varying reinforcement magnitude do not provide many clues as to what animals actually do when faced with the choice of one large versus many small items because in such studies total number of items and total amount of food provided are usually confounded. For instance, animals might be given one pellet as opposed to 10 pellets all of the same size (e.g., O'Connell & Rashotte, 1982) or one versus 10 seconds feeding time (e.g., Snyderman, 1983). Studies of pigeons' preferences among different natural food items, such as various kinds of grain (Brown, 1969; Moon & Zeigler, 1979), are also not very helpful because grains differ in many ways besides energy content. One hint as to what might happen with one big versus many small items is provided by a study of maze running in chickens conducted by Wolfe and Kaplon (1941). The chickens performed better for four one-quarter kernels of corn than for one whole kernel, though they performed better for the whole kernel than for one-quarter kernel. These results led Wolfe and Kaplon to conclude that the amount of pecking elicited was one determinant of the reinforcing value of food to chickens. Several similar studies with rats are reviewed by Bolles (1967).

The experiments discussed here involved choice in a shuttlebox similar to that used by Baum and Rachlin (1969). The first experiment tested pigeons' preferences for obtaining the same amount of food with different handling times on a concurrent variable-interval (VI) schedule, where a preference could be expressed without having much impact on the overall rate of feeding. Thus the situation differed in an important way from the item-selection problem depicted in foraging theory, because with relatively long concurrent VIs an animal can collect all the food that becomes available on both sides by changing sides sufficiently often. At the same time, however, a range of time allocations around 50:50 produces the same overall feeding rate (Houston & McNamara, 1981). The underlying assumption of the experiment was that any preferences the birds displayed would be the same ones that would govern their choices in a conventional diet-selection problem, where handling time is time lost from encountering further items. Using concurrent VIs allows the preference for some combinations of pellet sizes and numbers over others to be partially separated from a preference for rates of food intake per se. In effect, this type of experiment asks whether items are chosen on the basis of a simple rule of thumb by decoupling item choice from rate of energy gain. As is seen next, a second experiment confirmed that the same preference was expressed when choosing the preferred combination of pellet size and number not only did not increase the rate of energy gain but actually decreased it.

Experimentally naive White King pigeons (*Columba livia*) at 85% of their free-feeding weights were trained in a 62-centimeter-long shuttlebox with a turntable feeder at each end. The turntables held cups 2 centimeters in diameter containing various numbers of 300-milligram ("large") or 20-milligram ("small") Noyes pigeon pellets. When a reinforcer was programmed, a cup was presented for the designated handling time, then removed, allowing the schedule to go back into effect. Throughout the experiment, reinforcement was programmed at VI 60 seconds at both ends of the shuttlebox, and there was a signaled 3-second changeover delay (COD). An initial condition with alternating presentation of one 300-milligram pellet or 15 20-milligram pellets and 8-second handling times on both sides exposed the birds to both types of food items and established that there was no very strong bias for one side or the other (see Fig. 6.2).

The four main conditions included two with 300 milligrams of food per reinforcement on one side and 20 milligrams on the other. Each bird experienced each condition once for 10–15 sessions with a given alternative on the left and for the same number of sessions with it on the right. The programmed handling time for one item was 1.5 seconds, just long enough for the pigeon to detect and eat it. Programmed handling time for 15 items was 8 seconds, again just long enough for all the items to be consumed, as they usually were.

When the pigeons were offered one large versus one small item or 15 small items versus one small one, they spent more time on the side offering more food per reinforcement but visited the other side often enough to collect all the food there as soon as it became available. As a result, about half of all the reinforcers collected were from the less preferred side, even when only about 30% of the

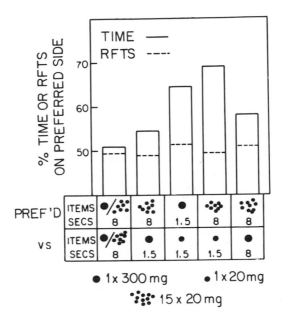

FIG. 6.2.   Mean results for five pigeons working on a concurrent VI60 VI60 schedule in a shuttlebox for the pairs of reinforcers depicted in the figure. "Seconds" for each reinforcer means the number of seconds for which the food cup was presented, or "handling time."

time was spent there (Fig. 6.2). But when the choice was between 15 small pellets and one big one, preference did not favor the side with the more profitable alternative. All five pigeons showed a small but consistent preference for the side with 15 small items, the less profitable reinforcer. All birds had a slightly greater preference in the case where identical, 8-second handling times were imposed on both sides so that the two alternatives differed only in the amount of pecking and numbers of items they offered. Perhaps, therefore, the preference for 15 small items is shown only when it results in no reduction in the rate of energy intake. Perhaps in a more natural situation, where accepting a longer handling time would reduce search time, this preference would be overridden by other factors tending to maximize rate of energy intake. This possibility was tested by exposing the pigeons to ratio-like schedules in the shuttlebox. Here, time spent on a given side counted only toward obtaining reinforcement on that side. The time requirement was very short, a fixed 10 seconds, so that there would be a substantial difference in rates of energy intake with 8-second versus 1.5-second handling times. Figure 6.3 depicts the procedure and mean results for the same five pigeons used in the first experiment.

When the sides differed only in the handling time imposed by the schedule, offering one large pellet with 1.5-second or 8-second handling time, an almost

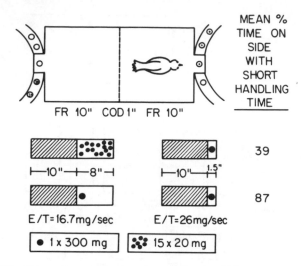

FIG. 6.3.   Schematic representation of a procedure in which pigeons worked for different sizes and numbers of food pellets by spending time on one side or the other of a shuttlebox. Results are means for five birds.

exclusive preference developed for the side with greater E/T. However, with this same difference in E/T and one large versus 15 small items, all birds shifted their preference toward the side offering more items even though it offered less than ⅔ the maximum rate of energy intake possible in the situation. On average there was a clear preference for the side with the smaller E/T (Fig. 6.3). Although the condition with one large versus 15 small items was run for 30 sessions of 40 reinforcers each, the birds showed no tendency to decrease their preference for the less profitable side with increased exposure to the situation.

These results can be summarized in several ways. One might wish to say that although pigeons use both size and number of items in assessing amount of food, like small children (Bruner, 1966) they weight number more heavily than size so that larger size of items does not completely compensate for reduced numbers. Thus, this part of the chapter might have been entitled, "Lack of conservation in the pigeon." The results also provide one of many illustrations of the fact that animals do not calculate E/T or profitability directly. They use rules of thumb (see Krebs et al., 1983) that may be good guides in natural situations but fail in artificial situations. The pigeon's rule in this situation seems to be something like "more items means more food." In a similar way, shrews choose large over small prey items even when the smaller ones are the more profitable (Barnard & Brown, 1981). It is of course impossible to say without further research how well the pigeon's rule of thumb fares in maximizing E/T in natural situations. It is also as yet unknown whether there are some additional costs of ingesting one big item versus many small ones so that preference for many small items over one large one does ultimately lead to greater net energy gain.

Choices between different forms of exactly the same amount of food must hardly ever occur in nature. More nearly natural might be an array of many small and many large items, all available simultaneously. The same pigeons run in the experiments already described selected the large pellets first in such a situation. Thus, far from being inherently aversive, the pea-sized large items used in these experiments were strongly preferred in a simultaneous choice test.

To return to the purpose of the experiments, pigeons, at least, do not assess all types of variations in E/h in the same way. In the operant simulations of successive encounters with food items of differing profitability, pigeons perform qualitatively as optimal-foraging theory predicts but tend to show a bias against accepting delayed food (Lea, 1979), although this bias may be overcome after extensive training (Snyderman, 1983). The present results suggest that, in contrast, pigeons successively encountering single large items and collections of small items would show a bias toward accepting the relatively unprofitable small items too often. Nevertheless, pigeons foraging for these sorts of items might still obey the qualitative prediction of optimal-foraging theory and switch from generalizing to specializing on the more profitable large items as density of large items increases. This prediction remains to be tested with pigeons and the types of items used here.

Assessment of Changing Food Availability

The second example of how foraging theory can stimulate analysis of unstudied learning problems is one discussed elsewhere in this volume (Dow & Lea; Kacelnik, Krebs, & Ens; Houston): how to assess food availability and choose foraging sites in a world that may be changing frequently. The problem of choosing foraging sites resembles the problem confronting an animal working on concurrent schedule of reinforcement in an operant laboratory. However, the results of most traditional studies of behavior on concurrent schedules are of limited usefulness in predicting behavior when patch densities are initially unknown to the animal or changing rapidly because such studies focus on behavior in the steady state, when food densities in the operant "patches" remain the same for many sessions. Consideration of natural foraging problems suggests that such a stable world is the exception. Animals should therefore be expected to be capable of adjusting fairly rapidly to changes in food availability within and between patches.

Consider, for example, the problem confronting an animal feeding in two patches of initially different densities that are unknown to the animal and that can only be discovered by feeding in the patches. Furthermore, the patches deplete as the animal feeds. The optimal behavior for an omniscient predator with a short or unknown time horizon would be to go immediately to the better patch and deplete it to the level of the second patch. If there were no cost to travelling between patches, the two patches should be exploited equally after this point. Given that there usually is some changeover cost, a predator that knows not only patch density but also time available for feeding can maximize total food intake by switching once between patches, allocating time between them in such a way that they are depleted to the same level at the end of the foraging bout (see Mellgren, this volume).

Clearly neither kind of behavior just described can be attained by an animal that first has to learn which is the better patch by sampling both. The need to gather information must constrain how close foragers can come to the optimal behavior when patch densities are unknown initially. If the rules describing how animals process information about food densities could be discovered, we could then begin to ask whether animals are optimizing net rate of energy gain or some other variable within the constraints of their information-gathering capabilities. A further question would then be whether animals are using information optimally (Houston, Kacelnik, & McNamara, 1982).

These kinds of considerations have inspired the recent development of a number of essentially similar reinforcement averaging models. These are outlined and compared in the chapter by Kacelnik, Krebs, and Ens. The work discussed here was inspired by the model developed by Nigel Lester (1984). His version was developed specifically to model an animal's responses to several patches that deplete as the animal feeds. The experiments were done jointly by him, Mary-Ann Beeby, and me (Lester et al., in preparation).

Lester's model combines a reinforcement averaging rule and a response rule for each of which there is some evidence as well as some a priori reasonableness. The reinforcement averaging rule is the familiar exponentially weighted moving average, the justification for which has been discussed by Killeen (1981). In terms of Lester's model, at time n the estimate of food availability in patch i, A_i, $_n$, is a weighted average of the number of past rewards, R_i, $_j$.

$$A_{i,n} = (1 - b)\sum_{j=1}^{n} b^{n-j}R_{i,j} \qquad 0 < b < 1. \tag{1}$$

The weighting factor b corresponds roughly to the "memory window" (Cowie, 1977) over which rewards are averaged. It ranges between zero and one. Smaller values correspond to relatively less influence of the past relative to the present, or a smaller memory window. In Lester's model the animal is assumed to update its average at constant small intervals of time independently of whether or where it has responded in the last such interval or "time bin." The similar models reviewed by Kacelnik et al. (this volume) each make slightly different assumptions in this regard.

The following form of the exponentially weighted mean shows that in any given time bin the current estimate is a function only of the most recent past estimate and current experience. Thus, averaging food availability in this way does not place a great load on memory. This is one reason why the exponentially weighted moving average is a plausible candidate for describing how animals might assess food availability.

$$A_{i,n} = b A_{i,n-1} + (1-b)R_{i,n}. \tag{2}$$

Lester applied this averaging principle to the case of two patches by assuming that animals match relative times, Ti, in two or more patches to estimates of relative availabilities, that is, for two patches:

$$\frac{T_{1,n}}{T_{1,n} + T_{2,n}} = \frac{A_{1,n-1}}{A_{1,n-1} + A_{2,n-1}}. \tag{3}$$

Lester referred to this response rule as dynamic matching. It might also be thought of as a description of how melioration (Herrnstein, 1982) could work. Because it does predict matching in the steady state, it seems a reasonable assumption for a response rule.

Lester's model makes straightforward predictions for two sorts of situations in which a forager encounters new patches (Fig. 6.4). The first is like the situation studied by Krebs, Kacelnik, and Taylor (1978). The animal encounters two nondepleting patches of different densities. It gradually develops a preference for the better one, but not an exclusive preference. Rate of preference development depends on both the ratio and the difference between densities in the two patches. Foragers in this situation are not predicted to switch abruptly from "sampling"

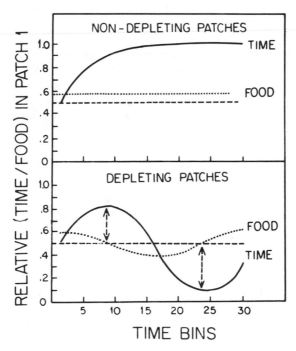

FIG. 6.4.   General form of the predictions of Lester's model for preference development when a forager confronts two patches and initially does not know which is better. Patch 1 is the patch with the greater density of food at the start.

both patches to "exploiting" the better (Krebs et al., 1978) but rather to absorb gradually in the better patch. In effect, Lester's model depicts the forager as choosing on the basis of a new weighted coin toss in each time bin. The closer the weighting is to 50:50, the more often the forager will switch from one patch to another, or "sample." However, in order to make realistic predictions about the changeover rate, it would be necessary to make assumptions about the length of the time bins as well as how the animal takes into account the cost of switching. In the simple form stated here, Lester's model makes only the qualitative prediction that the animal will sample more initially than after it has had time to assess unequal patch densities.

The second case considered by Lester is the more interesting. Initially the situation is the same as in the first case—densities are different and unknown to the animal—but the animal depletes both patches as it feeds. Preference should cycle from one patch to the other. An important prediction of Lester's model is that preference for the initially better patch should peak at the point where patch densities become equal. Then preference for that patch should begin to decrease toward indifference, lagging behind relative food density, which will favor the initially worse patch at this time.

Lester (1984) obtained a good fit between this simple model and data from groups of goldfish feeding in two areas of a tank ("patches") where food had been spread at different densities. In my laboratory, the model's predictions were tested on individual pigeons using computer-simulated depletion (a progressive random-ratio schedule, to use operant terminology). The purpose of the experiments was to discover whether pigeons would adjust their choices in a way qualitatively in accord with the model when they were exposed to rapid and frequent changes in food densities in two operant "patches." The results do not necessarily allow one to distinguish between Lester's model and its various alternatives, which had not all been reported when the experiments were done. However, they do provide descriptive data on pigeons' sensitivity to the variables dealt with by averaging theories, data that such theories should ultimately be able to deal with.

Experimentally naive White King pigeons at 85% of their free-feeding weights worked for single small food items (75-milligram Noyes pigeon pellets) in two simulated "patches" at the ends of a 2-foot-long shuttlebox. Because estimates of food availability are updated as a function of time in Lester's model, a pigeon had only to spend time in a patch to obtain food there. Food densities were defined as probabilities of a food item being delivered per second of residence in the patch. The probabilities in this initial experiment ranged between .20 and .025. When food was delivered, a signal light and then a feeder light were illuminated for a total of 2 seconds. Time spent in the patch during this period, the "handling time," did not count toward earning the next food item. Thus, the highest probability of food delivery was one item per 5 seconds of "search" or one per 7 seconds spent in the patch. In conditions where depletion was programmed, the initial probability decreased by .0025 with each item earned.

Four pigeons were exposed to three pairs of unequal food densities: .2-.1; .1-.05; and .1-.025. These were chosen to represent a range of relative and absolute food densities similar to those that Lester had used with fish. Throughout the experiment, daily sessions were 30 minutes long. Sessions with unequal densities alternated with sessions in which equal, .1, initial densities with depletion were programmed. This arrangement was designed to "neutralize" (Krebs et al., 1978) any preference that developed in one session with unequal densities before exposure to the next such session. In the first part of the experiment, food densities depleted continuously in unequal, as well as in equal, density sessions. In the second part, there was no depletion in unequal-density sessions. All pigeons were exposed to each pair of unequal densities four times in randomized order in each part of the experiment.

The group results for all the conditions are shown in Fig. 6.5. With unequal nondepleting patches, on average the birds began to develop a preference for the better patch within the first few minutes. Within 30 minutes they generally reached a high level of preference for the better patch. Although differences in the rate of preference development were not large with the parameters chosen, on average preference for the .1 patch developed somewhat faster when the alternative was .025 than when it was .05, as would be expected. The most rapid preference development and fewest changovers were seen in the .2:.1 condition.

The average behavior was very different in the case of unequal depleting patches. Again, preference developed quickly, but then it declined as the initially better patch depleted. Preference for the .1 density remained high for longer when the alternative was .025 than when it was .05, an outcome that would be expected because it takes longer for a .1 density to deplete to .025 than to .05. At the end of depletion sessions both patches had, on average, been depleted to the same level. There was no tendency for the initially better or worse patch to have the higher food density at the end of 30-minute sessions. Thus in one respect the birds approached the molar optimum for exploiting the experimental environment. However, they changed over from one patch to the other at least once a minute on average, more than would be optimal even with the small (1-second) changcover cost in effect in the experiment. This suggests that they are responding to some molecular variable like time since last reward.

Time allocation in individual trials was analyzed as 6-minute moving averages. In the majority of nondepleting trials preference for the better side developed nearly continuously. In 73% of cases it was possible to identify a point after which preference for the better side never fell below 90%. However, there were some cases where the bird never settled down on the better side, and occasionally birds settled down on the worse side.

Data from individual unequal-density depleting trials were analyzed for the relationship between the peak preference for the initially better side and the

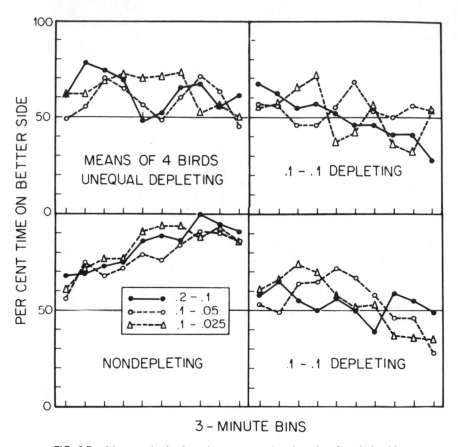

FIG. 6.5.   Mean results for four pigeons exposed to the pairs of patch densities indicated in the legend. Food densities are expressed as probabilities of receiving a food item per second spent at the specified end of the shuttlebox. For the equal-density sessions with depletion that were run in alternation with unequal-density sessions (right side of the figure), "better side" is the side that was better the previous day.

crossover in relative food density, i.e., the point where the initially worse side became the better side. Relative time spent on the initially better side and relative food density remaining there were analyzed in successive 3-minute intervals throughout the session. These were long enough to provide relatively smooth data but not so long as to obscure consistent short-term trends. Sometimes peak preference occurred in the same 3-minute interval as the crossover in density, as predicted by the model, but in about 80% of the cases where a peak could be identified, it preceded the crossover in relative density. (Details of this and other analyses are presented in Lester et al., in preparation). Thus, Lester's very simple version of the dynamic matching model seems to be inadequate in this situation.

Harley's (1981) relative-payoff sum model is identical to Lester's model except for an additional parameter corresponding to the animal's prior estimates of food availability. Experience is added to prior estimates, ei, as follows:

$$A_{i,n} = (1 - b) \, e_i + bA_{i,n-1} + R_{i,n}. \tag{4}$$

As in Lester's model, all estimates are updated at once, regardless of the amount of time spent in each patch since the last updating. In this case, however, the estimate for an unvisited or unrewarding patch will decay to the prior rather than to zero. When prior expectations are relatively high, the peak in preference for the originally better patch can precede the crossover in relative density (Lester, 1984). There may be no peak at all if the memory window is short. Thus, one thing that can be tested experimentally is whether manipulations that could be expected to alter prior expectations have the predicted effects on behavior in depleting schedules.

In contrast to Lester's assumption that the animal updates its estimates of both patch densities at regular intervals, Killeen (1984) suggests that updating occurs at each response. In order to apply this approach to our situation, it would be necessary to identify searching responses being made by pigeons in the shuttlebox or make assumptions about the rate of some sort of implicit foraging responses. Doing the latter would not be much different from making the assumption of Lester's model that animals update their estimates of food availability at regular time intervals.

Lester and Harley both assume implicitly that although the parameter b, the memory window, might change in the long term, it changes slowly in relation to estimates of food availability and therefore can be considered constant within any foraging bout. Their models do not incorporate any mechanism for changes in b. In contrast, Killeen's (1984) most recent version of the exponentially weighted moving average model does include a formal mechanism for changing b rapidly. High rates of feeding increase b (decrease the memory window), and low rates of feeding decrease b. A simulation of choice governed by this model in the two situations Lester and I used for pigeons gave results qualitatively similar to the group results shown in Fig. 6.5 (Killeen, personal communication).

One also might wish to modify Lester's "pessimistic animal" assumption (Kacelnik et al., this volume) that both estimates are updated at once no matter which patch the animal is in at the time. Intuitively, assuming instead that estimates are updated only when patches are visited seems likely to place the peak preference for the initially better of two depleting patches before the crossover in relative densities. This would approximate our data better than Lester's "pessimistic animal" model. If updating occurs only for the patch the animal is in, then the estimated density in the more visited of two depleting patches will decrease relatively faster than the estimated density in the less visited patch. In Lester's model, the estimate for the less preferred patch is decreasing when the animal is not visiting it, but if instead the estimate is frozen at its most recent value during this time, the animal should begin to switch preference toward it sooner than Lester originally predicted.

More detailed analysis of how well various models fit our data is presented elsewhere (Lester et al., in preparation). The models and our experiments with pigeons are discussed in the present context to illustrate how considerations of the problems that are likely to confront foragers can stimulate both laboratory experiments on learning and theoretical developments. In addition, analyzing learning problems in the context of optimal-foraging theory raises the issue of how close to optimal is the behavior both of real animals and of simulations of the various models. Houston discusses this problem in his contribution to the present volume (see also Houston et al., 1982). An additional consideration for future work is that linear-operator models deal only with the molar properties of behavior and not with the details of choices leading to the predicted outcomes. These need to be analyzed to try to determine what kind of moment-to-moment decision rule animals use.

CONCLUSIONS

This chapter presents two examples of how foraging theory can stimulate studies of processes of reinforcement and learning. Both still leave many unanswered questions. In the first case, it is not entirely clear why pigeons prefer a long to a short handling time when offered a choice of many small items versus one large one. The results also raise questions about possible differences in animals' responses to the different ways in which profitability can be varied. In the second example, unlike the first, pigeons seem to do more or less what they should, given the constraints imposed on behavior by the nature of memory processes. The exact means by which they do so remains to be worked out, however. It also might be noted that preferences develop very quickly in the situation we are using, and this may have some advantage for testing models of acquisition that are supposed to have some sort of ecological validity.

Bringing optimal-foraging theory into the laboratory to test its predictions and to analyze the means by which animals fulfill or fail to fulfill those predictions may entail testing foragers in an environment very different from that in which their foraging behavior evolved. Because optimal-foraging theory is an abstraction from particular foraging situations, testing it in the laboratory may appear to require only designing experiments that can be described in terms of parameters formally equivalent to those in the model. For example, rate of encounter with items is a quantity independent of how those items are encountered. Handling time is time lost from searching, no matter whether it is spent waiting or working. Different modes of encounter or of handling may have different energetic costs, but the predator is usually assumed to evaluate all costs or times equivalently (but see Krebs & Kacelnik, 1984). However, the first part of the chapter suggests that some modes of handling may be preferred to others that are formally equivalent. Ultimately, of course, a functional explanation of the differences may be forthcoming, but in the meanwhile, some caution may be advisable in designing laboratory foraging problems based on their formal properties alone. In spite of the many possible problems, however, there is a remarkable number of qualitative parallels between the established properties of food-reinforced operant behavior and the predicted or observed properties of optimal-foraging behavior (Lea, 1981). These point to rich possibilities for continuing and productive interactions between foraging theory and learning theory.

ACKNOWLEDGMENTS

The preparation of this chapter and the research reported in it were supported by a grant to the author from the Natural Sciences and Engineering Research Council of Canada. I thank John Krebs and Alex Kacelnik for comments on the manuscript.

REFERENCES

Barnard, C. J., & Brown, C. A. J. (1981). Prey size selection and competition in the common shrew. *Behavioral Ecology and Sociobiology, 8,* 239–243.

Baum, W. M. (1983). Studying foraging in the psychological laboratory. In R. L. Mellgren (Ed.), *Animal cognition and behavior* (pp. 253–283). Amsterdam: North Holland.

Baum, W. M., & Rachlin, H. C. (1969). Choice as time allocation. *Journal of the Experimental Analysis of Behavior, 12,* 861–874.

Bolles, R. C. (1967). *Theory of motivation.* New York: Harper & Row.

Brown, R. G. B. (1969). Seed selection by pigeons. *Behaviour, 34,* 115–131.

Bruner, J. S. (1966). On the conservation of liquids. In J. S. Bruner, R. R. Olver, & P. M. Greenfield (Eds.), *Studies in cognitive growth* (pp. 184–207). New York: Wiley.

Charnov, E. L. (1976). Optimal foraging: Attack strategy of a mantid. *American Naturalist, 110,* 141–151.

Cowie, R. J. (1977). Optimal foraging in great tits (*Parus major*). *Nature, 268,* 137–139.

Domjan, M., & Galef, B. G. (1983). Biological constraints on instrumental and classical conditioning: Retrospect and prospect. *Animal Learning & Behavior, 11,* 151–161.

Gibbon, J. (1977). Scalar expectancy theory and Weber's law in animal timing. *Psychological Review, 84,* 279–325.

Harley, C. B. (1981). Learning the evolutionary stable strategy. *Journal of Theoretical Biology, 89,* 611–633.

Herrnstein, R. J. (1982). Melioration as behavioral dynamism. In M. L. Commons, R. J. Herrnstein, & H. Rachlin, (Eds.), *Quantitative analyses of behavior* (Vol. 2, pp. 433–458). Cambridge, MA: Ballinger.

Houston, A. I., Kacelnik, A., & McNamara, J. (1982). Some learning rules for acquiring information. In D. J. McFarland (Ed.), *Functional ontogeny* (pp. 140–191). London: Pitman.

Houston, A. I., & McNamara, J. (1981). How to maximize reward rate on two variable-interval paradigms. *Journal of the Experimental Analysis of Behavior, 35,* 367–396.

Kamil, A. C. (1983). Optimal-foraging theory and the psychology of learning. *American Zoologist, 23,* 291–302.

Killeen, P. (1981). Averaging theory. In C. M. Bradshaw, E. Szabadi, & C. F. Lowe (Eds.), *Quantification of steady-state operant behaviour* (pp. 21–34). New York: Elsevier.

Killeen, P. R. (1984). Incentive theory III: Adaptive clocks. *Annals of the New York Academy of Sciences, 423,* 515–527.

Krebs, J. R., Erichsen, J. T., Webber, M. I., & Charnov, E. L. (1977). Optimal prey selection in the great tit *(Parus major)*. *Animal Behaviour, 25,* 30–38.

Krebs, J. R., & Kacelnik, A. (1984). Time horizons of foraging animals. *Annals of the New York Academy of Sciences, 423,* 278–291.

Krebs, J. R., Kacelnik, A., & Taylor, P. (1978). Test of optimal sampling by foraging great tits. *Nature, 275,* 27–31.

Krebs, J. R., Stephens, D. W., & Sutherland, W. J. (1983). Perspectives in optimal foraging. In G. A. Clark & A. H. Brush (Eds.), *Perspectives in ornithology* (pp. 165–216). New York: Cambridge University Press.

Lea, S. E. G. (1979). Foraging and reinforcement schedules in the pigeon: Optimal and non-optimal aspects of choice. *Animal Behaviour, 27,* 875–886.

Lea, S. E. G. (1981). Correlation and contiguity in foraging behavior. In P. Harzem & M. Zeiler (Eds.), *Advances in analysis of behavior* (Vol. 2, pp. 355–406). New York: Wiley.

Lester, N. P. (1984). The "feed–feed" decision: How goldfish solve the patch depletion problem. *Behaviour, 89,* 175–199.

Lester, N. P., Beeby, M. A., & Shettleworth, S. J. (in preparation). *Dynamic matching in the pigeon.*

Moon, R. D., & Zeigler, H. P. (1979). Food preferences of the pigeon *(Columba livia)*. *Physiology and Behavior, 22,* 1171–1182.

O'Connell, J. M., & Rashotte, M. E. (1982). Reinforcer magnitude effects in first and second order conditioning of directed action. *Learning & Motivation, 13,* 1–25.

Orians, G. H. (1981). Foraging behavior and the evolution of discriminatory abilities. In A. C. Kamil & T. D. Sargent (Eds.), *Foraging behavior: Ecological, ethological and psychological approaches* (pp. 389–405). New York: Garland.

Pyke, G. H., Pulliam, H. R., & Charnov, E. L. (1977). Optimal foraging: A selective review of theory and tests. *Quarterly Review of Biology, 52,* 137–154.

Rechten, C., Avery, M., & Stevens, A. (1983). Optimal prey selection: Why do great tits show partial preferences? *Animal Behaviour, 31,* 576–584.

Shettleworth, S. J. (1984). Learning and behavioural ecology. In J. R. Krebs & N. B. Davies (Eds.), *Behavioural ecology* (pp. 170–194). Oxford: Blackwell Scientific Press.

Shettleworth, S. J. (1985). Handling time and choice in pigeons. *Journal of the Experimental Analysis of Behavior, 44,* 139–155.

Sigmundi, R., & Shettleworth, S. J. (in preparation). *Item density and diet selection in an acquired foraging task.*

Snyderman, M. (1983). Optimal prey selection: Partial selection, delay of reinforcement and self control. *Behavior Analysis Letters, 3,* 131–142.

Staddon, J. E. R. (1980). Optimality analyses of operant behavior and their relation to optimal foraging. In J. E. R. Staddon (Ed.), *Limits to action: The allocation of individual behavior* (pp. 101–141). New York: Academic Press.

Stephens, D. W. (1981). The logic of risk-sensitive foraging preferences. *Animal Behaviour, 29,* 628–629.

Wolfe, J. B., & Kaplon, M. D. (1941). Effect of amount of reward and consummative activity on learning in chickens. *Journal of Comparative Psychology, 31,* 353–361.

7 Environmental Constraints on Optimal-Foraging Behavior

Roger L. Mellgren
Steven W. Brown
University of Oklahoma

Foraging behavior has become a popular topic of study for two important reasons. First, most if not all laboratory findings of behavioristically oriented psychologists can be tested in the foraging context. Understanding learning experiments on the basis of ecological considerations has become an important concern for a number of researchers (e.g., Baum, 1983; Domjan, 1983; Johnston & Turvey, 1980; Kamil & Yoerg, 1982). Foraging has heuristic value because it provides an ecologically relevant context for categorizing, through analogy, many of the phenomena studied in the laboratory. Second, optimal-foraging theory (OFT) provides the researcher with a means of quantitatively predicting and evaluating the responses of a forager to various problems encountered in the environment. A biologically based theory capable of predicting an individual organism's behavior needs an empirical test that will utilize the highly developed techniques of the behavioral laboratory.

Collier (1980, 1982) has argued that the foraging process often involves a number of distinct components including search, identification, procurement, and handling of prey. Consumption and utilization (digestion) of the ingested prey by the forager complete the process. An optimal forager is thus faced with a multidimensional problem and changes in the environment may alter one or more of the components of foraging, independent of other components. Because the foraging process can be analyzed into these separate components and each component potentially can be manipulated and studied, Collier's terminology seems preferable to alternatives that lump more than one of these components into one category. The components of chief concern in this chapter are search and procurement. Mellgren and Olson (1983) outline a general strategy for evaluating the possibility that different components of foraging are affected in different ways by the same environmental manipulation. For example, in a series of experiments (Mellgren & Olson, 1983) rats were allowed to run from one point to another where either food was found buried in sand every time each rat ran there (continuous reinforcement, CR) or, for different subjects, food was present half the time and absent the other half (partial reinforcement, PR). The environment then changed so that food was never again available (extinction). The animals that had experienced PR continued to run (search component) very rapidly even with repeated experience of extinction, but the CR animals showed a dramatic slowing with repeated extinction experiences. This is, of course, the well-known partial reinforcement effect (e.g., Amsel, 1967; Capaldi, 1967; Robbins, 1971). Interestingly, the PR-trained animals showed a large decline in the amount of time spent digging (procurement) in relation to the CR-trained animals, a result opposite to the normally observed partial reinforcement effect. Thus, prior experience with CR or PR schedules of prey availability had different effects on search (running to the food source) and procurement (digging in the sand for the food) components of foraging when environmental conditions changed.

Olson and Maki (1983) present data that they interpret as showing distinct memory capacities depending on the spatial arrangement of food. For example, their pigeons showed no disruption due to retroactive interference when using a spatial-delayed alternation task (T-maze) in contrast to drastic deficits produced by analogous manipulations in a nonspatial-operant task (e.g., Grant & Roberts, 1976). In another experiment, Maki, Gustavson, Berglund, and Thom (1983) report that search strategies are a function of the spatial separation of patchily distributed food. When the central compartment of a radial arm maze had long arms attached with food in the ends, the rats used place cues to avoid revisiting previously visited arms, but when the food was located in the central compartment with only small partitions separating each food source, the rats adopted the response-based strategy of going to immediately adjacent "arms." Maki et al. suggest that the "long-arm" maze represents the interpatch (search) component, whereas the partitioned compartment represents the intrapatch (procurement) component of foraging.

Thus, there is growing evidence suggesting that it is useful to distinguish search for food patches from search within food patches (what Collier would refer to as procurement). Furthermore, it has been suggested that search for food patches has been the main topic of study for investigators using mazes of various sorts, whereas search for food within a patch (procurement) has been the main topic of study for investigators using operant chambers (Mellgren & Olson, 1983; Olson & Maki, 1983).

EXPERIMENTAL SITUATIONS

There are two endpoints on a continuum of situations for testing models based on OFT. Field work on foraging offers the uncontested advantage of ecological validity. Laboratory simulations of foraging problems allow for control and precision of measurement usually unobtainable in the field. The most restrictive form of laboratory simulation involves using the operant chamber and imposing conditions normally associated with search by having the subject wait for a discriminative stimulus to appear, which would simulate arrival at a patch (e.g., Kamil & Yoerg, 1982; Killeen, Smith, & Hanson, 1981) or discovery of a prey item (Lea, 1979). The distinguishing characteristic that such simulations lack is the spatial distinctiveness usually associated with food sources in the natural environment (Baum, 1983). It has been demonstrated that the spatial separation of two keys may affect the conformity to the matching law of pigeons pecking at a response key in operant chambers (Baum, 1982; Boelens & Kop, 1983).

We believe that experimental situations that mimic the natural environment with respect to the spatial distinctness of food locations while maintaining the control of the laboratory situation will be most effective in testing models of OFT. Some laboratory procedures for studying foraging have a spatial component, whereas lacking spatially distinct prey locations or patches from which the subject may *choose*. Baum (1983) had pigeons fly to a location where they could then procure prey. Mellgren and Olson (1983) had rats run to a location where they then had to dig in sand for buried prey.

Mellgren (1982) reported an experiment in which the environment included multiple spatially distinct food sources (patches). These consisted of plastic boxes containing food pellets buried in sand. Each of nine patches was placed in a distinct geographical location and the subjects foraged by visiting the patches and digging for the available food. Travel costs between patches were deter-

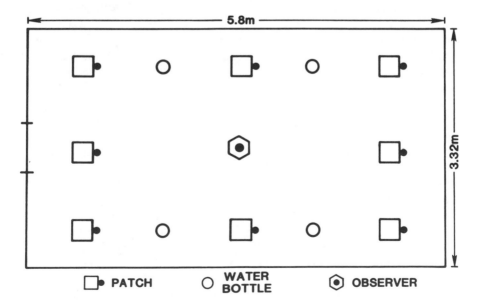

FIG. 7.1.   A floor plan of the experimental room.

mined by the distance involved (a large room was used) and by obstructions on the floor. Because of the long distances between patches and the obstructions on the floor, it was not possible for the experimenter to observe the subjects directly during foraging bouts. Thus, the data collected were limited to the patches visited and the amount of food obtained in each.

In the experiments described in this chapter, a smaller sized room was used and travel cost between patches was manipulated by requiring the subject to climb a vertical pole to reach the patch. Eight patches (plastic boxes) were available, each placed on a ledge that was attached to a vertical board that had nails partially driven into its length to form a ladder for climbing. The location of each pole-patch in the room is shown in Fig. 7.1. A more complete description of the room and the design may be found in Mellgren, Misasi, and Brown (1984).

This seminaturalistic situation allows for the spatial distinctiveness of food sources, and choice between food sources. But, because the distances are not great, an experimenter can record order of visits to patches, duration of stay, time to travel between patches, and number of prey consumed in each patch. Consideration is now given to OFT and what is expected of the behavior of an optimizing subject in this experimental situation.

Optimality Theory: Patch Utilization

The situation just described (one of patchily distributed prey) has received a good deal of theoretical attention. A main concern of theoretical development has been the nature of the decision rule the optimal forager should use to "decide" when to leave one patch in search of another. An early speculation as to this rule was that the predator would form a number expectation based on experience with available prey. "Hunting by expectation" means that the forager would utilize a patch until a fixed number of prey was obtained and then move off to look for a new patch (Gibb, 1962). This decision rule can maximize rate of energy gain only for the special situation when each patch contains nearly equal numbers of prey and the predator does not revisit patches. If the variability of number of prey per patch is substantial, then a hunting-by-expectation strategy is clearly inappropriate.

In a seminal paper, Charnov (1976) proposed the "marginal value theorem" as the optimal solution to the problem of determining how predators "decide" when to leave one patch to look for another. The idea is that, if we look across a habitat with a large number of patches, the average value of the patches can be estimated. Leaving a patch when the first derivative of the equation describing cumulative prey obtained over time equals the overall rate of gain for the environment provides a mathematical solution to the optimization problem. McNamara and Houston (this volume) provide a useful discussion of the marginal value theorem.

Krebs, Ryan, and Charnov (1974) presented data that supported an implication of the marginal value theorem. According to their analysis, the marginal value will be reached when the interval between successive prey captures reaches a criterion duration that is the same for all patches. This duration between the time that the last prey is captured and the predator's exit from the patch was referred to as the *giving-up time* (GUT) and, because it is potentially easily measured in the field or the lab, it has received considerable experimental attention (e.g., by Krebs, 1974; Smith & Dawkins, 1971).

Recently, McNair (1982) has challenged the appropriateness of GUT as an implication of the marginal value theorem. He has argued that residence time—total time spent in a patch before leaving—is the appropriate measure for testing the marginal value theorem. Iwasa, Higashi, and Yamamura (1981) claim that the optimal decision of when to leave a patch depends primarily on the spatial distribution of prey between patches.

Although there is controversy over the exact form taken by the optimal solution for foraging in a patchy environment, there is qualitative agreement with respect to general behavioral predictions. For example, as distance between patches (or costs of traveling between patches) increases, the residence time should increase.

The fact that different interpretations of optimality theory lead to very similar behavioral predictions has long been known in human-decision theory (von Winterfeldt & Edwards, 1973). The problem is that of the "flat maxima." Here a hypothetical set of behavioral strategies, each of which may be represented by different mathematical formulations, leads to roughly equivalent efficiency of behavior. Although there is one strategy that is optimal, there are several strategies, the application of which will approximate the same outcome and therefore be virtually indistinguishable from one another.

In the present context there were eight patches constituting the habitat. The behavior of main concern was how the forager utilized the patches when the number of prey initially available in each was variable. It is assumed that the forager is able to assess the overall rate of capture in the habitat. It also is assumed that as the prey in a patch are depleted, the time required to find the next prey item increases (on the average). A pilot study done under conditions where the forager was observed directly through plexiglas patch walls supports this assumption. For a patch with 20 prey items, a plot of interprey capture times as a function of the ordinal number of prey captured (the first, second, third, fourth, etc.) showed a linear relationship with a slope of 1.2.

Using the approach of curve fitting and adjustments to the curve based on energy cost considerations has been one method for making a quantitative test of an optimal-foraging theory model (Cowie, 1977). We choose to develop an alternative model of optimal-foraging theory to apply to our data for several reasons. First, the interprey capture interval in our pilot studies must be obtained under considerably different conditions than those in force in the foraging situation. Curve fitting based on the pilot study data to explain the actual foraging performance would be imprecise. Second, a number of parameters must be estimated using the curve-fitting approach and these parameters may or may not reveal important relationships between environmental conditions and the mechanisms of foraging (i.e., the parameters of the fitting equation do not represent some underlying mechanism directly related to foraging). In the approach we develop there is a direct and simple interpretation of the single free parameter used to fit the data. In a classic paper, Greeno and Steiner (1964) argued that having "observable states" for free parameters in a model allows for the most powerful test of a model. A model that has observable states is one in which the parameters must be in a one-to-one relationship with the theory and change in value in a predictable (qualitative) fashion as a result of changed conditions in the experiment. The model we develop meets these criteria. Finally, time-in-patch was used by Cowie as the data to be fit by his model, and we felt that time-in-patch was not the most precise data for testing the theory in our experimental situation because it included time spent foraging and also time spent in other activities such as grooming, monitoring the environment, etc. In the situation we use, the patches are boxes raised off the ground and therefore may serve not only as food sources, but also as "look-out posts." Thus, for our experimental situation time-in-patch was not necessarily the most accurate measure of patch utilization, and therefore we develop a model based on number of prey captured rather than time-in-patch as the dependent variable.

In his influential paper, Charnov (1976) assumed the forager is sensitive to the time between successive prey captures and may adopt a criterion time, called the giving-up time (GUT) that is the interval between captures for giving-up and leaving for another patch that leads to maximum long-term rate of gain. Attempting to observe directly the times between successive prey captures was impossible because of the obtrusiveness of the experimenter required by such observation. In addition, the stochastic nature of prey capture in the present situation makes questionable a direct application of Charnov's model to these data. However, we base our model on the assumption that the forager is sensitive to the time between successive prey captures. On the average, if patch exploitation is random rather than systematic, the interval between successive prey captures will reach the forager's criterion for giving-up when the patch has been depleted to a particular number of prey left. When this number of prey remains in the patch, the average interval between the end of handling the last prey and the capture of the next one exceeds the criterion interprey capture time (like Charnov's GUT). The number of prey left is called the left-over constant (LOC) because it should be the same between patches regardless of the number of prey available at the start (Krebs, Stephens, & Sutherland, 1983; Mellgren, 1982; Mellgren, Misasi, & Brown, 1984).

The LOC is a free parameter, to be estimated by using the available data. To use the data from the experiment to estimate a model parameter may seem like "cheating," but, in fact, the best available procedure for estimating parameters of a model must be used if an appropriate test of the model is to be made (see Restle & Greeno, 1970). If suboptimal parameter-estimation procedures are used and the model fails to fit, it will not be known whether the model or the parameter-estimation value is at fault.

The estimate of the LOC is made by calculating the a (= number of prey obtained per foraging session averaged across sessions), subtracting it from b (= the total number of prey available on each session), and dividing the difference by c (= the number of patches):

$$\text{LOC} = \frac{b - a}{c}. \tag{1}$$

A simple example might help to illustrate the LOC calculation. Suppose there are only three patches in the habitat, containing 15, 10, and 5 prey, respectively. In 10 foraging sessions the subject obtains an average of 20 prey per session. Thus, $a = 20$, $b = 30$, and $c = 3$, consequently LOC = 3.33. Therefore, the forager would average 11.67 prey taken from the 15 prey patch, 6.67 from the 10 prey patch, and 1.67 from the 5 prey patch.

The LOC model assumes that the value of the LOC is a function of several variables. For example, for a given environment, individuals who have greater energy requirements will have smaller LOCs than those with lower requirements. Such differential requirements could be due to different body sizes, metabolic rates, degrees of deprivation, etc. For an individual forager the LOC should increase with changes in environmental conditions such as reduced travel distances between patches, decreased risk of predation while traveling, and increased procurement (handling) time or effort. Mellgren et al. (1984) have shown that the predicted change in value of the LOC parameter was confirmed for differing travel requirements.

It should be noted that in order to get the LOC model and parameter estimation of equation (1) to work, the subject must visit all patches in the environment. Obviously this is not a good assumption if only one foraging session is considered. For this reason we average the utilization of each patch across several sessions for an individual subject. Thus the value of a in equation (1) is obtained by dividing the number of prey obtained by the number of times the patch was visited (not the number of foraging sessions unless the patch was visited on every session). It would not make sense to include occasions when a patch was not visited in our estimate of patch utilization.

If the number of prey initially available in each patch is plotted on the x-axis of a graph and the average number obtained is on the y-axis, this model of foraging predicts a linear relationship with a slope equal to 1.0 and y-intercept equal to $-\text{LOC}$. That is,

$$Y = -\text{LOC} + X + \epsilon \tag{2}$$

according to the LOC model of optimal-foraging theory. This relationship can be tested by first determining whether the relationship between number of prey available per patch and number obtained is indeed linear. Given that it is linear, then a test of the adequacy of the model can be made by comparing it to the least-squares linear-regression equation,

$$Y = \beta_0 + \beta_1 X + \epsilon \qquad (3)$$

where β_0 and β_1 are least-squares estimates of the y-intercept and the slope. The difference in number of free parameters between (2) and (3) is 2 (therefore, there are 2 degrees of freedom) and the error term from a standard analysis of variance has the number of observations made minus 2 as the degrees of freedom for making the model comparison.

Optimal Search

Patch utilization has been the topic of considerable theorizing and optimal-search strategies have also received corresponding attention (Krebs, 1978, gives a useful summary). At least one difficulty in the "search literature" is that the distinction between searching within a patch (procurement) and searching between patches (travel) is often not made. Thus, the finding that a stickleback increases the tortuosity of its movement after encountering a prey item may reflect a within-patch search (Thomas, 1974) rather than a between-patch search. Area-restricted search as evidenced by increased tortuosity has received considerable theoretical and empirical attention (Krebs, 1978). In an environment where prey within a patch do not replenish during each foraging period and the number of patches is large (so that repeat visits to patches within a foraging bout are not profitable), the best search strategy is to try new, unvisited patches (the so-called win-shift strategy, Olton, Handlemann, & Walker, 1981) and avoid those that have already been utilized. Thus, for the situation described here, the forager should choose a previously unvisited patch for each of the first eight patches visited. Although only a trivial mathematical derivation is needed to describe such perfect accuracy, it should be noted that what is demanded of the forager in order to achieve this accuracy is not trivial.

The extensive work done by Olton and his co-workers as well as numerous other investigators indicates that, when rats are confronted with eight options in a radial arm maze, their behavior approximates the optimal-search strategy, showing only a small probability of repeating visits to previously visited arms (e.g., Olton & Samuelson, 1976). Olton, Handelmann, and Walker (1981) have pointed out the importance of the radial arm maze data for foraging theory. In the present experiment the patch choices are spread over a 30-minute foraging session, so the rats' memory for places previously visited is severely tested (e.g., Olton, Walker, Gage, & Johnson, 1977).

Experimental Test of the LOC Model: Predictable versus Unpredictable Prey-Density Locations

The general procedure and the room have already been described. Hooded laboratory rats of Long–Evans descent (*Rattus norvegicus*) were selected as subjects because they are well adapted to the presence of humans, a great deal is known of their behavioral capacities in controlled situations, and they are well suited for both climbing and digging. Previous research had shown that foraging sessions every 12 hours would insure a fairly stable weight when all food is obtained in the experimental situation (e.g., in a closed economy, Hursh, 1980). Thirty-minute foraging sessions at approximately 0800 and 2000 hours were used. Each subject was individually placed in the foraging room with freshly provisioned patches, and the experimenter recorded the foraging activities of the subject with a stop watch (for timing).

Initially, there were 20 prey items available in each patch. The "prey" were a compressed cereal-grain food of somewhat variable size called Purina Startina. To insure that the rats had extensive experience with the foraging situation, they were allowed 12 hours of foraging time for a number of sessions. When it was clear that they were utilizing virtually all the food available during each foraging session, the time allowed for foraging was reduced to 30 minutes. The first phase of the experiment began by randomly distributing either 6, 8, . . . 20 (increments of 2) prey items into each of the eight patches. For 16 consecutive foraging sessions, the amount of food available in a particular location was systematically varied so that each location twice contained each number of prey. The number of prey in each patch was not predictable by the subject.

The second experimental phase also lasted for 16 foraging sessions, but the number of prey available in a particular location remained constant for all sessions. Each subject had a different, randomly determined distribution of prey items.

Phase 3 lasted for eight sessions and the number of prey available in each patch was randomly determined, and each patch location contained each number of prey once during the eight sessions of this phase.

Phase 4 also lasted for eight sessions and the number of prey available in each patch was randomly determined but remained constant for the eight sessions of this phase.

In sum, in Phases 1 and 3 the number of prey items available in a particular location varied systematically from session to session, whereas in Phases 2 and 4 the number of prey items available in a particular location was randomly determined but remained constant across the sessions of that phase.

The results of this experiment are shown in Figs. 7.2 and 7.3. The LOC model fits the data very well in the cases of Phases 1, 2, and 3 but statistically fails to fit the data of Phase 4. The LOC estimate is shown on each panel of Figs.

7.2 and 7.3. In all cases, the linear-regression component was highly significant whereas second-order (and higher order) regression was not. A comparison of the LOC model with the least squares regression analysis showed no significant differences between them at the .05 level of significance for Phase 1, $F(2,105)$ = 2.46 and $F(2,99)$ = 1.89 for subjects A and B, for Phase 2; $F(2,93)$ = 2.41 and $F(2,76)$ = 1.98, and for Phase 3, $F(2,50)$ = 1.17 and $F(2,49)$ = 1.05. Deviations from the LOC model were significant in Phase 4, $F(2,47)$ = 4.64 and $F(2,39)$ = 4.84, $ps < .05$. Thus, when a particular number of prey available has a fixed location across foraging sessions, the subject's utilization of the prey may or may not fit the LOC model, but when the number of prey and their location in the room is varied across sessions, the subjects do utilize the available prey in a manner consistent with the LOC model.

Exploratory data-analysis techniques on Phase 4 were done to determine if the order of visits to patches might somehow account for the discrepancy of patch utilization from the LOC model during this phase. Although the order of visit-patch utilization relationship was not helpful in understanding why under conditions of constant density location in Phase 4 there were significant deviations from the LOC model predictions, the analysis revealed a striking relationship between order of visit and geographical location. The four patches located in the

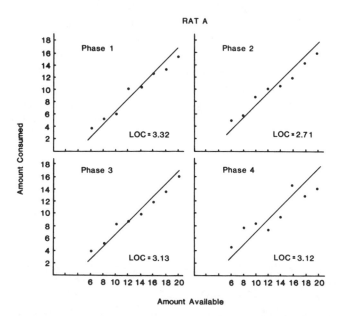

FIG. 7.2.   Mean number of prey consumed as a function of number available for subject A. In Phases 1 and 3 the location of a particular patch magnitude varied across sessions, but in Phases 2 and 4 the location of a patch magnitude remained constant for all sessions.

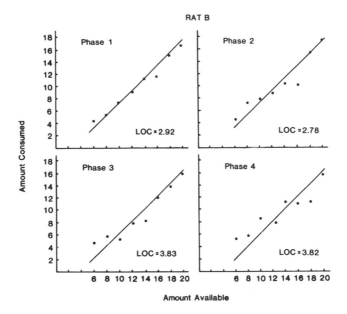

FIG. 7.3.   Mean number of prey consumed as a function of number available for subject B. In Phases 1 and 3 the location of a particular patch magnitude varied across sessions, but in Phases 2 and 4 the location of a patch magnitude remained constant for all sessions.

corners of the room had uniformly lower ranks (were visited first) than the noncorner ("wall" for convenience) patches. The probability of visiting a corner patch as a function of order of visit is shown in Fig. 7.4. The strong preference for corner patches is not dependent on the subject's having a high degree of hunger at the start of a session. Of the 20 patch revisits occurring near the end of sessions when the subject should have been reasonably satiated, 90% of them were revisits to a corner patch. Thus, the geographical location in the room was an important factor in determining the order of patch visits, but no consistent relationship was found between corner patches and predicted utilization of available prey. Deviations in utilization from that predicted by the LOC model were positive (the forager ate too much) in 3 of 4 corner cases for subject A, but negative (the forager ate too little) in 3 of 4 corner cases for subject B.

The memory capacity of these subjects appears to be excellent with respect to their ability to avoid revisiting patches within a session. The probability of a revisit as a function of ordinal visit number is shown in Fig. 7.5, for each of the 4 phases of the experiment.

It is interesting that the subjects show such an excellent memory for spatial locations within a foraging session as evidenced by the lack of repeat visits but show no alterations in the order of visiting patches from one session to the next

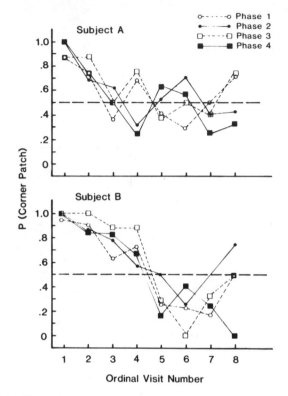

FIG. 7.4. The probability of visiting a corner patch plotted as a function of ordinal visit number. The dashed horizontal line represents no preference.

("search strategy") when the number of prey in a location was constant from session to session (i.e., Phases 2 and 4). Several exploratory analyses were done to determine if constant location of amounts of prey (Phases 2 and 4) resulted in altered search strategies. For example, it might be expected that the patches containing larger numbers of prey would be visited earlier in the session than those containing smaller numbers of prey. To test this hypothesis, we differentiated large from small patches by defining the large as those containing 20, 18, 16, or 14 prey items. We then counted the number of visits to large patches for the first four patch visits each session (2 would be expected by chance). Phase 2 lasted for 16 sessions, so a "learning effect" would be reflected by an increase in the number of large patches visited in the first four visits from the first 8 sessions to the last 8. One subject increased from 2.33 to 2.50, but the other decreased from 2.25 to 1.75 on this measure. During Phase 4 (8 sessions) there were means of 2.25 and 1.50 for visiting large patches in the first four visits of the sessions. Of course if the subjects were able to visit all 8 patches on each foraging session, then it might not make any difference if the larger patches were visited first or last. In fact, they did not typically visit all 8 patches within a session. The means for number of patches visited in Phase 2 were 6.38 and 5.31 (medians of 6 and 5) and were 6.50 and 5.63 in Phase 4 (medians of 6.5 and 6).

The fact that revisits could only occur on a 30-minute time scale and altered search strategies had to occur at 12-hour intervals suggests the possibility that multiple-memory systems may exist, one for more short-term problems and one for long-term ones. The idea that different memory systems are utilized depending on the duration of the interval has been well documented in the verbal learning abilities of humans (e.g., Baddeley, 1966). Another basis for different memory functions may be the distinction between memory for locations that have been visited within a foraging bout and memory for number of prey available at the locations from one bout to another. In this case it is the *function* of the

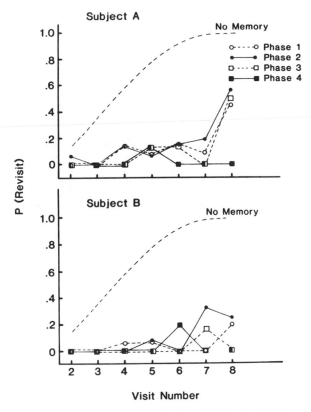

FIG. 7.5.   The probability of a revisit as a function of ordinal visit number for each of the four phases of the experiment. Note that a perfect memory is represented by zero revisits. The "no-memory" line assumes random sampling of patches with replacement.

memory system rather than the temporal duration of the sytem that is the distinguishing characteristic. Because memory for visits within a foraging bout involve a shorter time scale than memory for visits between foraging bouts, it may be difficult to distinguish temporal effects from functional effects in an experimental analysis.

Search Versus Procurement

In attempting to account for the deviations from the LOC model, it was discovered that the subjects had a strong preference for visiting patches in the corner of the room first and visiting those with only one wall in close proximity last (see Fig. 7.4). Although the order of searching is strongly influenced by the thigmotactic tendencies of rats, it is not clear if the procurement of food from a patch is also affected by the corner-wall factor. In order to evaluate this possibility, an experiment was conducted in which 4 amounts of prey were made available in the 8-patch habitat. There were 4, 8, 12, or 16 prey (Startina pellets), one amount in a corner patch and one in a wall patch on each session. The location of a particular concentration of prey changed from session to session, but there was always one corner and one wall patch with identical numbers of prey available.

A total of 6 rats was used in this experiment: 3 males and 3 females. Foraging sessions occurred every 12 hours for 30 minutes each. The data reported here were taken from a 16-session phase of the experiment where the number of prey available in a particular location changed randomly between sessions, but one 4-prey patch was located in a corner and the other along a wall, one 8-prey patch was located in a corner, and the other along a wall, and so on.

Consistent with the results of the previous experiment, these rats showed a preference for visiting corner patches first. Both males and females showed this preference.

Another way of demonstrating the preference for corner patches is to consider the *total* number of prey eaten from corner and wall patches. Figure 7.6 shows that, for each discrete number of prey available, there was more eaten from corner than from wall patches. This was due to the greater frequency of visiting corner patches. With respect to *mean* amount eaten, there was no difference between corner and wall patches averaged across male and female subjects (means for corner and wall for the 4, 8, 12, and 16 prey magnitudes were: 1.79–1.44, 4.12–4.46, 7.33–7.72, and 10.92–10.39, respectively). The total amount eaten between corner and wall patches differed because of the differential frequency of visits to them. But if procurement (i.e., behavior in the patch) alone is considered, the way in which the subjects utilized the food available in a patch was not a function of its location. Thus it can be concluded that searching for and procuring food were independent processes, search being influenced by the structure of the room, procurement being unaffected by the structure.

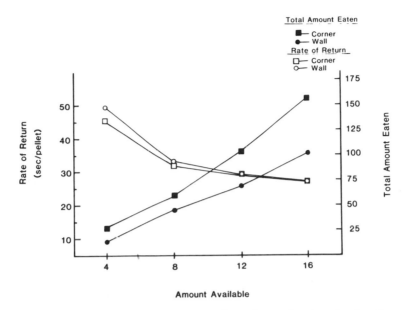

FIG. 7.6.   Total number of pellets eaten and rate of return plotted as a function of number available for corner, as opposed to wall, patches. Higher numbers of pellets were consumed in corner than in wall patches (closed symbols), but the rate of procurement was virtually the same regardless of location (open symbols).

It has been suggested that those variables that influence search may have different effects on procurement (Maki, Gustavson, Berglund, Thom, 1983; Mellgren & Olson, 1983; Olson & Maki, 1983). This experiment provides further support for this suggestion.

Summary and Conclusion

The approach represented by the LOC model is clearly different than other modeling approaches associated with the optimal-foraging perspective. Rather than searching for a detailed set of parameters that describe energy costs, caloric intake, etc. and then trying to fit a curve to data using parameters based on those estimated from extraexperimental contexts, the LOC model requires only one parameter to be estimated and the relationship between observed and predicted is completely specified. The modeling approach that utilizes a small number of parameters, estimated from existing data, and involving a quantitative evaluation of data versus theoretical prediction, has a long history in the "math models" approach within psychology (e.g., Atkinson, Bower, & Crothers, 1965; Restle & Greeno, 1970; Wickens, 1982). A one-parameter model is more parsimonious than a multiparameter model and is falsifiable in the logical positivist sense. The tradition within psychology has been to reduce behavior to the most fundamental processes and to then use these processes to describe (predict) behavior (performance). Within behavioral ecology, models have been developed to describe foraging behavior based on multiple parameters that determine performance. These parameters (caloric value of food, energy expended, etc.) may or may not reflect mechanisms that the animal actually uses in making foraging decisions. The differences in approaches are rooted in the historical heritage of each discipline. The behavioristic tradition of animal psychology is based on the premise that behavior is reducible to a set of basic, universal principles that underlie behavior. These basic principles are presumed to have generality across species and situations. This approach does not preclude exceptions and idiosyncratic phenomena but does emphasize the study and importance of common determinants of behavior. Behavioral ecology is a product of ethology and biology that stresses the uniqueness of species and the functional relationship between ecology and behavior. Because each organism occupies a unique niche, it may be assumed that each species has a unique set of principles that determines its behavior.

The translation of each of these traditions into models of foraging is exemplified by the LOC model developed in the present chapter for the animal psychology tradition and the curve-fitting models of Cowie (1977) and Kacelnik (1984) for the behavioral ecology tradition. At the present state of knowledge it seems reasonable to entertain both approaches because each has the potential of being useful in revealing the nature of the variables determining effective foraging behavior. With continued interactions between behavioral psychologists and behavioral ecologists as exemplified by this volume, the distinction between mechanisms accounting for behavior and the description of behavior (performance) will be clearer than in the past and the mechanistic-performance approaches will be understood to be compatible, not antagonistic.

The development of the LOC model based on optimal-foraging theory serves two functions in the work reported here. First, it suggests a methodology that includes aspects of both the natural and the laboratory environment. Second, it provides a yardstick for evaluating the foraging efficiency of the subject. Through the use of the LOC model of OFT as a criterion, the importance of various environmental constraints was revealed.

Patch location was an important variable because when patch density and patch location remain constant, the LOC model may fail to fit the patch utilization data, whereas, when patch density was systematically varied across all locations, the LOC model did fit the patch-utilization data. A search for the reason that constant locations of patch densities may result in a poor fit revealed that the subjects tended to go first to patches located in the corners of the room. Nevertheless, this preference for first searching corner patches did not result in the forager's overutilizing the food available in those patches. Thus, deciding which patch to go to is affected by the proximity of two walls but the utilization of available food in the patch is not. This conclusion is not inconsistent with the optimal-foraging perspective, but it does suggest that the currency that is optimized may be made up of several components.

The results suggest that those parameters that determine where to search for food and those that determine the extent of utilization of a discovered food source may be independent of each other. Mellgren and Olson (1983) have previously argued for making a distinction between search and procurement behaviors based on differential effects on each behavior as a function of the same independent variable manipulation. The present experimental results are consistent with the claim for making this distinction.

ACKNOWLEDGMENTS

We gratefully acknowledge the assistance of the following individuals: Linda Misasi, Maribeth Smith, Randy Stratton, and Michael Williams. The research was supported by the University of Oklahoma Research Council.

REFERENCES

Amsel, A. (1967). Partial reinforcement effects on vigor and persistence. In K. W. Spence & J. T. Spence (Eds.), *The psychology of learning and motivation* (Vol. 1, pp. 1–65). New York: Academic Press.

Atkinson, R. C., Bower, G. H., & Crothers, E. J. (1965). *An introduction to mathematical learning theory.* New York: Wiley.

Baddeley, A. D. (1966). Short-term memory for word sequences as a function of acoustic, semantic, and formal similarity. *Quarterly Journal of Experimental Psychology, 18,* 362–365.

Baum, W. M. (1982). Choice, changeover, and travel. *Journal of the Experimental Analysis of Behavior, 38,* 35–49.

Baum, W. M. (1983). Studying foraging in the psychological laboratory. In R. L. Mellgren (Ed.), *Animal cognition and behavior* (pp. 253–283). Amsterdam: North-Holland.

Boelens, H., & Kop, F. M. (1983). Concurrent schedules: Spatial separation of response alternatives. *Journal of the Experimental Analysis of Behavior, 40,* 35–45.

Capaldi, E. J. (1967). A sequential hypothesis of instrumental learning. In K. W. Spence & J. T. Spence (Eds.), *The psychology of learning and motivation* (Vol. 1, pp. 67–156). New York: Academic Press.

Charnov, E. L. (1976). Optimal foraging, the marginal value theorem. *Theoretical Population Biology, 9,* 129–136.

Collier, G. H. (1980). An ecological analysis of motivation. In F. Toates & T. Halliday (Eds.), *Analysis of motivational processes* (pp. 125–151). London: Wiley.

Collier, G. H. (1982). Life in a closed economy: The ecology of learning and motivation. In M. D. Zeiler & P. Harzem (Eds.), *Advances in analysis of behavior. Vol. 3: Biological factors in learning* (pp. 223–274). London: Wiley.

Cowie, R. J. (1977). Optimal foraging in great tits (*Parus major*). *Nature, 268,* 137–139.

Domjan, M. (1983). Biological constraints and the pursuit of general theories of learning. In R. L. Mellgren (Ed.), *Animal cognition and behavior* (pp. 319–344). Amsterdam: North-Holland.

Gibb, J. A. (1962). L. Tinbergen's hypothesis of the role of specific search images. *Ibis, 104,* 106–111.

Grant, D. S., & Roberts, W. A. (1976). Sources of retroactive inhibition in pigeon short-term memory. *Journal of Experimental Psychology: Animal Behavior Processes, 2,* 1–16.

Greeno, J. G., & Steiner, T. E. (1964). Markovian processes with identifiable states: General considerations and applications to all-or-none learning. *Psychometrika, 29,* 309–333.

Hursh, S. R. (1980). Economic concepts in the analysis of behavior. *Journal of the Experimental Analysis of Behavior, 34,* 219–238.

Iwasa, Y., Higashi, M., & Yamamura, N. (1981). Prey distribution as a factor determining the choice of optimal foraging strategy. *American Naturalist, 117,* 710–723.

Johnston, T. D., & Turvey, M. T. (1980). A sketch of an ecological metatheory for theories of learning. *The Psychology of Learning and Motivation, 14,* 147–205.

Kacelnik, A. (1984). Central place foraging in starlings (*Sturnus vulgaris*). I. Patch residence time. *Journal of Animal Ecology, 53,* 283–299.

Kamil, A. C., & Yoerg, S. J. (1982). Learning and foraging behavior. In P. P. G. Bateson & P. H. Klopfer (Eds.), *Perspectives in ethology* (Vol. 5, pp. 325–364). New York: Plenum.

Killeen, P. R., Smith, J. P., & Hanson, S. J. (1981). Central place foraging in *Rattus norvegicus. Animal Behaviour, 29,* 64–70.

Krebs, J. R. (1974). Colonial nesting and social feeding as strategies for exploiting food resources in the great blue heron. *Behaviour, 51,* 99–134.

Krebs, J. R. (1978). Optimal foraging: Decision rules for predators. In J. R. Krebs & N. B. Davies (Eds.), *Behavioural ecology: An evolutionary approach* (pp. 23–63). Sunderland, MA.: Sinauer.

Krebs, J. R., Ryan, J. C., & Charnov, E. L. (1974). Hunting by expectation or optimal foraging? A study of patch use by chickadees. *Animal Behaviour, 22,* 953–964.

Krebs, J. R., Stephens, D. W., & Sutherland, W. J. (1983). Perspectives in optimal foraging. In A. H. Brush & G. Clark (Eds.), *Perspectives in ornithology* (pp. 165–216). Cambridge: Cambridge University Press.

Lea, S. E. G. (1979). Foraging and reinforcement schedules in the pigeon: Optimal and non-optimal aspects of choice. *Animal Behaviour, 27,* 875–886.

Maki, W. S., Gustavson, C., Berglund, P., & Thom, J. (1983, November). *A laboratory model of foraging within and between patches.* Paper presented at the meeting of the Psychonomic Society, San Diego, CA.

McNair, J. N. (1982). Optimal giving-up times and the marginal value theorem. *The American Naturalist, 119,* 511–529.

Mellgren, R. L. (1982). Foraging in a simulated natural environment: There's a rat loose in the lab. *Journal of the Experimental Analysis of Behavior, 38,* 93–100.

Mellgren, R. L., Misasi, L., & Brown, S. W. (1984). Optimal foraging theory: Prey density and travel requirements in *Rattus norvegicus. Journal of Comparative Psychology, 98,* 142–153.

Mellgren, R. L., & Olson, M. W. (1983). Mazes, Skinner boxes, and feeding behavior. In R. L. Mellgren (Ed.), *Animal cognition and behavior* (pp. 223–252). Amsterdam: North-Holland.

Olson, D. J., & Maki, W. S. (1983). Characteristics of spatial memory in pigeons. *Journal of Experimental Psychology: Animal Behavior Processes, 9,* 266–280.

Olton, D. S., Handelmann, G. E., & Walker, J. A. (1981). Spatial memory and food searching strategies. In A. C. Kamil & T. D. Sargent (Eds.), *Foraging behavior: Ecological, ethological and psychological approaches* (pp. 333–354). New York: Garland STPM.

Olton, D. S., & Samuelson, R. J. (1976). Remembrance of places passed: Spatial memory in rats. *Journal of Experimental Psychology: Animal Behavior Processes, 2,* 97–116.

Olton, D. S., Walker, J. A., Gage, F. H., & Johnson, C. T. (1977). Choice behavior of rats searching for food. *Learning and Motivation, 8,* 315–331.

Restle, F., & Greeno, J. G. (1970). *Introduction to mathematical psychology.* Reading: Addison–Wesley Press.

Robbins, D. (1971). Partial reinforcement: A selective review of the alleyway literature since 1960. *Psychological Bulletin, 76*, 415–431.

Smith, J. N. M., & Dawkins, R. (1971). The hunting behavior of individual great tits in relation to spatial variations in their food density. *Animal Behaviour, 19*, 695–706.

Thomas, N. (1974). The influences of encountering a food object on subsequent searching behavior in gasterosteus aculeatusl. *Animal Behaviour, 22*, 941–952.

von Winterfeldt, D., & Edwards, W. (1973). *Flat maxima in linear optimization models* (Contract No. N00014-67-A-0181-0049). Ann Arbor: University of Michigan. Engineering Psychology Laboratory.

Wickens, T. D. (1982). *Models for behavior*. San Francisco: W. H. Freeman.

III OPERANT AND PAVLOVIAN PROCESSES

8 Mechanisms of Signal-Controlled Foraging Behavior

Michael E. Rashotte
Jeffrey M. O'Connell
Veljko J. Djuric
Florida State University

INTRODUCTION

It seems likely that in some foraging situations predators learn that certain types of feeding opportunities are signaled by the occurrence of environmental events. For example, Black-capped Chickadees learn that damaged leaves signal the presence of palatable caterpillars (Heinrich & Collins, 1983), and resident frugivorous birds may learn that changes in the nutritional value of ripening fruit are signaled by conspicuous changes in the color of the fruit (Stiles, 1982, 1984). The opportunity to learn that environmental events signal feeding opportunities is often explicitly arranged in laboratory simulations of foraging. Indeed, a predator's responsiveness to environmental signals is a principal datum when simulations are employed to test predictions derived from foraging models. For example, in many operant simulations where colored keylights signal differentially valued feeding opportunities, pigeons peck directly on the colored response key in order to indicate their willingness to accept the signaled feeding opportunity (see, for example, Fantino and Lea & Dow, this volume).

Although signal-controlled behavior seems to figure prominently in many settings where foraging is studied, and although it seems to involve learning, there has been little attempt to consider it from the viewpoint of research and theory about mechanisms of learning. This is partly because most foraging theories are functional in character, concerned with the ultimate causes rather than the mechanisms of behavior. However, the desirability of a mechanistic account of foraging is recognized, (e.g., Krebs, Houston, & Charnov, 1981; MacNamara & Houston, 1980), and the present chapter is intended to contribute to the development of such an account by examining the relationship between foraging behavior and the mechanisms of learned signal-controlled behavior as they have been understood by experimental psychologists. The main emphasis in this chapter is on mechanisms that can be identified in operant simulations of foraging. These simulations provide a good starting point for a mechanistic analysis because the procedures employed in them overlap greatly with the procedures employed in traditional experiments on mechanisms. This overlap facilitates the posing of some basic questions about mechanisms of signal-controlled performances in the foraging simulations and, by implication, in natural foraging.

TWO MECHANISMS OF LEARNED SIGNAL-CONTROLLED PERFORMANCE

For over 8 decades, the field of animal learning has been concerned with mechanisms of adaptive behavior (Mackintosh, 1974). As a result of this work there is a large body of research, theory, and experimental methodology, some of which might pertain to a mechanistic theory of foraging behavior. Notable points of contact between animal learning and foraging have already been made (e.g., Collier & Rovee-Collier, 1981; Hollis, 1982; Kamil, 1983; Krebs, 1978; Lea, 1983; Shettleworth, 1983), and some points of difficulty in the budding relationship have been thoughtfully analyzed (Kamil & Yoerg, 1982). Two ideas about mechanisms that influence the learned performances controlled by environmental signals are reviewed in the present section in order to provide background for experimental studies that are summarized later in this chapter.

One idea comes from research on Pavlovian conditioning (Pavlov, 1927). In the basic Pavlovian experiment, an animal experiences two events in succession, such as the illumination of a light followed by the presentation of food. The events are scheduled to occur independently of the animal's behavior. Through repetition of the events, the animal learns that opportunities to eat are signaled by the occurrence of the light and, as a result, the behavior of the animal changes in the presence of the light. The theoretical analysis of such learned behavioral reactions is usually made in terms of a learned association between the light and the food (termed, respectively, the *CS* and the *US*). The association is presumed to make it possible for presentation of the light to activate a neural representation of the food (Mackintosh, 1983; Rescorla, 1980). The process by which such a CS-activated representation of food exerts an influence on performance is not understood. However, there are many specific circumstances in which the effects of Pavlovian signals are well documented. In one that is of particular interest here, the CS occurs at a spatially localized site in a situation where the animal is free to move about. In those circumstances, animals of many species approach and direct consummatory responses towards a CS that signals food, and they withdraw from the vicinity of a CS that is explicity correlated with the absence of food (Hearst & Jenkins, 1974; Locurto, Terrace, & Gibbon, 1981).

As applied to foraging behavior, Pavlovian learning provides a mechanism by which an environmental event could activate a neural representation of prey items the predator has previously experienced in conjunction with that event. Damaged leaves, the color of fruit, and the sight of other animals in a certain feeding posture exemplify the kind of natural events that might signal differential feeding opportunities. They would be possible candidates for Pavlovian learning. Experimental analogues of these natural signaling events often are arranged in foraging simulations where, for example, the color of a keylight signals a particular type of prey item that is available. A predator's reaction to natural signals or to experimental signals for food often involves no more than would be expected if a Pavlovian mechanism were operative: The predator approaches and (if the situation permits) contacts the signal, or it withdraws from the vicinity of a signal indicating that no food is present. It seems reasonable, therefore, to consider the possibility that a Pavlovian learning mechanism influences signal-controlled foraging behavior.

A different mechanism derives from operant-conditioning research. The idea here is that the animal can learn *what to do in order to obtain food,* rather than simply learning about the properties of the signalled feeding opportunity as the Pavlovian mechanism allows. The experimental situation in which this "discriminative stimulus" (S^D) mechanism is identified is one where the animal is able to procure food by performing a designated response in the presence of a stimulus; when that stimulus is absent, the response is ineffective in producing food (Skinner, 1937, 1938). A large research literature indicates that animals learn to respond primarily when the stimulus is present, and there seem to be few limitations on the nature of the behaviors that can be bought under the control of an S^D (e.g., Honig, 1966; Honig & Staddon, 1977). Certainly, the range of behavioral topographies that can be controlled by an S^D goes well beyond the set of approach/contact/withdrawal behaviors that characterize motor reactions controlled by Pavlovian CSs. For example, an S^D might control intricate sequences of fine-motor manipulative responses that, in some situations, might be necessary to gain access to food. For reasons of experimental convenience, however, the behavioral repertoire employed in studies of discriminative stimuli is often confined to the relatively limited instances of motor behavior that comprise the Pavlovian set. Although the behavioral effectiveness of an S^D is well documented, the exact nature of the learning process that underlies its effectiveness is not well understood (e.g., Holland, 1983; Jenkins, 1977).

With regard to foraging behavior, the S^D mechanism is one by which the occurrence of an environmental stimulus could set the occasion for a specific foraging strategy that had previously resulted in prey capture under similar stimulus conditions. Viewed from a more cognitive perspective, the S^D mechanism could inform a predator about the behaviors that had been required to search for, procure, and handle the prey items found in similar stimulus conditions during past foraging episodes. Such information, about what might be called the "behavioral costs" of foraging, could influence the decisions that an experienced predator makes about whether or not to accept a particular feeding opportunity.

Although the CS and the S^D mechanisms of signal-controlled behavior are often studied separately, experimental psychologists have long recognized the possibility that both mechanisms could operate simultaneously in many situations (Hull, 1930, 1931, Mackintosh, 1983; Overmier & Lawry, 1979; Staddon, 1983); that is, a signal could inform the animal about *the properties of an expected feeding opportunity* (the CS mechanism) and about *the behavioral reaction that will deal efficiently with that opportunity* (the S^D mechanism). One question addressed in the present chapter concerns the extent to which both mechanisms operate in laboratory simulations of foraging behavior.

ECONOMIC CIRCUMSTANCES, FORAGING SIMULATIONS, AND THE STUDY OF BEHAVIOR MECHANISMS

The CS and S^D learning mechanisms described in the previous section have been studied under experimental conditions that differ in many ways from those under which the mechanisms might operate in natural foraging situations (Moran, 1975). In the typical experiment, an animal's body weight is reduced to about 80% of the free-feeding weight by restricting access to food. Experimental sessions last for only a short time each day, usually an hour or two, during which the animal obtains only a part of its already limited daily ration of food. The experimenter provides the remainder of the ration in the animal's home cage shortly after each daily session is completed.

One way to characterize the differences between the conditions in studies of mechanisms and those in natural foraging situations is in terms of the economic circumstances that each offers to the animal (Hursh, 1980). A distinction is made between closed and open economies. Natural situations are closed economies because in them the animal is responsible for obtaining all of its food through foraging behavior. The conditions of traditional mechanistic studies are open economies because in them the animal's total daily intake of food does not depend entirely on its behavior during the experimental sessions. In fact, the animal's body weight is explicitly held at some constant level by extraexperimental feedings.

For present purposes, the significance of this economic distinction lies in the fact that some familiar parameters of operant reinforcement schedules appear to have quite different behavioral effects in closed and in open economic circumstances (Hursh, 1980). Accordingly, in designing operant simulations for the study of mechanisms of signal-controlled foraging behavior, the choice of economic circumstances may be an important determinant of the kind of results obtained. Collier has pioneered in the use of closed-economy simulations in which the animal spends all 24 hours of each day in the experimental situation (e.g., Collier & Rovee-Collier, 1981; see also Logan, 1960, 1964). In these simulations, operant procedures are used to mimic various conditions of resource availability and, in many simulations, feeding opportunities are explicitly signaled by environmental events. The experimental work on mechanisms of signal-controlled foraging behavior that is summarized in the present chapter was conducted with pigeons living in such 24-hour, closed-economy circumstances. The intention was to bridge the economic gap between traditional mechanistic studies and the conditions in which natural foraging occurs.

In order to simulate foraging in the laboratory, it is necessary to partition foraging episodes into component parts and to identify specific experimental events that serve as analogues of each component. There are several schemes for partitioning foraging episodes (e.g., Collier & Rovee-Collier, 1981; MacArthur & Pianka, 1966; Orians, 1980; Schoener, 1971; Tinbergen, 1981). Figure 8.1 presents a scheme, based largely on Collier's partitioning, that represents the components of a foraging episode in a habitat where food is distributed in patches. The location of patches is assumed to be marked by distinctive features of the habitat ("patch signals") and, within a patch, the location of prey items is assumed to be signaled either by distinctive features of the prey items themselves or by spatially localized environmental stimuli such as damaged leaves ("prey signals"). The predator is assumed to be able to detect the relationships between these signals, on the one hand, and the behavioral responses and the feeding opportunities with which they are correlated.

Beginning at the top of Fig. 8.1, the predator is envisioned as initiating a foraging episode by traveling through its habitat after a transition from performing some other class of behavior, such as courtship. During its travels the animal encounters patch signals sequentially, identifying and rejecting some in favor of continued searching and, eventually, choosing to procure (i.e., to approach and enter) one of them. When the predator enters the stimulus context provided by a patch signal, the components of within-patch foraging can occur.

In the patch, the predator searches to identify stimuli correlated with the spatially localized prey items. Once the predator encounters such a stimulus, the within-patch foraging sequence involves rejection of that stimulus or attempted procurement of it, in which the predator approaches and contacts a prey item. Finally, the sequence progresses to the handling and the storage/consumption components. Most predators eat in discrete "bouts," at least when they live in laboratory circumstances where feeding opportunities can be searched out for many hours each day (e.g., Collier & Rovee-Collier, 1981). Accordingly, Fig. 8.1 shows that within-patch searching for prey signals might persist after the

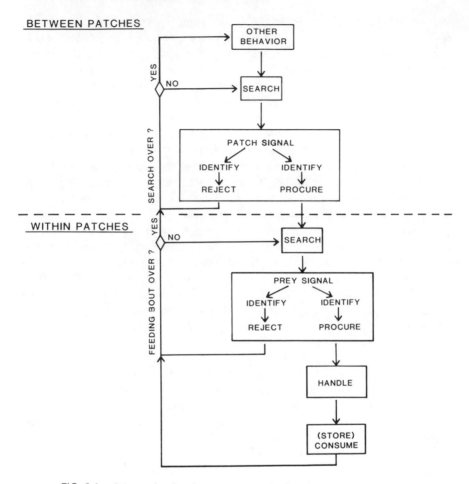

FIG. 8.1.   Scheme showing the components of a foraging episode.

consumption of a single prey item, continuing until the feeding bout is over. Then, the predator leaves that patch and travels to another one or returns to a behavior that does not involve foraging.

The basic experimental procedure used in the work described in this chapter illustrates one way that the partitioning scheme described in Fig. 8.1 is operationalized in laboratory simulations. Adult pigeons lived individually in chambers where an overhead light bulb was illuminated for 10 to 12 consective hours each day (depending on the experiment). The pigeons could initiate a foraging episode at any time in the light period by pressing some required number of times on a foot-treadle. In one of the experiments to be discussed, the pigeons worked through the complete hierarchical sequence shown in Fig. 8.1. In that case, presses were first required on one treadle in order to turn on a patch signal (a colored overhead light) that the pigeon could either reject (by continuing to treadle or by waiting a fixed period of time in order to terminate the signal) or procure (by pressing on the other treadle). When the patch was procured, the pigeon could begin within-patch foraging, which meant that it could search for signaled feeding opportunities by pressing on the second treadle some designated number of times. Within-patch foraging continued until the pigeon performed an explicit "patch exit" response (a return to pressing on the original treadle that terminated the current patch signal and allowed the animal to travel to other patches), or until it ceased foraging for a specified period of time.

In most of the experiments discussed in this chapter, however, patch signals were not included in the procedure and there was only one treadle in the chamber. In these cases, the pigeon was free to press the treadle at any time in order to "search" for signaled feeding opportunities in what is termed within-patch foraging in Fig. 8.1. The feeding opportunities were fixed-length periods of access to a hopper filled with mixed grains. The experimental analogues of the prey signals were always colored lights that illuminated a plastic response key on a wall 27.5 cm away from the treadle. Each keylight remained present for 10 seconds and its color was correlated with some aspect of the feeding opportunity, such as the duration of access to the food hopper. In most of the experiments, the keylights had a Pavlovian signaling relationship with the feeding opportunities. Consequently, the pigeon's behavior in the presence of the keylights did not affect the duration of the keylight or the presentation of the hopper. However, pecks made on the lighted response key were recorded as a measure of the strength of Pavlovian learning. In one experiment, the keylight was assigned an explicit S^D function: it signaled that the pigeon must *not* peck the key during the 10-second illumination period in order to receive the food at the offset of the keylight (an "omission" procedure). All the experiments included a variety of measures of feeding behavior because, as is explained in detail later, some important aspects of signal-controlled performance in these 24-hour closed-economy conditions seem to be closely related to the kinds of adjustments in feeding behavior that occur when various foraging circumstances are simulated.

It is emphasized that in the present foraging simulations it is the pigeon's pecking on colored keylights that is the signal-controlled behavior whose mechanisms are of primary interest. This type of signal-controlled behavior has been studied in a variety of open-economy simulations with pigeons (e.g., Fantino; Lea & Dow, this volume), and in some closed-economy circumstances, too (Fantino & Abarca, 1985; Lucas, 1981), but not from a mechanistic perspective. There is considerable evidence that when pigeons approach and peck on a keylight that signals access to grain, the topographical details of the behaviors are remarkably similar to those observed when pigeons react to a natural prey signal, the sight of grain at a distance (Goodale, 1983; Jenkins & Moore, 1973; LaMon & Zeigler, 1984; Zeigler, 1976; Zweers, 1982). In this respect, signal-controlled keypecking by pigeons seems to have ecologically relevant features that recommend it as a reasonable choice of response with which to begin a mechanistic analysis.

EXPERIMENTAL STUDIES OF CS AND S^D MECHANISMS IN CLOSED-ECONOMY FORAGING SIMULATIONS

Evidence for a CS Mechanism

The first indication that a Pavlovian mechanism could be responsible for the keypecking behavior of pigeons living in a closed-economy foraging simulation was provided by Rashotte, O'Connell, and Beidler (1982). Their experiments simulated only the within-patch sequence of events that was shown schematically in Fig. 8.1. In one experiment, the pigeons "searched" by performing a single treadle press that caused a keylight (CS) to be turned on. The color of the keylight signaled whether or not a feeding opportunity would become available at keylight offset.[1] Because the signaling relation was Pavlovian, the pigeons' behavior during the keylight had no influence on the duration of the keylight or on the likelihood that food would occur. However, the pigeon had to move across the chamber from the treadle to the hopper in order to eat, and it could minimize the delay to reach food by making its move during the keylight.

If Pavlovian learning occurred in this situation, the pigeon should approach and peck on keycolors that signal food. However, this same experimental arrangement might also permit the keylight to function as an S^D, even though this is not intended by the experimenter. Specifically, the keylight might signal the pigeon to approach the hopper in order to obtain food with the minimum of delay. If the keylight functioned as an S^D in this way, the pigeon would not peck when the keylight was presented but would position its head near the hopper.

In Rashotte et al.'s (1982) first experiment, there were two keycolors. One signaled food (CS+) and the other signaled no food (CS−). These two keycolors occurred equally often and in an irregular order across the sequence of trials that the animals produced each day by treadle pressing. In the experiment, the food hopper remained available for at least 60 seconds whenever it was presented and, if the pigeon ate during that time, the hopper presentation was extended until eating had ceased for 60 consecutive seconds. The results showed that all four pigeons in the experiment pecked on the CS+ keycolor, and that they did so at a higher rate than on CS−. These differential rates of pecking were maintained for about 2 weeks. When the signal–food correlation was then reversed (the former

---

[1]There was actually a sequence of two keycolors presented. The first keycolor was always the same and lasted for 20 seconds. It was followed immediately by one of two different 10-second keycolors that were differentially correlated with food or with no food. The role of the common stimulus is not relevant to the present considerations.

CS+ now signaling no food and the former CS− now signaling food), the rates of pecking on CS+ and CS− also reversed, indicating that the signal–food correlation was important in generating relatively high and sustained levels of pecking on the keylights. These findings demonstrate that a Pavlovian signal–food contingency is sufficient to establish and maintain signal-controlled key-pecking in a closed economy foraging simulation. There was also evidence that the pigeons did not move their head into the hopper area while CS+ was present, in contrast to what would be expected if the keycolor had acquired an S^D function.

In a second experiment, Rashotte et al. (1982) demonstrated the influence of a more subtle type of Pavlovian learning in which feeding opportunities are not directly involved. They arranged a Pavlovian "second-order conditioning" pro-cedure in which the pigeon's treadle-pressing occasionally produced trials on which one keylight (CS2) signaled only that another keylight (CS1) would soon be presented. CS1 was a well-established signal for food, but food was never presented on trials when that signal occurred in conjunction with CS2. The results showed that CS2 came to evoke keypecking responses by all three ani-mals studied, and a control condition indicated that this result was attributable to the Pavlovian pairings of CS2 with CS1. One implication of this finding is that Pavlovian learning could be responsible for signal-controlled behavior in forag-ing simulations even though food is not directly involved in the signaling rela-tionship. Other implications of this finding are discussed elsewhere (Rashotte et al., 1982).

In the Rashotte et al. experiments, the pigeons took advantage of the closed economy conditions to maintain their body weight and food intake at levels near those established in ad libitum feeding conditions. Also, the pigeons ate in several discrete "bouts" during the light period of each day. These feeding data indicate that the restrictions imposed on feeding and on body weight in open-economy experiments were truly absent here. Apparently, Pavlovian signal–food learning occurs readily in the relatively benign feeding conditions of the closed-economy foraging simulation.

Evidence for the Joint Influence of CS and S^D Mechanisms

There is much evidence that the keypecking behavior of pigeons is influenced by operant reinforcement contingencies in both open- and closed-economy foraging simulations (e.g., Abarca & Fantino, 1982; Lea, 1983; Lucas, 1981). It is possible, however, that some, or even most, of that keypecking is maintained by an unintended Pavlovian signaling relation between the keylight and the feeding opportunities (Moore, 1973). Just prior to the time that each feeding opportunity becomes available, the pigeon *must* be exposed to the lighted key on which it makes the final operant peck that causes food to be produced. Consequently, that keylight has an implicit Pavlovian signaling relation with food that might allow it to develop a CS function jointly with the experimentally specified S^D function. Rashotte and O'Connell (1986) employed the "omission procedure" as an analytical tool in order to explore whether a keylight in a closed-economy foraging simulation could control pecking through the *joint* action of CS and S^D mechanisms.

Four pigeons were studied in the experiment. Every time the pigeons completed six treadle presses, they produced one of three keycolors. One color was explicitly programmed to have an S^D function that is characteristic of omission schedules (e.g., Sheffield, 1965; Williams & Williams, 1969): In its presence, the pigeons were required *not* to peck the key in order to gain access to the food hopper at the end of the signal. If the pigeon pecked the lighted key, the hopper was not presented on that occasion, but if no peck was made, the hopper was presented at the time of keylight offset. A different keycolor (CS+) was programmed to have a Pavlovian function. Its occurrence simply indicated that the food hopper was likely to be presented at that keylight's offset, but the actual frequency with which food occurred was determined solely by the same pigeon's successes in obtaining food when the S^D was present; that is, whether or not the hopper was presented following a given CS+ presentation was determined by a yoking procedure that simply "replayed" the pigeon's own sequence of feeding opportunities that it had produced during earlier S^D presentations. On the average, the S^D presentations ran four trials ahead of the CS+ presentations. This arrangement guaranteed that at any given point in the experiment two of the keycolors had nearly identical histories of being paired with food, but one signal had a procedurally explicit S^D function and the other had a procedurally explicit Pavlovian CS+ function. The third keycolor was programmed as a Pavlovian CS− that simply signaled no food would be presented on that occasion. Throughout the experiment, the food hopper was presented for a fixed time of 10 seconds whenever the pigeons gained access to it.

The design of this experiment allows several comparisons of interest to a mechanistic analysis. If the S^D successfully informs the pigeons about what behavior is required in order to obtain food, they should learn not to peck the S^D color at all. In that event, the level of keypecking maintained by S^D should be less than or equal to that maintained by the CS−. Comparison of the levels of pecking maintained by S^D and by CS+ is also interesting because the yoking procedure ensures that the schedule of food presentations on CS+ trials will be identical to that on S^D trials. If the development of a Pavlovian function depends on the number of pairings of the keylights with food, CS+ and S^D should have equivalent Pavlovian status. For this reason, they should each control high, and approximately equivalent, levels of keypecking. The ability of the S^D to suppress keypecking should be judged with reference to the level of keypecking maintained by CS+, which presumably reflects the behavioral baseline against which the S^D function operates.

Figure 8.2 summarizes the results of the experiment by presenting representative data from an individual pigeon. The figure shows that, by the end of training, the pigeon pecked on only about 30% of the presentations of S^D and on about 95% of the presentations of CS+. The disparity in responsiveness to these two signals indicates that, in a closed-economy foraging simulation, an S^D mechanism can influence the behavior controlled by a keylight analogue of prey signals. However, the S^D was not successful in eliminating keypecking or even in reducing it to the level maintained by CS− and, therefore, the pigeon clearly failed to maximize its access to food by learning not to peck when S^D was present; that is, on the approximately 30% of trials on which the pigeon pecked on S^D, it cancelled the opportunity to eat that it had already gained by treadle pressing.

The fact that the pigeon was more responsive to S^D than one would expect if the S^D mechanism alone were controlling its behavior is understandable if keypecking were *jointly* controlled by the S^D and the CS mechanisms. On the 70% of occasions when the pigeon successfully used the information conveyed by the S^D in order *not* to peck, the resulting pairing of the keycolor with food could have been responsible for Pavlovian learning. As a consequence, whenever the S^D was presented, the S^D and CS mechanisms would compete for control of behavior and, for these reasons, the pigeons would be unable to maximize the frequency with which they gain access to food in the presence of S^D. Of course, the omission procedure is a laboratory tool for analyzing the different mechanisms of signal-controlled performance, and it is not meant to simulate a natural foraging circumstance. For present purposes, it is valuable because it reveals that

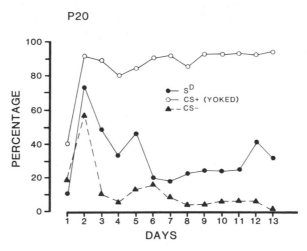

FIG. 8.2.   Keypecking by a representative pigeon in the omission experiment of Rashotte and O'Connell (1986).

CS and S^D mechanisms could jointly influence signal-controlled foraging behavior in closed-economy simulations. In this regard, the procedure helps identify the joint action of two mechanistic "rules of thumb" that can operate in foraging simulations (Houston, 1980).

Mechanisms of Signal-Controlled Foraging in Simulations Where the Duration of Feeding Opportunities is Uniform Within Days and Varies Between Days

Lucas (1981) reported that in a 24-hour closed-economy situation the rate at which pigeons pecked on a response key in order to make fixed-duration feeding opportunities available was inversely related to the duration of those feeding opportunities. In Lucas' experiments, keypecking was an operant response that had to be performed in accordance with the requirements of some schedule of reinforcement in order that a hopper filled with grain would be presented. The duration of the hopper presentations was always uniform on a given day, but between days the duration was varied in the range from 1.5 to 24 seconds. In an operant simulation with rats, Collier and Kaufman (cited in Collier, 1980) also found that the rate of barpressing was inversely related to the duration of the feeding opportunities available. Recently, Rashotte and O'Connell (in press) have demonstrated that even when a keylight has a Pavlovian-signaling relationship with food, the rate of keypecking is inversely related to the duration of the feeding opportunity signaled. This recent result raises the possibility that keypecking data of the sort Lucas described, and, possibly barpressing data of the sort obtained by Collier and Kaufman, reflect the influence of the Pavlovian mechanism of signal-controlled foraging behavior. Certain aspects of Rashotte and O'Connell's data also indicate that in order to understand the operation of the CS mechanism in closed-economy simulations such as these, it will be necessary to take into account various aspects of the pigeon's feeding behavior. The experiment and the main issues surrounding it are described here.

Rashotte and O'Connell (in press, experiment 1) studied 6 pigeons in a 24-hour closed-economy situation where the completion of six treadle presses at any time in the daily 12-hour light period resulted in the presentation of a keylight whose color identified which of three possible feeding opportunities would occur. One key color, CS+, was always followed by presentation of the food hopper. Another color, CS+/−, was a less reliable predictor of food: food or no food followed this keylight equally often in a quasirandom sequence across trials. Finally, a third color, CS−, was never followed by food. The likelihood of encountering CS+/− was twice as great as for the other stimuli in order to allow experimental comparisons that are not of primary interest here.

In four separate experimental phases, each lasting about 10 days, the hopper was presented for one of four durations. For half the pigeons, the initial duration was the shortest one (3 seconds), and it was increased to 7.5 seconds, then 30 seconds, and finally to an unlimited duration across the phases. The remaining pigeons experienced the same four durations, but in a decreasing sequence (unlimited, 30, 7.5, and 3 seconds). The unlimited duration was operationalized by presenting the hopper for a minimum of 30 seconds on each trial and, if the pigeon ate during that interval, by leaving the hopper present until the pigeon stopped eating for 30 consecutive seconds. In practice, the pigeons averaged about 140 seconds of eating time per hopper presentation in the unlimited condition.

The main results of the experiment are summarized in Fig. 8.3. Panel A shows the rate of pecking on each of the three keycolors. These data are averaged across all six animals and across the last 4 days of each phase. The most striking feature of the data is that the rate of pecking to the signals for food (CS+ and

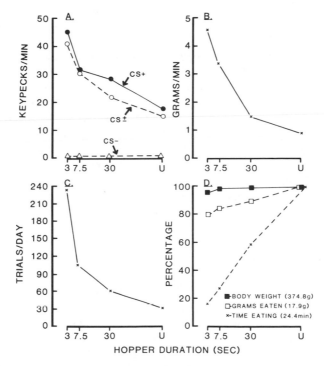

FIG. 8.3.   Keypecking and feeding behavior in the experiment of Rashotte and O'Connell (in press). The rate-of-eating data shown in panel B were computed by dividing "total number of grams of food eaten each day" by "total amount of time the photobeam in the raised food hopper was interrupted each day." Each measure in panel D is expressed as a percentage of the value recorded at the unlimited duration. Absolute values at the unlimited duration are given for each measure in parentheses.

CS+/−) was inversely related to the duration of the hopper presentations. This effect was large and statistically significant and it is similar to Lucas' (1981) operant keypecking data. Two other aspects of the keypecking data shown in panel A deserve brief note. One is that at every duration of hopper presentation the pigeons pecked at a higher rate on CS+ and CS+/− than they did on CS−. The other is that the CS+ and CS+/− curves did not differ statistically. These two findings indicate, respectively, that a keylight must be correlated with feeding opportunities in order to support signal-controlled pecking, and that the present manipulation of signal–food reliability had no impact on the strength of signal-directed behavior.

The other panels of Fig. 8.3 summarize some aspects of feeding behavior in the experiment. Both the average rate at which the pigeons consumed grain from the hopper (panel B), and the average number of trials produced by the pigeons each day (panel C), were inversely related to the duration of the hopper presentations. Lucas (1981) found similar effects in his operant keypecking experiment. Panel D presents three additional measures, each expressed as a percentage of the level achieved when the duration of access to the hopper was unlimited. At the shorter durations of hopper presentation, the time spent eating each day (cumulative time the photobeam in the raised hopper was interrupted) decreased as much as 80%, the amount of food eaten decreased by about 20%, but the greatest body weight loss was only about 5%. Apparently, the reason the pigeons were able to maintain relatively high levels of food intake in the face of the severe reduction in feeding time (panel D) was that the overall rate at which they consumed the grain increased so greatly (panel B). The relatively small decrease in body weight under these feeding conditions is consistent with the fact that the pigeon's body weight is very resistant to change when food intake is reduced (e.g., Lucas, 1981; Rashotte, 1985; Zeigler, Green, & Siegel, 1972).

From the perspective of Pavlovian theory, the inverse relationship between rate of keypecking and duration of hopper presentation that is shown in Fig. 8.3 is surprising. As a general rule in Pavlovian experiments, the amount of conditioned behavior evoked by a CS is directly related to the size of the food item signaled (e.g., Mackintosh, 1974), and this includes experiments on signal-directed keypecking with pigeons (O'Connell & Rashotte, 1982). Some factors that might have contributed to the inverse relationship between keypecking and the duration of feeding opportunities do not seem to play an important role. In particular, a variety of data indicate that the trial frequency (panel C) is unlikely to be a major influences on rate of keypecking (Lucas, 1981; Rashotte & O'Connell, in press). Also, the fact that very little body-weight loss occurred (panel D) indicates that increased motivation is not responsible for the enhanced rate of keypecking at the shorter hopper durations, at least when motivation is operationalized in the traditional way by the percentage of loss in body weight. The most interesting possibility is that the rate at which food is consumed from the hopper (panel B) determines the rate at which the pigeon pecks on the keylight. In traditional Pavlovian terms, this amounts to saying that the characteristics of the unconditioned response (eating) determine the characteristics of the conditioned response (keypecking). In the present case, the short-duration feeding opportunities may trigger an increased rate of eating that, in turn, enhances the rate at which the key is pecked (Rashotte & O'Connell, in press). The closed economy seems to offer more opportunity for the pigeon to alter its eating rate in response to experimental manipulations than is the case in open-economy situations where the birds are kept in a chronic state of hunger. To the extent that this is true, the present line of reasoning suggests that in an open economy, it may be difficult or impossible to obtain an inverse relationship between the rate of pecking on a Pavlovian keylight and the duration of hopper presentations.

Rashotte and O'Connell's (in press) data suggest that Pavlovian learning might have been a factor in other 24-hour closed-economy simulations where the duration of the feeding opportunities was varied between days. Lucas' (1981) operant simulation in which pigeons were required to peck on a lighted key in order to gain access to the hopper has been described earlier. In Collier and Kaufman's (cited in Collier, 1980) simulation, rats barpressed in order to obtain a fixed time of access to food. In that experiment, the rate of barpressing was inversely related to time of access (range: 0.5 minutes to 64 minutes). Because of the operant contingencies imposed in Lucas' and in Collier and Kaufman's experiments, the rate of responding directly affected the availability of food. In Rashotte and O'Connell's experiment, of course, the Pavlovian contingency ensured that keypecking was completely nonfunctional. Collier and Kaufman interpreted the increased rate of barpressing in their experiment as being in agreement with a theoretical prediction that the rats would defend the rate of caloric intake per unit of time. Rashotte and O'Connell's experiment implies that a Pavlovian mechanism of signal-controlled performance could mediate this defense of intake. From a mechanistic perspective, the bar in an operant procedure can be viewed as a stimulus that rats always encounter shortly before they eat food, and it has been recognized, and empirically demonstrated, that this inherent Pavlovian relation between the bar (as a signal) and the opportunities to eat may influence the barpressing performance that is maintained by operant schedules (e.g., Locurto, 1981). On these grounds, Rashotte and O'Connell's (in press) keypecking data suggest that the increased levels of barpressing observed in Collier and Kaufman's procedure could at least partly reflect the influence of a Pavlovian mechanism. A similar account of Lucas' operant keypecking is possible as well. Apparently, in foraging simulations where the duration of the signaled feeding opportunities available is uniform, predators respond more vigorously to the signals as the duration of the feeding opportunities is reduced. The mechanism underlying this change in signal-controlled behavior may be Pavlovian.

The CS Mechanism as a Factor in Simulations That Test Optimal-Diet Models

Optimal-diet models make predictions about the conditions under which a predator will include differentially valued prey items in its diet (Charnov, 1976). These predictions have sometimes been tested with pigeons in operant simulations where colored keylights signal the value of feeding opportunities that are currently available. In order to procure a feeding opportunity, the pigeon must peck on the signaling keycolor according to the requirements of some operant reinforcement schedule. The probability that the pigeon pecks on the various keycolors is the behavioral indicant of the pigeon's willingness to include the differentially valued feeding opportunities in its diet (e.g., Abarca & Fantino, 1982; Lea, 1979).

For example, Lea (1979) tested some predictions in an open-economy foraging simulation where the behavioral cost involved in finding prey items was varied across phases of the experiment. Lea required the pigeons to wait for a specified period of time in a "search state" before a peck on a white keylight would result in the presentation of a red or a green keycolor. Both keycolors signaled that a brief period of access to a grain hopper was available, but the red color indicated a short delay to food and the green color indicated a long delay. Accordingly, the red and the green keycolors signaled feeding opportunities with high and low relative values, respectively. When the pigeon saw one of the colored keylights, it was able to accept or reject the available feeding opportunity by keypecking. In order to accept the feeding opportunity signaled, it pecked on the keycolor and thereby initiated the delay period. At the end of the delay, the pigeon gained access to the food hopper by pecking on the colored key once again. In order to reject the signaled feeding opportunity, the pigeon pecked on the white key and immediately was returned to the search state where it was required to wait the specified time until another keypeck could produce a red or a green keycolor on the next trial.

The manipulation of primary interest in Lea's (1979) experiment concerned the effect of varying the length of time the pigeon was required to search before a keycolor would be presented. From the perspective of a cost–benefit analysis, the "cost" of searching increased as the time spent in the search state increased. Given the theoretical assumption that the pigeons will maximize rate of energy intake per unit time, optimal-diet models make it possible to pinpoint that duration of time in the search state at which it would become profitable for the pigeon to include the long delayed (hence lower valued) feeding opportunity in its diet. More specifically, the pigeon should not peck on the green keycolor when the time required to find other feeding opportunities is short, but it should always peck on that keycolor once the required search time exceeds some critical length. The search time should not affect the pigeon's acceptance of the high-valued feeding opportunity; the red keycolor should always be pecked when it occurs.

The results of Lea's experiment did not show the step-function change in responsiveness to the green keycolor that was predicted by optimal-diet theory. Instead, the likelihood that the pigeons would peck on that keycolor increased gradually as the search time increased. The implications of Lea's (1979) and of others' similar findings for optimal-diet models are discussed in detail elsewhere (e.g., Abarca & Fantino, 1982; Fantino & Abarca, 1985; Lea, 1979). The question of interest here concerns the mechanisms of signal-controlled behavior that operate in simulations where the behavioral costs involved in finding prey items are manipulated. In particular, might the effect of different search costs on the pigeon's responsiveness to a keycolor that signals a relatively low-valued feeding opportunity reflect the operation of the Pavlovian CS mechanism? A large experimental literature indicates that the length of time animals are forced to wait between signals for food in Pavlovian experiments has an important effect on responsiveness to those signals (e.g., Gibbon & Balsam, 1981; Jenkins, Barnes, & Barrera, 1981; Mackintosh, 1974). The general direction of the effect is similar to Lea's: There is heightened responsiveness as the waiting time increases. It is rare, however, that a Pavlovian experiment requires the animal to perform some motor response in the time between signals in order to make the signal–food pairings occur. In the few cases where this has been done (e.g., Ellison & Konorski, 1964; Jenkins, Barrera, Ireland, & Woodside, 1978), the behavioral cost of producing the Pavlovian signals has not been studied. Consequently, it is uncertain how the pecking controlled by Pavlovian keylights would be affected by behavioral costs incurred in producing the keylight–food pairings. Recently, several closed-economy experiments conducted in this laboratory with pigeons have investigated this question. As discussed later, these findings suggest that Pavlovian learning may mediate at least some of the signal-controlled keypecking on which operant tests of optimal-diet theory have depended.

A good illustration of the kind of result obtained in these experiments is found in O'Connell's (1985) dissertation research. During each foraging episode in his simulation, the pigeons completed the entire hierarchical sequence of foraging that was described in Fig. 8.1. By pressing on one treadle a fixed number of times, the pigeons could "travel" between two separate patches. The color of an overhead light that was turned on by these treadle presses identified which one of two patches had been encountered. In both patches, high- and low-valued feeding opportunities could be searched out by performing the treadle-press response. These two feeding opportunities were equally likely to occur and were signaled in a Pavlovian fashion by different keycolors. The value of the feeding opportunities was manipulated by varying the duration of the hopper presentation: A 30-second presentation defined the high-valued opportunity and a 3-second presentation defined the low-valued opportunity.

For purposes of the present discussion, the most interesting aspect of O'Connell's procedure was that different behavioral costs of searching out individual feeding opportunities were imposed in the two patches. The search cost was manipulated by varying the number of treadle presses that produced each of the keylight–hopper pairings. Across successive phases of the experiment, the cost of searching in one patch varied whereas it remained fixed at a low value in the other patch. The question of interest concerned how the search cost affected the pigeons' responsiveness to the Pavlovian keylights and to the feeding opportunities themselves in the two patches.

Pertinent data from a representative pigeon in O'Connell's experiment are presented in Fig. 8.4. The upper panels show how the pigeon responded to the Pavlovian keylights in the patch where the search cost varied across phases (left-hand panel) and in the patch where the search cost remained fixed at a low value (i.e., three treadle presses were always required to produce each keylight–food pairing; a fixed-ratio 3 schedule). The data indicate that, in both patches, the pigeon always pecked on the keycolor that signaled the high-valued feeding opportunity (open circles). However, the likelihood that the pigeon would peck on the keycolor that signaled the low-valued feeding opportunity in each patch (closed circles) depended on the search cost in the respective patches. When the

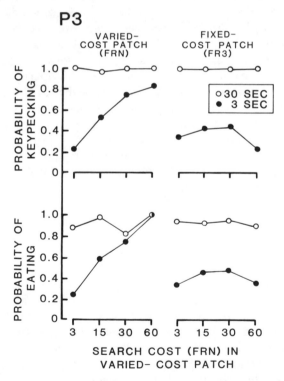

FIG. 8.4.   Keypecking and eating in two patches by a representative pigeon in O'Connell's (1985) experiment. The eating data are based on responding during the first 3 seconds of each hopper presentation.

search cost was lowest (FR3) in the varied-cost patch, the pigeon pecked on about 20% of the occasions on which the low-valued keycolor occurred, but when the search cost increased to FR15, FR30, and finally to FR60, the pigeon gradually became more responsive to that keycolor. At FR60, it pecked more than 80% of the times that keycolor occurred. Figure 8.4 shows that the effect of varying the search cost was confined to the varied-cost patch. In the fixed-cost patch, the pigeon always responded on a low percentage of occasions when the keycolor that signaled the low-valued feeding opportunity occurred. One implication of these results is that the pigeon's keypecking is not governed by the average search cost in the habitat, but by the localized search costs in the various patches it encounters.

O'Connell's (1985) keypecking data, which are very similar to Lea's (1979), demonstrate that when differentially valued feeding opportunities are encountered with equal frequency in a patch, the likelihood that the pigeon will respond to a keycolor that signals a low-valued feeding opportunity is greatly influenced by the costs involved in finding another feeding opportunity. Apparently, this effect of search cost is the same whether it is operationalized by specifying the time to be spent (Lea) or the number of responses to be made (O'Connell) in the search state. More importantly, this effect of search cost is the same whether the pigeon is *required* to peck on the keycolor in order to indicate its acceptance of the feeding opportunity (Abarca & Fantino, 1982; Fantino, this volume; Fantino & Abarca, 1985; Lea, 1979; Lea & Dow, this volume) or whether the keycolor simply has a Pavlovian signaling relationship with the feeding opportunity (O'Connell). The possibility suggested by these findings is that in operant foraging simulations that are designed to test optimal-diet theory, the signal-controlled keypecking behavior on which the test hinges could originate from a Pavlovian learning mechanism. Because signal-controlled lever pressing by rats is also known to be influenced by Pavlovian signaling relations (Locurto, 1981), it seems possible that the Pavlovian mechanism operates in closed-economy tests of optimal-diet theory where rats are required to press a lever in order to include a signaled feeding opportunity in their diet (Kaufman, cited in Collier & Rovee-Collier, 1981). If a Pavlovian mechanism *is* responsible for these kinds of signal-controlled behaviors, the mechanistic "rule of thumb" responsible for prey selection in these simulations would be one that simply involves learning *to expect a particular kind of feeding opportunity* (the CS mechanism) rather than learning *what to do in order to get food* (the S^D mechanism).

Another aspect of O'Connell's data is notable because it provides striking evidence that keylights with a Pavlovian signalling relation play a functional role in closed-economy foraging simulations. He measured the probability that the pigeons ate from the food hopper during the first 3 seconds of each feeding opportunity. Because the high- and low-valued feeding opportunities were identical during the first 3 seconds, a pigeon's decision to eat or not had to be based on information provided by the keylight about the duration of the impending hopper presentation. The data are shown in the bottom panels of Fig. 8.4 where it is clear that the probability of eating when the low-valued feeding opportunity occurred was affected by search cost in the same manner as was the probability of pecking on the Pavlovian keylights. The functional significance of the Pavlovian CSs is clearly indicated by the fact that on a sizable proportion of the low-valued feeding opportunities that were produced when the search cost was low, the pigeon didn't even bother to eat when the food hopper was presented.

The likelihood of keypecking and of eating when the pigeons encountered a low-valued feeding opportunity were each influenced in the same way by the search cost manipulation in O'Connell's (1985) experiment. On the basis of the present data it cannot be determined whether search cost acts directly on both keypecking and eating, or whether it acts directly on only one of those behaviors, the other one changing as a consequence of the changes in the first (e.g., search cost might directly affect some aspect of feeding behavior that, in turn, mediates the changes in keypecking). An answer to this question could be useful in understanding the mechanisms of signal-controlled keypecking in this type of simulation.

Fine-Grained Analysis of the Pigeon's Feeding Behavior in a Closed Economy: Effects of Search Cost

One change in feeding behavior that is reported when food becomes less readily available in a 24-hour closed-economy simulation is that pigeons eat at a faster rate when food is presented (Lucas, 1981; Rashotte & O'Connell, in press). The measurement of eating rate in these previous reports has been derived from two measures: the amount of food consumed during the entire day, and the time spent eating each day as estimated from photobeam breaks in the food hopper. Using a new measurement technique, Djuric (1984) has recently obtained some relatively detailed information about how the pigeon's eating rate changes when different search costs are imposed in a 24-hour closed-economy foraging simulation. His findings represent the kind of information that might ultimately be valuable for understanding the mechanisms of signal-controlled foraging behavior.

Djuric suspended a standard food hopper from an electronic load beam that was monitored by a computer in order to measure the hopper's weight on a continuous basis (Smith, Rashotte, Austin, Henderson, Oliff, & Bloom, 1984). The resolution of the weighing system was 0.10 grams and the weighing accuracy was 0.01 grams. The hopper contained only Canadian peas instead of the usual mixed-grains diet in an attempt to minimize differences in the topography of food pecks made by the pigeons when they were eating seeds of different sizes (Zeigler, 1976; Zweers, 1982). On the average, the Canadian peas weighed about 0.10 grams, which meant that the system was nearly capable of detecting the removal of individual peas from the hopper. It could also measure the time at which individual pecks were made in the food hopper. Using the peck-time and the amount-removed data that were obtained during each feeding opportunity, it was possible to quantify several measures of feeding behavior that contribute to the increased rate of eating observed when the search cost is relatively high.

In the experiment, Djuric trained four pigeons to press a treadle during the 10-hour light period of each day in order to produce a hopper presentation that was signaled by a keycolor. The food hopper was always presented for 15 seconds, and the pigeons were free to produce the hopper as often as they wished. The manipulation of interest was the cost of producing the hopper which was increased across successive phases of the experiment from FR3, to FR15, and finally to FR30. (Subsequently, the original FR3 search cost was imposed and the original baseline of feeding behavior was recovered. The recovery data are not discussed here.)

Djuric (1984) found, as expected, that as the search cost increased, the pigeons produced fewer feeding opportunities each day and ate at a faster rate when food became available. Figure 8.5 presents a detailed picture of how the increased rate of eating was accomplished. Panel A simply quantifies the increased eating rate. It shows that there was approximately a three-fold increase in the number of grams consumed during the actual time spent eating on each trial when the search cost was raised from FR3 to FR30. The pigeons accomplish this increase by reducing the latency with which they begin to eat on each feeding opportunity, and by spending a greater portion of the 15-second period of each hopper presentation engaged in actual eating behavior (panel B). However, it is also clear that they increase their rate of food intake by making more pecks in the hopper per unit time of eating (panel C), and by improving the efficiency with which they handled the food, picking up more grams of food per peck at the high search costs (panel D). In all the measures shown in Fig. 8.5, the effect of search cost had a statistically significant effect. However, there were some suggestions

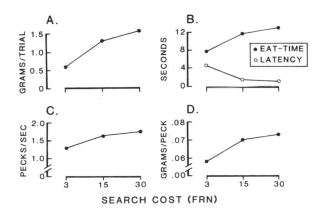

FIG. 8.5.   Feeding behavior at three different search costs as measured with an electronic weighing device in Djuric's (1984) experiment.

in the data that the overall increase in feeding rate might be achieved in different ways by individual pigeons. For example, one pigeon increased its handling efficiency more than the rate at which it pecked at food in the hopper, whereas another did the reverse.

Djuric's (1984) data indicate that various aspects of the pigeon's feeding behavior change in response to a change in the cost of finding food in 24-hour closed-economy foraging simulations. From a mechanistic perspective, these findings are interesting because they raise questions about which of these changes, if any, are causally related to the changes in signal-controlled keypecking that are observed at various search costs. It is possible, for example, that the likelihood of pecking on a keycolor is determined by the rate at which pecks are made at food when the grain hopper is presented following that keycolor. It will be interesting to see the extent to which the currently available array of keypecking data from both closed- and open-economy simulations can be understood in terms of the relationship between feeding behavior and keypecking. The nature of a mechanistic account of signal-controlled foraging behavior seems likely to be influenced by the way that relationship operates, whether it is the Pavlovian CS mechanism, the operant S^D mechanism, or some other one that is involved.

CONCLUSION

The experiments summarized in the present chapter indicate that in a closed-economy foraging simulation, pigeons approach and peck on a keycolor encountered during a search for food if, in the past, that keycolor has had a Pavlovian signaling relationship with opportunities to eat. Furthermore, the keypecking that occurs on the Pavlovian signal is affected by changes in the value of the feeding opportunity signaled, and by changes in the cost involved in searching for those opportunities, in essentially the same way as has been reported in other simulations where pecking was established and maintained by an operant reinforcement contingency. The operant contingency would seem to require that the pigeon learn *what to do* in the presence of the keylight in order to obtain food (the S^D mechanism), but in Pavlovian signaling situations the pigeon would seem to learn only *to expect food* when the keylight occurs (the CS mechanism). The similarity between the behavioral effects observed in the two cases suggests several possibilities about the mechanisms of signal-controlled keypecking in operant simulations of foraging.

One possibility is that the operant and the Pavlovian procedures do, in fact, engage different mechanisms of signal-controlled performance, but that in the typical simulation where keypecking is studied, the behavioral effects of the mechanisms cannot be differentiated without analytical techniques such as the omission procedure. When that procedure was employed in one of the simulations summarized here, it was possible to show that the pigeon can learn *what to do* in order to obtain food when a keylight is present. However, in many experimental situations the omission procedure is one in which the S^D mechanism competes with the CS mechanism for control of keypecking, and in the present omission experiment the S^D mechanism was not able to dominate completely. In these experimental circumstances, at least, joint control by the S^D and CS mechanisms seems indicated.

There is another interpretation of the similarity between the keypecking that occurs in Pavlovian procedures and the keypecking that occurs in traditional operant simulations. It is that the CS mechanism alone is responsible for keypecking in the operant simulations. This interpretation is consistent with the view that many instances of keypecking performance that occur when operant contingencies are imposed in open-economy experiments result from the CS mechanism (Moore, 1973). Certainly, the Pavlovian repertoire of signal-controlled motor behavior (i.e., approach to, contact with, and withdrawal from signals) encompasses the behaviors demanded of pigeons in most operant simulations. This fact indicates that for purpose of understanding the limitations of the CS mechanism in operant simulations, signal-controlled behavior should also be studied in simulations where the responses required of the animal are not included in the Pavlovian set (cf. Jenkins, 1977). It may be noted, however, that a substantial portion of the foraging behavior of many species in natural situations could be accounted for by a Pavlovian mechanism (Hollis, 1982).

It might be argued that the Pavlovian mechanism has been selected for its energetic advantage, although there is no evidence that bears on the question of whether the energetic costs involved in learning *what to do* (the S^D mechanism) are different from those involved in learning *to expect food* (the CS mechanism). Conceivably, predators could rely on Pavlovian learning as a mechanistic rule of thumb that guarantees, say, maximum net energy returns from signal-controlled foraging behavior in most circumstances. When the situation requires behavior other than those in the Pavlovian set, however, predators may be able to fall back on the (possibly more costly) S^D mechanism in order to achieve the best returns possible. General questions about the costs involved in learning, and specific questions about the costs involved in using some learning mechanisms rather than others in certain foraging situations, are ones that deserve attention (Orians, 1981).

Some of the experimental results summarized in this chapter suggested that an understanding of the mechanisms of learned signal-controlled foraging behavior will require a better understanding of the relationship between that behavior and the feeding behavior that occurs following the signals. Djuric's (1984) detailed measurements of the pigeon's eating behavior in closed-economy foraging simulations represent one kind of data that should be useful in this work. For example, Rashotte and O'Connell (in press) have discussed how some basic questions about the Pavlovian mechanism could be resolved if the time-course of the changes in feeding behavior and in signal-controlled keypecking that occur immediately following a shift in search cost were known. Another example is provided by O'Connell's (1985) experiment, summarized earlier, in which it is theoretically important to know how keypecking relates to various aspects of feeding beheavior in patches where different search costs are imposed.

The CS and S^D mechanisms of signal-controlled behavior that have been examined in the context of closed-economy foraging simulations in the present chapter comprise only a small fraction of the behavioral mechanisms studied by experimental psychologists. In considering only these two mechanisms here, and only in a limited number of situations, it is difficult to judge how much the animal learning literature can contribute to the development of a mechanistic theory of foraging. However, earlier attempts to account for adaptive behavior in terms of traditional mechanisms of learning and motivation indicate that it will be difficult to account for instances of complex behavior (Amsel & Rashotte, 1984), including behavior in closed-economy foraging simulations (Logan 1960, 1964). In the process of trying to relate animal learning to foraging, it seems likely that insights will be gained about the mechanisms of foraging behavior and about the limitations of mechanisms that have heretofore been studied in open-economy experiments.

ACKNOWLEDGMENTS

The authors thank Michael Commons, Alex Kacelnik, and Sara Shettleworth for their helpful comments on an earlier version of this manuscript. Veljko Djuric was supported by a Fulbright predoctoral fellowship.

REFERENCES

Abarca, N., & Fantino, E. (1982). Choice and foraging. *Journal of the Experimental Analysis of Behavior, 38,* 117–123.

Amsel, A., & Rashotte, M. E. (1984). *Mechanisms of adaptive behavior: Clark L. Hull's theoretical papers, with commentary.* New York: Columbia University Press.

Charnov, E. L. (1976). Optimal foraging: Attack strategy of a mantid. *The American Naturalist, 100,* 141–151.

Collier, G. H. (1980). An ecological analysis of motivation. In F. M. Toates & T. R. Halliday (Eds.), *Analysis of motivational processes* (pp. 125–151). London: Academic Press.

Collier, G. H., & Rovee-Collier, C. K. (1981). A comparative analysis of optimal foraging behavior: Laboratory simulations. In A. C. Kamil & T. D. Sargent (Eds.), *Foraging behavior: Ecological, ethological and psychological approaches* (pp. 39–76). New York: Garland Press.

Djuric, V. J. (1984). *Search cost and feeding behavior of pigeons in a closed-economy foraging simulation.* Unpublished master's thesis, Florida State University.

Ellison, G. D., & Konorski, J. (1964). Separation of the salivary and motor responses in instrumental conditioning. *Science, 146,* 1071–1072.

Fantino, E., & Abarca, N. (1985). Choice, optimal foraging, and the delay-reduction hypothesis. *The Behavioral and Brain Sciences, 8,* 315–330.

Gibbon, J., & Balsam, P. (1981). Spreading association in time. In C. M. Locurto, H. S. Terrace, & J. Gibbon (Eds.), *Autoshaping and conditioning theory* (pp. 219–253). New York: Academic Press.

Goodale, M. A. (1983). Visually guided pecking in the pigeon (*Columbia livia*). *Brain, Behavior and Evolution, 22*, 22–41.

Hearst, E., & Jenkins, H. M. (1974). *Sign-tracking: The stimulus-reinforcer relation and directed action*. Austin, TX: The Psychonomic Society.

Heinrich, B., & Collins, S. L. (1983). Caterpillar leaf damage, and the game of hide-and-seek with birds. *Ecology, 64*, 592–602.

Holland, P. C. (1983). Occasion-setting in Pavlovian feature positive discriminations. In M. L. Commons, R. J. Herrnstein, & A. R. Wagner (Eds.), *Quantitative analyses of behavior: Vol. IV., Discrimination processes* (pp. 183–206). New York: Ballinger.

Hollis, K. L. (1982). Pavlovian conditioning of signal-centered action patterns and autonomic behavior: A biological analysis of function. In J. S. Rosenblatt, R. A. Hinde, C. Beer, & M. Busnel (Eds.), *Advances in the study of behavior* (Vol. 12, pp. 1–64). New York: Academic Press.

Honig, W. K. (Ed.). (1966). *Operant behavior: Areas of research and application*. New York: Appleton–Century–Crofts.

Honig, W. K., & Staddon, J. E. R. (Eds.). (1977). *Handbook of operant behavior*. Englewood Cliffs, NJ: Prentice-Hall.

Houston, A. (1980). Godzilla v. the creature from the black lagoon. Ethology v. psychology. In F. M. Toates & T. R. Halliday (Eds.), *Analysis of motivational processes* (pp. 297–318). London: Academic Press.

Hull, C. L. (1930). Knowledge and purpose as habit mechanisms. *Psychological Review, 37*, 511–525.

Hull, C. L. (1931). Goal attraction and directing ideas conceived as habit phenomena. *Psychological Review, 38*, 487–506.

Hursh, S. R. (1980). Economic concepts for the analysis of behavior. *Journal of the Experimental Analysis of Behavior, 34*, 219–238.

Jenkins, H. M. (1977). Sensitivity of different response systems to stimulus-reinforcer and response-reinforcer relations. In H. Davis & H. M. B. Hurwitz (Eds.), *Operant-Pavlovian interactions* (pp. 47–62). Hillsdale, NJ: Lawrence Erlbaum Associates.

Jenkins, H. M., & Moore, B. R. (1973). The form of the auto-shaped response with food or water reinforcers. *Journal of the Experimental Analysis of Behavior, 20*, 163–181.

Jenkins, H. M., Barnes, R. A., & Barrera, F. J. (1981). Why autoshaping depends on trial spacing. In C. M. Locurto, H. S. Terrace, & J. Gibbon (Eds.), *Autoshaping and conditioning theory* (pp. 255–284). New York: Academic Press.

Jenkins, H. M., Barrera, F. J., Ireland, C., & Woodside, B. (1978). Signal-centered action patterns of dogs in appetitive classical conditioning. *Learning & Motivation, 9*, 272–296.

Kamil, A. C. (1983). Optimal foraging theory and the psychology of learning. *American Zoologist, 23*, 291–302.

Kamil, A. C., & Yoerg, S. J. (1982). Learning and foraging behavior. In P. P. G. Bateson & P. H. Klopfer (Eds.), *Perspectives in ethology* (pp. 325–346). New York: Plenum.

Krebs, J. R. (1978). Optimal foraging: Decision rules for predators. In J. R. Krebs & N. B. Davies (Eds.), *Behavioural ecology: An evolutionary approach* (pp. 23–63). Oxford, England: Blackwell Scientific Publication.

Krebs, J. R., Houston, A. I., & Charnov, E. L. (1981). Some recent developments in optimal foraging. In A. C. Kamil & T. D. Sargent (Eds.), *Foraging behavior: Ecological, ethological and psychological approaches* (pp. 3–18). New York: Garland Press.

LaMon, B. C. & Zeigler, H. P. (1984). Grasping in the pigeon (*Columbia livia*): Stimulus control during conditioned and consummatory responses. *Animal Learning & Behavior, 12*, 223–231.

Lea, S. E. G. (1979). Foraging and reinforcement schedules in the pigeon: Optimal and non-optimal aspects of choice. *Animal Behaviour, 27,* 875–886.

Lea, S. E. G. (1983). The mechanism of optimality in foraging. In M. L. Commons, R. J. Herrnstein, & H. Rachlin (Eds.), *Quantitative analyses of behavior: Vol. II, Matching and maximizing accounts* (pp. 169–188). Cambridge, MA: Ballinger.

Locurto, C. M. (1981). Contributions of autoshaping to the partitioning of conditioned behavior. In C. M. Locurto, H. S. Terrace, & J. Gibbon (Eds.), *Autoshaping and conditioning theory* (pp. 101–135). New York: Academic Press.

Locurto, C. M., Terrace, H. S., & Gibbon, J. (Eds.). (1981). *Autoshaping and conditioning theory.* New York: Academic Press.

Logan, F. A. (1960). *Incentive: How the conditions of reinforcement affect the performance of rats.* New Haven, CT: Yale University Press.

Logan, F. A. (1964). The free behavior situation. In D. Levine (Ed.), *Nebraska symposium on motivation* (pp. 99–128). Lincoln: University of Nebraska Press.

Lucas, G. A. (1981). Some effects of reinforcer availability on the pigeon's responding in 24-hour sessions. *Animal Learning & Behavior, 9,* 411–424.

MacArthur, R. H., & Pianka, E. R. (1966). On optimal use of a patchy environment. *American Naturalist, 100,* 603–609.

Mackintosh, N. J. (1974). *The psychology of animal learning.* London: Academic Press.

Mackintosh, N. J. (1983). *Conditioning and associative learning.* New York: Oxford University Press.

McNamara, J., & Houston, A. (1980). The application of statistical decision theory to animal behaviour. *Journal of Theoretical Biology, 85,* 673–690.

Moore, B. R. (1973). The role of directed Pavlovian reactions in simple instrumental learning in the pigeon. In R. A. Hinde & J. Stevenson-Hinde (Eds.), *Constraints on learning* (pp. 159–186). London: Academic Press.

Moran, G. (1975). Severe food deprivation: Some thoughts regarding its exclusive use. *Psychological Bulletin, 82,* 543–557.

O'Connell, J. M. (1985). *The cost of food and feeding behavior in the pigeon (Columba livia).* Unpublished doctoral dissertation, Florida State University.

O'Connell, J. M., & Rashotte, M. E. (1982). Reinforcement magnitude effects in first and second-order conditioning of directed action. *Learning and Motivation, 13,* 1–25.

Orians, G. H. (1980). *Some adaptions of marsh-nesting blackbirds.* Princeton: Princeton University Press.

Orians, G. H. (1981). Foraging behavior and the evolution of discriminatory abilities. In A. C. Kamil & T. D. Sargent (Eds.), *Foraging behavior: Ecological, ethological and psychological approaches* (pp. 389–405). New York: Garland Press.

Overmier, J. B., & Lawry, J. A. (1979). Pavlovian conditioning and the mediation of behavior. In G. H. Bower (Ed.), *The psychology of learning and motivation.* (Vol. 13, pp. 1–55). New York: Academic Press.

Pavlov, I. P. (1927). *Conditioned reflexes.* Oxford, England: Oxford University Press.

Rashotte, M. E. (1985). *A hard day's night: Nocturnal hypothermia in response to high food costs in the 24-hr closed economy.* Paper delivered at the 26th annual meeting of the Psychonomic Society, Boston, MA.

Rashotte, M. E., & O'Connell, J. M. (in press). Pigeons' reactivity to food and to Pavlovian signals for food in a closed economy: Effects of feeding time and signal reliability. *Journal of Experimental Psychology: Animal Behavior Processes.*

Rashotte, M. E., & O'Connell, J. M. (1986). *Pigeon's reactivity to Pavlovian signals for food in a closed economy: Effects of omission training and food cost.* Unpublished manuscript.

Rashotte, M. E., O'Connell, J. M., & Beidler, D. L. (1982). Associative influence on the foraging behavior of pigeons (*Columba livia*). *Journal of Experimental Psychology: Animal Behavior Processes, 8,* 142–153.

Rescorla, R. A. (1980). *Pavlovian second-order conditioning: Studies in associative learning.* Hillsdale, NJ: Lawrence Erlbaum Associates.

Schoener, T. W. (1971). Theory of feeding strategies. *Animal Review of Ecology and Systematics, 2,* 369–404.

Sheffield, F. D. (1965). Relation between classical conditioning and instrumental learning. In W. F. Prokasy (Ed.), *Classical conditioning: A symposium* (pp. 302–322). New York: Appleton-Century-Crofts.

Shettleworth, S. J. (1983). Function and mechanism in learning. In M. D. Zeiler & P. Harzem (Eds.), *Advances in analysis of behaviour.* (Vol. 3, pp. 1–37). London: Wiley.

Skinner, B. F. (1937). Two types of conditioned reflex: A reply to Konorski and Miller. *Journal of General Psychology, 16,* 272–279.

Skinner, B. F. (1938). *The behavior of organisms.* New York: Appleton-Century-Crofts.

Smith, J. C., Rashotte, M. E., Austin, T., Henderson, R., Oliff, G., & Bloom, L. (1984). An apparatus for making fine-grained measurements of canine feeding behavior. *Neuroscience & Biobehavioral Reviews, 8,* 239–242.

Staddon, J. E. R. (1983). *Adaptive behavior and learning.* Cambridge, England: Cambridge University Press.

Stiles, E. W. (1982). Fruit flags: Two hypotheses. *American Naturalist, 120,* 500–509.

Stiles, E. W. (1984, August). Fruit for all seasons. *Natural History, 93,* 42–50.

Tinbergen, J. M. (1981). Foraging decisions in starlings (*Sturnus Vulgaris L.*). *Ardea, 69,* 1–65.

Williams, D. R., & Williams, H. (1969). Auto-maintenance in the pigeon: Sustained pecking despite contingent non-reinforcement. *Journal of the Experimental Analysis of Behavior, 12,* 511–520.

Zeigler, H. P. (1976). Feeding behavior of the pigeon. In J. S. Rosenblatt, R. A. Hinde, E. Shaw, & C. Beer (Eds.), *Advances in the study of behavior* (Vol. 7, pp. 285–389). New York: Academic Press.

Zeigler, H. P., Green, H. L., & Siegel, J. (1972). Food and water intake and weight regulation in the pigeon. *Physiology & Behavior, 18,* 127–134.

Zweers, G. A. (1982). Pecking of the pigeon (*Columba livia l.*). *Behaviour, 81,* 173–230.

9

Choice and Optimal Foraging: Tests of the Delay-Reduction Hypothesis and the Optimal-Diet Model

Edmund Fantino
University of California, San Diego

Nureya Abarca
Pontificia Universidad Católica de Chile
Santiago, Chile.

Masato Ito
City University of Osaka
Japan

The parameter-free delay-reduction hypothesis, developed in studies of choice, states that the strength of a stimulus as a conditioned reinforcer is a function of the reduction in time till reinforcement correlated with the onset of that stimulus (Fantino, 1969, 1977, 1981; Fantino & Davison, 1983; Squires & Fantino, 1971). Expressed differently, the greater the improvement, in terms of temporal proximity or waiting time till reinforcement, correlated with the onset of a stimulus, the more effective that stimulus will be as a conditioned reinforcer. Although the hypothesis has been extended to areas such as observing (Case & Fantino, 1981), self-control (Ito & Asaki, 1982; Navarick & Fantino, 1976), elicited responding (Fantino, 1982), and three-alternative choice (Fantino & Dunn, 1983), the hypothesis was first developed to account for choice for two variable-interval schedules of reinforcement (Fantino, 1969; Squires & Fantino, 1971). The simplest form of the delay-reduction hypothesis may be stated as:

$$\text{Reinforcing strength of stimulus } A = f\left(\frac{T - t_A}{T}\right), \qquad (1)$$

where t_A represents the temporal interval between the onset of stimulus A and primary reinforcement, T represents the total time between reinforcer presentations and the function is montonically increasing.

181

The application of equation (1) to two-alternative choice (equation 2, following) is introduced because most of the operant analogs to foraging that are discussed here involve similar types of choice. Assume the subject is choosing between two reward outcomes, one involving an average delay of t_{2L} seconds, the other an average delay of t_{2R} seconds (L and R for "left" and "right," respectively; t_{2L} and t_{2R} may be thought of as "handling times"). The subject produces the two outcomes by responding in the search state (signaled by concurrent white lights) of the choice procedure depicted in Fig. 9.1. Responses made in the presence of the concurrently available white lights are reinforced according to variable-interval (VI) schedules of reinforcement by a change in the color of

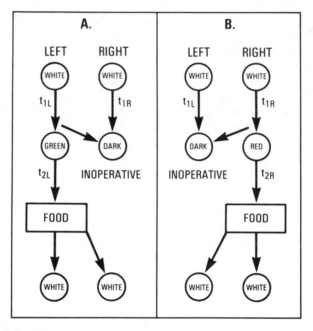

FIG. 9.1. The concurrent-chains procedure for the study of choice. *A* (left) depicts the sequence of events when responses on the left key are reinforced. *B* (right) depicts the analogous sequence on the right key. Responses in the presence of the colored lights (the stimuli of the outcome phase) are reinforced with food according to some schedule of reinforcement (generally the independent variable; the schedule is often a VI schedule). The measure of choice is the relative rate of responding in the presence of the concurrently available white lights (number of responses to one white light divided by the sum of responses to both). Typically, equal VI schedules arrange access to the outcome schedules. The mean scheduled duration for the left and right white lights are t_{1L} and t_{1R}, respectively. The mean scheduled durations for the green and red lights are t_{2L} and t_{2R}, respectively. After Fantino (1969).

the keylight from white to either green (left key) or red (right key). The mean scheduled durations of the schedules associated with the green and red lights are t_{2L} and t_{2R}, respectively. The corresponding durations in the initial links are t_{1L} and t_{1R}, the mean scheduled durations associated with the left and right white lights, respectively. Typically, the independent variable is some difference in the amount of food provided. The dependent variable, the measure of choice, is the relative rate of responding in the presence of the concurrently available white lights, the number of responses made to the left white light (R_L) divided by the number of responses made to both white lights ($R_L + R_R$).

Numerous studies have shown that the strength of preference for one alternative is an inverse function of the length of the choice (or "search") phase (see Fantino, 1977, for a review; see also Fantino & Davison, 1983). This finding follows from the delay-reduction hypothesis. To see this one need calculate how far in time from primary reinforcement the organism is during the choice phase (or "initial links" of the concurrent-chains procedure). Let T stand for the average scheduled overall time till primary reinforcement from the onset of the choice phase. Thus, T equals the average time in the choice phase plus the average time in the outcome phase. For example, when the equal VIs in the choice phase are VI 120-seconds schedules, the mean time in the choice phase equals 60 seconds (because the two VI 120-seconds schedules operate simultaneously). If t_{2L} equals 30 seconds and t_{2R} equals 90 seconds, the average time in the outcome phase also equals 60 seconds (the average of 30 seconds and 90 seconds, the two equiprobable outcome times). Thus, T equals 60 seconds plus 60 seconds or 120 seconds. The delay reduction correlated with the onset of t_{2L} (entering the outcome phase on the left) then equals ($T - t_{2L}$) or (120 seconds − 30 seconds) or 90 seconds. Similarly, the delay reduction correlated with the onset of t_{2R} equals ($T - t_{2R}$) or (120 seconds − 90 seconds) or 30 seconds. According to the delay-reduction hypothesis (henceforth, the DRH), the subjects' choice proportions should match proportions of delay reductions. In the example given, because the onset of t_{2L} is correlated with three times the amount of delay reduction as the onset of t_{2R}, the subject should respond three times as often on the left during the choice phase. More generally, Fantino (1969) hypothesized that the following equation should describe choice:

$$\frac{R_L}{R_L + R_R} = \frac{T - t_{2L}}{(T - t_{2L}) + (T - t_{2R})} \quad \text{(when } t_{2L} < T, \ t_{2R} < T\text{).} \quad (2)$$

$$= 1 \quad \text{(when } t_{2L} < T, \ t_{2R} > T\text{)}$$

$$= 0 \quad \text{(when } t_{2L} > T, \ t_{2R} < T\text{)}$$

Note that, when either outcome represents an increase in average delay to reinforcement (either $t_{2L} > T$ or $t_{2R} > T$), equation (2) requires the subject to choose the other outcome exclusively.[1] Only when choice is exclusive, or nearly so, does choice affect the experienced rates of reinforcement. Otherwise, concurrent-chains schedules permit choice to vary over a wide range (say, choice proportions between .10 and .90) without materially affecting the rates of reinforcement the subject encounters. Two other procedural points should be clarified. First, there is no delay between the end of a food presentation and the beginning of the next exposure to the white lights of the choice phase. Second, the VI schedules associated with the choice phase operate only during the choice phase. After reinforcement, when the choice phase is reinstated, the VI schedules continue from the point they had been when last operative. This feature of concurrent VI schedules helps keep experienced rates of reinforcement close to scheduled rates.

It follows from equation (2) that the longer the choice phase (that is, the longer t_{1L} and t_{1R}), the greater the value of T. As the value of T becomes indefinitely large, $R_L/(R_L + R_R)$ approaches 0.5. An intuitive justification for this prediction is presented in Fantino and Logan (1979, p. 231). Next consider what equation (2) predicts when the outcome durations or handling times (t_{2L} and t_{2R}) are increased for a given choice phase duration (say one that lasts 30 seconds, on the average). If the ratio of t_{2L} to t_{2R} is kept constant while both are increased (say from 10 seconds and 20 seconds to 30 seconds and 60 seconds), preference for the shorter outcome should increase (in the example given, from .58 to .75). Thus, increasing the duration of the outcome phases (while

---

[1]Note that t_{2L} and t_{2R} cannot *both* be greater than T. Also, equation (2) has been modified by Squires and Fantino (1971) and by Fantino and Davison (1983). For the sake of clarity we discuss only the simpler, unmodified version (equation 2), because all versions make comparable qualitative predictions in most of the procedures discussed in this chapter and make *identical* quantitative predictions for the successive-choice procedure used in two sets of experiments. In the special case of different initial-link durations, however, it is necessary to weight the terms in the right-hand side by the overall food rate scheduled on each key so that:

$$\frac{R_L}{R_L + R_R} = \frac{r_L(T - t_{2L})}{r_L(T - t_{2L}) + r_R(T - t_{2R})} \quad t_{2L} < T, t_{2R} < T, , \qquad (2a)$$

$$1, \qquad\qquad\qquad t_{2L} < T, t_{2R} > T,$$

$$0, \qquad\qquad\qquad t_{2L} > T, t_{2R} < T,$$

where r_L and r_R are the overall rates of food on the left and right keys, respectively. This extension is also valuable because equation (2a) requires matching of choice to rate of reinforcement when there are no terminal links—that is, when $t_{2R} = t_{2L} = 0$. Fantino and Davison (1983) have shown that even better fits to choice data may be obtained by using the square root of the overall rates of reinforcement ($\sqrt{r_L}$ for r_L and $\sqrt{r_R}$ for r_R). Finally, note that equations (2) and (2a) represent molar descriptions of choice as opposed to molecular ones, that is the DRH says nothing about momentary changes in preference within particular choice phases.

maintaining a constant ratio between them) relative to the duration of the choice phase has the same effect as decreasing choice phase duration in relation to that of the outcome phase; that is, preference for the favored alternative should increase. Both of these predictions have been confirmed (see Fantino, 1977, and Fantino & Logan, 1979, for reviews). Later they are assessed in light of more recent experiments from our laboratory that investigate operant analogs to foraging.

Because foraging behavior involves choice, the DRH may also be extended in an attempt to describe aspects of foraging. The present chapter discusses the strategy of assessing parameters of foraging through analogs to foraging developed in the context of the operant conditioning laboratory, compares the predictions of the DRH, other theories developed in the operant laboratory, and optimal-foraging theories, and presents data on the effects of several factors thought to be centrally involved in foraging. A critical question is this: Are principles that have evolved from the study of decision making in the operant laboratory consistent with decision making in situations that share important properties with foraging?

Much theoretical work in foraging has focused on the idea that natural selection favors the most economic of alternative foraging patterns (e.g., MacArthur & Pianka, 1966). Optimality theory has been applied to a number of foraging decisions that a predator may make, such as how and where to feed (Pyke, Pulliam, & Charnov, 1977). Although most of the foraging studies have been carried out in the natural environment or in laboratory studies that simulate the field situation, there have been several successful simulations of foraging that have used operant conditioning (e.g., Abarca & Fantino, 1982; Collier & Rovee-Collier, 1981; Krebs, Kacelnik, & Taylor, 1978; Lea, 1979). Although such studies have potential limitations, which are discussed following, they also permit rigorous control of variables in practical, accessible settings and the application of laboratory technology developed over several decades (Fantino & Logan, 1979). Moreover, the experimental analysis of foraging appears to be a ripe area in which to combine the assumptions and methodologies of the laboratory and the field. This approach may successfully encourage an interdisciplinary or "integrated" approach to behavior (Fantino & Logan, 1979, pp. 473–499).

A study of foraging in the operant conditioning laboratory mimics foraging through procedures that have been studied exhaustively in the laboratory. The technology and data base developed in the operant laboratory over the past several decades (Ferster & Skinner, 1957; Honig & Staddon, 1977) may help assess the effects of variables believed to influence foraging in the field. In moving an experiment on foraging from the field into the laboratory one is using *manipulative* research in the hope of increasing *internal validity* of the conclusions drawn (though much field work is also manipulative). Altmann (1974) has assessed the relative merits of manipulative versus *nonmanipulative* research (corresponding in a very rough way to experimental versus field research). As Fantino and Logan (1979) have noted:

> this newer usage conveys the understanding that control is not lacking in the nonmanipulative (observational) situation. Rather, naturally occurring controlling variables, not artificially manipulated factors, determine the course of behavior. In either case, control is inherent in the situation; manipulative procedures simply facilitate the task of *identifying* the controlling variables. Altmann's comparison of the relative virtues of manipulative versus nonmanipulative methods centers on the degree of internal versus external *validity* associated with each . . . Internal validity refers to the validity of conclusions drawn about changes in the behavior of the sample of organisms on which the investigation was conducted. *External validity*, on the other hand, refers to the validity of generalizations from these internally valid conclusions (drawn on the basis of sample results) to some other population or situation. Both types of validity are essential to the overall validity of any conclusion. (p. 478)

The strategy used here thus far has been to maximize internal validity, even at the risk of sacrificing external validity. By studying variables thought to influence a forager's choice behavior (and by testing theoretical implications of the effects of these variables) in the context of well-established laboratory procedures, the attainment of a degree of empirical rigor more difficult to achieve in natural settings is hoped for. It is also believed that the rich data base accumulated from prior work with similar procedures will permit the selection of those parameters that are most likely to aid in the fair assessment of theoretical predictions.

Charnov's (1976) optimal-diet model (ODM) derives an equation giving the rate of energy intake in a random encounter model. This model is deterministic and assumes that the forager possesses complete information concerning the relevant variables. Few contemporary ecologists and psychologists accept this assumption except as an approximation (Kamil & Sargent, 1981; Staddon, 1983). Nonetheless, the approach presented here is to use this simple model and the DRH to propose some basic experimental analogs. Moreover, in the experiments discussed here, subjects are exposed to each condition for thousands of trials so that they become relatively familiar with the relevant variables. Thus, the assumption of a "knowledgeable" subject becomes more tenable. In terms of the ODM note that foraging time, T, is made up of T_s (time searching) and T_h (time handling all food items). A net rate of energy intake (E/T) is

$$\frac{E}{T} = \frac{E}{(T_s + T_h)}.$$

While the predator searches, assume it encounters the ith food type at a rate λ_i and that P_i is the probability that the predator will seek and consume an item of type i when one is encountered (that is, escape of items is not considered). It may be helpful to think of P as being under the forager's control whereas rate of energy gain (E/T) is maximized by choice of P. Also, because optimal choice is always all-or-none, P should equal either 0 or 1. If E_i is the net energy gain and h_i the handling time for the ith food type, then the total energy gain E, in time T, is given by:

$$E = T_s \sum_{i=1}^{n} \lambda_i E_i P_i$$

and the total handling time T_h, by

$$T_h = T_s \sum_{i=1}^{n} \lambda_i h_i P_i .$$

The rate of energy intake is then given by

$$\frac{E}{T} = \frac{T_s \sum_{i=1}^{n} \lambda_i E_i P_i}{T_s + T_s \sum_{i=1}^{n} \lambda_i h_i P_i} = \frac{\sum_{i=1}^{n} \lambda_i E_i P_i}{1 + \sum_{i=1}^{n} \lambda_i h_i P_i}$$

It can be shown that if two food types, "L" and "R," are available and

$$\frac{\lambda_R E_R}{1 + \lambda_R h_R} > \frac{\lambda_R E_R + \lambda_L E_L}{1 + \lambda_R h_R + \lambda_L h_L},$$

exclusive preference for type "R" is predicted. This can be rearranged to give:

$$\frac{1}{\lambda_R} < \frac{E_R}{E_L} h_L - h_R. \tag{3}$$

Inequality (3) may also be derived from equation (2). First the preceding inequality is simplified by considering $E_R = E_L$ (in most laboratory studies the quality of food is the same for both alternatives). Next equivalent terms must be found. The rate of encounter with food type "R," in terms of equation (2), equals $1/t_{1R}$ and the rate of encounter with food type "L" equals $1/t_{1L}$ where t_{1R} and t_{1L} are the average durations of the search state for the left and right key, respectively. The handling times for these alternatives are represented by:

$$h_R = t_{2R}; h_L = t_{2L}.$$

Thus, the last inequality, written in terms of equation (2), representing exclusive preference for food type "R," may be given as:

$$t_{1R} < t_{2L} - t_{2R}. \tag{4}$$

May this inequality be derived from equation 2? If so, the ODM and the DRH make equivalent predictions in terms of the conditions that should produce exclusive preference. Equation (2) requires exclusive preference for outcome "R" under two conditions:

$$t_{2L} > T; \; t_{2R} < T.$$

Because t_{2R} must be less than T when $t_{2L} > T$, only the latter inequality need be considered. First replace T:

$$T = \frac{1}{1/t_{1L} + 1/t_{1R}} + \frac{t_{1L}}{t_{1L} + t_{1R}} t_{2R} + \frac{t_{1R}}{t_{1L} + t_{1R}} t_{2L}.$$

$t_{2L} > T$ may then be shown equivalent to:

$$t_{2L}(t_{1R} + t_{1L}) > t_{1L}t_{1R} + t_{1L}t_{2R} + t_{1R}t_{2L}$$
$$t_{2L} > t_{1R} + t_{2R}$$
$$t_{1R} < t_{2L} - t_{2R},$$

which is inequality (4) aforementioned. Thus, inequalities (3) and (4) are equivalent, and the ODM and the DRH require exclusive preference under the same conditions.

Inequality (4), when written as

$$t_{1R} + t_{2R} < t_{2L}$$

has a simple biological interpretation. Given an encounter with an item of type L, the less preferred prey, that prey should be rejected if it takes longer to handle that item (t_{2L}) than it does to find (t_{1R}) and handle (t_{2R}) an item of type R (on the average of course). The important point is that the identical inequality may be derived from the ODM and the DRH, that is they require exclusive preference under the same conditions. In a sense, the ODM and the DRH complement one another. Many optimality models assume that natural selection has shaped organisms to maximize rate of energy intake per unit time (other relevant conditions held constant). The DRH states a principle by which this may be generally accomplished: Outcomes will be chosen in terms of their correlation with a reduction in time till the onset of the next reinforcer. The complementarity of the two approaches appears important: A model of natural selection for foraging efficiency makes several predictions consistent with an hypothesis of a more proximate phenomenon (reduction in time till reinforcement).

What can be done about the potential problem of external validity? That is, do results from operant simulations of foraging shed light on behavior in more natural settings? Certainly there are "unnatural" aspects of laboratory simulations. The nature of feeding in the experimental chamber differs in at least three potentially important ways from feeding in the wild. One involves the use of fixed-duration (usually 3 seconds) access to a hopper filled with grain, even though birds generally obtain a single grain at a time in the wild (Baum, 1983). It is possible that this difference in reinforcer presentation might produce different functional relations between choice and the temporal variables under study. The primary advantage of retaining the conventional food-hopper presentation, at least in our initial work, is to maintain comparability with a large body of work done in this manner (for example, virtually all work with schedules of reinforcement, including tests of equation 1, has used this approach). It is hoped eventually to assess the importance of differences such as this through direct comparisons. A second example is the use of experimental sessions of fixed, short (1-hour) durations as opposed to continuous 24-hour sessions that may more closely resemble foraging in the wild. Collier and Rovee-Collier (1983) assert that in "nature, deprivation is a rare occurrence and a condition of an animal in an 'emergency' state" (p. 429). They propose that by studying behavior in short sessions every 24 hours researchers are focusing on emergency behavior. These speculations are difficult to evaluate. A more general and closely related issue involves the use of open versus closed economies, one that is discussed as evaluated in several of the experiments reviewed next. The third, and potentially most important, limitation involves the assessment of foraging under conditions that resemble those of within-meal, rather than between-meal, behavior, a distinction raised cogently by Collier and Rovee-Collier (1981). In the tradition of virtually all studies of choice in the operant laboratory and of the prior operant simulations of foraging (work from Dr. George Collier's laboratory the most notable exception), "portions" of meals (e.g., 3-seconds access to food) are utilized as reinforcers rather than entire meals. For reasons outlined in the Collier and Rovee-Collier paper, it is important to assess the generality of the conclusions that are drawn here when the reinforcers are meals. It is likely, however, that where pigeons and many other birds are concerned, "portions" of meals are the natural bill of fare. It would be interesting to determine whether rewards consisting of portions of meals versus entire meals would be differentially effective with subjects of different species, depending on the species' natural foraging habits.

Baum (1983) has noted the following "three artificialities" of the "typical experiment in operant behavior . . . : it occurs inside a small box, rather than outdoors, (2) it occupies only a small portion of the organism's active hours, and (3) it presents food on a schedule that bears little resemblance to the occurrence of food in nature" (p. 259). These limitations all apply, to some extent, to the present work. It should be acknowledged that Baum also points out the similarities in the results of what has been done inside and outside of the "little box" and of what has been done with 1-hour and 24-hour sessions (pp. 259 & 266–267). In general, the present approach moves slowly from the use of well-established procedures to the use of those that better mimic or represent natural settings. In this way it is hoped to increase the external validity of the obtained results without eliminating valuable connections to the well-studied operant-choice procedures. Morever, only through a gradual alteration of these procedures will researchers be in a position to assess which variables are responsible for any changing results.

Overview of Experimental Results

Four sets of experiments are considered. The first two utilize varients of concurrent-chains procedures such as that shown in Fig. 9.1. Although those provide tests of the DRH, it is noted later that they are not well suited to test the ODM (Fantino, 1984). The final two sets of experiments use a successive-choice procedure, developed by Lea (1979). Results from these experiments are relevant for both the DRH and the ODM.

Travel Time

Prior work has shown that increasing search duration should decrease selectivity in accordance with the ODM and the DRH (e.g., Abarca & Fantino, 1982; Collier & Rovee-Collier, 1981; Fantino, Abarca, & Dunn, in press; Lea, 1979). Because increases in the time taken to travel between alternatives ("travel time") increase search duration, these increases should also decrease selectivity.

In order to assess the effect of varying the size of the travel requirement, the present studies examined choice using a modified concurrent-chains procedure. It differed from the standard concurrent-chains procedure, shown in Fig. 9.1, in that only one alternative was available at a given moment and that a changeover requirement had to be fulfilled to change from one alternative to the other. The changeover requirement consisted of a fixed-interval X-seconds (FI X-seconds). In a FI X-seconds schedule, the first response after X seconds have elapsed is reinforced, in this case with a change in alternatives. In particular, the changeover requirement was arranged on a switching key that required an FI of X-seconds for a changeover (the first peck darkened one of the main keys, the first peck after X-seconds lighted the alternate one). In each of two experiments, half the subjects were maintained in a standard open economy and half in a closed economy (e.g., Hursh, 1980). In one, the closed-economy condition was arranged by having longer reinforcement duration (5-seconds access to food) than for the open-economy group (3-seconds access to food). In the second, the closed-economy condition was arranged by having longer sessions for the birds maintained in this system (80 food reinforcements rather than 50 for the open-economy subjects). Both ways of arranging closed economies fulfilled the requirements of a closed economy. Subjects received sufficient food within the experimental session so that they required no supplementation outside of the experimental session. These experiments also differed in the durations of the outcome phases that is $t_{2L} \neq t_{2R}$ (VI 5 seconds vs. VI 20 seconds in the first experiment; VI 30 seconds vs. VI 60 seconds in the second). Both studies examined the effect of varying the length of the changeover requirement in concurrent-chains schedules.

In each experiment preference for the preferred alternative (VI 5 seconds in the first; VI 30 seconds in the second) decreased significantly as travel time increased, i.e., the subjects became less selective (in one experiment $F(2, 8) = 8.41, p < .05$; in the second, $F(2, 8) = 7.14, p < .05$). Choice was unaffected, however, by the type of economic condition employed. Similar results were obtained using a second dependent variable. After each reinforcement the initial-link alternative present upon return to the choice phase was selected on a random basis (to insure equal exposure to both alternatives). The second measure is the probability of remaining in the presence of the stimulus that led to the less preferred outcome (VI 20 seconds in the first experiment; VI 60 seconds in the second). Although the DRH does not make quantitative predictions in terms of this measure, one would expect that the likelihood of remaining in the presence of the stimulus that led to the longer VI should increase with increases in travel time. This prediction was confirmed. The data in Fig. 9.2 represent the mean

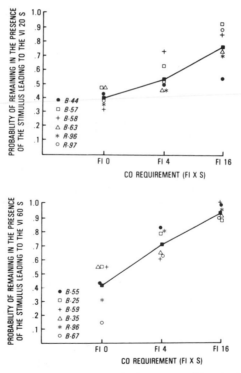

FIG. 9.2.   The probability of remaining in the presence of the stimulus leading to the less preferred outcome (VI 20 seconds, top; VI 60 seconds, bottom) as a function of the duration of the changeover requirement (travel time) in each of two experiments. Each data point represents the mean value of this probability averaged over the last five sessions in each condition for each of six birds. The line is drawn through the means of the group data (data from Abarca, 1982).

value of the probability of remaining in the presence of the stimulus that lead to the longer VI over the last five sessions in each condition for each of the six birds. This measure of preference was obtained by dividing the number of times the subject remained in the presence of the stimulus that led to the long VI (VI 20 seconds in the first experiment) by the number of times this alternative was presented during the initial links. The probability of remaining in the presence of the stimulus leading to the shorter terminal link is not included, because it was always in the range of .90 to 1.0. The top portion of the graph shows data for the first experiment; the bottom portion for the second experiment. These data appear to be related to the number of changeovers in a session. As the duration of the FI requirement increased, the rate of changeovers decreased. Thus, the subjects became more indifferent to the two alternatives as the FI duration increased. These results are thus qualitatively consistent with the DRH, because with longer changeover requirements, the average overall delay to primary reinforcement (T) increases (averaged over the 12 subjects in the present experiments, the mean time till reinforcement was 75 seconds, 82 seconds, and 92 seconds, with changeover requirements of 0, 4, and 16 seconds, respectively).

Asymmetric Effects of Accessibility

When one of two unequal choice schedules is varied in the concurrent-chains procedure, with unequal outcome durations (that is, with $t_{2L} \neq t_{2R}$), equation (2) requires a different rate of change in choice proportions depending on whether the choice-phase schedule that was changed has led to the shorter or longer outcome phase. For example, let t_{2L} equal 5 seconds, t_{2R} equal 20 seconds, and t_{1L} and t_{1R} (the durations of the choice schedules) each equal 60 seconds. T, the scheduled time till reinforcement from the onset of the choice phase, is 42.5 seconds and, according to equation (2a), the predicted choice proportion for the 5-second outcome in this baseline condition is .67. Now change the duration of the choice schedule leading to the VI 5-second schedule from 60 seconds to 120 seconds, while keeping t_{1R} equal to 60 seconds. T is now 55 seconds and the predicted choice proportion for the 5-second outcome is now only .48, a change of .19 from baseline. Next, consider instead changing the duration of the choice schedule leading to the VI 20-second schedule from 60 seconds, to 120 seconds, while keeping t_{1L} equal to 60 seconds. T is now 50 seconds and the predicted choice proportion for the 5-second outcome is .77, a change of .10 from baseline.

In each condition of these experiments the length of only one of the initial links was varied with respect to a baseline condition. In the first experiment, the duration of the initial links was increased; in the second, it was decreased. According to the DRH, varying the initial link that leads to the short schedule (preferred outcome) should produce a marked change in the choice proportion and varying the initial link that leads to the long schedule (less preferred outcome) should have a smaller effect.

The independent variable was the duration of the choice schedules (t_{1L} and t_{1R}). The outcome schedules (t_{2L} and t_{2R}) were VI 5 seconds and VI 20 seconds. In a baseline condition the choice schedules were both VI 60 seconds. In condition 1 of the first experiment, the choice schedule that lead to the VI 5-second schedule was changed to VI 120 seconds. In condition 2, after a return to baseline, the choice schedule that led to the VI 20-second schedule was changed to VI 120 seconds. In the second experiment, after returning to baseline the choice schedule that led to the VI 5-second schedule was changed to VI 30 seconds and, after a return to baseline, the choice schedule that led to the VI 20-second schedule was changed to VI 30 seconds.

The major findings from this experiment were: (a) in each experiment an analysis of variance showed that the difference between behavior in the open and closed economies was not significant; (b) in each experiment changing accessibility of the preferred outcome had a greater effect on choice than changing accessibility of the less preferred outcome (in the first experiment, however, changing accessibility of either outcome produced a statistically significant effect on choice; in the second experiment only the change in accessibility of the preferred outcome was significant); (c) in each experiment, an analysis of variance showed that choice proportions in each condition did not differ significantly

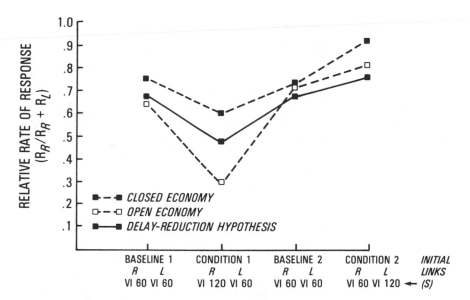

FIG. 9.3. Relative rate of responding in the choice (or search) state in each of four conditions averaged separately over subjects maintained on a closed and on open economies. The relative rate of responding was obtained by dividing the rate of responding for the preferred alternative by the total rate of responding for both alternatives ($R_r/R_r + R_1$). The figure also shows relative rates required by the delay-reduction hypothesis (equation 2a). After Abarca (1982).

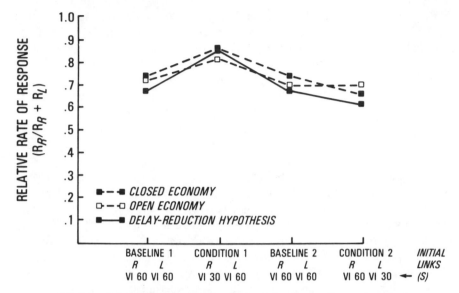

FIG. 9.4.   Relative rate of responding in the choice (or search) state in each of four conditions (different from those shown in the previous figure), averaged separately over subjects maintained on a closed and an open economies. The relative rate of responding was obtained by dividing the rate of responding for the preferred alternative by the total rate of responding for both alternatives ($R_r/R_r + R_1$). The figure also shows relative rates required by the delay-reduction hypothesis (equation 2a). After Abarca (1982).

from the values required by the DRH for both the open- and closed-economy groups (mean absolute deviation averaged over all subjects was 0.07). The basic results are illustrated in Figs. 9.3 (first experiment) and 9.4 (second experiment), which plot the choice proportions over the last five sessions for the closed- and open-economy groups and those required by the DRH in each condition.

Killeen's incentive theory (Killeen, 1982) also predicts how choices should be distributed between two acceptable outcomes. According to Killeen: $S = R(P + C)$ where S is the "strength" of responding on a schedule, R is the rate of arousal motivating responding, P is the primary directional effect of a reinforcer, and C is the directional effect of conditioned reinforcement. R is itself the overall rate of reinforcement on a key, P decreases exponentially with delay of reinforcement, and C is a function of the immediacy of the primary reinforcer signaled by the onset of the terminal link (Killeen, 1982, has the relevant equations and details). It may be readily shown that this theory and the DRH make virtually indistinguishable predictions over a wide range of conditions (e.g., Killeen, 1985). The two may be distinguished, however, by separately varying the accessibility of the more and less profitable outcomes. In the first place Killeen predicts comparable effects of varying accessibility of the two outcomes where the DRH requires variation of the more profitable outcome to have a greater effect. Whereas the results shown in Fig. 9.3 and 9.4 appear to support the DRH in this regard, Killeen (1985) has shown that these results do not permit adequate differentiation between the two models' predictions. In the second place, however, sharply different predictions may be derived from the two accounts by varying accessibility of the less profitable outcome over a wider range.

Consider an experiment in which pigeons' keypecks are reinforced according to equal VI 60-second search schedules (initial links) that lead to either VI 10-second (left) or VI 20-second (right) outcomes. The duration of the right initial

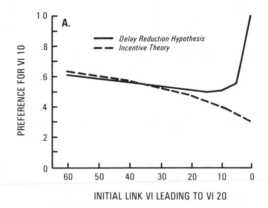

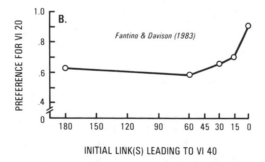

FIG. 9.5.   A. Predicted choice proportions for the more profitable of two outcomes (VI 10 seconds) as the accessibility of the less profitable outcome (VI 20 seconds) increases, according to the DRH (equation 2a) and to Killeen's (1982) theory.

B. Although not addressing this problem, data from five conditions in Fantino and Davison (1983) show the change of choice proportions for the shorter VI schedule (here, VI 20 seconds) as the accessibility of the longer VI schedule (here, VI 40 seconds) increased (the accessibility of the VI 20-second schedule was constant at VI 180 seconds). Data averaged over six pigeons.

link (that leads to VI 20 seconds) is then decreased until zero (CRF choice). According to incentive theory, decreasing the initial link should produce increasing preference for VI 20 seconds throughout the range (see Appendix). The DRH predicts first an increase and then a decrease in preference for VI 20 seconds as its initial link is decreased (see Fig. 9.5A, which plots preference in terms of the VI 10-second schedule). The prediction of the DRH that preference for the less profitable outcome should decrease as it becomes sufficiently more accessible seems intuitively implausible to all individuals with whom the authors have discussed it. All assume that this experiment will prove the DRH incorrect and strengthen the generality of Killeen's model. However, Ray Preston, a collaborator in this experiment, has discovered that several data points (conditions 25, 38, 40, 42, and 45 from a study by Fantino & Davison, 1983) are consistent with the DRH view. Preston has plotted these points in Fig. 9.5B. The experiment just outlined is now being carried out. As the data in Fig. 9.5B suggest, support for incentive theory and rejection of the DRH is by no means as foregone a conclusion as one's intuitions suggested originally.

Varying Handling Times with Different Reinforcer Amounts

Ito and Fantino (1984) have investigated the effects of varying search and handling times with differing reinforcer amounts. Navarick and Fantino (1976) have applied equation (2) to the case of different reinforcer amounts. The following inequality, analogous to inequality (3), may be derived from either the DRH or the ODM theory for equal handling times and unequal rewards ($E_R > E_L$):

Specialize on R and reject L if:

$$(1/\lambda_R) < h\left(\frac{E_R}{E_L} - 1\right). \tag{5}$$

In this expression, E_R and E_L are net energy gains from alternatives R and L, h represents handling time, and λ_R the encounter rate for R. It can be seen that increasing the density of the preferred prey type (greater λ_R) or increasing the common handling time makes specialization more likely.

In a test of the latter assertion, Ito varied the duration of the equal handling times when reward durations were unequal in a successive-choice procedure patterned after that used by Lea (1979) and modified by Abarca and Fantino (1982). Unlike the concurrent-chains procedure (Fig. 9.1), in the successive-choice procedure the subject may accept or reject on outcome (t_{2L} or t_{2R}) when it first becomes available. In the concurrent-chains procedure, on the other hand, once an outcome is presented the subject cannot return to the search phase without first completing the schedule requirement associated with that outcome. The successive-choice procedure is shown in Fig. 9.6. Note that in the choice phase the subject may either respond to return to the search phase or may respond

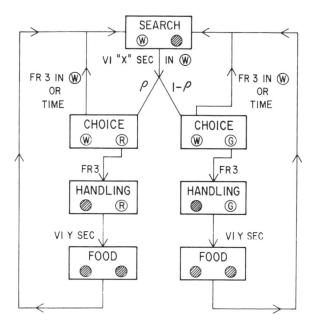

FIG. 9.6. Flowchart of procedure used in experiments with different reinforcer amounts. The rectangles indicate the different states of the schedule; the state-transition requirements are indicated by the legends. The circle indicates the keys and the letters the corresponding colors (R:red; G:green; W:white). After Lea (1979) and Abarca and Fantino (1982).

to enter the available handling phase (noted by VI Y seconds, where Y is the counterpart to t_{2L} and t_{2R} in the concurrent-chains procedure). This procedure permits tests of both the DRH and the ODM. The VI value in the Search State was maintained at VI 5 seconds and the reward durations were 3 and 6 seconds. What varied across three conditions was duration of the equal handling times (VI Y seconds in Fig. 9.6): from VI 20 seconds to VI 5 seconds and back to VI 20 seconds. As noted in the introduction, equation (2) requires that preference move closer to indifference (less selectivity) as the handling times are decreased. A comparable prediction follows from inequality (5) and from Killeen (1982) and Staddon (1983). Figure 9.7 shows that the prediction is confirmed for each of three pigeons, because each subject was more likely to accept the shorter duration reward (less selectivity) with the shorter handling time.

Although the present results may be taken as successful confirmation of the ODM and inequality (5), application of this theory to the procedure used requires assumptions that may or may not seem plausible. For example, is handling time equal to time in the outcome phase as assumed previously (that is, $h = t_{2L} = t_{2R}$)? Kacelnik and Krebs (1985) have argued cogently that a more direct prediction from a rate maximization perspective may be derived by avoiding such

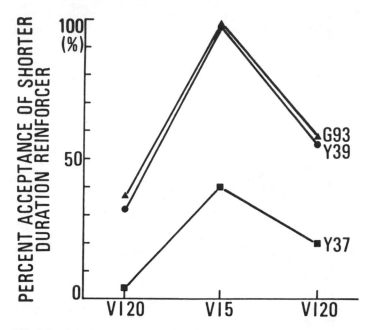

FIG. 9.7.   Percentage acceptance of the shorter duration reinforcer as a function of the VI values in the handling state (shown on abscissa) for each of three subjects (data from Ito & Fantino, 1984).

assumptions and calculating rates of energy gain "from scratch." They proceeded to develop an optimality account specially tailored for successive-choice procedures of the type used in the present experiments. Their basic strategy was to calculate the rate of energy gain for a subject always accepting both the more and less profitable outcomes (a "generalist" subject) and for one accepting only the more profitable outcome (a "specialist" subject). By comparing the energy gain rates one can determine whether it is optimal to be a generalist or a specialist under any given set of conditions. When reinforcer durations are 6 seconds ("big items") and 3 seconds ("little items"), they find that it "pays to specialize" in big items when the following inequality is satisfied:

$$p < 1 - (x + t + C)/y. \qquad (6)$$

In this expression, p is the probability that a little reward is available, x equals search duration (as in Fig. 9.6), t equals time between the end of reinforcement and the start of a new trial, C equals time in the choice phase, that is the time to complete the FR 3, and y equals time in the outcome phase (as in Fig. 9.6).

How does inequality (6) compare to comparable predictions from the DRH? For $t = 0$, its value in all these studies, the inequality reduces to

$$\frac{X + C}{(1 - p)} < Y.$$

In terms of the DRH, $Y = t_2$ and $X + C/(1 - p)$ is equivalent to t_{1R}, giving $t_{1R} <$ t_2. But $t_{1R} < t_2$ represents the equivalent inequality derived from the DRH. For the DRH,

$$t_{1R} < \frac{E_R}{E_L} t_{2L} - t_{2R} \tag{7}$$

or, because $E_R = 2E_L$, and $t_{2L} = t_{2R} = t_2$ in this example,

$$t_{1R} < t_2.$$

It is of some interest that the formulation arrived at by two preeminent behavioral ecologists is fundamentally comparable to one developed in the operant conditioning laboratory. This point is embellished in the paper's concluding remarks.

Results from the rest of Ito's experiments (Ito & Fantino, 1984) are also consistent with the DRH. For example, the rate of acceptance of the shorter reinforcer increased as the search duration increased. This finding is analogous to that of Lea (1979) and of Abarca and Fantino (1982) in the case of equal reinforcement durations but unequal handling times. In this portion of Ito and Fantino, reinforcer durations were unequal whereas handling times were equal. Their finding follows from inequalities (5), (6), and (7). For inequality (5), as search time increases λ_R decreases and, therefore the left side of the inequality increases. Because the right side of the inequality is unaffected by changes in search duration, the difference between the two sides decreases and, with sufficiently long search times, the inequality is no longer satisfied. For inequality (6), the larger X (search duration) the smaller the p required for specialization. Finally, for inequality (7) the argument is entirely comparable as that for inequality (5).

The results from Ito's studies, in conjunction with prior work, show that, at least in the context of procedures such as that shown in Fig. 9.6, the predictions of the DRH are qualitatively consistent with the effects of variations in both search and handling times, and with procedures involving both equal and unequal handling times and reward times.

Effects of Percentage Reward

In the natural environment, the probability that the sampling of a given prey or patch will provide food varies. On many occasions a "good" patch or prey is difficult to obtain and the subject may not obtain food. The classical foraging models assumed that animals rank food sources according to average rate of obtaining rewards. These models effectively ignored possible sensitivity to environmental variation (but see Houston & McNamara, 1982). Thus, a simple application of such models assumes that a forager has no preference between obtaining variable amounts of reward and always obtaining the average of these variable amounts. Caraco, Martindale, and Whittam (1980) in a laboratory simulation of foraging showed, however, that variation in rate of food intake may sometimes have an important effect on choice (see also Caraco & Lima, this volume). For example, a series of studies by Caraco (1981, 1982, 1983) working with small birds such as juncos and sparrows showed that when birds' energy intake was greater than that minimally required to meet daily energy costs, they generally preferred more constant to more variable rewards ("risk-aversion"). When their energy intake was less than the minimally required rate, however, more variable rewards were preferred ("risk proneness").

Abarca, Fantino, and Ito (1985) examined the effects of varying the percentage of reinforcement for the preferred alternative in a laboratory simulation of foraging. The procedure was a variant of that shown in Fig. 9.6. The schedules in the handling states were VI 5 seconds and VI 20 seconds, which initially terminated in food reward in all trials. In subsequent conditions, however, the percentage of reinforcement for the preferred outcome (VI 5 seconds) varied. On a certain (random) proportion of trials, $(1 - p)$, food presentation was replaced by presentation of a blackout (elimination of all chamber lights for 3 seconds). The independent variable was the percentage of reward for the VI 5-second schedule. The probabilities employed were, in order, 1.0, 0.10, 0.25, 0.63, 1.0, 0.63, 0.25, and 0.10. Each of these values defined a condition. Each condition was maintained for 20 sessions. Half the subjects were maintained in an open economy and half in a closed economy. The measures of choice were the mean probabilities of accepting the VI 5-second outcome when it was available and the VI 20-second outcome when it was available.

The preferences obtained for both the longer and shorter VIs varied as a function of the percentage of reinforcement for the shorter VI (the VI 5-second) for each of the five subjects. Figure 9.8 depicts the mean data averaged over subjects and over the two replications at each percentage reinforcement value. These data represent the mean probability of accepting the longer and the shorter VI averaged over the last five sessions in each condition. Although these data show that subjects were sensitive to variations in the percentage of reinforcement, they also show that subjects always preferred the outcome associated with the higher rate of reward.

In the condition where the percentage reward was 25%, both alternatives provided the same mean reward and both were accepted almost equally. If anything, subjects preferred the certain outcome (VI 20 seconds), thus showing a risk-averse pattern of behavior, a result ostensibly opposite to that expected from the work of Kendall (1974) and Fantino, Dunn, and Meck (1979). Whereas it is true that the two alternatives provided the same mean rate of reinforcement in the handling state (one food presentation every 20 seconds), from another perspective the certain but longer alternative provided a higher mean rate of reinforcement. This resulted from the fact that the birds had to cycle through the entire chain more often per reward on the uncertain schedule. The median obtained interreinforcement intervals for each complete chain averaged over replications in each condition were: 12 seconds (left) and 28 seconds (right) in the 100%

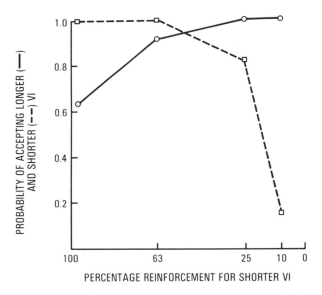

FIG. 9.8. Probability of accepting the longer (VI 20 seconds) and shorter (VI 5 seconds) schedules as a function of percentage reinforcement for the shorter VI schedule. Percentage reinforcement was always 100 for the VI 20-second schedule. Each point represents the mean data averaged over subjects and replications (after Abarca et al., 1985).

condition; 18 seconds (left) and 28 seconds (right) in the 63% condition; 54 seconds (left) and 28 seconds (right) in the 25% condition; 106 seconds (left) and 26 seconds (right) in the 10% condition. These data, taken together with the results in Fig. 9.8, support the following conclusion: subjects preferred whichever alternative provided the higher overall mean rate of reinforcement.

The probability of accepting the longer VI as a function of percentage reinforcement for the shorter VI is given for the closed- and open-economy groups separately in Fig. 9.9. The analogous data in terms of the probability of accepting the shorter VI is given in Fig. 9.10. There was no significant difference between the results obtained when subjects were maintained on open and on closed economies. In this respect, these data are similar to those from other operant simulations of foraging reported in this chapter: The generality of the functional relations obtained in the experiments on travel time and on assymetric accessibility did not appear to depend on the economic context in which the relations were obtained. However, the other studies involved concurrent-chains procedures, not the successive-choice procedure of Fig. 9.6, and they did not involve percentage reinforcement. In the present study at least a suggestive difference in the behavior of subjects maintained in open versus closed economies was found when the percentage reinforcement for the shorter VI was 100%: Namely subjects in the closed economy were more likely to accept the longer VI schedule (0.71 vs. 0.51).

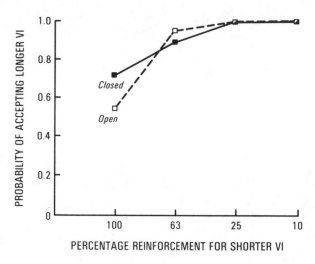

FIG. 9.9. Probability of accepting the longer (VI 20 seconds) schedule as a function of percentage reinforcement for the shorter (VI 5 seconds) outcome for subjects in open- and closed-economy conditions. Each point represents the mean data averaged over subjects and replications (after Abarca et al., 1985).

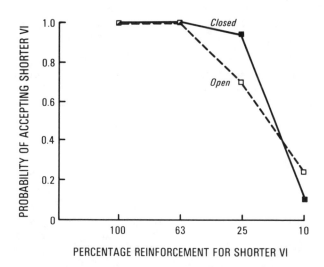

FIG. 9.10. Probability of accepting the shorter (VI 5 seconds) schedule as a function of percentage reinforcement for that outcome for subjects in open- and closed-economy conditions. Each point represents the mean data averaged over subjects and replications (after Abarca et al., 1985).

Although this difference is not significant, it is consistent with Caraco's studies that show that adequate food consumption promoted risk aversion. In terms of the present experiment, subjects maintained on a closed economy should be more likely to accept an available alternative than those maintained on an open economy because: (a) they receive their entire food supply in the experimental session, whereas those on open economies do not receive enough to maintain themselves at 80% of their free-feeding body weight (and need to be supplemented in their home cages); and (b) subjects maintained on our closed economies come to have higher body weights than those maintained on open economies, (i.e., body weights above 80%). Thus, when presented with the opportunity to accept the longer handling time, they may be more likely to do so than their open-economy counterparts. However, as noted earlier differences between performance in closed and open economies was at best only suggestive and, in any event, not statistically significant. The primary conclusion based on the present results is that choice was well accounted for, at least qualitatively, but the mean rates of reinforcement associated with the alternatives.

CONCLUDING DISCUSSION

Staddon (1983) has developed a comprehensive treatment of adaptive behavior and learning that has explicit application to work on foraging and that also deals with choice in the concurrent-chains procedure (Fig. 9.1). Staddon points out that an optimality analysis is not only useful for understanding much about foraging (consistent with the view presented here) but is also illuminating when applied to choice in situations not generally considered analogs to foraging. In terms of the present experiments, Staddon develops an inequality equivalent to that of the present equation (4). He notes that this equation predicts what should happen when either search duration or handling-time duration is varied. In each case the predictions are identical to those of the present approach. Staddon goes on to acknowledge that his analysis "cannot account for variations in the degree of preference within the 'both' region" (p. 502), i.e., within the region where both outcomes are acceptable (where the inequality in equation 3 is not satisfied). He notes that the models of Fantino (1969, 1981) and Killeen (1982) are applicable here, however. As noted earlier (Fig. 9.5 and its discussion) experiments are now being carried out to differentiate between the predictions of Killeen's model and the DRH. In any case, Abarca (1982) and Staddon (1983) have independently shown that for choice in concurrent-chains procedures, predictions from a rate-maximization analysis, such as the ODM, coincide with those of the DRH. In this chapter it is shown that for choice in successive-choice procedures, predictions from a rate-maximization analysis, that of Kacelnik and Krebs (1985), again coincide with those of the DRH. These correspondences are not surprising because the DRH is itself a rate-maximization hypothesis.

The experiments reported in this chapter were all guided by the theoretical framework suggested by the ODM and the DRH. Results from experiments with varying search state durations, varying travel-time durations, varying rates of accessibility of rewards, varying handling-time durations, and varying percentage reward are all qualitatively accounted for by the DRH and the ODM. This conclusion applies to studies where rewards differ in handling time and in amount and where deprivation conditions resemble those of open or closed economies. The results suggest that the technology of the operant conditioning laboratory may have fruitful application in the study of foraging.

APPENDIX

For Killeen (1982) the strength of a schedule (S) is a combination of three factors: the rate of primary reinforcement on the schedule (R), the primary effect of the reinforcer (P), and any conditioned reinforcement (C). Specifically,

$$S = R (S_D) = R (P + C),$$

where S_D equals the sum of the directive effects $(P$ and $C)$ of the schedule.

The primary effects of the reinforcer are exponentially decayed by any delay imposed between a given response (e.g., the choice response producing the outcome phase) and the reinforcer such that:

$$P = \exp(-qt),$$

where q is a rate constant and t is the delay between the response and the reinforcer. When there is no delay, $P = 1$. As applied to the concurrent-chains procedure (Fig. 9.1), t equals the duration of the outcome phase. The conditioned reinforcement provided by the terminal-link stimuli of concurrent chains is usually immediate and therefore not decayed. But, conditioned reinforcers are not as effective as primary reinforcers. This assumption is incorporated by considering the conditioned reinforcement (C) to be equal to the immediacy of the primary reinforcement such that

$$C = 1/t.$$

Finally, the rate of reinforcement on a key is

$$R = 1/(I + t),$$

where I represents the average duration of the initial link. The complete model, then, predicts that

$$\frac{B_L}{B_R} = \frac{S_L}{S_R} = \frac{R_L(S_{DL})}{R_R(S_{DR})} = \frac{[\exp(-qt_L) + (1/t_L)]/(I_L + t_L)}{[\exp(-qt_R) + (1/t_R)]/(I_R + t_R)}$$

where B_L and B_R are rates of responding on the left and right alternative, and the subscripts L and R designate the left and right alternatives, respectively. In summary, incentive theory predicts relative response rates in a choice phase as a function of the relative strengths of the separate schedules. In particular, incentive theory postulates that relative response rates in the choice phase of the schedule will match the relative schedule strength.

In the case of varying the accessibility of the less profitable outcome the predictions of incentive theory are straightforward: assuming that $S_{DR} < S_{DL}$, varying the initial link leading to S_{DR} has its full effect by increasing or decreasing I_R.

ACKNOWLEDGMENTS

This research was supported by National Science Foundation Grant BNS 83–02963 and by NIMH Grant MH-20752 to the University of California at San Diego and was conducted while all three authors were at the University of California, San Diego. We thank the editors for many constructive, invaluable suggestions.

REFERENCES

Abarca, N. (1982). *On the mechanism of foraging*. Unpublished doctoral dissertation, University of California, San Diego.

Abarca, N., & Fantino, E. (1982). Choice and foraging. *Journal of the Experimental Analysis of Behavior, 38*, 117–123.

Abarca, N., Fantino, E., & Ito, M. (1985). Percentage reward in an operant analogue to foraging. *Animal Behaviour, 33*, 1096–1101.

Altmann, J. (1974). Observational study of behavior: Sampling methods. *Behavior, 49*, 227–262.

Baum, W. M. (1983). Studying foraging in the psychological laboratory. In R. L. Mellgren (Ed.), *Animal cognition and behavior* (pp. 253–283). Amsterdam: North–Holland.

Caraco, T. (1981). Energy budgets, risk and foraging preferences in dark-eyed juncos (*Junco hyemalis*). *Behavioral Ecology and Sociobiology, 8*, 213–127.

Caraco, T. (1982). Aspects of risk-aversion in foraging white-crowned sparrows. *Animal Behaviour, 30*, 710–217.

Caraco, T. (1983). White-crowned sparrows (*Zonotrichia leucophrys*): Foraging preferences in a risky environment. *Behavioral Ecology and Sociobiology, 12*, 63–69.

Caraco, T., Martindale, S., & Whittam, T. S. (1980). An empirical demonstration of risk-sensitive foraging preferences. *Animal Behaviour, 28*, 820–830.

Case, D., & Fantino, E. (1981). The delay-reduction hypothesis of conditioned reinforcement and punishment: Observing behavior. *Journal of the Experimental Analysis of Behavior, 35*, 93–108.

Charnov, E. L. (1976). Optimal foraging: Attack strategy of a mantid. *The American Naturalist, 110*, 141–151.

Collier, G. H., & Rovee-Collier, C. K. (1981). A comparative analysis of optimal foraging behavior: Laboratory simulation. In A. C. Kamil & T. Sargent (Eds.), *Foraging behavior: Ecological, ethological, and psychological approaches* (pp. 39–76). New York: Garland Press.

Collier, G. H., & Rovee-Collier, C. K. (1983). An ecological perspective of reinforcement and motivation. In E. Satinoff & P. Teitelbaum (Eds.), *Handbook of behavioral neurobiology* (Vol. 6, pp. 427–441). New York: Plenum.

Fantino, E. (1969). Choice and rate of reinforcement. *Journal of the Experimental Analysis of Behavior, 12,* 723–730.

Fantino, E. (1977). Conditioned reinforcement: Choice and information. In W. K. Honig & J. E. R. Staddon (Eds.), *Handbook of operant behavior* (pp. 313–339). Englewood Cliffs, NJ: Prentice-Hall.

Fantino, E. (1981). Contiguity, response strength, and the delay-reduction hypothesis. In P. Harzem & M. D. Zeiler (Eds.), *Advances in analysis of behavior, Vol. 2: Predictability, correlation and contiguity* (pp. 169–201). Chichester, England: Wiley.

Fantino, E. (1982). Effects of initial-link length on responding in terminal link. *Behaviour Analysis Letters, 2,* 65–70.

Fantino, E. (1984). *Operant conditioning simulations of foraging and the delay-reduction hypothesis.* Paper presented at the Foraging Behavior Conference, Brown University, Providence, Rhode Island.

Fantino, E., & Abarca, N. (1985). Choice, optimal foraging, and the delay-reduction hypothesis. *The Behavioral and Brain Sciences, 8,* 315–362.

Fantino, E., Abarca, N., & Dunn, R. (in press). The delay-reduction hypothesis. Extensions to foraging and three-alternative choice. In M. L. Commons, J. E. Mazur, J. A. Nevin, & H. Rachlin (Eds.), *Quantitative analyses of behavior, Vol. 5: Reinforcement value: Delay and intervening events.* Hillsdale, NJ: Lawrence Erlbaum Associates.

Fantino, E., & Davison, M. (1983). Choice: Some quantitative relations. *Journal of the Experimental Analysis of Behavior, 40,* 1–13.

Fantino, E., & Dunn, R. (1983). The delay-reduction hypothesis: Extension to three-alternative choice. *Journal of Experimental Psychology: Animal Behavior Processes, 9,* 132–146.

Fantino, E., Dunn, R., & Meck, W. (1979). Percentage reinforcement and choice. *Journal of the Experimental Analysis of Behavior, 32,* 335–340.

Fantino, E., & Logan, C. (1979). *The experimental analysis of behavior: A biological perspective.* San Francisco: W. H. Freeman.

Ferster, C. B., & Skinner, B. F. (1957). *Schedules of reinforcement.* New York: Appleton-Century-Crofts.

Honig, W. K., & Staddon, J. E. R. (1977). *Handbook of operant behavior.* Englewood Cliffs, NJ: Prentice-Hall.

Houston, A. I., & MacNamara, J. (1982). A sequential approach to risk-taking. *Animal Behaviour, 30,* 1260–1261.

Hursh, S. R. (1980). Economic concepts for the analysis of behavior. *Journal of the Experimental Analysis of Behavior, 34,* 219–238.

Ito, M., & Asaki, K. (1982). Choice behavior of rats in a concurrent-chains schedule: Amount and delay of reinforcement. *Journal of the Experimental Analysis of Behavior, 37,* 383–392.

Ito, M., & Fantino, E. (1984). *Choice, foraging, and reinforcer duration.* Manuscript in preparation.

Kacelnik, A., & Krebs, J. R. (1985). Rate of reinforcement matters in O.F.T. *The Behavioral and Brain Sciences.*

Kamil, A. C., & Sargent, T. D. (1981). *Foraging behavior: Ecological, ethological, and psychological approaches.* New York: Garland Press.

Kendall, S. B. (1974). Preference for intermittent reinforcement. *Journal of the Experimental Analysis of Behavior, 21,* 463–473.

Killeen, P. R. (1982). Incentive theory: II. Models for choice. *Journal of the Experimental Analysis of Behavior, 38,* 217–232.

Killeen, P. R. (1985). Delay-reduction: A field guide for optimal foragers? *The Behavioral and Brain Sciences.*

Krebs, J. R., Kacelnik, A., & Taylor, P. (1978). Test of optimal sampling by foraging great tits. *Nature, 275,* 27–31.

Lea, S. E. G. (1979). Foraging and reinforcement schedules in the pigeon: Optimal and non-optimal aspects of choice. *Animal Behaviour, 27,* 875–886.

Lea, S. E. G. (1981). Correlation and contiguity in foraging behaviour. In P. Harzem & M. D. Zeiler (Eds.), *Advances in analysis of behaviour, Vol. 2: Predictability, correlation, and contiguity* (pp. 355–406). Chichester, England: Wiley.

MacArthur, R. H., & Pianka, E. R. (1966). On optimal use of a patchy environment. *American Naturalist, 100,* 603–609.

Navarick, D. J., & Fantino, E. (1976). Self-control and general models of choice. *Journal of Experimental Psychology: Animal Behavior Processes, 2,* 75–87.

Pyke, G. H., Pulliam, H. R., & Charnov, E. L. (1977). Optimal foraging: A selective review of theory and tests. *The Quarterly Review of Biology, 52,* 137–154.

Squires, N., & Fantino, E. (1971). A model for choice in simple concurrent and concurrent-chains schedules. *Journal of the Experimental Analysis of Behavior, 15,* 27–38.

Staddon, J. E. R. (1983). *Adaptive behavior and learning.* Cambridge, England: Cambridge University Press.

IV
SPECIAL FORAGING ADAPTATIONS

10 Foraging for Stored Food

David F. Sherry
University of Toronto

Most models of foraging require that animals possess information about the distribution and abundance of food in their environment (Krebs, 1978; Pyke, Pulliam, & Charnov, 1977; Schoener, 1971). Animals that search for food they have stored themselves might be expected to possess a great deal more information about its distribution than animals foraging for food distributed in ways they cannot control. Some birds, notably marsh tits (*Parus palustris*), black-capped chickadees (*Parus atricapillus*), and Clark's nutcrackers (*Nucifraga columbiana*), are capable of remembering hundreds of locations where they have cached food, and in some cases the current status and contents of these caches. They are able to retain this information in memory for several days, and probably much longer, and they rely on it to guide the accurate and efficient recovery of their stored food supply.

Although the spatial memory of food-storing birds seems remarkable, the differences between food cachers and foragers may be more apparent than real. In both cases animals have the opportunity to acquire information about where food is to be found, and, if they are able to retain it, can use this information to direct their searching. The study of food storing allows us to determine what information can be retained and how it is used to guide search. It may provide an indication of the kind of information processing that is available to other foraging animals.

NATURAL HISTORY

Chickadees and tits will store food most of the year, but in fall and winter their caching reaches its peak (Ludescher, 1980). The birds store hundreds of prey items per day and may thus establish thousands of caches over the course of a winter. Single food items, such as seeds, pieces of nut, insects, spiders, and other invertebrates are each placed in a separate site in hollow stems, moss, crevices in bark, dry leaves, clusters of conifer needles, and other cache sites (Fig. 10.1). Storage sites are not reused, and they tend to be evenly spaced throughout the territory. In a study in Wytham Wood, Oxford, the mean distance between neighboring marsh tit storage sites was 7 meters, with little variation about this mean either within or between birds (Cowie, Krebs, & Sherry, 1981). Clark's nutcrackers store the seeds of whitebark and other pines by burying them in the ground, and it has been estimated that a typical bird may establish over 9,000 separate caches in late summer and fall (Tomback, 1982). Nutcrackers usually store several seeds at each site and prefer to store them on steep south-facing slopes, on which little snow accumulates and which experience early spring melt-off (Tomback, 1977).

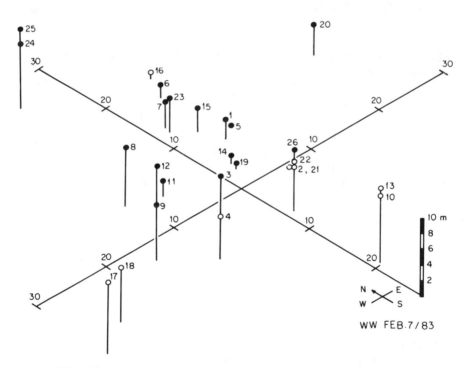

FIG. 10.1. A three-dimensional representation of storage sites established by a black-capped chickadee during 2 hours of observation in a mixed conifer-hardwood forest. Open circles represent sunflower seeds, closed circles, safflower seeds. Numbers indicate the sequence in which seeds were taken from a feeder located at the origin of the axes. Horizontal and vertical scales are given in meters. Points on the same vertical line represent seeds stored in the same tree. Seeds 2 and 21 were stored on different branches at the same height in the same tree.

Is Stored Food Recovered?

Cowie, Krebs, and Sherry (1981) were able to locate marsh tit storage sites in the wild by offering the birds sunflower seeds radioactively labeled with technetium (Tc^{99m}) and then hunting for stored seeds using a portable scintillation meter. To determine whether cached seeds were later collected by the bird that cached them, we placed control seeds at every site we found: a "near" control 10 centimeters away from the stored seed and a "far" control 100 centimeters away. These control seeds were placed in the same type of site and at the same height as the cached seed. If seeds are not taken by the animal that cached them, or if marsh tits re-encounter their caches only by chance in the course of normal foraging, hoarded and control seeds should all disappear at the same rate. The procedure was replicated a total of eight times, with three territorial marsh tit pairs. Inspection at intervals of 3 hours showed that the mean survivorship of cached seeds was 7.7 daylight hours from the time of storage, 13.5 hours for near-control, and 20.4 hours for far-control seeds. (Daylight hours alone were measured because marsh tits are not active at night.) The simplest explanation for this result is that the bird that cached the seeds returned and recovered them. Any other animal foraging in the area would have taken stored and control seeds with equal likelihood, as would a marsh tit that merely re-encountered its stored food at random. On 121 occasions we knew whether the cached seed or its near control had disappeared first. Ninety-three times it was the cached seed, which indicates that despite the nearness of the two seeds, the one cached by a marsh tit was taken preferentially.

A mean survivorship of 20.4 daylight hours for far-control seeds is roughly equal to the expected survivorship of seeds placed a meter apart and subject to normal predation by birds and rodents. But the spacing between neighboring seeds does affect loss to other animals, and marsh tits appear to be influenced by this. Sherry, Avery, and Stevens (1982) laid out square arrays of 25 sunflower seeds in Wytham Wood and systematically varied the spacing of neighboring seeds within an array. We found that survivorship increased with increasing spacing in an array, up to about 7 meters between neighboring seeds. Seeds stored in arrays with nearest neighbor distances of 1.8, 3.6, or 7.2 meters survived for means of 16.2 ± 4.8, 18.5 ± 3.7, or 78.4 ± 29.6 daylight hours (± 1 SEM), respectively. Additional spacing (10.8 and 14.4 meters between seeds) did not significantly increase the survivorship of seeds. As noted earlier, the mean nearest neighbor distance between marsh tit caches is about 7 meters, the spacing at which the maximum survivorship of artificial caches was found. Chewed hulls and droppings at seed sites in the experimental arrays indicated heavy predation by mice and voles. It appears that marsh tits cannot prevent loss of some stored food to other animals but space their caches sufficiently far apart to minimize this loss. Spacing caches is probably energetically costly, because it requires a return trip from the food source to the cache site, and the birds do not incur the energetic cost of spacing caches farther apart when the increased spacing results in no additional reduction of loss to other animals.

Clark's nutcrackers establish groups of caches within an area of a few meters and establish many such groups (Tomback, 1977). They are better at locating caches than they would be if they searched at random, as Tomback (1980) was able to show from the proportions of successful and unsuccessful bill probes in the soil. Probes into the soil were 75% successful in the spring, as indicated by discarded hulls around probe holes, but this success rate declined over the summer as more caches were recovered or lost to rodents. Similar, though less systematic, field observations have been made of Eurasian nutcrackers (*Nucifraga caryocatactes;* Swanberg, 1951) and European jays (*Garrulus glandarius;* Bossema, 1979).

Nutcrackers use food stored in the fall to survive the winter and to feed their young in the spring (Vander Wall & Balda 1981; Vander Wall & Hutchins, 1983). Compared to this, the interval of 7 daylight hours between caching and recovery that was found for marsh tits seems surprisingly short. Even if one allows for 15 hours or more of darkness at the latitude of Oxford in winter, most cached seeds were recovered within 1 or 2 days of hoarding. Why then should marsh tits store food at all if it is collected after such a short interval?

One possibility is that storing confers independence from fluctuations in the supply of food. Animals able to use a supply of cached food are buffered from the effects of scarcity. Whether food availability fluctuates from season to season or is prone to vary from day to day, or even within days, caching food when it is abundant and harvesting it during scarcity should be beneficial. The South Island robin (*Petroica australis*) of New Zealand caches invertebrate prey and recovers it within a few days. Caching occurs most often in the morning, and recovery in the afternoon (Powlesland, 1980). Kestrels (*Falco sparverius* and *F. tinnunculus*) also show a daily pattern of capturing and caching prey when they are available, and recovering them later the same day (Collopy, 1977; Mueller, 1974; Rijnsdorp, Daan, & Dijkstra, 1981).

Another possibility is that caching provides some independence from fluctuations in energy requirements. Energy requirements may vary seasonally, as mean daily temperature varies, or when an energetically costly activity, such as raising young, is underway. Acorn woodpeckers rarely feed acorns to young in the nest, but, instead, rely on stored acorns to meet their own energy requirements while collecting insects to feed to the young (Koenig, 1978). But energy requirements can also vary over shorter periods. Low overnight temperature, for example, may raise the energy requirements of small birds (Chaplin, 1974; Reinertsen, 1983), and hence the amount of food that must be consumed. Buffering from variation in energy requirements, even very short-term variation, may be beneficial.

Finally, there may be benefits from decoupling the requirements for food from the need to forage for it. When other activities like defending a territory or searching for mates compete with foraging for time, some animals reduce or abandon foraging and rely on energy reserves stored as fat (Mrosovsky & Sherry, 1980; Sherry, 1981). Access to cached food, whether it has been stored days or months before, may provide a similar flexibility in the allocation of time between foraging and other activities.

Laboratory Studies of Memory and Cache Recovery

The field study described earlier showed that marsh tits do not re-encounter their stored food by chance in the course of normal foraging, and hints that memory for the site is involved, but it does not show unequivocally that memory is the mechanism of retrieval. The birds could, for example, have a rule about the *types* of site in which to cache and later search only sites satisfying this rule. Or they could cache and recover at regular intervals along a fixed route and remember only their movement rule and not the locations of many storage sites.

Marsh tits in captivity readily store seeds, and in the laboratory it is possible to control the conditions under which they search for and recover stored food (Sherry, Krebs, & Cowie, 1981). In the laboratory experiments, a bird was admitted into an aviary containing three trays of moss, each divided into four sectors, and was observed for 15 minutes. No food was available, and the time the bird spent in each sector of moss was recorded. The purpose of this prestorage observation period was to measure baseline preferences and biases to search each sector of moss. Birds were next given sunflower seeds and allowed to store for 15 minutes, after which they were allowed to leave the aviary. After 24 hours, birds were readmitted to the aviary for 15 minutes to search for the seeds they had stored. The seeds had been removed in the interval to eliminate the possibility that partially concealed seeds could be spotted from a perch or detected directly by olfaction or some other means. The amount of time spent searching moss sectors where storage had occurred, and the frequency at which they were visited, was compared to the time spent at, and visits made to, these sectors during the baseline prestoring period (Fig. 10.2a). Because a mean of 5.5 sectors out of the 12 available was used for storage per trial, birds searching at random would be expected to allocate 46% of their time and visits to sites where they had cached food. However, during the search phase of the experiment about 90% of the birds' searching time was spent in these sectors.

For each bird, the distribution of stored seeds was different on every trial, but each moss sector was used for storage in the course of the experiment, and no significant preference was shown by the birds to cache seeds in particular sectors of moss or regions of the aviary. These findings indicate the birds were not caching and recovering along a regular route, nor were they caching and recovering only from preferred sites. There was no indication that birds marked storage sites or covered stored seeds with moss or other material, as do crested tits

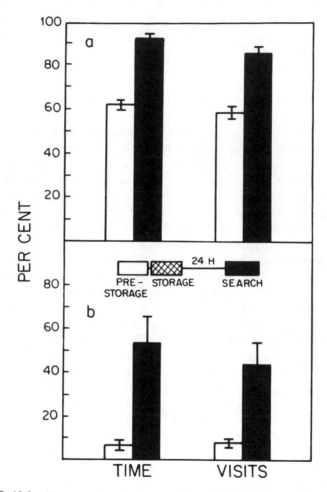

FIG. 10.2. Memory and cache recovery. Time and visits at sites used for storage, as a percentage of time and visits at all available sites. Marsh tits (a), chickadees (b). In this and following figures error bars equal ± 1 SEM and all statistical tests are on arcsin transformed percent data. Marsh tits ($N = 3$) stored a mean of 9.5 seeds in a mean of 5.5 of the 12 available 40 × 35 cm moss sectors. Chickadees ($N = 4$) stored a mean of 4.4 seeds in 4.4 of 72 available holes on artificial trees. All differences between prestorage and search behavior are significant at the .05 level by 2-tailed t test. Redrawn from Sherry, Krebs, & Cowie (1981) and Sherry (1984a).

(*Parus cristatus*) and boreal chickadees (*Parus hudsonicus;* Haftorn, 1953, 1974).

Thus the search for stored food is more successful than chance encounter would account for. It can occur without direct detection of the stored food item and is accurate up to 24 hours after storage. More recent experiments of similar design show that black-capped chickadees also use memory to relocate storage sites (Fig. 10.2b).

Laboratory studies by Vander Wall (1982) and Balda (1980) have shown that nutcrackers also relocate caches using memory. One of Vander Wall's (1982) experiments showed that Clark's nutcrackers use local landmarks to relocate caches, and that displacing these landmarks in the aviary causes the birds to displace their search probes in the same direction by the appropriate amount.

Interocular Transfer and Memory

A further experiment with marsh tits, which relies on a peculiar feature of the avian visual system, also points to spatial memory as the important mechanism in cache recovery. In some birds there is limited interocular transfer for some kinds of visual discriminations. If one of a pigeon's eyes is covered with an opaque shield, and the bird is trained monocularly on a jumping stand or keypeck discrimination, it must relearn the discrimination in order to perform correctly with the naive eye (Graves & Goodale 1977; Green, Brecha, & Gazzaniga, 1978; Levine 1945). If each eye is trained and tested singly, conflicting discriminations can be trained to the two eyes simultaneously. Not all visual discriminations fail to transfer, however. Recent research with pigeons indicates that failure of interocular transfer occurs when visual information falls on the area of the retina serving monocular vision, by far the largest region on the retina of birds with panoramic vision (Goodale & Graves, 1982). Complete decussation of the optic nerves at the chiasm, along with limited commissural decussation of fibres serving monocular vision, may be responsible for this. In addition, task difficulty may also affect the degree of interocular transfer (Green et al., 1978). If marsh tits too have limited interocular transfer for visual information, an experiment can be performed to determine whether visual information acquired during caching is necessary for successful cache recovery.

Marsh tits that had one of their eyes covered with a small opaque plastic cap readily flew, ate, and stored seeds in trays of moss. The eye cap was attached to the feathers around the eye with cosmetic eyelash adhesive. After seeds had been stored, it could be removed and placed over the eye that had been open during storage or, in a control procedure, replaced on the same eye that had been covered during storage. Birds that stored seeds and later searched for them using the same eye performed as well as birds using both eyes (Fig. 10.3). Birds that were forced to use the ''naive'' eye during search performed no better than the chance level. This experiment shows that when visual information acquired during storage, presumably information about the spatial location of storage

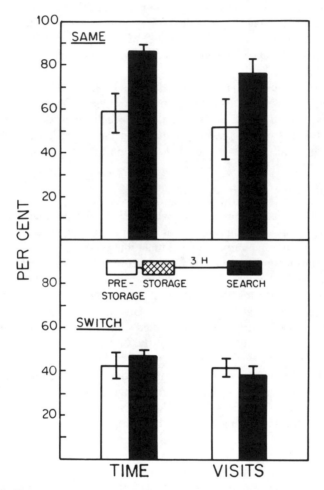

FIG. 10.3. Interocular transfer and memory in marsh tits. After storage, the eyecap was removed and replaced on either the eye covered during storage (SAME condition) or on the eye open during storage (SWITCH condition). The figure shows time and visits to sites used for storage, as a percentage of time spent at, and visits to, all available sites. Marsh tits ($N = 2$) stored a mean of 6.4 seeds in a mean of 4.4 of the 12 available 40×35 centimeter moss sectors. The difference between prestorage and search behavior is significant in the SAME condition at the .05 level by 1-tailed paired t test but is not significant for the SWITCH condition. From Sherry, Krebs, & Cowie (1981) and Sherry (1984b).

sites, is unavailable, storage sites cannot be readily relocated (Sherry et al., 1981).

Using Memory

Marsh tits and black-capped chickadees may be able to remember where they have cached food, as indicated by the foregoing results, but for the food-storing strategy to succeed, memory for cache sites must possess a number of additional properties. As noted earlier, these birds recover food a few days after storing it. Storage sites are not reused in the wild, so that in a short period of time a large number of sites that were accurately remembered become empty former cache sites. We can predict that to recover stored food efficiently birds that have recovered some caches should be able to avoid revisiting these empty sites, while continuing to accurately relocate caches that still contain food.

Caches can also be emptied by other animals (Sherry et al., 1982; Tomback, 1980). We can predict, in a similar fashion, that birds should be able to avoid revisiting cache sites they have returned to once and found to be empty.

Finally, marsh tits and chickadees store a variety of foods. Seeds, nuts, insects, and other invertebrate prey differ in their caloric and nutrient composition, handling times, and availability in the environment. Myton and Ficken (1967) report that black-capped chickadees' preference for different types of seed is affected by air temperature. Recovering some kinds of food and not others may be advantageous in the wild. We can predict that when more than one kind of food is hoarded, birds can remember what kind of food is stored at which site. These three predictions have been tested in the laboratory, as described next.

Avoiding Revisiting

As marsh tits and chickadees recover the food they have cached, some of the remembered storage sites change in status, from full to empty. Other storage sites that have not been visited, or have been visited and merely inspected, remain intact. Laboratory experiments with marsh tits and chickadees indicate that these sites are distinguished in memory.

Birds stored sunflower seeds and 24 hours later were allowed to recover half of them. After an additional 24-hour interval the birds were allowed to return to the aviary and search for their caches. All remaining seeds had been removed in the interval, and the amount of time spent searching at the two categories of storage site was recorded. More time was spent searching at sites where no recovery had occurred. At sites where recovery had occurred 24 hours previously (and 24 hours after the initial storage bout), the time spent searching did not exceed control levels (Fig. 10.4; Sherry, 1982, 1984a). Simple performance rules do not account for the avoidance of emptied sites. The sites visited and emptied were not spatially clustered, at least not in the laboratory, and there was

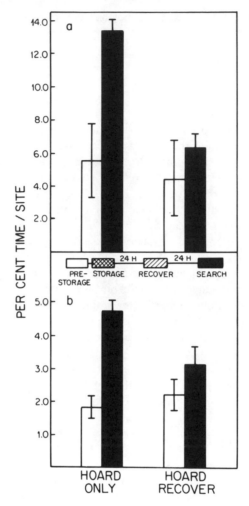

FIG. 10.4. Avoiding revisits. Time spent at storage sites, as a percentage of time spent at all available sites for marsh tits (top) and black-capped chickadees (bottom). At hoard-recover sites birds stored seeds and recovered them before the search phase. At hoard-only sites seeds were stored but not recovered by the bird. Results are shown as percentage per site, because the number of hoard-only and hoard-recover sites was not always equal. Marsh tits ($N = 4$) stored a mean of 9.3 seeds in 6.4 of the 27 available 23×27 centimeter moss sectors and recovered 4.8 of them from 3.1 sectors. Chickadees ($N = 4$) stored a mean of 12.0 seeds and recovered 6.0 of them from among 72 available holes on artificial trees. Differences between prestorage and search are significant for hoard-only sites at the .05 level by 1-tailed t test. Differences are not significant for hoard-recover sites. From Sherry (1984b).

no correlation between the sequence of recovery and the sequence of storage. In the field, successive storage sites are established in loose aggregations and may be recovered as a group at about the same time (Cowie et al., 1981). The aviary experiments show, however, that neither spatial clustering nor recovery based on the sequence of storage is necessary for birds successfully to avoid revisiting caches they have emptied.

Shettleworth and Krebs (1982) have looked at 12-minute bouts of cache recovery and found that marsh tits also avoid revisiting storage sites over this shorter time period. It is not clear whether the birds avoid revisiting in the short run by using the same memory process they use to avoid sites emptied on the previous day.

Balda (1980) has found that, in contrast to chickadees and tits, Eurasian nutcrackers do not avoid cache sites where they have already harvested stored food. He offered several possible explanations. Nutcrackers range widely and do not normally remain in the area where they have collected stored food. They may not, therefore, normally retain information about which caches they have previously visited. Because more than one seed is stored in a cache by nutcrackers, revisiting may sometimes uncover food that was missed during the first recovery attempt. Nutcrackers often husk recovered seeds at the cache site and so are provided with a visual cue to which sites they have already visited. Because this cue is available they may not need to retain in memory information about previous visits. It would be valuable to determine whether these differences between tits and nutcrackers in recovery behavior have produced different mnemonic rules for cache recovery.

Avoiding Revisiting Lost Caches

In the wild, stored food may be taken by other animals (Sherry et al., 1982; Tomback 1980) or lost for other reasons. We have found that chickadees sometimes push sunflower seeds so deeply into bark that they cannot be removed. Wind and rain occasionally dislodge the stored seeds of marsh tits or destroy the cache site. Food-storing birds should be able to avoid searching at sites that they have already discovered to be empty as readily as they avoid sites that they have emptied themselves. To test this, captive black-capped chickadees were allowed to store sunflower seeds in artificial trees and then visit these sites 24 hours later. In the meantime, one third of their cached seeds had been removed at random by the experimenter. The birds visited most of these random removal sites and also recovered some of the stored seed that had been left undisturbed. After a further 24 hours the birds were allowed to return to the aviary to search for storage sites (all remaining seeds having been removed by the experimenter). Birds were as successful at avoiding the sites that they discovered had been pilfered as they were at avoiding sites they had emptied themselves. Time spent searching at storage sites where neither recovery by the bird nor random removal had occurred exceeded the baseline control level, as in previous experiments (Sherry, 1984a).

Loss of stored food not only affects subsequent recovery behavior but also influences the way food is cached during later episodes of storing. Stevens (1984) has investigated marsh tits' memory for the kind of storage sites that are subject to loss or pilfering by other animals. In an aviary, he offered marsh tits different types of material in which to cache including moss, hollow stems, and bark. Cached food was then systematically removed from one of these site types, for example from all patches of moss. On succeeding storage bouts, the birds responded by storing fewer seeds in moss and more in the other kinds of site available. Comparable results were obtained by systematically pilfering other types of site.

In the wild, marsh tits have preferences for certain types of storage site, but these preferences change from day to day (Cowie et al., 1981). These changes may be responses to the behavior of rodents or birds that prey on stored food. By varying the types of site used for caching and by remembering where loss has occurred, marsh tits may be able to keep a step ahead of such competitors.

Although the birds avoid revisiting both the caches they have already recovered and caches that have been lost to other animals, their response to these events should differ in other ways, because the loss of stored food to other animals reduces the profitability of caching. Mott-Trille (1983) has examined the effect of random pilfering on the bird's willingness to store additional food. The variable measured was how many seeds birds in an aviary would add to the total amount of stored food, when given ad lib access to seeds. Birds spent about 1 hour per day in a large aviary adjoining their home cage, where they could freely store, recover, eat and recache sunflower seeds. The number of seeds stored in a bout of caching was found to vary with the rate of pilfering experimentally imposed on the previous trials. The higher the level of random pilfering (0, 25, and 50% imposed in random order), the lower the number of seeds stored during a bout. The number of seeds recovered and eaten did not differ significantly among conditions, which indicates that the effect is specific to hoarding and not a general motivational effect. Thus, not only are the spatial locations of both recovered and lost caches remembered, but how the site came to be empty influences subsequent storage behavior.

The Contents of Caches

Marsh tits and chickadees store a variety of foods in the wild. It can be predicted that food-storing birds would benefit from remembering what type of food was stored in a cache. In the laboratory black-capped chickadees prefer sunflower seeds with the shells removed to safflower seeds with the shells on. They will, however, eat and store both types of seeds. In an experiment to establish the nature of this preference, 80.0% of the seeds cached by the birds and 79.6% of the seeds eaten were sunflower seeds when both types of seeds were offered ad lib. When only six seeds of each type were offered in a second experiment on cache recovery, however, all seeds were taken and either cached or eaten. The birds created roughly equal numbers of storage sites of each type in artificial trees. Twenty-four hours following this storage episode birds were allowed to return to the aviary to search for stored seed. All seeds had been removed in the

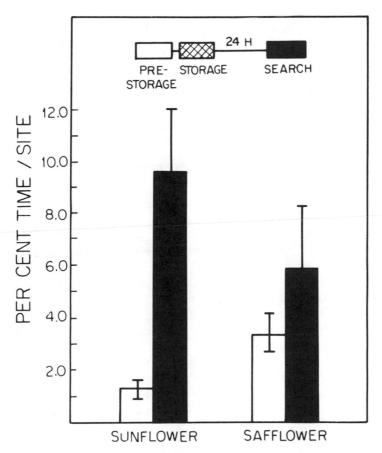

FIG. 10.5.   The contents of caches. Time at sunflower and safflower storage sites, as a percentage of time spent at all of 72 available storage holes on artificial trees. Results are shown as percentage per storage site because the number of sunflower and safflower sites was not always equal. Chickadees ($N = 5$) stored a mean of 3.2 sunflower seeds and 2.2 safflower seeds. For sunflower sites the difference between prestorage and search is significant at the .01 level by 2-tailed t test, but this difference is not significant for safflower sites. Redrawn from Sherry (1984a).

interval to control for visual or other detection of the stored seed itself. Storage sites containing safflower seeds were not searched at a level significantly above the control level, but sunflower sites were (Fig. 10.5).

Although sunflower seeds tended to be stored first, storage sites were not necessarily searched in the same order in which they had been created. This is in agreement with the findings of previous experiments in which there was no tendency to search first the caches that had been established first. Sunflower and safflower caches were not established in spatially distinct clumps, nor were different types of seed stored at different heights. Whillans-Browning (1983), in a field study of two populations of color-banded black-capped chickadees, has found no tendency to store mealworms, sunflower seeds, or safflower seeds at different heights or in different types of site. The laboratory results thus provide some indication that chickadees, in the absence of site-type cues and of the stored food itself, are able to recall which of two seed types was stored at a site and search preferentially at sites containing seeds known from an independent test to be preferred (Sherry, 1984a).

AVOIDING REVISITS: MEMORY AND FORAGING

I have suggested that memory in food-storing birds can give us some indication of the kind of mechanisms that foraging animals may have available for retaining and processing information about the abundance and distribution of food. I will briefly discuss one area where foraging animals face a problem directly comparable to that of food-storing birds.

The ability of marsh tits and chickadees to avoid places where they have already collected stored food or previously found their cache gone resembles behavior observed in two other well-known foraging studies. Nectar-feeding birds avoid revisiting flowers they have depleted of nectar because, once depleted, nectar is not available again from these flowers for some time. Gill and Wolf (1977) found that successive visits by territorial golden-winged sunbirds (*Nectarinia reichenowi*) to inflorescences differed from a Poisson random distribution of visits and revisits in about half of their observations. In most cases, the difference was due to birds revisiting depleted influorescences less often than would be expected by chance.

Likewise, it was found that amakihi (*Loxops virens*) avoided revisiting individual clusters of flowers for about 1 hour after their initial visit, when a similar criterion of a non-Poisson distribution of visits and revisits was used to detect avoidance (Kamil, 1978). Kamil reported that ''no obvious spatial pattern mediates the avoidance of recently visited clusters (of flowers)'' (p. 393).

Avoiding patches where food availability has been depressed, either by depletion or disturbance to the prey, is probably a very common problem for foraging animals (Charnov, Orians, & Hyatt, 1976). Avoiding all previously visited patches by remembering exactly which patches have been visited is one obvious solution to the problem, if such a solution is at all feasible. The results from studies of chickadees, tits, and nutcrackers suggest that it may be. There is also evidence suggesting that for other animals a memory solution to the problem of revisiting depressed patches is possible.

Olton, Roberts, and others have shown in a number of studies that laboratory rats can remember where they have been in mazes of 8, 16, or more radial arms, and avoid re-entering those arms they have depleted of food (Olton & Samuelson, 1976; Olton & Schlosberg, 1978; Roberts, 1979; Roberts & Dale, 1981). This has been called a *win-shift* strategy of foraging, though Gaffan and her colleagues have recently pointed out it might be better labeled a *shift* strategy because it occurs whether the rat collects food (''wins'') or simply finds that food is not available at the end of an arm of the maze (Gaffan & Davies, 1981; Gaffan, Hansel, & Smith, 1983). Various experiments have shown that spatial memory for the layout of the maze, based on visual cues that lie outside the maze such as objects in the room or overhead lights, is responsible for the nearly error-free performance of rats on this task (see Olton, 1982 for a recent review). Memory of the precise location and identity of depleted patches, even when the number of patches is very large, does not seem unreasonable in light of these results.

Memory, however, is not the only mechanism animals can use to avoid revisiting depleted patches. The pied wagtail (*Motacilla alba*) avoids revisiting streambanks it has depleted of food by the simple method of following a regular route along the bank (Davies & Houston, 1981). Bibby and Green (1980) have shown that pied flycatchers (*Ficedula hypoleuca*) avoid trees they have depleted of prey by patrolling their feeding territories in long circuits of clockwise or counterclockwise moves. Baum (1982) has also found systematic searching in pigeons.

A combination of memory and movement rules is a further possibility. Pyke (1979) found that the bumblebee *Bombus appositus* was able to avoid flowers that it had previously visited, in this case flowers within inflorescences of monkshood (*Aconitum columbianum*). Pyke was able to specify the bees' movement rule within inflorescences and construct a number of hypothetical movement rules that generated sequences of visits with low rates of revisiting. Rules with no memory component, such as ''Choose the closest flower in the same direction as the initial direction,'' led to revisiting rates as low as rules with a minimal involvement of memory, such as ''Choose the closest flower that is not one of the last two flowers visited'' or rules with more detailed memory of the previous visiting pattern, for example, ''Choose the closest flower not previously visited.'' Mean rate of energy gain calculated by simulation of foraging behavior based on these movement rules did not differ from that of bumblebees observed foraging.

An additional finding from Pyke's analysis of movement rules is that a ''shift'' strategy alone does not produce a low rate of revisiting. Rules such as ''Always choose the closest flower'' or ''Always choose the closest flower not just visited'' embody a shift strategy but produce more revisiting than that observed in foraging bumblebees and rates of energy gain lower than observed. Thus, although animals that forage in depleting environments may have strong "shift" or spontaneous alternation biases (Cole, Hainsworth, Kamil, Mercier, & Wolf, 1982; Gaffan & Davies, 1981), shifting alone does not necessarily prevent revisits to depleted patches.

A major difference between the foraging studies mentioned and the behavior of food-storing birds lies in the time elapsed between the initial visit and the onset of later avoidance of depleted sites. Beatty and Shavalia (1980) have shown that rats' ability to avoid previously visited maze arms begins to deteriorate after about 8 hours. Honeycreepers avoid flowers they have visited for about 1 hour but revisit after this. (It is not clear if revisits are errors, or whether replenishment of floral nectaries occurs in this interval.) Avoidance of revisits over long intervals, comparable to that found in chickadees, occurs in flocks of brent geese (*Branta bernicla*) that forage in salt marshes on the plant *Plantago* (Prins, Ydenberg, & Drent, 1980). In about 4 days after cropping, *Plantago* regrows to the height preferred by the geese. The brent revisit regions of the salt marsh on which they have previously foraged at intervals that peak at about 4 days. Their means of spacing revisits is unknown, and the social nature of their foraging may pose additional problems, but memory over this interval is a possibility.

These examples show that the use of memory to avoid depleted patches may vary from species to species, or with the nature of the task and the pattern of resource depression produced by foraging. The work with food-storing birds and laboratory rats shows, however, that hypotheses involving memory can be made sufficiently explicit to permit direct testing.

CONCLUSION

It is possible that spatial memory in food-storing birds is a unique specialization adapted to the particular task of recovering scattered caches, but I suspect that it is not (see also Sherry, 1984b). Instead, it may be that memory for locations and events, over intervals of several days or more, is used by foraging animals to solve a variety of problems. There is evidence that memory is used by some animals to avoid depleted patches of food. Memory may also be used to solve other foraging problems. There would be many advantages in recalling where particular food items are to be found, the travel times between patches, the quantity of food likely to be found in particular patches, and the patterns of variation in food abundance for a number of previously visited patches. Using memory to perform these tasks requires that information be acquired during foraging, that it be retained for hours, days, or possibly months, and that it be available during foraging. Studies of food storing show that such information processing is within the capabilities of a variety of birds.

ACKNOWLEDGMENTS

I would like to thank foremost John Krebs, who introduced me to the problem. Karen Whillans-Browning and Rachel Mott-Trille gave permission to quote from unpublished research. Karen Hollis, Diana Tomback, Michael Commons, and Alex Kacelnik offered many helpful comments on the manuscript. Research at the Edward Grey Institute in Oxford was supported by a Science Research Council grant to John Krebs and research at the University of Toronto was supported by grants to the author from the Natural Sciences and Engineering Research Council, and the Connaught Fund. Joint work at both institutions was supported by a NATO Collaborative Research Grant.

REFERENCES

Balda, R. P. (1980). Recovery of cached seeds by a captive *Nucifraga caryocatactes*. *Zeitschrift für Tierpsychologie, 52*, 331–346.

Baum, W. M. (1982). Instrumental behavior and foraging in the wild. In M. L. Commons, R. J. Herrnstein, and H. Raichlin (Eds.), *Quantitative analyses of behavior:* Vol. II, Matching and maximizing accounts (pp. 227–240). Cambridge, MA: Ballinger.

Beatty, W. W., & Shavalia, D. A. (1980). Spatial memory in rats: Time course of working memory and effect of anesthetics. *Behavioral and Neural Biology, 28*, 454–462.

Bibby, C. J., & Green, R. E. (1980). Foraging behaviour of migrant pied flycatchers, *Ficedula hypoleuca*, on temporary territories. *Journal of Animal Ecology, 49*, 507–521.

Bossema, I. (1979). Jays and oaks: An eco-ethological study of a symbiosis. *Behaviour, 70*, 1–117.

Chaplin, S. B. (1974). Daily energetics of the black-capped chickadee, *Parus atricapillus*, in winter. *Journal of Comparative Physiology, 89*, 321–330.

Charnov, E. L., Orians, G. H., & Hyatt, K. (1976). Ecological implications of resource depression. *American Naturalist, 110*, 247–259.

Cole, S., Hainsworth, F. R., Kamil, A. C., Mercier, T., & Wolf, L. L. (1982). Spatial learning as an adaptation in hummingbirds. *Science, 217*, 655–657.

Collopy, M. W. (1977). Food caching by female American kestrels in winter. *Condor, 79*, 63–68.

Cowie, R. J., Krebs, J. R., & Sherry, D. F. (1981). Food storing by marsh tits. *Animal Behaviour, 29*, 1252–1259.

Davies, N. B., & Houston, A. I. (1981). Owners and satellites: The economics of territory defence in the pied wagtail, *Motacilla alba*. *Journal of Animal Ecology, 50*, 157–180.

Gaffan, E. A., & Davies, J. (1981). The role of exploration in win-shift and win-stay performance on a radial maze. *Learning and Motivation, 12*, 282–299.

Gaffan, E. A., Hansel, M. C., & Smith, L. E. (1983). Does reward depletion influence spatial memory performance? *Learning and Motivation, 14*, 58–74.

Gill, F. G., & Wolf, L. L. (1977). Nonrandom foraging by sunbirds in a patchy environment. *Ecology, 58*, 1284–1296.

Goodale, M. A., & Graves, J. A. (1982). Retinal locus as a factor in interocular transfer in the pigeon. In D. J. Ingle, M. A. Goodale, & R. J. W. Mansfield (Eds.), *Analysis of visual behavior* (pp. 211–240). Cambridge, MA: MIT Press.

Graves, J. A., & Goodale, M. A. (1977). Failure of interocular transfer in the pigeon (*Columba livia*). *Physiology & Behavior, 19*, 425–428.

Green, L., Brecha, N., & Gazzaniga, M. S. (1978). Interocular transfer of simultaneous but not successive discriminations in the pigeon. *Animal Learning and Motivation, 6*, 261–264.

Haftorn, S. (1953). Contribution to the food biology of tits especially about storing of surplus food. Part I. The crested tit (*Parus c. cristatus* L.). *Det Koniglik Norske Videnskabers Selskabs Skrifter, 4*, 1–123.

Haftorn, S. (1974). Storage of surplus food by the boreal chickadee *Parus hudsonicus* in Alaska, with some records on the mountain chickadee *Parus gambeli* in Colorado. *Ornis Scandanavica, 5*, 145–161.

Kamil, A. C. (1978). Systematic foraging by a nectar-feeding bird, the amakihi (*Loxops virens*). *Journal of Comparative and Physiological Psychology, 92*, 388–396.

Koenig, W. D. (1978). *Ecological and evolutionary aspects of cooperative breeding in acorn woodpeckers of central coastal California*. Doctoral dissertation, University of California, Berkeley.

Krebs, J. R. (1978). Optimal foraging: Decision rules for predators. In J. R. Krebs & N. B. Davies (Eds.), *Behavioural ecology: An evolutionary approach* (pp. 23–63). Oxford, England: Blackwell Scientific Publication.

Levine, J. (1945). Studies of interrelations of central nervous structures in binocular vision. I. The lack of binocular transfer of visual discriminative habits acquired monocularly by the pigeon. *Journal of Genetic Psychology, 67*, 105–129.

Ludescher, F.-B. (1980). Fressen und Verstecken von Sämereien bei der Weidenmeise *Parus montanus* im Jahresverlauf unter konstanten Ernährungsbedingungen. *Ökologie der Vögel, 2*, 135–144.

Mott-Trille, R. (1983). *Food storage: An inventory model*. B.A. Thesis, University of Toronto, Canada.

Mrosovsky, N., & Sherry, D. F. (1980). Animal anorexias. *Science, 207*, 837–842.

Mueller, H. C. (1974). Food caching behaviour in the American kestrel (*Falco sparverius*). *Zeitschrift für Tierpsychologie, 34*, 105–114.

Myton, B. A., & Ficken, R. W. (1967). Seed-size preference in chickadees and titmice in relation to ambient temperature. *Wilson Bulletin, 79*, 319–321.

Olton, D. S. (1982). Spatially organized behaviors of animals: Behavioral and neurological studies. In M. Potegal (Ed.), *Spatial abilities: Development and physiological foundations* (pp. 335–360). New York: Academic Press.

Olton, D. S., & Samuelson, R. J. (1976). Remembrance of places passed: Spatial memory in rats. *Journal of Experimental Psychology: Animal Behavior Processes, 2*, 97–116.

Olton, D. S., & Scholsberg, P. (1978). Food-searching strategies in young rats: Win-shift predominates over win-stay. *Journal of Comparative and Physiological Psychology, 92*, 609–618.

Powlesland, R. G. (1980). Food-storing behaviour of the South Island robin. *Mauri Ora, 8*, 11–20.

Prins, H. H.Th., Ydenberg, R. C., & Drent, R. H. (1980). The interaction of brent geese *Branta bernicla* and sea plantain *Plantago maritima* during spring staging: Field observations and experiments. *Acta Botanica Neerlandica, 29*, 585–596.

Pyke, G. H. (1979). Optimal foraging in bumblebees: Rule of movement between flowers within inflorescences. *Animal Behaviour, 27*, 1167–1181.

Pyke, G. H., Pulliam, H. R., & Charnov, E. L. (1977). Optimal foraging: A selective review of theory and tests. *Quarterly Review of Biology, 52*, 137–154.

Reinertsen, R. E. (1983). Nocturnal hypothermia and its energetic significance for small birds living in the arctic and subarctic regions: A review. *Polar Research, 1*, 269–284.

Rijnsdorp, A., Daan, S., & Dijkstra, C. (1981). Hunting in the kestrel *Falco tinnunculus*, and the adaptive significance of daily habits. *Oecologia, 50*, 391–406.

Roberts, W. A. (1979). Spatial memory in the rat on a hierarchical maze. *Learning and Motivation, 10*, 117–140.

Roberts, W. A., & Dale, R. H. (1981). Remembrance of places lasts: Proactive inhibition and patterns of choice in rat spatial memory. *Learning and Motivation, 12*, 261–281.

Schoener, T. W. (1971). Theory of feeding strategies. *Annual Review of Ecology and Systematics, 2*, 369–404.

Sherry, D. (1981). Adaptive changes in body weight. In L. A. Cioffi, W. P. T. James, & T. B. Van Itallie (Eds.), *The body weight regulatory system: Normal and disturbed mechanisms* (pp. 161–168). New York: Raven Press.

Sherry, D. F. (1982). Food storage, memory, and marsh tits. *Animal Behaviour, 30,* 631–633.
Sherry, D. F. (1984a). Food storage by black-capped chickadees: Memory for the location and contents of caches. *Animal Behaviour, 32,* 451–464.
Sherry, D. F. (1984b). What food-storing birds remember. *Canadian Journal of Psychology, 38,* 304–321.
Sherry, D. F., Avery, M., & Stevens, A. (1982). The spacing of stored food by marsh tits. *Zeitschrift für Tierpsychologie, 58,* 153–162.
Sherry, D. F., Krebs, J. R., & Cowie, R. J. (1981). Memory for the location of stored food in marsh tits. *Animal Behaviour, 29,* 1260–1266.
Shettleworth, S. J., & Krebs, J. R. (1982). How marsh tits find their hoards: The roles of site preferences and spatial memory. *Journal of Experimental Psychology: Animal Behavior Processes, 8,* 354–375.
Stevens, T. A. (1984). *Food storing by marsh tits.* Unpublished doctoral dissertation, University of Oxford, England.
Swanberg, P. O. (1951). Food storage, territory and song in the thick-billed nutcracker. *Proceedings of the 10th International Ornithological Congress* (pp. 545–554). Uppsala.
Tomback, D. F. (1977). Foraging strategies of Clark's nutcracker. *The Living Bird, 16,* 123–161.
Tomback, D. F. (1980). How nutcrackers find their seed stores. *Condor, 82,* 10–19.
Tomback, D. F. (1982). Dispersal of whitebark pine seeds by Clark's nutcracker: A mutualism hypothesis. *Journal of Animal Ecology, 51,* 451–467.
Vander Wall, S. B. (1982). An experimental analysis of cache recovery in Clark's nutcracker. *Animal Behaviour, 30,* 84–94.
Vander Wall, S. B., & Balda, R. P. (1981). Ecology and evolution of food-storage behavior in conifer-seed-caching corvids. *Zeitschrift für Tierpsychologie, 56,* 217–242.
Vander Wall, S. B., & Hutchins, H. E. (1983). Dependence of Clark's nutcracker, *Nucifraga columbiana,* on conifer seeds during the postfledging period. *Canadian Field-Naturalist, 97,* 208–214.
Whillans Browning, K. V. (1983). *The influence of food type on hoarding behaviour in black-capped chickadees (Parus atricapillus).* Unpublished manuscript, University of Toronto.

11 The Influence of Context on Choice Behavior: Fruit Selection by Tropical Birds

Timothy C. Moermond, Department of Zoology
Julie Sloan Denslow*, Departments of Zoology and Botany
Douglas J. Levey, Department of Zoology
Eduardo Santana C., Department of Wildlife Ecology
University of Wisconsin

INTRODUCTION

According to Ivlev (1961), "Feeding and the attitude of the animals toward food occupy an exceptional position [in ecology]. One may assert with complete confidence that other . . . questions are entirely of secondary importance . . . compared with questions of a trophic nature" (p. 2).

The study of animal feeding behavior has played an important role in ecological studies of animal population and community dynamics (Hutchinson, 1957; Ivlev, 1961; Krebs, Stevens, & Sutherland, 1983; Pulliam, 1976; Schoener, 1971) and has also been central to psychological studies of animal motivation (Revusky, 1977; Rozin, 1976; Shettleworth, 1975; Staddon, 1983; Zeigler, 1977). An increasing number of studies have begun to incorporate both psychological and ecological perspectives (e.g., Collier, Hirsch, & Hamlin, 1972; Hirsch & Collier, 1974; Kamil & Sargent, 1981).

What determines which foods an animal eats? This question is central to both ecological and psychological studies of feeding behavior. The answer is widely assumed to be a function of the properties of both the food and the internal state of the animal (e.g., Rozin, 1976) and therefore is assumed to be investigable through experiments in which both the animals and their foods are controlled. Food-choice tests under controlled conditions usually show that animals have definite preferences, but the underlying factors that lead to those preferences are often difficult to determine (e.g., Brown, 1969; Moon & Ziegler, 1979). Al-

---

*Present address: New York Botanical Gardens, Bronx, New York

though laboratory experiments are assumed to deal with adaptive responses of the animals (at least implicitly), few studies have attempted to test interpretations derived from laboratory experiments against field observations. Among the few cases in which such direct comparisons have been made, preference ranks of food items determined in the laboratory are usually found to be poor predictors of diet observed in the field (e.g., Best, 1981; Brown, 1969; Mitchell, 1975; Pulliam, 1980; Sorensen, 1981). This lack of correspondence is often ascribed to the scarcity of preferred items in the field (e.g., Brown, 1969). The issue of availability of food—what factors determine it and its influence on food selection—is often overlooked and only rarely investigated directly, but availability is an important issue to which ecological perspectives have much to offer.

At its most general level, availability of food items in the field must affect diet in the simple sense that an animal cannot eat items that are not present or can eat very rare items only occasionally. However, even taking differential abundance of food items into account (Ivlev, 1961; Johnson, 1980) does not often improve the ability to determine the bases for food selection in the field (e.g., Eggers, 1982; Vedder, 1985). Here it is suggested that not only does this lack of fit result from the difficulties in measuring availability, it also underscores the present lack of understanding of all the factors that influence the availability of food items for a given organism.

"Availability" is used not only to mean the relative and absolute abundances of potential food items, it also includes their relative detectabilities (i.e., that proportion of each item usually encountered) and their relative exploitabilities (e.g., the ease of capture). The question thus becomes, how many of each food type are actually encountered and able to be caught by the forager? This question has been addressed from the sensory side of the question (i.e., what types of items can be detected at what distance given a forager's sensory capabilities; e.g., O'Brien, Slade, & Vinyard, 1976; Pietrewicz & Kamil, 1977; Rice, 1983) but also depends on which items the forager is looking for. A forager can affect the rates at which different food items are encountered by varying hunting techniques (Rice, 1983) or microhabitats searched (Tinbergen, 1981) or by employing different search images (Dawkins, 1971; Pietrewicz & Kamil, 1979; Staddon & Gendron, 1983).

Hunting in different microhabitats may incur different costs that in turn influence the availability of food items. If the cost of obtaining a given food item defines its availability, then it may be said that factors external to both the consumer and the food influence that availability. For example, when good food items are scarce, the items may be less common in the forager's diet either because it is unable to find many or because the costs of searching for and moving between the rare food items are too high. If the latter, then increased costs of obtaining rare food items may affect the value of those items in the diet and hence influence the preference patterns of the consumer. In this context, the problem of the bases for diet selection becomes an economic one of relative costs and benefits.

The economic approach used in optimal-foraging theory offers a useful way of evaluating food items on a cost–benefit basis. A number of optimal-foraging models present convenient ways to quantify differences among diverse food items by employing a common currency (energy or time) and by dividing the process of obtaining items into useful components: search, capture, handling, and ingestion. Capture, handling, and ingestion are usually assumed to be properties of the food item, and search a property of its availability (e.g., density). Using any of several models (e.g., Estabrook & Dunham, 1976; MacArthur & Pianka, 1966; Schoener, 1969, 1971), one can calculate benefit/cost values for each type of food item (e.g., net energy per time) and thus rank the food items and predict the set of food items that should be taken in a given situation to maximize net energy intake (e.g., Sorensen, 1981).

Considerations of the consumer as a complex biological entity rather than simply an energy-gathering "machine" (e.g., Clark, 1982; Glander, 1981; Sibly, 1981) have led to more elaborate models that take into account an animal's diverse nutrient requirements (e.g., Pulliam, 1975; Westoby, 1974) and/or include more of its constraining internal physiological and morphological characteristics such as limitations due to gut volume or gut passage rate (e.g., Belovsky, 1978; Demment & Van Soest, 1983). Nevertheless, many diet-choice models still assume choice to be determined primarily by the needs of, and internal constraints on, the animal in conjunction with the properties of the food items themselves.

Yet it is known that, in the field, animals must search for food items and that the search often involves considerable time and effort. A number of optimal-foraging models have incorporated search costs in models of diet selection (e.g., Charnov, 1976; Krebs, Erichsen, Webber, & Charnov, 1977; Norberg, 1977; Orians & Pearson, 1979; Schoener, 1969, 1971). Of these, Charnov's model of optimal patch use (1976) has generated a number of new theoretical developments as well as a number of laboratory tests by behavioral ecologists and psychologists (see Krebs et al., 1983 and several chapters in this volume). Search is included only as a time cost in these models (and in many of the laboratory experiments). Only a few models have included energy costs as a function of search distance or time traveling. Norberg (1977) has gone further to incorporate different costs of searching in different situations. Careful observations of animals in the field show that moving through the environment to search for and collect food items is a complex process involving coordination of locomotory morphology and behavior to fit the physical characteristics of the microhabitat being searched (e.g., Fitzpatrick, 1978; Leisler & Thaler, 1982; Moermond, 1979a, b; Norberg, 1979, 1981; Pearson, 1977; Robinson & Holmes, 1982; Tyser & Moermond, 1983; Williamson, 1971). The additional maneuvers or specialized foraging techniques needed to capture food items may be considered an important component of search (e.g., Davies & Green, 1976; Denslow & Moermond, in press; Fitzpatrick, 1978, 1980; Moermond, 1981; Newton, 1967) and certainly influence the availability and costs of food items in the field. Such factors need to be included in investigations of the bases of food selection. The interaction of foraging behavior and prey availability together with the intrinsic properties of the prey and internal conditions of the forager is not only likely to be complex but will be affected by the context in which prey choices are made.

This chapter examines food choice behavior for one set of foragers (tropical fruit-eating birds) to illustrate some of the subtle ways in which the abundances and costs of obtaining food items influence their selection. The work on fruit-eating birds summarized in the following sections may be found in detail elsewhere (Denslow & Moermond, 1982, in press; Levey, Moermond, & Denslow, 1984; Moermond & Denslow, 1983, in press; Santana, Moermond, & Denslow, 1985).

Why Birds and Fruits?

One major difference distinguishing psychological from ecological investigations of feeding behavior of animals is the diversity of animal species examined. The white rat and the white Carneau pigeon are the principal subjects of many psychological studies whereas ecological studies employ a seeming potpourri of animals. In the experiments described here, over 20 species from six families of tropical birds were used. Comparison of the responses of several species with varying degrees of relationship provides much additional information otherwise unavailable (e.g., Kear, 1962; Newton, 1967). The comparative approach is one of the most effective methods of investigating questions of adaptation (cf. Krebs & Davies, 1981). The utility of this approach is expressed no better than by Niko Tinbergen (1972), who says the ethologist (or the ecologist) "interprets differences between allied species in terms of adaptive evolutionary divergence; and similarities between otherwise dissimilar species in terms of adaptive convergence. This is applying to behavior an old method which has been so extremely fertile in the past for our understanding of structure—a lesson which, unfortunately, is in danger of being forgotten" (p. 211).

Often the decision to study a particular species is based on its suitability in the examination of a particular question. In this case, fruit-eating birds are particularly appropriate for a study of the determinants of diet composition. Not only is there an incredible diversity of tropical birds and fruits, but the particular interactions between fruit eaters and their foods offers an unusually promising situation in which to compare field observations to laboratory results and to examine the contribution of food availability to their choice patterns.

A diverse set of arboreal tropical fruit-eating birds have been used in the experiments discussed next. The principal groups referred to here are the tanagers, manakins, araçaris, and trogons. For those unfamiliar with these groups a brief synopsis follows. For a more extensive description of these families see Harrison (1978), and for more detailed comparisons of their feeding behavior see Moermond and Denslow (in press) and references therein.

Trogons (Trogonidae) are medium-large with large heads, short necks, prominant large eyes, and short, broad, strong bills. They have very small, weak legs and feet but large, well-slotted wings. They take nearly all their food on the wing, plucking large insects and fruits from vegetation. Araçaris (Ramphastidae) are medium-sized toucans with long necks and very large and long, colorful bills. Their wings are relatively short and rounded. Their legs are short, but their feet are very strong, enabling them to reach far out from a perch. Virtually all their food items, including many fruits, are plucked from a perched position. Tanagers (Thraupinae; Emberizidae) are small, active, often brightly colored birds that feed on both insects and fruits. Most are good flyers and have strong legs and feet (examples of the varied feeding abilities in this diverse group are described in Snow and Snow, 1971, and Moermond and Denslow, in press). Manakins (Pipridae) are small, compact birds with large heads, large gapes, and broad, short, flat bills. The males are brightly colored; the females nearly all a uniform olive green. They show great maneuverability on the wing, but their legs and feet are weaker than most tanagers and do not usually permit the agile reaches from perches characteristic of many tanagers.

Diet and Fruits: A Supermarket

Fruit-eating birds of diverse types and sizes are known to include a wide variety of fruit species in their diets (Jenkins, 1969; Leck, 1971; Moermond & Denslow, in press; Snow, 1981). Likewise, most fruiting plants are dispersed by many species of birds as shown most dramatically through observations of birds feeding at fruiting trees (e.g., Denslow & Moermond, in press; Eisenmann, 1961; Herrera & Jordano, 1981; Howe, 1977, 1981; Kantak, 1979; McDiarmid, Ricklefs, & Foster, 1977; Snow & Snow, 1971; Stiles, 1979; Wheelwright, Haber, Murray, & Guindon, 1984; Willis, 1966). Fruits are generally a poor food: low in protein with a low protein-to-carbohydrate ratio, and with a high proportion of water and a large indigestible seed mass (Moermond & Denslow, in press). Yet most species of fruits are taken by many species of birds, which demonstrates that fruits nevertheless fill an important role in the birds' diets (cf. Foster, 1978; Jenkins, 1969; Moermond & Denslow, in press). Because plants benefit when fruits are taken by birds that eat the plup and disperse the seed, numerous characteristics have evolved that make fruits conspicuous and attractive to birds. Plants dispersed by birds are characterized by fruits with a fleshy pulp, bright color, and conspicuous display (Ridley, 1930; Van der Pijl, 1969). Despite a recognizable general "bird-dispersed seed" syndrome, fruits of related species differ in details of the syndrome in consistent, species-specific ways such that most fruits appear to be readily identifiable to species or species-groups (e.g., see Fig. 1 in Denslow & Moermond, in press). Thus a fruit eaten by a bird can be recognized as a known quantity in future foraging bouts. In the tropics, fruit is often available the year around, and individual shrubs or trees may have large crops of fruits available for several days to several weeks and some plants produce fruit at regular intervals for many years (Crome, 1975; Denslow, unpubl. data; Foster, 1982a,b; Frankie, Baker, & Opler, 1974; Hilty, 1980; Howe, 1977; Opler, Frankie, & Baker, 1980; Snow, 1965). Given the presumed longevity and sedentary habits of tropical birds (Fogden, 1972; Karr, 1971; Snow, 1962), it is likely that individual birds readily learn where and when particular plants will produce fruits. Fruit may sometimes be so abundant that large quantities of fruit remain uneaten (Denslow & Moermond, 1982, in press; Foster, 1977).

The salient image is of a bird selecting fruits arrayed as if in a supermarket: numerous food items (fruits) of known value, conspicuously marked, in known locations, and simultaneously available for relatively long periods of time (several days to weeks). Some authors have suggested that, given an abundant source of easily harvestable but low-quality foods, fruit-eaters may show little discrimination and feed opportunistically (McKey, 1975; Morton, 1973) or randomly (Worthington, 1982, personal communication) as they encounter the fruits. However, Denslow and Moermond have maintained that the "supermarket" situation offers the ideal opportunity in which to observe discrimination and selection (Denslow & Moermond, in press; Moermond & Denslow, 1983). Optimal-foraging theory leads one to expect that these birds are good shoppers (e.g., Krebs, 1978; Tullock, 1970).

In fact, several lines of evidence have shown discrimination or selectivity by fruit-eating birds. First, although different bird species feeding in the same habitat overlap widely in the species of fruits they eat, different birds do not consume those fruits in the same proportions (e.g., Hartley, 1954; Snow & Snow, 1971; Sorensen, 1981; i.e., they have individual utility functions). Secondly, birds show some degree of selectivity from among fruits of the same species but of varying quality (e.g., Best, 1981; Herrera, 1981; Howe & Vande Kerckhove, 1980; Moermond & Denslow, 1983). Lastly, experiments with several species of fruit-eaters have shown that they make systematic choices (i.e., rational decisions in a technical sense, Kaufman, 1968) among many species of fruits offered (Moermond & Denslow, 1983).

The questions to be addressed here are (1) what are the criteria or decision rules for the observed selectivity, and (2) how does the context in which the fruits are presented affect those criteria?

Choice Experiments: Selectivity and Consistency

Three questions are fundamental to a determination of selection criteria: (1) Do the birds make clear-cut choices from among different species of fruits?; (2) are those choices consistent from trial to trial?; (3) are the choices arrayed in a linear hierarchy (i.e., are they transitive)? These questions are addressed by administering a series of pairwise choice tests. These tests approximated two-choice trials used in operant psychology. They are described here in sufficient detail to show the protocol and, importantly, to point out how they match or differ from choice situations encountered in the field.

Fruits are most frequently born in clusters, termed infructescences. The shape and appearance of these clusters vary considerably, both in terms of the fruits and the arrangement and colors of the branches and stalks holding the fruits. To standardize conditions in the choice tests, fruits were uniformly presented by mounting them on standard artificial holders that resemble natural infructescences in many respects. With all fruits thus displayed, the differences between fruits are restricted to differences in the fruits per se: color, size, shape, texture, and nutrient content. Natural infructescences add additional variables such as number of fruits per infructescence, spacing between fruits on the infructescence, size and flexibility of the stalks holding the fruits, proximity of rigid perches, and presence of colored unripe fruits, leaves, or bracts that increase the conspicuousness of the display. Such factors may affect both the attractiveness of the fruits and the costs of obtaining the fruits, irrespective of the qualities of the fruits themselves. The possible influence of such components of the fruit display is the subject of additional experiments and observations described next.

Several versions of the artificial holders were tested until the birds' behavior toward the fruits and fruit holders resembled that observed in the field. Because it was believed, and has since been shown, that the fruit presentation influences a bird's fruit selection, it was necessary that the fruit holders mimic natural infructescences in several critical ways such as the size of the display, the spacing of fruits, the flexibility of the holder, and the firmness of attachment of the fruits. The necessity of this close match with nature was illustrated by an early version of fruit holders devised by the authors in which the fruits were firmly seated on the holders. Although the fruits were not so firmly attached as to prevent the birds from removing them, they nevertheless were frequently rejected. Most ripe fruits are very easily removed from the plant whereas unripe fruits are more tightly attached (consider the case of humans picking raspberries). In many plants the difficulty of fruit removal is a clear clue that the fruit is unripe and therefore (for most fruit-eating birds) not ready to eat (Snow, 1971). Such seemingly subtle differences in experimental design may influence its outcome in ways not desired, not planned, and perhaps not even detectable by researchers (e.g., Hawkins, 1977). Such deficiencies in design are an important source of Type II errors in interpreting the results of any food-choice experiments.

Choice-Trial Protocol.   In each session, a bird was presented with two holders, one with 16 fruits of one species and the other with 16 fruits of another species (Fig. 11.1). During the session, a detailed chronology was kept of all fruits touched, handled, and eaten by the birds as well as all other foraging movements. The session was terminated when all fruits had been eaten, or after a previously specified time period (1 hour or less) if the bird ceased to show

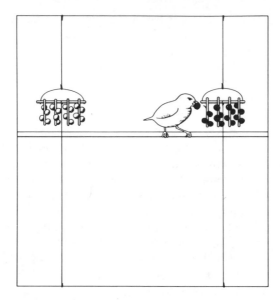

FIG. 11.1.   Diagram of arrangement of fruit-choice trial. The artificial holders are suspended 2 centimeters out from the perch so that a bird landing directly in front of either holder can move freely along the perch.

interest in the fruits. The birds usually consumed nearly all of one of the fruit types offered. The time allotted to eat the fruits was more than sufficient. The birds were not starved or deprived of food before experiments but were fed ad libitum on a maintenance diet of soy protein isolate, banana, agar, and selected additives (Moermond, Denslow, Levey, & Wentworth, unpubl. data). The food dish was removed only during the running of the choice trial to eliminate a third food choice.

Preference was determined by the number and order in which the fruits were eaten. At the end of each trial all fruits eaten and still remaining on the holders were tabulated. The number of each species of fruit eaten among the first half of all fruits available was compared to the number of each species of fruit either eaten or remaining in the second half. The numbers were cast in a 2 × 2 contingency table and tested with the Fisher's Exact Test (Siegal, 1956). The null hypothesis assumed fruits were chosen with equal probability. This statistic was conservative because it assumed a constant availability of fruits of each species throughout the trial. However, fruits were removed without replacement so that the probability of taking the favored species by chance alone decreased during the course of the trial. Thus, our statistics introduced in the analyses a conservative bias against detection of preference.

The statistics used assume independence of choice. Although birds often took several fruits in one sitting (i.e., without leaving the experimental perch), the behavioral responses suggested that each choice involved a separate decision (cf. Moermond & Denslow, 1983). Both fruit holders were displayed next to the same perch so that a bird sitting on that perch could reach fruits on each side with little difficulty (Fig. 11.1). Independence was maximized also by offering only two sets of fruits in each trial. Cafeteria-style trials with several alternatives would have presented more difficulty in this regard.

Consistency of choices was gauged by running a condition over with the positions of the fruits on left and right sides of the cage reversed. Although cage-side preferences were observed in other sessions and could be induced, no such preferences were detected in the choice trials reported here.

All birds tested were caught in the wild. One or 2 days were required for the birds to become accustomed to the maintenance diet, during which time some birds lost weight, usually less than 10% of their capture weight. The birds were disturbed as little as possible for the first week in order to allow them to adjust to the cages and the researchers and to return to capture weight. Most birds were presented with choice trials early in the second week of captivity. Nearly all the birds quickly learned to take fruits from the artificial holders, usually within a few minutes to an hour of being offered the fruits for the first time. With few exceptions, the birds were not offered the fruit species to be tested before they were used in the choice trials. Because all fruits used were taken from the same forest areas as the birds, it was assumed that the birds had previously encountered most or all of those fruits. It is not known whether the birds recognized particular species as presented on the artificial holders either before or after eating the fruits.

Choice Patterns: Selectivity and Consistency.   Pairwise choice sessions were conducted with more than 20 species of fruit-eating birds (usually with two individuals of each species) and 26 species of fruits (Moermond & Denslow, 1983). All the birds showed significant preferences in most of the choice sessions (in 70% of the initial sessions and 80% of replication sessions, Fig. 11.2). When preferences in initial sessions were compared to those of replicate sessions, it was found that preferences demonstrated in 70% of the replicates were the same as those in the initial session. In only 4% of the cases did a bird reverse its preference in the replication session. In all other cases the birds showed a preference in one session but none in the other. In three out of four cases, the session in which no preference between fruits was detected was the initial one ($p < .05$, Sign Test, Siegal, 1956). The sessions showing this seeming lack of preference for any of the fruits used in the first session appeared to be the result of sampling by the bird.

It is suspected that the birds are more consistent in choice and more selective than these trials indicate. Although the attempt was made to select a uniform set of fruits in terms of ripeness, size, and color for each species, some variation was often detected by the birds. It was often observed that birds preferentially took

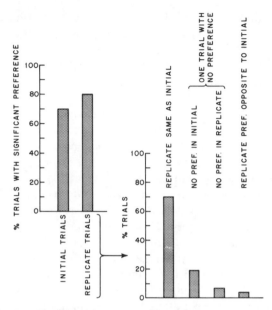

FIG. 11.2.   Results of 77 initial and 70 replicate choice trials for tanagers (11 individuals of 5 species) and manakins (3 individuals of 1 species) combined. A single choice test, Fig. 11.1, is scored as showing preference if one fruit species is taken more frequently in the first 50% of all fruits eaten than expected by chance ($p = .05$). Replicate trials are defined as consistent with the initial trial with the same pair of fruits if the replicate showed the same preference as the initial trial.

the ripest fruits (as indicated by color) and avoided fruits that had slight marks of spoilage or that were slightly flaccid. From all this, the present inclination is to believe that preference for one species over another depended on the relative ripeness of the fruits offered. Such fine scale selection was difficult to document but could have contributed to the inconclusive results observed in some choice sessions.

Systematic Decision Making.   Despite the high frequency of selection and consistency of preference, establishing the bases of the choices is difficult. Even if nutritional information were available on all the fruits, other properties remain difficult to quantify and compare across species. For example, pulp texture probably affects the birds' assessment of ripeness, nutrient content, and digestibility. This, however, is very difficult to quantify in a meaningful way. Nevertheless, given the consistency of their preferences, one can determine whether the birds employ an underlying decision criterion by looking for transitivity among the choices. Choices are considered transitive and form a simple order if the preferences are arrayed in a consistent hierarchy. For example, choices are transitive if fruit A is preferred over fruit B, fruit B over fruit C, and fruit A over fruit C (Kaufman, 1968). Triplets—all pairwise comparisons of three species of fruits—are a useful format for determining the character of diet selection. Because the choices of individual birds may differ and both fruits and individual birds may vary seasonally, all tests of transitivity for each individual are performed over a relatively short period of time (less than 1 month). Under such constraints 24 different triplets were examined. The choices were transitive in all 24 (see Fig. 2 in Moermond & Denslow, 1983). One can thus conclude that the birds were basing their choices on some underlying decision criterion that is likely based on a maximization principle (Kaufman, 1968; McCleery, 1978).

Behavioral Titrations

Most optimal-foraging models assume that items are ranked in preference according to costs and benefits accruing at the encounter or capture of the item (e.g., net energy/time = (assimilable energy–handling cost)/handling time; Schoener, 1969, 1971, 1979). In the field, birds must often be faced with the choice of a low-ranked food item nearby versus a high-ranked item further away. Does the bird discount the value of the distant good item such that some low-ranked items nearby have an immediate relative higher value? Here one may define the net energy/time (or some similar energy- and time-based value) of the item as its value, and then assume that availability acts as a cost that diminishes the value of the item being considered. If the birds behave so as to maximize the net value of the fruit, then a near item should be preferred over the same item farther away. The inclusion of search cost in the equation decreases the value of the food item in proportion to its distance. This is an approximation of the choice between scarce, high-ranking items and common, low-ranking items, a choice that has been investigated experimentally.

Distance Titrations. Wild-caught birds in large flight cages (3.5 meters × 7.5 meters × 2.5 meters high) were offered four simultaneous choices (Fig. 11.3; Levey, Moermond, & Denslow, 1984). In each session two fruit species were used that the bird had already eaten readily in captivity and between which the bird had already demonstrated a clear difference in preference (using 12 individuals of 6 species, in a total of 64 of 64 tests the birds showed a preference of fruit A over B with $p < .005$, calculated as described earlier). A cluster of each fruit species was offered side by side above a perch near to the bird's "home perch" (= starting point for the trial) and another pair of such clusters were placed similarly over a second perch further away. When the bird was released from a small cage within the large flight cage, the bird always flew immediately to the closest perch in view and ate the preferred fruits on that perch (here called "A" fruits). Next the bird either ate the less preferred ("B") fruits on the same perch or flew to the distant perch to eat more of the A fruits (Fig. 11.3). For the initial runs, the two perches were placed close together (0.3 meters). After completion of five replications with the same bird for a given

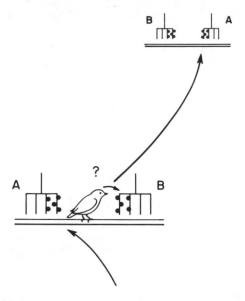

FIG. 11.3.   Diagram of a distance-titration trial. A bird on the first perch typically eats all the preferred A fruits (see Table 11.1), then eats either the adjacent, less preferred B fruits, or flies directly to the more distant perch to eat the other set of A fruits.

distance between perches, the perches were moved farther apart. Four distances between the perches were used in succession (0.3, 0.9, 3.4, and 6.4 meters).

When the perches were closest together, all the birds (2 individuals each of 6 species) chose distant (i.e., 0.3 meters) preferred fruits over the near, less preferred fruits. However, as the distance to the preferred fruits was increased, all but one of the 12 birds tested eventually switched to choose the nearby less preferred fruits over the other more distant fruits. The "switching point" was defined as the distance at which one could accept a null hypothesis of no difference between the number of A and B fruits among the first half of all the fruits taken (chi-square test, $p < .05$). The switches observed were dramatic with the preference test changing from a show of consistent preference for fruit A at one perch distance to nearly a 50:50 ratio of fruits taken at the next longer perch distance. The occurrence of these switches demonstrated that in the selection of fruits birds do take into account not only the value and properties of the items themselves but also the costs of obtaining them—costs that are determined by the environment or context in which the foods are found.

Two further results from these experiments are of interest. First, different individuals switched their choice pattern at different distances and in general the two individuals of each species were consistent in their behavior (Table 11.1). Notably, the four manakins (*Pipra mentalis* and *Manacus candei*) switched at greater distances than most of the tanagers. Although no explanation emerged as to why these birds differed in their response, it was shown that the degree of preference of fruit type A over type B was significantly correlated with the distance between perches at which the birds switched their choice pattern ($r = .75, p < .01$, Spearman rank correlation coefficient; Table 11.1). Those with the strongest preference for A over B were more willing to fly longer distances to take fruit A in place of the nearby B fruits. The four manakins all showed very strong preferences for fruit A when compared to the tanagers, a difference that is somewhat expected from consideration of differences between manakins and tanagers in their morphology, their flight and their feeding techniques (Moermond & Denslow, in press). Manakins take most of their fruits on the wing and pay a high cost for each fruit when compared with many tanagers that can often reach several fruits from one perch at a low cost per fruit. The high cost paid per fruit may lead manakins to reject some low-quality fruits that are worthwhile for a tanager to take.

The second point is that the switch distance of the dusky-faced tanagers (*Mitrospingus cassinii*) differed depending on the pair of fruits offered. The implication is that the relative qualities of the fruits influence the choice patterns of the birds. This also is to be expected if the birds are assessing the relative benefits and costs of alternative fruits.

TABLE 11.1
Fruit Preferences and Switch Points in Tanagers and Manakins

Bird Species	Individual	Fruit Choice	Preference Index	Switch Point (m)
Tanagers				
Mitrospingus cassinii	1	6B/150A	0.96	3.4
	2	6B/143A	0.96	3.4
Habia fuscicauda	1	15B/140A	0.89	3.4
	2	6B/149A	0.96	3.4
Tachyphonus delatrii	1	14B/137A	0.90	0.9
	2	0B/153A	1.00	3.4
Ramphocelus passerinii	1	5B/147A	0.97	6.4
	2	13B/139A	0.91	3.4
Manakins				
Manacus candei	1	0B/152A	1.00	6.4
	2	0B/159A	1.00	6.4
Pipra mentalis	1	0B/156A	1.00	6.4
	2	0B/150A	1.00	no switch

Note: Total number of fruits of A (more-preferred) and B (less-preferred) taken when both were available at the same perch. Preference index is defined as 1 − (number of B/number of A). The switching point is that distance between perches at which birds switched to the nearby less-preferred B fruits over the distant more preferred A fruits (Levey et al., 1984)

This point was further examined in cage experiments with a much larger fruit-eating bird, the collared araçari (a small toucan, *Pteroglossus torquatus;* Santana C., Moermond, & Denslow, unpublished manuscript). Two perches separated by a fixed distance were used and the relative values of the two fruits offered were changed. If the birds are using a cost–benefit basis for selecting fruits, then the relative value of the nearby low-ranked fruit compared to the distant higher ranked fruit should determine the sequence of fruit selection (see Fig. 11.3).

Because fruit quality is difficult to evaluate, fruits of the same species of plant were chosen that differed only in ripeness. All birds tested so far prefer ripe over partially ripe or unripe fruits (Moermond & Denslow, 1983). In this case, fruits of *Hamelia patens* (Rubiaceae) were used that change color from green to yellow to red to maroon to black as they ripen. The collared araçaris demonstrated strong preferences for black fruits over maroon and for maroon fruits over red. In addition, digestion trials with each color of fruit showed that the araçaris were able to more fully digest black fruits than the maroon or red. They thus presumably obtained more benefit from the riper fruits (Santana C., Moermond, & Denslow, unpublished manuscript).

The araçaris were offered four fruits, two of each color, attached to each of two perches spaced 1.5 meters apart (Fig. 11.4). When offered black and maroon fruits, the bird first ate a black fruit then a maroon, hopped to the other side of the

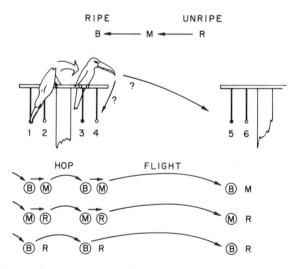

FIG. 11.4. Diagram of distance titration with the araçari (toucanet) and *hamelia patens* fruits. Individual fruits are denoted by letters indicating their color: B = black, M = maroon, R = red. The three lines of arrows show three observed fruit-selection sequences with the different combinations of fruit colors as indicated. See text for details.

same perch, ate the other black fruit then the other maroon, and then flew to the other perch and repeated the same selection sequence as shown diagrammatically in Fig. 11.4. When maroon and red fruits were offered, the selection sequence followed the same pattern. However, when black fruits were offered with red ones, the bird often ate all four black fruits on both perches before eating the red ones.

The strength of the choice pattern shown diagrammatically in Fig. 11.4 can be analyzed by examining three different choices within the overall sequence: (1) a choice between each pair of fruits, (2) a choice between a less ripe fruit on one half of the perch versus a riper fruit on the far half of the same perch, and (3) a choice between a less ripe fruit on one perch versus a riper fruit on the other perch. In the first two sequences (i.e., those with B versus M or M versus R fruits) the bird tested ate all the riper fruits before the less ripe fruits in 71 of 92 choice pairs ($p < .01$), in 8 of 14 choices between perch sides (n.s.), and in only 1 of 5 choices between perches (n.s.). In contrast, in the third sequence with B versus R fruits, the bird ate all the B fruits in 15 of 18 choices ($p < .01$), in 12 of 12 choices between perch sides ($p < .01$), and in 4 of 6 choices between perches (n.s.). The stronger preference for B fruits when compared with R fruits was shown for all three types of choices (Santana C., Moermond, & Denslow, unpublished manuscript). The fact that the sequence of fruit selection depends on the relative value of the two fruits again strongly suggests that fruits are evaluated in a cost–benefit manner incorporating the search or travel costs incurred in obtaining the fruits. In the cases where the bird ate all four B fruits first, the bird then ate the remaining R fruits on both perches. It is presumed that, in a field situation, the bird may have not returned for the low-quality R fruits on the first perch but might have continued on to other nearby fruit clusters in search of riper fruits.

We called the preceding choice experiments "titrations" because one could potentially change the values of fruits or the distance between them until one found the indifference point. At this point the difference in value of the two fruits could be estimated by the cost (in distance in this case) incorporated into the value of the high-ranked fruit that equalized the net values of the two fruits to the bird (Baerends & Kruijt, 1973; Moermond & Denslow, 1983).

Accessibility as a Cost of Availability. The titration procedure was used to test other components of availability. For instance, how does the cost of reaching from a perch for fruits influence fruit selection? The araçari, with its large size, strong legs, and long beak, could easily reach the fruits shown in Fig. 11.4, but a smaller bird like a tanager or manakin would have had difficulty. By offering different sets of fruits different distances above or below perches we were able to demonstrate that birds prefer to take the fruits that are easiest to reach, given that the fruits are otherwise of equal value (Denslow & Moermond, 1982, in press &

in preparation, Moermond & Denslow, 1983). Even birds, like araçaris, that easily reach hanging fruits prefer to take the same fruits close to a perch (Fig. 11.5a; Santana C., Moermond, & Denslow, unpublished manuscript).

The ease or difficulty with which a fruit can be taken from an infructescence is referred to as its accessibility. Proximity of fruits to a perch is one obvious component of accessibility. Fruits very close to a sturdy perch are easily accessible to most birds, whereas those hanging several centimeters from a perch are less accessible. Perch diameter, flexibility, and angle also influence a given bird's ability to reach fruits. The preference that birds show for the most accessible fruits is consistent with the hypothesis that foragers maximize benefit-to-cost ratios of their food selections but perhaps could also partially be explained by physical limitations of their reaching ability as dictated by their morphology (without reference to the costs of such reaches). If the bird is using a cost–benefit assessment to select fruits, then differences in accessibility of fruits are expected to influence fruit selection.

The degree of accessibility does influence which fruits the araçaris choose. Like other birds offered a favored type of fruit, araçaris preferred an easy to reach (accessible) fruit over the same fruit when it was difficult to reach (Fig. 11.5a). However, they took other, less preferred fruits only when they were

FRUIT-◉   PREFERRED OVER FRUIT-☐

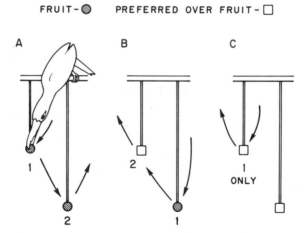

FIG. 11.5.   Fruit-accessibility trials with the araçari (toucanet). Three separate tests are diagrammed using the same fruits indicated by symbols defined at the top of the figure. The arrows indicate the movement of the bird to and from the fruits taken. Two individual araçaris made the choice indicated in condition A in 78 of 86 trials ($p < .01$, binomial test). When choosing between papaya cubes (preferred) and cubes of our synthetic banana-protein diet (less preferred), the birds made the choice indicated in condition B many times without a single exception. When offered only cubes of the synthetic diet as indicated in condition C, the birds always chose the near cube and only very rarely took the far cube when there were no other choices present.

relatively easy to reach (Fig. 11.5c). Although, in the case illustrated, the araçari chose to reach far for the preferred fruit over the more accessible less preferred fruit (Fig. 11.5b), one also expects to find cases in which an easy-to-reach, less preferred fruit is taken before a less accessible but otherwise preferred fruit. The additional cost imposed by the accessibility of the fruits should determine not only whether a given fruit is taken, but also which fruit(s) are taken. As with distance, degree of accessibility as a cost can be used to "titrate" the difference between fruits (Moermond & Denslow, 1983).

Accessibility Titrations. Initial preference for one of two different fruit types was determined by offering sets of both types just above a sturdy perch (i.e., both types easily and equally accessible). After a bird demonstrated a preference for one of the fruits, the fruits taken were replenished but with the preferred fruits made slightly more difficult to reach by suspending the fruit holder just below the experimental perch (Fig. 11.6). If the bird showed a preference for the same fruits again, the fruits were again replenished and the set of the preferred fruit was made even more difficult to reach by suspending them farther below the experimental perch. If the same fruit was still preferred when placed at the limit of the bird's reach, the difficulty of reaching them could be further magnified by increasing the diameter of the experimental perch, which made it more difficult for the bird to hang from the perch to take those fruits (Fig. 11.6). In 9 of 16 such titration series the bird switched its preference, taking the initially less preferred fruit before the more difficult to reach, but initially preferred, fruit. These switches in preference were repeatable, reversible, and in each case occurred consistently when the initially preferred fruit was presented at a particular degree of difficulty (Moermond & Denslow, 1983).

In all cases each bird ate both sets of fruits, preference being determined by the order in which the two sets were eaten. The level of accessibility necessary to induce a switch in preference by a given bird depended on the particular pair of fruits being compared. This can be seen in the example of the three titrations with a small tanager (*Euphonia gouldi*) (Fig. 11.6). This bird switched preference at a lesser degree of difficulty when choosing between its two least preferred fruits than it did when choosing between the most preferred fruit and either of the others.

These experiments provide strong evidence that the degree of accessibility functions as a cost in a cost–benefit assessment by the bird. That all fruits in most trials are eaten demonstrates that the switch is not due to the initially preferred fruit simply becoming unreachable. The reversibility of the switch shows that the switch was not due to a temporal change in preference or to satiation with the initially preferred fruit. The dependence of level of accessibility causing a switch on the particular set of fruits argues against the notion that a switch is occurring only at some limit of reach determined by the bird's morphology and further supports a similar finding in the distance titrations just

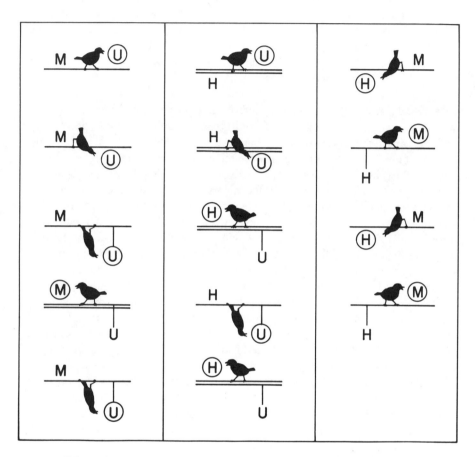

FIG. 11.6.   Accessibility titration with a *euphonia qouldi* tanager. Each figure is a diagrammatic representation of the placement of fruits above or below a 12-millimeter (double line) or 3-millimeter (single line) diameter perch during a single test. Each column, beginning at the top, shows the sequence of tests in a single titration series. The preferred fruits in each test are circled. Preference was determined by the bird eating all or nearly all the circled fruit type before eating the other fruit type (16 berries of each type were presented in each test, and each test was replicated with the left and right sides reversed to control for cage-side bias). This bird preferred fruit species U to species H and M and preferred species H to species M (figure reproduced with permission from Moermond & Denslow, 1983).

described for the araçari. These points, plus the consistency and repeatability of the responses in each trial, support the validity of the claim of the phenomenon to be a cost–benefit assessment.

It is also important to note that the degree of accessibility is not likely to be a linear measure. For example in the tanager example (Fig. 11.6), the same degree of difficulty of access resulted in a switch of preference in the first two sequences even though the strength of preference between the two pairs was not equal (the M fruits clearly had a lower preference rank than the H fruits). The cost of reaching a fruit depends on the distance to be reached, the direction of the reach (i.e., above or below a perch), the diameter and angle of the perch and the type of maneuver required to obtain the fruit (Denslow & Moermond, in press & in preparation). The responses to such differences in accessibility depend on the locomotory morphology of the bird (Moermond & Denslow, in press). Thus, for each bird there must exist a scale of costs to be applied to each fruit according to its degree of availability. Whereas some poor fruits may only be taken when most easily accessible, other highly preferred fruits may be taken even when access is very difficult.

The insights gained from these experiments were considerably enhanced by comparing responses to several different fruit combinations and similar combinations with different bird species. For example, in the case with the araçari illustrated in Fig. 11.5, if only those two fruit types had been used, the observation of a switch in fruit preference associated with accessibility would not have been made. Accordingly, no such switches in titrations using unripe fruits as the less preferred fruits were observed (Moermond & Denslow, 1983). Some birds, such as manakins and trogons, show much stronger aversions to eating unripe fruits than other species. For example, although two unripe stages of *Hamelia patens* fruits were used in the titration trials described with the araçaris (Fig. 11.4), similar results would not have been shown if a bird such as the slaty-tailed trogon (*Trogon massena*) had been used. The trogon readily ate the fully ripe black *Hamelia* berries in captivity but consistently refused all unripe stages, including dark maroon berries after periods of food deprivation (on black berries chosen in 27 of 27 choice tests with two individuals, $p < .01$; Santana C., Moermond, & Denslow, unpublished manuscript). The reasons for such differences among the birds are not arbitrary but rather are predictable manifestations of the differences in the birds' morphologies and, hence, the differences in their costs of obtaining fruits (Moermond & Denslow, in press). The comparative method here has not only led to interesting results, it has been essential to the proper interpretation of the experimental results.

Conclusions: Availability and Context

Our experiments have revealed, not too surprisingly, that fruit-eating birds make consistent, transitive, systematic choices from among the fruits they eat. The food-selection problem for a frugivorous bird would seem apparently simple—

multiple types of fruits displayed so as to be found and taken by birds. Yet, upon closer examination, the problem appears almost insolubly complex, with nutrient content, ripeness, accessibility, and spacing all influencing fruit selection. This system is certainly no less complex than that experienced by many types of animals searching for food, although the "supermarket" aspect of the fruit availability and the amenability of the food and the consumers to experimentation and manipulation may make the complexity easier to intergrate and interpret in the case of some fruit eaters. The results of our experiments are clearly applicable to studies of frugivory and seed dispersal, but they also provide important cautions and clues to many laboratory feeding experiments.

For example, the approach used here differs most from previous food-choice experiments in the handling of different types of variables. Variables, such as the effort needed to pluck a fruit, are not easy to equate with the nutrient content of the fruit. Yet it has been shown here that these fruit-eating birds do equate these types of variables and that they treat them as if they were using a cost–benefit calculation. This was shown in this study by using the systematic series of choice trials and situations described here as "behavioral titrations." A second point, essential to this approach, is that the variables to be tested were not simply chosen arbitrarily, but rather that the variables chosen were those known to be important to these kinds of birds foraging under natural conditions. This connection to the field is particularly important when attempting to interpret the results.

Other experimenters have used variables that alter the availability of a preferred item; perhaps the most frequently used is a time delay. For example, Logan (1965) has shown that rats choose a less preferred small reward if there is a sufficiently long time delay to receive the more preferred large reward. Interpretation of the role of such a time delay is far from clear. If one considers the lab variables as directly relevant to the animal's expectations, then time delays can easily be incorporated as a direct time cost when evaluating optimal-foraging hypotheses and other possibilities such as the delay reduction hypothesis (Fantino & Abarca, in press). From an ecological viewpoint, however, time delays are unlikely to function simply as a time cost. Other experimenters have shown that the choice of food involving time delays depends on the "ecological" history of the individual animal and interpretation of the response behavior depends on the evolutionary history of the animal (Christensen-Szalanski, Goldberg, Anderson, & Mitchell, 1980). Other types of laboratory studies have also usefully applied ecological perspectives to interpret behavioral patterns or responses not easily (or correctly?) explained on the basis of the lab experiments alone (e.g., Cole, Hainsworth, Kamil, Mercier, & Wolf, 1982; Hirsch & Collier, 1974; Shettleworth, 1975).

The close correspondence of the experimental questions and design to the ecology of the animals is essential but easier to give lip service to than it is to bring into practice. There is no set formula as to how such connections should be handled but there is a mode of approach that has been proven to be successful:

the comparative approach. Several different comparisons can be made to obtain information about numerous aspects of natural complexity that would otherwise be rather difficult to deduce. Three different comparisons were used in this study: Different types of fruits were obviously needed to test for preference patterns; different species of birds allowed us to see how differences in morphology or ability of the birds influenced their response to specified choice situations and, hence, allowed us to gauge the relative importance of certain types of availability variables; different types of experiments such as the three versions of titrations all played a crucial role in guiding our interpretation of the nature of the constraints that influence the birds' responses. The comparative approach allows a sifting and testing among sets of hypotheses with a focus on the ecological problems to which the animals are adapted.

Our focus on availability of food items served to emphasize the influence of ecological factors. Not only does availability have many different dimensions (e.g., abundance of food items, spacing, association with other foods, ease of capture), but each of these dimensions seems to play an important role in determining food choice. How great a role each plays is in part determined by characteristics of the food item and consumer, as well as external aspects of the environment (Collier & Rovee-Collier, 1981). Thus, the assessment and interpretation of choices made by animals in laboratory tests depend critically on the response of the animals to combinations of such factors in their natural habitat. Clearly, diet choice is a matter of context—context that can rarely be realistically simulated in the lab. Nevertheless, a solid understanding of an animal's ecology and a comparative approach allow one to make more valid interpretations from the results of laboratory studies. The answer to our original question, "What determines which food animals eat?," depends on an understanding of the disparate costs and contingencies faced by an animal in its natural environment. Designing studies that take these factors into account, and that ask how the animals deal with them, will lead to more fruitful answers in both ecology and psychology.

ACKNOWLEDGMENTS

We thank M. L. Commons, S. J. Shettleworth, and C. T. Snowdon for comments on the manuscript. T. C. Moermond and C. M. Hughes drew the figures. D. E. Stone, D. A. Clark, and D. B. Clark of the Organization for Tropical Studies provided much assistance at the La Selva Biological Station in Costa Rica. The research was supported in part by a National Science Foundation grant to T. C. Moermond and J. S. Denslow, a grant from the Organization for Tropical Studies to E. Santana C., a grant from P. and M. Hess to T. C. Moermond, and by the Graduate School and the Department of Zoology of the University of Wisconsin. This chapter has benefitted from comments and discussions with many people including J. R. Baylis, M. S. Foster, C. L. Gass, A. C. Kamil, C. T.

Snowdon, A. E. Sorensen, F. G. Stiles, A. L. Vedder, N. T. Wheelwright, and A. Worthington. We are grateful to those and the many others who have aided these studies.

REFERENCES

Baerends, G. P., & Kruijt, J. P. (1973). Stimulus selection. In R. A. Hinde & J. Stevenson-Hinde (Eds.), *Constraints on learning* (pp. 23–50). New York: Academic Press.

Belovsky, G. E. (1978). Diet optimization in a generalist herbivore, the moose. *Theoretical Population Biology, 14,* 105–134.

Best, L. S. (1981). *The effect of specific fruit and plant characteristics on seed dispersal.* Unpublished doctoral dissertation, University of Washington, Seattle, Washington.

Brown, R. G. B. (1969). Seed selection by pigeons. *Behaviour, 34,* 115–131.

Charnov, E. L. (1976). Optimal foraging: The marginal value theorem. *Theoretical Population Biology, 9,* 129–136.

Christensen-Szalanski, J. J. J., Goldberg, A. D., Anderson, M. E., & Mitchell, T. R. (1980). Deprivation, delay of reinforcement, and the selection of behavioral strategies. *Animal Behavior, 28,* 341–346.

Clark, D. A. (1982). Foraging behavior of a vertebrate omnivore (*Rattus rattus*): Meal structure, sampling, and diet breadth. *Ecology, 63,* 763–772.

Cole, S., Hainsworth, F. R., Kamil, A. C., Mercier, T., & Wolf, L. L. (1982). Spatial learning as an adaptation in hummingbirds. *Science, 217,* 655–657.

Collier, G. H., Hirsh, E., & Hamlin, P. H. (1972). The ecological determinants of reinforcement in the rat. *Physiology and Behavior, 9,* 705–716.

Collier, G. H., & Rovee-Collier, C. K. (1981). A comparative analysis of optimal foraging behavior: Laboratory simulations. In A. C. Kamil & T. D. Sargent (Eds.), *Foraging behavior: Ecological, ethological and psychological approaches* (pp. 39–76). New York: Garland STPM Press.

Crome, F. H. J. (1975). The ecology of fruit pigeons in tropical northern Queensland. *Australia Wildlife Research, 2,* 155–185.

Davies, N. B., & Green, R. E. (1976). The development and ecological significance of feeding techniques in the reed warbler (*Acrocephalus scirpaceus*). *Animal Behaviour, 24,* 213–229.

Dawkins, M. (1971). Perceptual changes in chicks: Another look at the "search image" concept. *Animal Behaviour, 19,* 566–574.

Demment, M. W., & Van Soest, P. J. (1983). Body size, digestive capacity and feeding strategies of herbivores. *Winrock International Livestock Research Publication,* Morrilton, Arkansas.

Denslow, J. S. (1983). *Unpublished data.*

Denslow, J. S., & Moermond, T. C. (1982). The effect of accessibility on rates of fruit removal from neotropical shrubs: An experimental study. *Oecologia, 54,* 170–176.

Denslow, J. S., & Moermond, T. C. (in press). The interaction of fruit display and the foraging strategies of small frugivorous birds. In W. D'Arcy & M. D. Correa (Eds.), *The botany and natural history of Panama: La botánica e historia natural de Panamá.* St. Louis: Missouri Botanical Garden.

Eggers, D. M. (1982). Planktivore preference by prey size. *Ecology, 63,* 381–190.

Eisenmann, E. (1961). Favorite foods of neotropical birds: Flying termites and *Cecropia* catkins. *Auk, 78,* 636–637.

Estabrook, G. F., & Dunham, A. E. (1976). Optimal diet as a function of absolute abundance, relative abundance and relative value of available prey. *American Naturalist, 110,* 401–413.

Fantino, E., & Abarca, N. (in press). Choice, optimal foraging, and the delay-reduction hypothesis. *Behavioral and Brain Sciences.*

Fitzpatrick, J. W. (1978). *Foraging behavior and adaptive radiation in the avian family Tyrannidae.* Unpublished doctoral dissertation, Princeton University, Princeton, New Jersey.

Fitzpatrick, J. W. (1980). Foraging behavior of neotropical tyrant flycatchers. *Condor, 82,* 43–57.

Fogden, M. P. L. (1972). The seasonality and population dynamics of equatorial forest birds in Sarawak. *Ibis, 114,* 307–343.

Foster, M. S. (1977). Ecological and nutritional effects of food scarcity on a tropical frugivorous bird and its fruit source. *Ecology, 58,* 73–85.

Foster, M. S. (1978). Total frugivory in tropical passerines: A reappraisal. *Tropical Ecology, 19,* 131–154.

Foster, R. B. (1982a). The seasonal rhythm of fruit fall on Barro Colorado Island. In E. G. Leigh, Jr., A. S. Rand, & D. Windsor (Eds.), *The ecology of a tropical forest* (pp. 151–172). Washington, DC: Smithsonian Institution Press.

Foster, R. B. (1982b). Famine on Barro Colorado Island. In E. G. Leigh, Jr., A. S. Rand, & D. Windsor (Eds.), *The ecology of a tropical forest* (pp. 201–212). Washington, DC: Smithsonian Institution Press.

Frankie, G. W., Baker, H. G., & Opler, P. A. (1974). Comparative phenological studies of trees in tropical wet and dry forests in the lowlands of Costa Rica. *Journal of Ecology, 62,* 881–919.

Glander, K. E. (1981). Feeding patterns in mantled howling monkeys. In A. C. Kamil & T. D. Sargent (Eds.), *Foraging behavior: Ecological, ethological and psychological approaches* (pp. 231–257). New York: Garland STPM Press.

Harrison, C. J. O. (Ed.). (1978). *Bird families of the world.* New York: Harry N. Abrams.

Hartley, P. H. T. (1954). Wild fruits in the diets of British thrushes: A study in the ecology of closely allied species. *British Birds, 47,* 97–107.

Hawkins, R. C. (1977). Effects of method of presentation and fluid deprivation upon drinking of sucrose and saline solutions by pigeons. *Behavioral Biology, 19,* 35–44.

Herrera, C. M. (1981). Fruit variation and competition for dispersers in natural populations of *Smilax aspera. Oikos, 36,* 51–58.

Herrera, C. M., & Jordano, P. (1981). *Prunus mahaleb* and birds: The high-efficiency seed dispersal system of a temperate fruiting tree. *Ecological Monographs, 51,* 203–218.

Hilty, S. L. (1980). Flowering and fruiting periodicity in a premontane rain forest in Pacific Colombia. *Biotropica, 12,* 292–306.

Hirsch, E., & Collier, G. (1974). The ecological determinants of reinforcement in the guinea pig. *Physiology and Behavior, 12,* 239–249.

Howe, H. F. (1977). Bird activity and seed dispersal of a tropical wet forest tree. *Ecology, 58,* 539–550.

Howe, H. F. (1981). Dispersal of a neotropical nutmeg (*Virola sebifera*) by birds. *Auk, 98,* 88–98.

Howe, H. F., & Vande Kerckhove, G. A. (1980). Nutmeg dispersal by tropical birds. *Science, 210,* 925–927.

Hutchinson, G. E. (1957). Concluding remarks. *Cold Spring Harbor Symposium on Quantitative Biology, 22,* 415–427.

Ivlev, V. S. (1961). *Experimental ecology of the feeding of fishes.* New Haven, CT: Yale University Press.

Jenkins, R. (1969). *Ecology of three species of Saltators in Costa Rica with special reference to their frugivorous diet.* Unpublished doctoral dissertation, Harvard University, Cambridge, Massachusetts.

Johnson, D. H. (1980). The comparison of usage and availability measurements for evaluating resource preference. *Ecology, 61*(1), 65–71.

Kamil, A. C., Peters, J., & Lindstrom, F. J. (1982). An ecological approach to the study of the distribution of behavior. In M. L. Commons, R. J. Herrnstein, & H. Rachlin (Eds.), *Quantitative analyses of behavior: Vol. II. Matching and maximizing accounts* (pp. 189–203). Cambridge, MA: Ballinger.

Kamil, A. C., & Sargent, T. D. (Eds.). (1981). *Foraging behavior*. New York: Garland STPM Press.

Kantak, G. E. (1979). Observations on some fruit-eating birds in Mexico. *Auk, 96,* 183–186.

Karr, J. R. (1971). Structure of avian communities in selected Panama and Illinois habitats. *Ecological Monographs, 41,* 207–233.

Kaufman, A. (1968). *The science of decision-making*. New York: McGraw–Hill.

Kear, J. (1962). Food selection in finches with special reference to interspecific differences. *Proceedings of the Zoological Society of London, 138,* 163–204.

Krebs, J. R. (1978). Optimal foraging: Decision rules for predators. In J. R. Krebs & N. B. Davies (Eds.), *Behavioural ecology: An evolutionary approach* (pp. 23–63). Sunderland, MA: Sinauer.

Krebs, J. R., & Davies, N. B. (1981). *An introduction to behavioural ecology*. Sunderland, MA: Sinauer.

Krebs, J. R., Erichsen, J. T., Webber, M. I., & Charnov, E. L. (1977). Optimal prey selection in the great tit, Parus major. *Animal Behavior, 25,* 30–38.

Krebs, J. R., Stevens, D. W., & Sutherland, W. J. (1983). Perspectives in optimal foraging. In A. H. Brush & G. A. Clark, Jr. (Eds.), *Perspectives in ornithology* (pp. 165–221). Cambridge, England: Cambridge University Press.

Leck, C. F. (1971). Overlap in the diet of some neotropical birds. *Living Bird, 10,* 89–106.

Leisler, B., & Thaler, E. (1982). Differences in morphology and foraging behaviour in the goldcrest and the firecrest. *Annales Zoologici Fennici, 19,* 277–284.

Levey, D. J., Moermond, T. C., & Denslow, J. S. (1984). Fruit choice in neotropical birds: The effect of distance between fruits on preference patterns. *Ecology, 65,* 844–850.

Logan, G. A. (1965). Decision making by rats: Delay versus amount of reward. *Journal of Comparative Physiological Psychology, 59,* 1–12.

MacArthur, R. H., & Pianka, E. R. (1966). On optimal use of a patchy environment. *American Naturalist, 100,* 603–609.

McCleery, R. H. (1978). Optimal behaviour sequences and decision making. In J. R. Krebs & N. B. Davies (Eds.), *Behavioural ecology: An evolutionary approach* (pp. 377–410). Sunderland, MA: Sinauer.

McDiarmid, R., Ricklefs, R. E., & Foster, M. S. (1977). Dispersal of *Stemmadenia donnell-smithii* (Apocynaceae) by birds. *Biotropica, 9,* 9–25.

McKey, D. (1975). The ecology of coevolved seed dispersal systems. In L. E. Gilbert & P. H. Raven (Eds.), *Coevolution of animals and plants* (pp. 159–191). Austin: University of Texas Press.

Mitchell, J. E. (1975). Variation in food preferences of three grasshopper species (Acrididae: Orthoptera) as a function of food availability. *American Midland Naturalist, 94,* 267–283.

Moermond, T. C. (1979a). Habitat constraints on the behavior, morphology, and community structure of *Anolis* lizards. *Ecology, 60,* 152–164.

Moermond, T. C. (1979b). The influence of habitat structure on *Anolis* foraging behavior. *Behaviour, 70,* 147–167.

Moermond, T. C. (1981). Prey-attack behavior of *Anolis* lizards. *Zeitschrift für Tierpsychologie, 56,* 128–136.

Moermond, T. C., & Denslow, J. S. (1983). Fruit choice in neotropical birds: Effects of fruit type and accessibility on selectivity. *Journal of Animal Ecology, 52,* 407–420.

Moermond, T. C., & Denslow, J. S. (in press). Neotropical avian frugivores: Patterns of behavior, morphology and nutrition with consequences for fruit selection. In P. A. Buckley, M. S. Foster, E. S. Morton, R. S. Ridgely, & F. G. Buckley (Eds.), *Neotropical ornithology. Ornithological Monographs,* No. 36 (pp. 865–897).

Moermond, T. C., Denslow, J. S., Levey, D. J., & Wentworth, B. C. (1985). *Unpublished data.*

Moon, R. D., Ziegler, H. P. (1979). Food preferences in the pigeon (*Columba livia*). *Physiology and Behavior, 22,* 1171–1182.

Morton, E. S. (1973). On the evolutionary advantages and disadvantages of fruit eating in tropical birds. *American Naturalist, 107,* 8–22.

Newton, I. (1967). The adaptive radiation and feeding ecology of some British finches. *Ibis, 109,* 33–98.

Norberg, R. A. (1977). An ecological theory on foraging time and energetics and choice of optimal food-searching method. *Journal of Animal Ecology, 46,* 511–529.

Norberg, U. M. (1979). Morphology of the wings, legs and tail of three coniferous forest tits, the goldcrest, and the treecreeper in relation to locomotor pattern and feeding station selection. *Philosophical Transactions of the Royal Society of London. Series B, Biological Sciences, 287,* 131–165.

Norberg, U. M. (1981). Flight, morphology and the ecological niche in some birds and bats. *Symposia of the Zoological Society of London, 48,* 173–197.

O'Brien, W. J., Slade, N. A., & Vinyard, G. L. (1976). Apparent size as the determinant of size selection by bluegill sunfish (*Lepomis macrochirus*). *Ecology, 57,* 1304–1310.

Opler, P. A., Frankie, G. W., & Baker, H. G. (1980). Comparative phenological studies of treelet and shrub species in tropical wet and dry forests in the lowlands of Costa Rica. *Journal of Ecology, 68,* 167–188.

Orians, G. H., & Pearson, N. E. (1979). On the theory of central place foraging. In D. J. Horn, R. D. Mitchell, & G. R. Stairs (Eds.), *Analysis of ecological systems* (pp. 155–177). Columbus: Ohio State University Press.

Pearson, D. L. (1977). Ecological relationships of small antbirds in Amazonian bird communities. *Auk, 94,* 283–292.

Pietrewicz, A. T., & Kamil, A. C. (1977). Visual detection of cryptic prey by blue jays (*Cyanocitta cristata*). *Science, 95,* 580–582.

Pietrewicz, A. T., & Kamil, A. C. (1979). Search image formation in the blue jay (*Cyanocitta cristata*). *Science, 204,* 1332–1333.

Pulliam, H. R. (1975). Diet optimization with nutrient constraints. *American Naturalist, 109,* 765–768.

Pulliam, H. R. (1976). The principle of optimal behaviour and the theory of communities. In P. P. G. Bateson & P. H. Klopfer (Eds.), *Perspectives in ethology* (Vol. 2, pp. 311–332). New York: Plenum.

Pulliam, H. R. (1980). Do chipping sparrows forage optimally? *Ardea, 68,* 75–82.

Revusky, S. H. (1977). Learning as a general process with emphasis on data from feeding experiments. In N. W. Milgram, L. Krames, & T. M. Alloway (Eds.), *Food aversion learning* (pp. 1–51). New York: Plenum.

Rice, W. R. (1983). Sensory modality: An example of its effect on optimal foraging behavior. *Ecology, 64,* 403–406.

Ridley, H. N. (1930). *The dispersal of plants throughout the world.* Ashford, Kent, England: L. Reeve.

Robinson, S. K., & Holmes, R. T. (1982). Foraging behavior of forest birds: The relationships among search tactics, diet, and habitat structure. *Ecology, 63,* 1918–1931.

Rozin, P. (1976). The selection of foods by rats, humans, and other animals. *Advances in the Study of Behavior, 6,* 21–76.

Santana C., E., Moermond, T. C., & Denslow, J. S. (1985). *Fruit choice in neotropical birds: Contrasts between the collared aracari and the slaty-tailed trogon.* Unpublished manuscript.

Schoener, T. W. (1969). Models of optimal size for solitary predators. *American Naturalist, 103,* 277–313.

Schoener, T. W. (1971). Theory of feeding strategies. *Annual Review of Ecology and Systematics, 2,* 369–404.

Schoener, T. W. (1979). Generality of the size–distance relation in models of optimal foraging. *American Naturalist, 114,* 902–914.

Shettleworth, S. J. (1975). Reinforcement and the organization of behavior in golden hamsters' hunger, environment and food reinforcement. *Journal of Experimental Psychology, 104*, 56–87.

Sibly, R. M. (1981). Strategies of digestion and defecation. In C. R. Townsend & P. Calow (Eds.), *Physiological ecology: An evolutionary approach to resource use* (pp. 109–139). Sunderland, MA: Sinauer.

Sigel, S. (1956). *Nonparametric statistics for the behavioral sciences.* New York: McGraw–Hill.

Snow, B. K., & Snow, D. W. (1971). The feeding ecology of tanagers and honeycreepers in Trinidad. *Auk, 88*, 291–322.

Snow, D. W. (1962). A field study of the black and white manakin, *Manacus manacus*, in Trinidad. *Zoologica* (N. Y.), *47*, 65–104.

Snow, D. W. (1965). A possible selective factor in the evolution of fruiting seasons in tropical forests. *Oikos, 15*, 274–281.

Snow, D. W. (1971). Evolutionary aspects of fruit-eating by birds. *Ibis, 113*, 194–202.

Snow, D. W. (1981). Tropical frugivorous birds and their food plants: A world survey. *Biotropica, 13*, 1–14.

Sorensen, A. E. (1981). Interactions between birds and fruits in a temperate woodland. *Oecologia, 50*, 242–249.

Sorensen, A. E. (1984). Nutrition, energy and passage: Experiments with fruit preference in European blackbirds (*Turdus merula*). *Journal of Animal Ecology, 53*, 545–557.

Staddon, J. E. R. (1983). *Adaptive behavior and learning.* Cambridge, England: Cambridge University Press.

Staddon, J. E. R., & Gendron, R. P. (1983). Optimal detection of cryptic prey may lead to predator switching. *American Naturalist, 122*, 843–848.

Stiles, F. G. (1979). Notes on the natural history of *Heliconia* (Musaceae) in Costa Rica. *Brenesia, 15*, 151–180.

Tinbergen, J. M. (1981). Foraging decisions in starlings (*Sturnus vulgaris* L.) *Ardea, 69*, 1–67.

Tinbergen, N. (1972). *The animal in its world. Vol. 2: Laboratory studies.* Cambridge, MA: Harvard University Press.

Tullock, G. (1970). The coal tit as a careful shopper. *American Naturalist, 104*, 77–80.

Tyser, R. W., & Moermond, T. C. (1983). Foraging behavior in two species of different-sized sciurids. *American Midland Naturalist, 108*, 240–245.

van der Pijl, L. (1969). *Principles of dispersal in higher plants.* New York: Springer–Verlag.

Vedder, A. L. (1985). Movement patterns of a group of free-ranging mountain gorillas (*Gorilla gorilla beringei*) and their relation to food availability. *American Journal of Primatology, 7*, 73–88.

Westoby, M. (1974). An analysis of diet selection by large generalist herbivores. *American Naturalist, 108*, 290–304.

Wheelwright, N. T., Haber, W. A., Murray, K. G., & Guindon, C. (1984). Tropical fruit-eating birds and their food plants: A survey of a Costa Rican lower montane forest. *Biotropica, 16*, 173–192.

V METHODOLOGY

12

Detecting and Eliminating Spatial Bias When Tracking Foraging Behavior in a Laboratory Experiment

Peter Cahoon
Department of Interdisciplinary Studies
University of British Columbia

INTRODUCTION

In all natural systems, particularly biological systems, space and time are interrelated. Currently, the analytical techniques available to biologists do not deal adequately with spatial correlation. A great many studies of foraging and population dynamics are carried out on some sort of grid, regular or irregular, such as Latin squares. These are designed so that any treatment results are orthogonal, thus removing the effects posed by the grid geometry. Another standard technique for removing grid bias is to enter a dummy treatment effect both for rows and columns of the experiment to see whether this makes any difference to the statistical model being tested. If the geometry is irregular or if there is some interpolation or extrapolation to be done, then these spatial biases present a much more complex situation. Dealing with these biases as the experiment evolves through time becomes a major statistical difficulty.

Space and time may be taken theoretically as having dimensions of R^n, where R indicates that the space is real and n indicates that it can have n dimensions. Because both temporal and spatial characteristics are derived from a space having the same dimension and characteristics, they can be treated in analogous ways. In practice, however, the spatiotemporal framework of the organism may have little to do with the framework applied by the researcher's experimental design.

The purpose of this chapter is to present some analytical techniques that dealt with some of these problems as they arose in laboratory foraging experiments.

This experiment had an intentional spatial bias included in its experimental design, plus an unintentional spatially directional bias.

The Experiment

The idea behind this laboratory experiment was to reproduce the periodic variation in the abundance of available nectar in meadow flowers encountered by a hummingbird during the course of a day. In addition, the experiment attempted to simulate the inherently patchy, spatial distribution of the flowers. The objective was that from this time-varying and patchy environment some measurable behavior stereotypes would emerge. The hummingbirds used in the experiment (*Selasphorus rufus*) were allowed to forage in this controlled environment for periods of 30 seconds. After each foraging period the spatial arrays were reallocated and refilled. This process was repeated for a total of 38 trials and the results were recorded. The foraging experiment was designed and run by Tom and Chris Getty of the Biological Sciences Department of the University of Michigan. The experimental room was located in the foraging laboratory of Lee Gass at the University of British Columbia.

The experiment was run on 4 consecutive days, with several "training" days preceding the actual experiment. Both females and males were used as subjects. The results presented here are for a single female, and they represent the best tracking behavior by any bird.

The Experimental Design

A U-shaped room (Fig. 12.1) was fitted with two arrays of single-dose feeders on the western and eastern walls. The locations to be filled were allocated by means of a random-number generator on an APPLE II microcomputer. The number of loaded feeders for both sides for any trial was 35. The feeding arrays were made from small hollow tubes attached to individual reservoirs containing a 15% concentration of sugar in water. Each tube with its reservoir was attached to a base that in turn was attached to a metal panel having a regular array of holes. The assembled feeders were attached so as to be even with the mounting board and had no markings to distinguish one from another. The numbers of filled feeders allocated on each side were made to vary sinusoidally, as indicated in Fig. 12.2. Each trial started with the bird positioned as in Fig. 12.1, with a pair of window blinds covering the feeder arrays. At the beginning of each trial the bird was alerted by sound and the blinds were raised simultaneously.

Each touch of the bird's beak to a feeder location was conveyed *via* a serial processor to the APPLE II. The location was converted to integer-numbered units and the duration of the touch was recorded. This information was then down-loaded to a Digital 11/45 minicomputer and reprocessed and reformatted for further analysis.

Experiment Setup

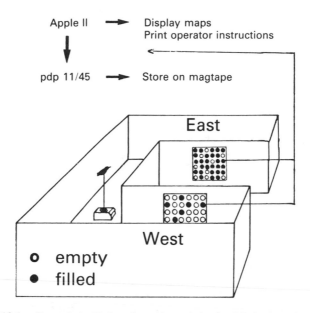

FIG. 12.1.   Shown is the U-shaped experimental chamber. At the start of a given trial, blinds covered both feeder arrays. The bird began each trial perched as illustrated.

The results presented in Fig. 12.2(a,b,c,d) represent proportions of the total number of touches to a given side on a 30 second trial. This proportion was calculated for each of the 38 trials and appears as the histogram under the sinusoid that represents the experimental design. Note that on the second day of the experiment the sinusoid was assigned a different phase, to see whether the bird's response would change.

A different perspective can be seen in Fig. 12.3,4,5,6(a,b,c,d). These three-dimensional histograms represent the total occurrences of visitations to location (x,y) for all the day's trials. The three-dimensional histogram of the experimental design represents the total number of times that location (x,y) was filled during the course of the day.

The techniques used to identify, describe, and correct these spatial-biasing problems are the two-dimensional Fourier transform, and the singular-value decomposition. Before describing the application of these techniques to this experiment, some background introduction to their mechanics is required.

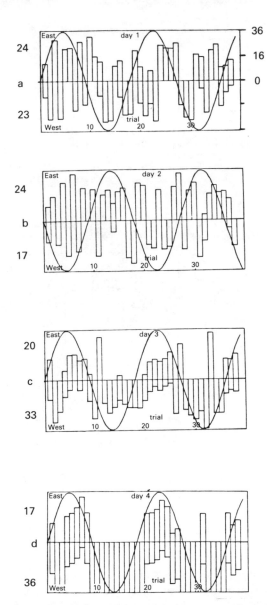

FIG. 12.2. Shown are the sinusoidally varying experimental design (solid line) and the total number of touches by the bird during each of the 38 trials (histograms) under the solid line). The figures on the left indicate the average number of feeders touched per trial on each of the two sides. The figures on the right indicate the total number of feeders available on a side.

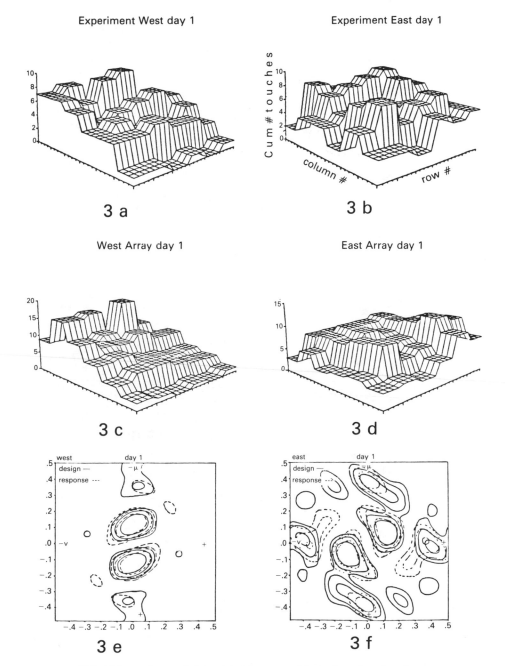

FIG. 12.3. *a*, *b*, *c*, and *d* show the histograms of the total number of touches at any location of the eastern and western feeder arrays on experimental day-one. The columns and rows number from 1 to 6, beginning at the x, y, z origin. *e* and *f* show the two-dimensional responses represented in *a*, *b*, *c*, and *d*.

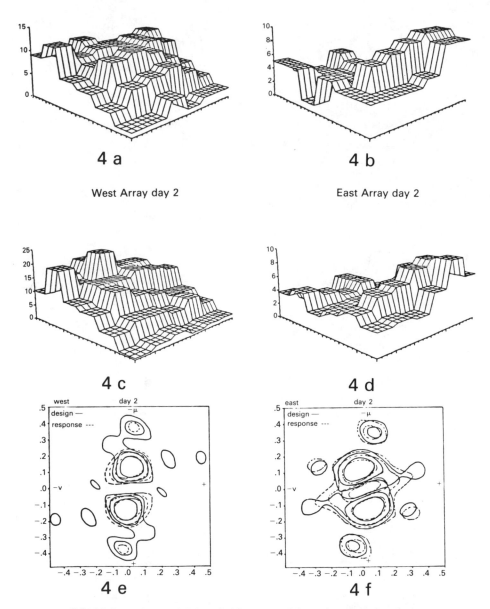

FIG. 12.4. *a, b, c,* and *d* show the histograms of the total number of touches at any location of the eastern and western feeder arrays on experimental day-two. The columns and rows number from 1 to 6, beginning at the x, y, z origin, *e* and *f* show the two-dimensional responses represented in *a, b, c,* and *d*.

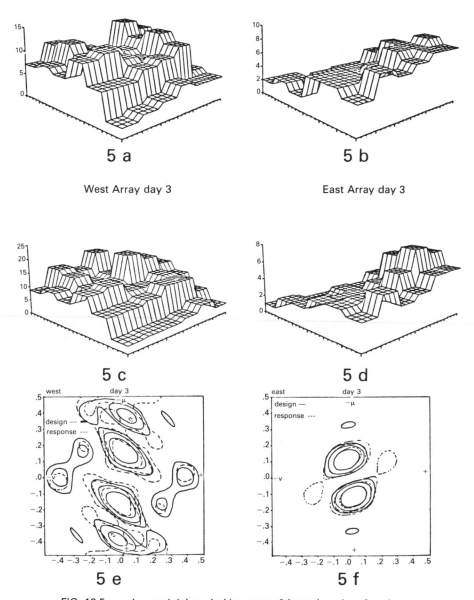

Experiment West day 3   Experiment East day 3

5 a   5 b

West Array day 3   East Array day 3

5 c   5 d

west   day 3

east   day 3

5 e   5 f

FIG. 12.5.   *a, b, c,* and *d* show the histograms of the total number of touches at any location of the eastern and western feeder arrays on experimental day-three. The columns and rows number from 1 to 6, beginning at the x, y, z origin. *e* and *f* show the two-dimensional responses represented in *a, b, c,* and *d.*

261

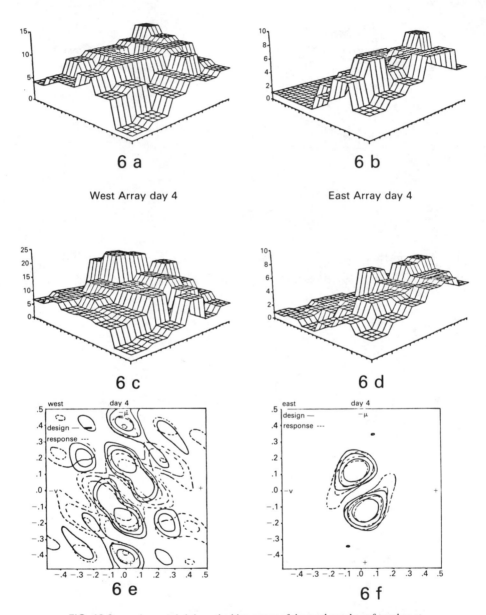

Experiment West day 4   Experiment East day 4

6 a   6 b

West Array day 4   East Array day 4

6 c   6 d

6 e   6 f

FIG. 12.6. *a, b, c,* and *d* show the histograms of the total number of touches at any location of the eastern and western feeder arrays on experimental day-four. The columns and rows number from 1 to 6, beginning at the x, y, z origin. *e* and *f* show the two-dimensional responses represented in *a, b, c,* and *d.*

Using the Two-Dimensional Fourier Transform to Interpret Spatial Grids

Using the Fourier transform to analyze spatial grids assumes that the time vary-ing spatial components can be modeled with a sum of sinusoids. In this setup the experiment itself was designed to vary sinusoidally over time. Therefore, the expected response was some approximation to sinusoidal components. The searching responses, delineated as numbers of touches at the locations within a grid are not a priori periodic. However, through computer animation, an exam-ination of the recorded movements of these birds during the period of several weeks in their natural habitat was conducted. From this study it was discovered that their search sequences are periodic. In addition the type of searching se-quence employed in a particular situation was discovered to be highly stereo-typed as well. This, then, is the empirical justification behind the use of the techniques about to be introduced.

One way to illustrate the two-dimensional spatial-field concept is by means of the following example: Let $z(i,j)$ be the measure of an array of point densities of the total number of visits to feeder location (i,j) on a grid having m rows and n columns. The Fourier transform represents these as $z(i,j) = \sin(2\pi(ui + vj))$, for $i = 1, \ldots , m$ and $j = 1, \ldots , n$.

The frequency components u and v represent the rate of oscillation of these sinusoids in the row and column directions, respectively. They correspond to the rate of row and column searches conducted by the hummingbird as it moves about the experimental grid. For example, if $u = 0.5$ and $v = 0.25$, the column search rate varies twice as much as the row component. Therefore, a point would appear in the spectrum at $(u,v) = (0.5, 0.25)$ having a height representing a covariation of that frequency pair. A grid made up of many of these components would be analogous to a snapshot of the ripples generated by throwing a rock into a quiet pond.

Interpreting a Two-Dimensional Spectrum

The transformed point density maps change the basis from (x,y) coordinates to (u,v) coordinates. The (u,v) coordinates vary from $-1/2\Delta, \ldots , +1/2\Delta$, where Δ represents the data-sampling interval. The grids under study here had a sam-pling rate of 1 measurement per spatial interval. Therefore, $\Delta = 1$. The $+$ to $-$ range can be explained as follows.

If the bird were searching in a sinusoidal pattern, and its search was progress-ing parallel to the u plane, then the row frequency would be constant. A state such as this would imply that the oscillations in the covariance were progressing in either a right-to-left or a left-to-right direction. Because only the peak spatial covariance is ever available, several time frames are necessary to ascertain the direction of the search movement.

Reading a Spectral Map

The actual form taken by the cumulative data maps before transformation is that of a two-dimensional lagged covariance in the (x,y) coordinate plane.

The lagged covariance is defined as

$$E[x(i,j)x(i - r, j - s)] = \sum_{i\,j=1}^{mn} x(i, j)x(i - r, j - s),$$

where $E[-]$ denotes expectation, and

$$r = -m/2, \ldots, +m/2 \text{ and } s = -n/2, \ldots, +n/2.$$

Geometrically this consists of moving the point-density map $x(i,j)$ around itself in a counterclockwise, positive direction for each of the various lags. The range from $+$ to $-$ in each direction insures that there is no directional bias in the resulting covariance. A schematic of the operation is shown next.

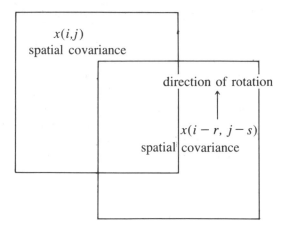

This lagged two-dimensional spatial-covariance map is then Fourier transformed. The two-dimensional spatial-covariance has now been mapped onto the (u,v) plane. The resulting map that now has coordinates of $1/2\Delta$ spatial units is then reoriented so that the frequency $(0.,0.)$ lies at the center of the grid to insure that the proper symmetry is maintained.

The Fourier transform also has a reflective symmetry about $(0.0,0.0)$. This means that, if a peak appears in the top left quadrant, its mirror image will appear in the lower right-hand quadrant. Similarly, if a peak appears in the lower left quadrant, its mirror image will appear in the upper right quadrant. Therefore, when reading these maps one need only look at one half of the entire plane. A typical (u,v) map is illustrated here.

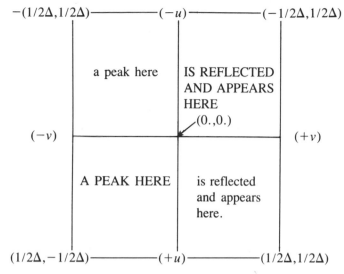

The two-dimensional Fourier-transform maps are displayed in Fig. 12.4,5,6(e and f). The solid line represents the experimental design whereas the dotted line represents the bird's responses.

Aliasing on a Spatial Grid

The term *aliasing* refers to sampling a grid at one rate and having this rate reappear in the sampled data at lower frequency multiples of itself. For example, if the bird took samples at the 10 grid points, then the rate of sampling is 1/10 per spatial increment. The Nyquist sampling theorem states that the experimenter cannot resolve those components having a repetition rate greater than $1/(2\times10)$ per spatial increment. The resulting point-density array has one set of frequency components due to fluctuations in the point-density amplitudes, plus another set that is strictly due to the sampling rate. These two appear together in the sampled data base. Therefore, in order to analyze those components that represent the actual point density amplitude fluctuations, the spurious components resulting from the sampling must be removed. More generally, one must have the ability to remove numerically any suspected aliases at any arbitrary frequency.

A general solution to the multidimensional problem was presented by Russell Mersereau (1983). He demonstrated that aliasing due to sampling on any grid shape in any number of dimensions can be removed from any raw, interpolated, or decimated grid. His arguments are quite direct. Therefore, only a simple outline is presented here.

Let the sampling grid be considered to be made up of a set of S linearly independent column vectors denoted as

$$[c(1), \ldots , c(S)] = C.$$

Each location in c can be expressed as $t = Cn$, where n represents a vector with integer entries. For this rectangular case C is diagonal. Neither the basis nor the sampling grid is unique. However, if E is a S $\times$ S matrix of integers, such that,

$$|\det E| = 1,$$

(det means determinant, $|-|$ denotes magnitude) is unimodular, then the original matrix C has been aliased and now has the form C = EC.

Now consider the Fourier transform of the point-sample grid to be defined by

$$y(\Omega) = (1/T) \sum_{-\infty}^{+\infty} y(n)\exp[-j\Omega^t Cn],$$

t denotes transpose, $j = \sqrt{-1}$, and C represents a matrix having the rank of the sampling grid with independent columns. Ω represents a vector of spatial frequencies and has a length that corresponds to the number of spatial dimensions (in this case 2). The determinant of C is unique for a given grid and is equal to the reciprocal of the sampling density.

This is equivalent to saying that the spatial Fourier transform has been aliased by Cn, where C is due to the geometry of the grid. What one wants to do is recover the unaliased version of the transform.

In order to achieve this the following calculation is made

$$y(\Omega) = (1/\det C) \sum_{-\infty}^{+\infty} y(\Omega - U(r)).$$

$U^t C = 2\pi I$, and I represents the identity matrix. The matrix U defines the amount of aliasing present in the sampling due to the shape of the grid. U has elements

$$\begin{vmatrix} 2\pi/T(1) & 0.0 \\ 0.0 & 2\pi/T(2) \end{vmatrix}$$

T(1) represents the row sampling rate, and T(2) the column rate. The spectrum is, therefore, scaled by 1/det U.

For those not familiar with the two-dimensional Fourier transform, Bracewell (1965) offers an excellent treatment of the subject as well as its applications.

Singular-Value Decomposition

The hummingbird visited any number of locations an arbitrary number of times during a given trial, and also during the course of the entire 38 trials. This means that there was much redundant information on any particular row or column on the grid. "Redundant," as applied here, means that the majority of the amplitudes measured on the rows and columns of the grid are linearly dependent and do not contribute in any useful way to explaining the dynamics of the problem.

In order to demonstrate this redundancy, the decomposition of the component grid fields has been provided through the use of the singular-value decomposition algorithm. Forsyth (1977) devotes an entire chapter to this algorithm as well as its applications to least squares problems.

The singular-value decomposition (SVD) is used to decompose a field represented by a matrix C into two orthogonal matrices U and V. An examination of the singular values of C, denoted as D, will indicate which of those components of C is independent, and which of those is linearly dependent. If the singular values D are zero, or less than some desired tolerance ξ, then the singular vector columns corresponding to U and V are deemed linearly dependent, and thus redundant to the description of the characteristics of C. This implies, therefore, that the matrix C is rank-defective in that there exists a set of row and column transformations that will reduce C to a lesser rank at which none of the rows or columns are linearly dependent. This is also known as the effective rank of C. It is this reduced effective rank that contains all the active information on the field.

The second part of this decomposition is to determine the condition number of C. If C is of full rank the condition number of C, denoted as cond(C), is defined as d_{max}/d_{min}, where d_{max} and d_{min} are respectively the largest and smallest singular values of C. If C is orthogonal, then cond(C) = 1 and the columns are as independent as possible. In addition, if cond(C) = 1, then it turns out that C must be a scalar multiple of an orthogonal matrix.

If we now define the length of a vector (its norm) to be

$$\| x \| = \surd \, (x^t x),$$

where t denotes transpose, and $\|-\|$ denotes norm. The quantity

$$\| Cx \| \, / \, \| x \|$$

measures the amount by which C extends x. What one wishes to know from this relation is, how much does this extending factor vary over x?

This extension tells the experimenter whether all row and column components are equal, and if they are not, in which directions they are dominant. The larger the separation in the amplitudes of the singular values, the larger the spatial bias.

A more explicit way of presenting the amount and direction in which things are extended can be illustrated as follows. Geometrically, the matrix C maps the unit sphere, which is the set of vectors x for which $\| x \| = 1$, onto a set of vectors defined by $b = Cx$, which have varying lengths. The result is a multidimensional ellipsoid having major and minor axes d_{max} and d_{min}.

If one lets C = UDV^t and $y = V^t x$, then, because orthogonal matrices preserve length, $\| y \| = \| x \|$ and

$$\| Cx \| = \| UDV^t x \| = \| Dy \|.$$

Because D is diagonal,

$$d_{\min} \le \| Cx \| / \| x \| \le d_{\max}.$$

This indicates that $d_{\max}$ is the largest extension of C and $d_{\min}$ the smallest.

The ellipsoids of the various experimental designs and foraging grids are illustrated in Fig. 12.7, 12.8, 12.9, 12.10(a,b,c,d). Each axis of these ellipsoids has two components: the major-axis (longest) component and the minor-axis (shortest) component. Because there are only three singular values that turn out

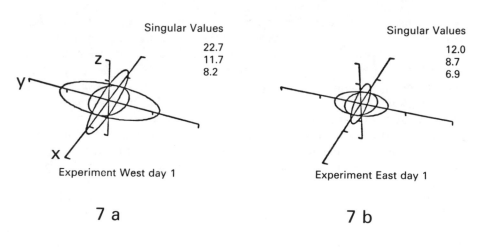

Singular Values

22.7
11.7
8.2

Experiment West day 1

7 a

Singular Values

12.0
8.7
6.9

Experiment East day 1

7 b

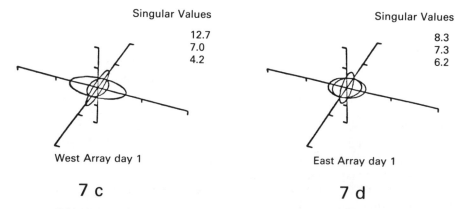

Singular Values

12.7
7.0
4.2

West Array day 1

7 c

Singular Values

8.3
7.3
6.2

East Array day 1

7 d

FIG. 12.7.   *a, b, c,* and *d* show the singular values of the data arrays in Figure 3 (*a, b, c, d*). The singular values listed are those for the y-, x-, and z-axes. respectively. The amount of elongation of an axis indicates the selection of a preferred direction of search.

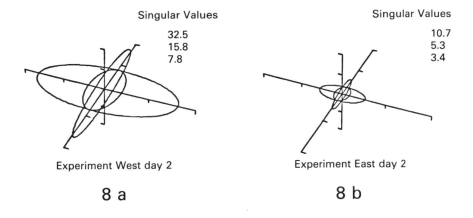

Singular Values

32.5
15.8
7.8

Experiment West day 2

8 a

Singular Values

10.7
5.3
3.4

Experiment East day 2

8 b

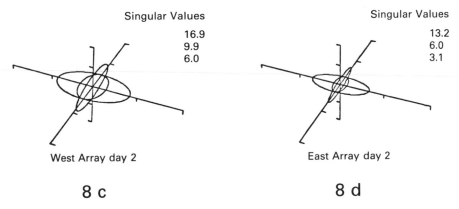

Singular Values

16.9
9.9
6.0

West Array day 2

8 c

Singular Values

13.2
6.0
3.1

East Array day 2

8 d

FIG. 12.8. *a, b, c*, and *d* show the singular values of the data arrays in Fig. 12.4 (*a, b, c, d*). The singular values listed are those for the y-, x-, and z-axes, respectively. The amount of elongation of an axis indicates the selection of a preferred direction of search.

to be important, the major/minor singular value pairs are (1,2) corresponding to (*x,y*), (1,3) corresponding to (*x,z*), and (2,3) corresponding to (*y,z*). These are represented on the *x,y,z* orthogonal axes in their respective orders.

Outer Product Expansions

The composition of any two-dimensional scalar or vector field, denoted as C, can be expressed as:

$$C = UDV'.$$

In such an expansion the unitary matrices U and V are arbitrary and D is a matrix made up of the expansion coefficients of the rows and columns of the field, so these expansion coefficients will appear as

$$d_{ij} = u^t_i \, C \, v_j.$$

In this expression u_i denotes the i-th component vector of U; v_j the j-th component vector of V; d_{ij} the i,j-th element of the matrix D. The expansion coefficients are also known as singular values. By means of the singular-value

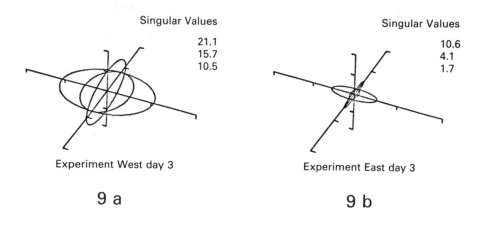

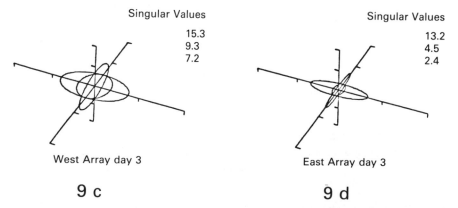

FIG. 12.9. *a, b, c,* and *d* show the singular values of the data arrays in Fig. 12.5 (*a, b, c, d*). The singular values listed are those for the y-, x-, and z-axes, respectively. The amount of elongation of an axis indicates the selection of a preferred direction of search.

Singular Values

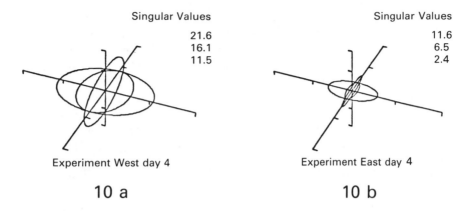

Singular Values
21.6
16.1
11.5

Experiment West day 4

10 a

Singular Values
11.6
6.5
2.4

Experiment East day 4

10 b

Singular Values

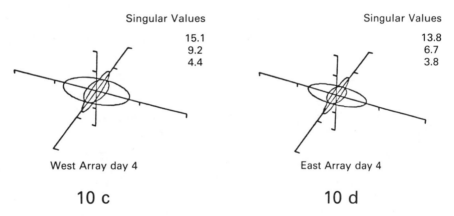

Singular Values
15.1
9.2
4.4

West Array day 4

10 c

Singular Values
13.8
6.7
3.8

East Array day 4

10 d

FIG. 12.10.   *a, b, c,* and *d* show the singular values of the data arrays in Fig. 12.6 (*a, b, c, d*). The singular values listed are those for the y-, x-, and z-axes, respectively. The amount of elongation of an axis indicates the selection of a preferred direction of search.

decomposition (SVD), D can be made diagonal. Therefore the composition of C expressed as

$$C = d_1u_1v_1{}^t + d_2u_2v_2{}^t + \ldots + d_ru_rv_r{}^t.$$

The "*r*" denotes the number of "significant" singular values that have been determined. "Significant", in this case, indicates how much of the total covariance of the grid can be accounted for using only "*r*" of the singular values to reconstruct the grid.

The SVD is applied to analyzing the output grids of this experiment as a means of demonstrating the salient features of the SVD properties, and illustrating the interrelationship between observed tracking behavior and the corresponding experimental design. If the bird tracks the experiment exactly, the amplitudes and number of "significant" singular values will be the same for both the experimental design and the data array. If it tracks the experimental design but is unsure of the exact shape, then the proportions of the singular values will be larger, with more variance, but their relative proportion will remain the same. These responses are quite apparent in the geometry of the singular value plots. Where there should be no difference in the experimental designs, there are very sizable geometric differences. The foraging responses, on the other hand differ little from the experimental designs.

There were six singular values for each grid. Out of these six, only three were large enough to affect the amount of variation accounted for in the grids. This meant that each grid was recontructed by means of an outer product expansion as previously described. The sum of squares of the variance accounted for by the reconstruction done with three of the six singular values differed by less than 5% of the total sum of squares of variance on the original grid. These three singular values are now labeled the "significant" singular values of the corresponding grid.

Results

The first indication of spatial biasing can be seen in the three-dimensional histograms of the experimental design (Fig. 12.3, 12.4 & 12.5,a,b,c,d).

It is immediately apparent from the experimental design that there is a great deal of difference in the eastern and western sides. This subsequently turns up in the bird's responses. What is not apparent from the histograms, however, is exactly how well the bird tracked the bias. When one looks at Fig. 12.2(a,b,c,d) it appears that on the whole the bird did not follow the experimental sinusoid very well. If one looks at the spectra in Fig. 12.3, 12.4, 12.5, 12.6(e,f), quite another picture develops.

If a spatial design were unbiased, then the spectrum of feeder variance would be a white-noise spectrum. This means that no discernible structure would be apparent. However, because there were only 35 feeders, repetitions were unavoidable. Thus, the appearance of clusters of preferred feeders is justified. These are plotted as a set of concentric circular contours over some (u,v) frequency range. The experimental design sinusoid will only appear in the cross spectrum between the east and west arrays.

The presence of an array bias will appear as an ellipsoid of concentric ring contours. The contours plotted here can be visualized as squashed cones the tops of which form the most central rings and the bases of which are the outermost rings. The amount of spatial biasing in a particular direction can be seen in the differences in the singular values (Fig. 12.7, 12.8, 12.9, 12.10(a,b,c,d)). Again, if all the singular values were the same, then there would be no directional bias. This also illustrates the concept of the extending of the unit sphere along one or more of its axes. The dashed lined contours represent the bird's response to the experimental design. Here it can be seen that the bird tended to pool patches of preferences, established what it somehow perceived to be their boundaries, and remained within them.

In order to establish the fact that this bird actually did group these patches, the experiment was animated so that every movement was indicated by a vector. The entire set of movements was run and their trajectories were observed as they unfolded through time. It became clear that entirely systematic search sequences were occurring. These began with a visit to the last rewarded feeder location and ended after no more than 10 successive failures. However, what was not apparent from the animation, but is clearly indicated here, is the reason that the bird moved almost diagonally down an array. From looking at the spectra of the experiment's spatial biasing and the degree to which the foraging tracked the bias, it becomes apparent that the hummingbird is better adapted to utilizing trends in patterns than the human experimenters.

More scatter in the covariation occurred on the western side as the experiment unfolded, along with an ever increasing directional slant. The pattern on the eastern array was exactly the opposite. The reason for this is beyond the capability of this researcher. It should be noted that the bird's tracking became researcher. It should be noted that the bird's tracking became better as time progressed (Fig. 12.2d). This perhaps was a direct result of the increasing directional bias from the points at which the preferred feeders were located.

The difference in the detectibility of these patterns is clearly demonstrated in the three-dimensional histograms of the same information. Although a definite bias is discernible in the experiments, the degree to which the bird adhered to them is not.

Conclusions

Spatial aliases are recurrent problems in the experimental designs of foraging studies. Leaving these in the design has been shown in Fig. 12.2(a,b,c,d) to yield misleading results.

When the two-dimensional Fourier transform is used in conjunction with the geometrical aspects of the SVD it is possible to detect and correct spatial biases before the trial commences. In addition they can provide immediate indications of directional preferences in the bird's foraging. In this particular case, correction of the array allocations at the time of their assignment would have obviated the ambiguity in the tracking results.

Hummingbirds are extremely adept at utilizing these context-dependent clues quickly in order to aid in effective searches for food. My preliminary conclusions were that the bird did not track the experimental design as well as had been expected. Secondary analysis demonstrates, however, that cumulatively over the 4-day span of the experiment, the bird had indeed "learned" the experimental design as it actually was.

The removal of spatial aliasing is not restricted to the simple geometry of a rectangle. The alias matrix for the rectangle has a very simple (diagonal) structure. If the grid occurred in a natural habitat it is highly unlikely that a rectangle would suffice as an approximation to the experimental boundaries. Whatever the shape of these natural boundaries, they all can be represented as integer line segments. The segments form an enclosing map of the spatial configuration of the particular experimental design. The map of these segments is then coded as a set of observations having all amplitudes equal to 1. The observational data must then be scaled to have peak amplitude 1 as well. Because both the experimental map and the observational map now have the same scale, the experimental design map can be deconvolved from the observational map. Deconvolution here means unfolded at all spatial lags. Thus, by following the procedures outlined by Mersereau (1983), foraging patterns can be separated from their experimental designs. This permits a far more accurate and detailed study of the experimental results. In addition, one can return to the experimental design map and selectively remove some of the segments, recompute the spectrum, and observe the changes in the contours and the corresponding set of singular values. By selectively isolating segments of the geometry that appear to have large effects on the spectrum as well as the corresponding singular values, a direct sensitivity analysis of any experiment is possible. Therefore, those features that appear to harbor contextual clues for the forager can quickly be isolated. This general type of feature is essential in analyzing any type of foraging that follows a two, three, or multidimensional pattern.

REFERENCES

Bracewell, R. (1965). *Fourier transform and its applications*. New York: McGraw–Hill.
Forsyth, G. (1977). *Computer methods for mathematical computation*. Englewood, NJ: Prentice–Hall.
Mersereau, R. (1983). The processing of periodically sampled multidimensional signals. *IEEE Transactions on Acoustics Speech and Signal Processing, ASSP-31,* No. 1, 188–194.

Author Index

A

Abarca, N., 15, 19, 48, 58, 117, 118, 159, 161, 168, 169, 171, 176, 181, 185, 190,191, 193, 194, 196, 197, 199, 200, 201, 202, 203, 205, 206, 248, 250
Allen, T., 13, 17
Altmann, J., 185, 186, 205
Amsel, A., 134, 149, 176
Anderson, M. E., 248, 250
Asaki, K., 181, 206
Atkinson, R. C., 147, 149
Austin, T., 172, 179
Avery, M., 117, 132, 211, 219, 226
Axelrod, R., 56, 58

B

Baerends, G. P., 243, 250
Baddeley, A. D., 145, 149
Baker, H. G., 234, 251, 253
Balda, R. P., 212, 215, 219, 225, 227
Balsam, P., 169, 177
Barnard, C. J., 15, 18, 122, 131
Barnes, R. A., 169, 177
Barrera, F. J., 169, 177
Battalio, R. C., xx, xxii, 42, 43, 60
Baum, W. M., 43, 46, 58, 89, 112, 119, 131, 133, 135, 149, 188, 189, 223, 225, 295

Beatty, W. W., 224, 225
Beeby, M. A., 118, 124, 128, 130, 132
Beidler, D. L., 160, 161, 178
Bellman, R., 7, 18, 34, 38
Belovsky, G. E., 150, 231
Berglund, P., 134, 147, 150
Best, L. S., 230, 234, 250
Bibby, C. J., 223, 225
Bloom, L., 173, 179
Bobisud, L. E., 91, 112
Boelens, H., 42, 58, 135, 149
Boitano, G. A., 64, 86
Bolles, R. C., 119, 131
Bossema, I., 225
Bower, G. H., 147, 149
Bracewell, R., 266, 274
Breck, J. E., 26, 38
Brecha, N., 226
Brown, C. A. J., 15, 18
Brown, R. G. B., 119, 122, 131, 229, 230, 250
Brown, S. W., 133, 136, 138, 139, 150
Bruner, J. S., 122, 131
Bush, R. R., xv, 51, 51, 58, 64, 85, 91, 112

C

Cahoon, P., 255
Calder, W. A., 12, 19

S

Samuelson, R. J., 140, 150, 223, 226
Santana, C., 229, 231, 242, 243, 244, 247, 249, 253
Sargent, T. D., 186, 206, 229, 252
Savage, L. J., 18, 19
Schaffer, W. M., 7, 21
Schlosberg, P., 223, 226
Schoener, T. W., 17, 21, 157, 179, 209, 226, 229, 231, 234, 253
Shavalia, D. S., 224, 225
Sheffield, F. D., 162, 179
Sherry, D. F., 209, 210, 211, 213, 214, 216, 217, 218, 219, 220, 221, 222, 224, 225, 226, 227
Shettleworth, S. J., 10, 21, 51, 85, 91, 115, 118, 119, 124, 128, 130, 132, 154, 176, 179, 219, 227, 229, 248, 249, 254
Shimp, C. P., 44, 46, 61
Sibly, R. M., 90, 113, 231, 254
Siegal, S., 236, 237, 254
Siegel, J., 166
Sigmundi, R., 119, 132
Silberberg, A., 108, 113
Silverfine, E., 5, 14, 17, 20
Simon, H. A., 91, 113
Skinner, B. F., xv, 165, 179, 185, 206
Sadle, N. A., 230, 253
Smith, J. C., 172, 179
Smith, J. N. M., 137, 151
Smith, J. P., 135, 150
Smith, L. E., 223, 225
Snow, B. K., 233, 234, 254
Snow, D. W., 233, 234, 235, 254
Snyderman, M., xvii, xx, xxii, 48, 61, 119, 123, 132
Sorenson, A. E., 230, 231, 234, 250, 254
Squires, N., 181, 184, 207
Staddon, J. E. R., xx, xxii, 2, 17, 20, 21, 42, 44, 46, 59, 61, 81, 87, 115, 132, 155, 156, 177, 179, 185, 186, 197, 203, 206, 207, 229, 230, 254
Stearns, S. C., 7, 21
Steiner, T. E., 138, 150
Stephens, D. W., 1, 2, 3, 4, 7, 17, 20, 21, 23, 36, 38, 39, 41, 49, 60, 61, 63, 83, 86, 87, 116, 118, 122, 132, 138, 150
Stevens, A., 117, 132, 211, 219, 227
Stevens, D. W., 229, 232, 252
Stevens, T. A., 220, 227
Stewart-Oaten, A., 26, 39

Stiles, E. W., 153, 179
Stiles, F. G., 233, 250, 254
Stuart, R. A., 23, 39
Suppes, P., 13, 16, 20
Sutherland, W. J., 17, 20, 23, 38, 41, 49, 60, 63, 86, 116, 122, 138, 229, 231, 252
Swanberg, P. O., 212, 227

T

Tarpy, R., 43, 79, 87
Taylor, P. J., 1, 10, 16, 20, 60, 68, 83, 86, 91, 94, 112, 125, 126, 127, 132, 185, 207
Taylor, R., 43, 61
Templeton, A. R., 17, 21
Terrace, H. S., 65, 86, 155, 178
Thaler, E., 231, 252
Thom, J., 134, 147, 150
Thomas, N., 140, 151
Tinbergen, J. M., 157, 179, 230, 254
Tinbergen, L., xv, xix, xxii
Tinbergen, N., 41, 61, 232, 254
Tolman, E. C., 91, 113
Tomback, D. F., 210, 212, 217, 219, 225, 227
Trumbule, G. H., 45, 46, 59
Tullock, G., 234, 254
Turelli, M., 17, 21
Turvey, M. T., 133, 150
Tversky, A., 3, 5, 18, 20, 21
Tyler, D. W., 79, 86
Tyser, R. W., 231, 254

V

van der Pijl, L., 233, 254
van Santen, J. P. H., 13, 21
Van Soest, P. J., 231, 250
Vande Kerkhove, G. A., 234, 251
Vander Wall, S. B., 212, 215, 227
Vaughan, W., Jr., xx, xxii, 17, 19, 42, 52, 55, 56, 59, 61, 93, 112
Vedder, A. L., 230, 250, 254
Vinyard, G. L., 230, 253
vom Winterfeldt, D., 137, 151
Voxman, W. L., 91

W

Waddington, K. D., 13, 17, 21
Walker, J. A., 140, 150
Webber, M. I., 48, 60, 117, 118, 132, 231, 252

Subject Index